The Curatorial Conundrum

Edited by:
Paul O'Neill,
Mick Wilson,
Lucy Steeds

This book was set in Unica77, Larish Neue, Julien, and Hermes, and was printed and bound in Belgium.

Library of Congress Cataloging-in-Publication Data

Names: O'Neill, Paul, 1970- editor. | Wilson, Mick, editor. | Steeds, Lucy, editor.
Title: The curatorial conundrum : what to study? what to research? what to practice? / edited by Paul O'Neill, Mick Wilson, and Lucy Steeds.
Description: Cambridge, Massachusetts : The MIT Press, 2016. | Includes bibliographical references.
Identifiers: LCCN 2015050424 | ISBN 9780262529105 (pbk. : alk. paper)
Subjects: LCSH: Museums--Curatorship--Philosophy. | Art museum curators.
Classification: LCC N408 .C877 2016 | DDC 708--dc23
LC record available at http://lccn.loc.gov/2015050424

10 9 8 7 6 5 4 3 2 1

The Curatorial Conundrum

What to Study? What to Research? What to Practice?

LUMA Foundation and The Center for Curatorial Studies, Bard College

The MIT Press
Cambridge, Massachusetts
London, England

Edited by:
Paul O'Neill,
Mick Wilson,
Lucy Steeds

The Curatorial Conundrum
What to Study? What to Research?
What to Practice?

What to Study?

What to Research?

What to Practice?

Preface
Maja Hoffmann

The Curatorial Conundrum: What to Study? What to Research? What to Practice? offers a broad and searching set of essays and papers that evolved out of the symposium *The Future Curatorial What Not And Study What, Conundrum*. Organized collaboratively with the LUMA Foundation as part of a series of symposiums hosted in Arles, this third conference was held at the Center for Curatorial Studies at Bard College in November 2014, and brought together many of today's leaders in the field of curatorial studies, an area of intellectual inquiry that has emerged over the past 25 years, and transformed the landscape of exhibition-making.

For the LUMA Foundation* the questions and responses in *The Curatorial Conundrum* are particularly urgent in regard our LUMA Arles project of an experimental cultural center in the Parc des Ateliers in the city of Arles, France, for which we are already working with an international core group of artistic consultants (Tom Eccles, Liam Gillick, Hans Ulrich Obrist, Philippe Parreno, Beatrix Ruf), the architects Frank Gehry and Annabelle Selldorf, and landscape architect Bas Smets, always in close relation with artists and thinkers.

While the first two conferences and the publications that followed—*The Human Snapshot* (2011), and *The Flood of Rights* (2013)—addressed the burgeoning distribution of photographic imagery, and its effect of human rights claims today (human rights and the environment are significant areas of focus for the LUMA Foundation, both in Arles and internationally), this publication asks three fundamental questions related to curating: *What to Study?, What to Research?,* and *What to Practice?*

The responses point to the vitality, diversity, and criticality of the field, to shared concerns—and some disputes—across broad geographies, particularly with regard to the public nature of exhibitions and how these structures shape and frame the art of our time. The responses published in this book should be interesting not only to student curators, but to art institutions, museums, and schools generally speaking, and raise many of the fundamental issues that face any arts institution today. They question many of the assumptions of research programs in the visual arts, and the global expansion of exhibitions. In addition to *The Curatorial Conundrum*, a fourth conference to further study the difficulties arising from questions that arts institutions are facing in our current world, was presented in Arles under the title *How Institutions Think* in February 2016, and will be the subject of a further publication.

I am particularly grateful to the organizers of the curatorial conferences, Paul O'Neill and Tom Eccles (CCS Bard/LUMA Foundation), in partnership with Mick Wilson (Valand Academy of Arts, University of Gothenburg); Lucy Steeds, Yaiza Hernández, Charles Esche, and Alison Green (MRes Art: Exhibition Studies/Afterall Books: Exhibition Histories and BA/MA Culture, Criticism and Curation at Central Saint Martins, London); and Lorenzo Benedetti and Guus van Engelshoven (de Appel Arts Centre, Amsterdam). This publication has been astutely shepherded by editors Paul O'Neill, Mick Wilson, and Lucy Steeds, and together we would like to thank the authors and participants who have reshaped their presentations into expanded essays for this publication. These new texts have benefited from the careful oversight and copy-editing of Gerrie van Noord, London, and innovative design of Prem Krishnamurthy and Grace Robinson-Leo of Project Projects in New York. I would also like to acknowledge the support and direction provided by Roger Conover at The MIT Press with whom we co-publish this edition.

As a long-standing board member of the Center for Curatorial Studies at Bard College, I would conclusively like to express my gratitude to the leadership, faculty, and graduate students of the program, who for the past ten years have been an important partner in the evolution of LUMA Arles.

Maja Hoffmann
President, LUMA Foundation

*The LUMA Foundation was established in 2004 in Switzerland to support the activities of independent artists and pioneers, as well as institutions working in the fields of art and photography, publishing, documentary, and multimedia. The foundation specializes in artistic projects, combining a particular interest in environmental issues, human rights, education, and culture in the broadest sense. In 2014, LUMA Arles was founded in support of the project in Arles, which as of 2018 will become an epicenter permanently open to the public and dedicated to the production and presentation of exhibitions, archives, and ideas with special emphasis on education and research.

The Curatorial Conundrum Introduction

Paul O'Neill, Mick Wilson, Lucy Steeds

What to Do?

The contributors to this volume all respond in one way or another to the following core question: Given that curating has come to occupy a central critical and practical space within the global 'contemporary,' how will its unfolding futures be imagined and actualized? This overarching question references a series of complex developments over the last quarter century that have positioned critical work in general, and curating in particular, in a potentially inescapable conundrum; that of the 'damned if you do, damned if you don't' variety.

One phenomenon that frames the contributions herein is the rapid expansion of curatorial educational programs and platforms following on from initiatives first appearing in the late 1980s and early 1990s. These new programs and platforms are not reducible to a singular formula; however, the question of how they will shape future practices is a recurrent concern across the literature on contemporary curating. The emergence of an increasingly global circuit for curatorial education—tending to generate canonical understandings and a Eurocentric professionalization of practices with thicker and thicker veneers of criticality—both allows for the publication of a volume such as this, *and* is an integral part of the problematics that are elaborated on in the chapters to follow. This volume responds not only to the presumed presence of a globally dispersed readership, but also to the horizon of the thinkable that is delimited by curatorial 'training' and professionalization—a horizon that most of the contributions herein wish to contest or re-orient in some way.

A second series of developments framing these texts has been the re-setting of the tension between curating-as-display-making (the exhibitionary) and curating-as-expanded-practice (the curatorial). While in the early 1990s the role of the curator was discussed largely through the gloss of the 'exhibition-maker,' and the expansion of the curatorial role since that time may be understood as the overcoming of the authorial function of the curator, the problematization of the exhibitionary complex—and particularly the development of a substantial new historiography of exhibition-making—has arguably given rise to a less dichotomous construal of the exhibitionary and the curatorial. A notable point of interchange emerges around thinking through exhibition-making, and the interrogation of curatorial knowledges—made manifest in the increased profile given to questions of curatorial labor or exhibition-making when this work is broadly understood, for instance, as actions of practical inquiry congruent with, but not reducible to, other modes of scholarship and experimental research.

Third and most prominent among the framing developments relevant here is a mode of globalization effected by various corporate neo-imperialisms, underpinned by the neoliberal state and inter-state regulatory apparatuses that have produced the conditions for a massively expanded, integrated (though regionalized and segmented) international art system. This inflated art system is entangled with dispersed and divergent critical fronts that contest the hegemonic construction of 'the contemporary' exclusively in terms of globalizing capital, and (Eurocentric) normative 'development' narratives. Such critical fronts, or points of resistance, are often engendered by alter-globalizing and counter-globalizing cultural imaginaries that refuse the 'endless growth' optimism/pessimism of a futurity based on an absolutizing global society as the networking of all monetized existences, and the monetizing of all dimensions of existence. However, an art system that thrives on the extraction and nullification of alterity—an art system that seems blissfully integrated into the all-flattening regime of frictionless financial flows—appears all too willing and eager to swallow whole the raw tenderness of this independent critical culture, or to pre-digest it by removing and disposing of anything that might impede its easy maceration and ingestion.

Operative at very different registers, these sets of developments provide the context within which the current curatorial conundrum arises. This conundrum may then be re-stated as follows: Given that curating has come to occupy a central critical and practical space within a global 'contemporary,' characterized by an assimilation of critical practices as simply more 'value' to be extracted and monetized, what is to be done? Each of the processes outlined above frames this central question, and supplements its formation via translation into a series of sub-questions: What to study? What to research? What to practice?

What to Study?

Turning to the questions of educational provision, one can see that in recent decades broader educational debates have been preoccupied with the impact of the neoliberal re-construction of public education as a space for private enterprise, metric competition, and the formation of human capital. During the same period—and ostensibly wishing to move in a very different direction—many emergent curatorial education practices have sought to renew education as a kind of public cultural work in its own right, with a particular openness to situating student learning outside the academy, at multiple sites, both institutional and non-institutional. Furthermore, many of these educational initiatives and programs aim for a global reach in recruitment, in a curriculum that is aligned with the increasingly globally integrated art system, suggesting the tensions between a globalizing public culture and globally integrated markets. One particular strategy emerging in the face of a potentially globalized flattening is attendance to the local and historical/genealogical dimensions of practices, positioning close study and close reading of exhibitionary systems as a way to re-assert the specificity and difference of concrete instances against abstract globalizations. The eight contributions gathered here under the heading "What to Study?" demonstrate the critical differentiation possible when one turns to the re-construction of particular exhibition histories, and the differential constructions of the archives of practices that provide a basis for introducing students to the critical study of exhibitions. In the same movement, however, they also problematize the assumption of 'the' exhibition as the paradigmatic object of curatorial studies.

Opening this section of the volume, Lucy Steeds's contribution sounds a note of concern: namely that the teaching of exhibition histories might become a kind of hagiography fixating students on the careers of quasi-canonized curators. Steeds advocates an alternative strategy, drawing provocatively upon Benjamin's critical historical poetics, while citing the different material means and formats of exhibition histories as well as the current vogue for exhibition reconstructions. Rather than naturalize the notion of the 'exhibition,' this strategy entails the investigation and analysis of the political importance of the events by which art becomes public, and the examination of art's intellectual and ethical force in these contexts, both historically and in relation to the present. Next, David Teh considers the obstacles to exhibition histories as a strategy in the context of Southeast Asia, and critically re-frames the 'national' as a differential operator that problematizes any aspirations toward global conditions for exhibition histories. Teh declares unequivocally that—for many contemporary art formations, national, and transnational—"it is not exhibitions but independent *organizations* that are the more significant and influential forms in the landscape." In their contribution, Jelena Vesić and Vladimir Jerić present a critical-imaginary of futures-past that provides a dramatized polylogue of educational reconstruction, satirizing the self-referentiality of the curatorial field, while also highlighting the critical impulses that animate the wish to overcome "the vicious cycle of anthropological curators studying other curators." Moving in an opposite direction—but with a similar critical drive to protest the exclusions and repressions naturalized in the canonization of contemporary curatorial citations and exhibition histories—Eddie Chambers addresses the archival erasures and art-historical exclusions of Black-British artists and exhibitions. Working both to reconstruct history, and to mark the exclusions that make such reconstruction all but impossible, Chambers underlines continuing processes of exclusion—noting, for example, that the generation of Black-British artists who achieved prominent visibility in the 1990s have already been 'disappeared' from the current dominant frames of reference. Next, Nikita Yingqian Cai provides a close reading of the 'paradoxes of autonomy' through a consideration of the dynamics of institutional critique, and a version of artistic autonomy that has been elaborated by contemporary artists contemporaneous with the emergence and marketization of an experimental critical contemporary scene in China from the 1980s onward. Cai demonstrates the need to read the specificity of the regional dynamics of art marketization, rather than imposing a normative reading based on a narrow conception of institutional critique derived from specific North American histories of practice. Miguel A. López continues this practice of redistributing how 'globality' is oriented, exploring two exhibition-events that called into question the political role of exhibitions as mediators of Latin America in a global system. Examining the first and only edition of the Latin American Biennial of São Paulo (1978) and the Coloquio De Arte No-Objetual in Medellín (1981), López describes how these two projects reset the focus of globality in the context of exhibition histories, and remapped the ways in which the politics of the exhibitionary are construed. João Ribas proposed a renewed address to the genre of the solo exhibition, arguing that this particular form has been repressed within curatorial discourse and education. Although Ribas's account of the solo show begins in the eighteenth-century imperial center of London, his call for a critical investigation of this form is also put forward as a way to overcome Eurocentric practices, arguing that from "a global art historical perspective, the importance of such exhibition might also act as a corrective to the kinds of totalized history—both global and revisionist—that is often presented in group or survey exhibitions." Finally, in the essay "On the Case of Curatorial History," Jeannine Tang takes a pedagogical approach, examining the teaching of historical approaches within a particular curatorial course, to draw attention to the languages by which exhibition and curatorial histories have been deemed significant, and the differentials of value and power inhering within curatorial history's source materials and practices of study.

What to Research?

The question of curatorial practice has long been entwined with those of different ideas of knowledge, ranging from an art historical model—in which the curator is the one who knows in detail the specificity of a particular collection and archive—to the transdisciplinary constructions of knowledge that position 'knowing' as embedded in the life-world rather than isolated in narrow institutional enclaves, and thus place the curator as a co-worker with artists and others in making, translating, and experimenting with different ways of knowing, and, ultimately, different forms of living.

Opening the "What to Research?" section, Luis Camnitzer's contribution bridges the question of pedagogy and the question of inquiry, problematizing the rampant quantification of life that he presents as working against questions of quality and the processes of living. His wide-ranging essay touches upon almost all of the themes that were used to frame the invitation to the authors, but ultimately resolves upon a fundamental two-fold task: to deal with things, and to deal with those who reify and own things. This 'dealing' with things is to be understood not as a matter of quantitative education, but rather of practical qualitative and lived inquiry. Mélanie Bouteloup's reflections on *The Day After* (a program elaborated through Maryam Jafri's exhibition at Bétonsalon—Centre for Art and Research, Paris), provides a counterpoint and rejoinder to Camnitzer's text by advocating curatorial practice as a form of inquiry that seeks to move beyond a "globalized world full of abrasions, frictions, and tensions hidden behind false reciprocities and hegemonic historiographies." Bouteloup describes a practice of research-based curating that "is not just about articulating material, but also about experimenting and inventing form." Next, Galit Eilat's text begins by describing the research ethos adopted by the curatorial team in developing the 31st Bienal de São Paulo, before exploring how inquiry conducted through the public modalities of exhibition unfolds when the question of the boycott of Israel (called for in 2004 by the Palestinian Campaign for the Academic & Cultural Boycott of Israel) intersected with the Bienal, as the majority of participating artists demanded that the Bienal Foundation boycott Israeli state funding in solidarity with the Palestinian people. Eilat's alert analysis of the public dimensions of boycott positions collective reflection within a 'live' process of critique that *must* be 'made public,' while also demonstrating the difference between an idea of research practice that seeks to position inquiry in a space apart from its subject—or bracketed and held outside the flow of living social practices—and a curatorial research practice that is situated within the processual dynamics of the complex entanglement of social, economic, political, and cultural specificities that produce 'public-ness.' Eilat's text is followed by an interrogative and reflective piece by What, How & for Whom that extends this further, pointing to the way in which practitioners are entangled and implicated in the dynamic of power between the particular knowledge required to be constantly present within the global network, and the limitation of access to this resource. What, How & for Whom's proposed strategy is one of durable local institutions operating in critical international solidarities, and engages in a shared process of multiple reflexivities. Next, these various strategies of curatorial inquiry and curatorial reflexivity are subjected to a systematic and playfully pointed challenge by Liam Gillick's deconstruction of "The Incomplete Curator." This text, rehearsed in a satirical-critical-familial voice worthy of Swift or Sterne, takes the reader through the various steps of curatorial reflexivity—as through the progressive steps in a manual of spiritual exercises, or a *Bildungsroman*—to reach an omega point, variously constructed as freedom, madness, poetry, or love. This second section of the volume is then brought to a close by Simon Sheikh's "Curation and Futurity," echoing in its breadth the opening contribution by Camnitzer, and similarly weaving together the questions of education, research, and practice as it asks us to consider what kinds of futurity the current education and research field invokes, constitutes, or requires. In pursuing this analysis, Sheikh is brought to questions of care for the world, and a framing of the curatorial with reference to the wider life-world, and not simply to its internal problematics or canons of reflexivity.

What to Practice?

The third section of this volume gathers a series of texts under the heading "What to Practice?" The purpose of this section, however, is not to provide a prescription for, but rather to consider the different modes of practice—and modes of disclosure of practice—that are seen by the authors to indicate possible ways through, beyond, or elsewise to the conundrum presented above.

This section opens with Nancy Adajania's reflection on both her own practice as an autodidact, and on the practice of the exhibition designer and experimental media artist Dashrath Patel. Excavating a key, but obscured, moment within the pre-history of new media art in India, Adajania proposes a genealogy that must be thought beyond a simple binary of the national and the cosmopolitan, citing the intersection of the history of exhibition design with that of World Expos, Cold War transcultural encounters, nationalistic politics, and grassroots activism. The question of the translocation of practice is continued by Tobias Ostrander's contribution, which discloses his own curatorial practice as a "Strategic Regionalism" that emerges in dialogue with other geopolitical and regional orderings of curatorial practice, centering on his recent work at the Pérez Art Museum in Miami—a city oriented to the Caribbean, and to Central and South America, while also directly linked to the Southern United States. Continuing this attendance to the regional specificities of practice, and to the differential operations within the overarching narratives of globalization, Koyo Kouoh asserts the emergence of different canons, economies, dialectics, and new audiences that has been especially apparent in Africa since the mid-1990s, with a variety of independent and/or private art initiatives setting themselves apart from the state and the market in order to create alternative frameworks of practice. Zasha Cerizza Colah introduces a similar kind of analysis, pointing to the specificity of artist-initiated and alternative platforms in terms of negotiations of the translocal that are not oriented to a narrative of 'normal' cultural development from elsewhere, by describing the operational modes and concerns of Clark House, Mumbai, and by projecting comparisons and solidarities beyond traditional geopolitical imaginaries. Sumesh Sharma develops this imaginary further, providing a partner text to Cerizza Colah's by describing the multiple layerings of mobility, displacement, diaspora, and colonization that resonate behind the encounters orchestrated in Village Des Arts, Senegal, and in the curatorial practices of Clark House. Moving in a different direction, and addressing the future of the institution as such, Hans Ulrich Obrist draws on a range of sources, from Édouard Glissant to Cedric Price, and from Sergei Diaghilev to Etel Adnan, to advocate a reimagining of the institution that can escape the stasis engendered by the hyper-saturated contemporary digital mediascape, and at the same time give us access to our condition beyond the atrophizing effects of a static culture. Vivian Ziherl provides a counterpoint to Obrist's call for reimagining the institution beyond the saturation/stasis of the contemporary mediascape by locating her own performative intervention within the longstanding processes of cultural political contestation. Ziherl cites recent controversies around the concrete labor conditions and interests of artist and curators, and the challenge of constructing workaday solidarities within the actualities of everyday practice, while also invoking the post-identity disruptive force and demand of queer politics.

The volume concludes with Sarah Rifky's exquisitely realized "Oalqalah: Falling out of Memory." This text unfolds as an account of an act of listening to language as reverberant sound, growing into a complex narrative of futures past. It discloses a science-fiction futurity and invokes an ethos and practice of care that—in relation to all core questions posed here—encourages hope.

What to Study?

Lucy Steeds
David Teh
Jelena Vesić & Vladimir Jerić
Eddie Chambers
Nikita Yingqian Cai
Miguel A. López
João Ribas
Jeannine Tang

What Is the Future of Exhibition Histories?

Or, toward Art in Terms of Its Becoming-Public

Lucy Steeds

the explosive force of this thought, which Engels carried with him for half a century, goes deeper. It places the closed unity of the disciplines and their products in question.
—Walter Benjamin[1]

In this text I want to address the possibilities offered by exhibition histories. I won't argue for this promising field of research and inquiry as being a discipline, not least since part of the promise stems from *in*discipline—that is, in responding to contemporary art with whatever modes and terms it makes historically necessary. Instead I will look at exhibition histories operating within universities, museums, and beyond, reviewing work in three overlapping realms: pedagogy, scholarship, and practice.

At the heart of my own current work in the field lies an attempt to rethink the dialectic between "exhibition value" and "cult value," as proposed by Walter Benjamin in 1930s Paris.[2] Starting to develop that here, I will revisit his insistence on art's "exhibitability," to see how this might be repurposed for the present technological and globalized era.[3] Before doing that, however, I will reflect on the teaching and writing of exhibition histories to date.

To set the tone it is useful to reflect on Benjamin's critique of art history and cultural history as disciplines in his time. The quote above shows that he troubled the limits of academic disciplinarity, on the basis of a letter written by Friedrich Engels in 1893, and he goes on to question "the unity of art itself," as an object of study. He writes: "the reception of a work of art by its contemporaries is part of the effect that the work of art has on us today."[4] This might argue precisely in favor of the field of exhibition histories—indeed he goes on to point out how the initial becoming-public of a work of art cannot be considered an isolated moment, but operates in tandem with subsequent public events in which it takes part. However, Benjamin also warns us of the risks of pursuing "a new and even more problematic" disciplinary unity, and by extension we must further question the unity of exhibitions themselves.[5] To be clear: the object of focus for exhibition histories remains unsettled for me—as unsettled as the boundaries of contemporary art, or indeed, it points to the problems of defining the latter.

1. Teaching Exhibition Histories

It would be flawed, to the point of perversity, to teach contemporary art curators-in-the-making *only* about past shows—as nonsensical, in fact, as training artists *only* in art history. Nevertheless, it clearly constitutes one potentially useful way to stimulate students to think through their own work on new shows, and to understand the potential impact of the methodologies they

1
Walter Benjamin, "Eduard Fuchs: Collector and Historian" (1937), trans. Howard Eiland and Michael W. Jennings, in *Walter Benjamin: The Work of Art in the Age of its Technological Reproducibility, And Other Writings on Media*, eds. Michael W. Jennings, Brigid Doherty, and Thomas Y. Levin (Cambridge, MA: The Belknap Press of Harvard University Press, 2011), p. 117.

2
Walter Benjamin, "The Work of Art in the Age of its Technological Reproducibility" (1935), trans. Michael W. Jennings, *Grey Room*, No. 39, Spring 2010, pp. 17-19. I refer readers to later versions of this famous essay for variations on the ideas in this initial draft.

3
Ibid., p. 18. I appreciate this translation of Benjamin's essay for its insistence on Benjamin's term "exhibitability" [*Austellbarkeit*].

4
Benjamin, "Eduard Fuchs: Collector and Historian," p. 118.

5
Ibid., p. 124. Benjamin is describing the risks of pursuing cultural history in particular.

may apply. I worry, though, if the teaching of this material veers toward hagiography, with students becoming fixated on the career trajectories of quasi-canonized curators—even more so when contact with such curators plays a dominant or preferred role on curatorial courses. In many ways these concerns apply more generally to the transformation of higher education—that is, to its ceasing to operate as a public sphere, underwritten by open and active debate, and its becoming business-like, underwritten by a stubborn faith in markets, brands, and their controlling elites. They are relevant specifically, however, when we take into account that curators assume the role of creating publics for art—of mediating in public spheres on behalf of art—since the values of publicness are precisely in jeopardy in higher education. In these circumstances we may turn to teaching exhibition histories—to discussion of the becoming-public of art, in disparate historical instances—in order to insist on the importance of public spheres, and to reassert the notion of discourse over a roll-call of names, insisting on open discussion over the closed-off flexing of privilege.

In the art college where I teach, and indeed across the umbrella organization (or the subsuming corporate entity, which takes the form of a university), all postgraduate students find themselves graded for 'Personal and Professional Development.' Here the study of exhibition histories might play a surprise role in the 'professional development' of art students—surprising because it may reactivate pedagogical principles over business priorities. Through interrogating exhibition histories, art students can critically explore how the way in which their work meets its publics determines the way in which it will be seen and discussed. As a result, the public manifestation of their artwork becomes the issue, in tandem with its production, instead of the training in careerist self-promotion.

In universities and colleges where art history is taught as an academic subject without the applied element that is fundamental to curatorial and art students, exhibition histories typically constitute a particular direction for study, incorporated as a sub-genre. However, there is reason to ask whether exhibition histories might in fact be a spur to rethink some core concerns of art history today—as I'll explore further on. To conclude at this point: whether within curatorial studies, exhibition studies, the teaching of art, or art history, the promise of exhibition histories is an education in the public life of art. A promise that, when fulfilled, puts it beyond sheer strategic usefulness in relation to professional practice.

2. Writing Exhibition Histories

The writing of exhibition histories may develop from within the writing of art history,[6] or it may be annexed to the latter.[7] Both possibilities were anticipated by T.J. Clark in 1974, when calling for "the social history of art" to be written, and specifically not just the ideological "history of the conditions of artistic production," but also "an account of how the work [of art] took on its public form."[8] Yet there are exciting possibilities if we make the publicness, or the becoming-public of art our *primary* concern, only then turning to the matter of production. What I'd like to explore is whether exhibition histories may thereby further complicate the diverse current understandings of what art history might be. The point here is not to go through a branding exercise, to make a territorial claim, or—as Clark accused various diversifications of art history in the 1970s of doing—to chase "hot-foot in pursuit of the New."[9] Instead, I first want to tease out an idea that I've floated before, which draws on the understanding of "minor literature," proposed by Gilles Deleuze and Félix Guattari in their 1975 celebration of the writings of Franz Kafka.[10] As a Prague-born Jew who published in German, Kafka is hailed by Deleuze and Guattari for making strange and subverting ("deterritorializing") that familiar language, concomitantly with issuing a political program and collective utterance. Among the more direct summary statements they offer is the following: "A minor literature is not the literature of a minor language but the literature a minority makes in a major language."[11]

Let me try and draw some analogies without squeezing all the power from Deleuze and Guattari's famous essay. In my experience, when writing exhibition histories most effectively it is not primarily art history that curators, artists, and other non-historians produce. For instance, when curator Lisette Lagnado reflected recently on the 24th Bienal de São Paulo, curated in 1998 by Paulo Herkenhoff, she not only explained the key curatorial influence of a notion borrowed from François Lyotard—that of *épaisseur*, a quality that might be paraphrased as a density loaded with silent meaning—but in describing the installation of the show she put this very concept to work in her prose.[12] The crux of her historical project was to reinvigorate in text what she had perceived to be significant when visiting the Bienal exhibitions.

Or consider artist Martin Beck's analysis of *an Exhibit*—the 1957 installation in Newcastle and London by Richard Hamilton and Victor Pasmore (with the involvement of Lawrence Alloway)—in which he deals with the fact that he knows the show best through a succession of recreations, addressing these as so many 'ghosts' to be probed and questioned.[13] The historical task

6
See, for instance, Bruce Altshuler, *The Avant-Garde in Exhibition* (New York, NY: Harry N. Abrams, 1994); *Salon to Biennial, Exhibitions that Made Art History, 1863-1959* (London: Phaidon, 2008); and *Biennials and Beyond, Exhibitions that Made Art History, 1962-2002* (London: Phaidon, 2011). In addition, within the *Exhibition Histories* book series, see Rachel Weiss, "A Certain Place and a Certain Time: The Third Bienal de La Habana and the Origins of the Global Exhibition," in *Making Art Global (Part 1): The Havana Biennial 1989*, Rachel Weiss *et al.* (London: Afterall, 2011).

7
See, for instance, Claire Bishop's history of participatory art, *Artificial Hells* (London and New York, NY: Verso, 2012).

8
T.J. Clark, "The Conditions of Artistic Creation," *Times Literary Supplement* (May 24, 1974) pp. 561-562.

9
Ibid.

10
See Lucy Steeds, "Contemporary Exhibitions: Art at Large in the World," in *Exhibition*, ed. Lucy Steeds (London and Cambridge, MA: Whitechapel Gallery and The MIT Press, 2014) p. 18.

11
Gilles Deleuze and Félix Guattari, *Kafka: Toward a Minor Literature* (1975), trans. Dana Polan (Minneapolis, MN: University of Minnesota Press, 1986) p. 16.

12
Lisette Lagnado, "Anthropophagy as Cultural Strategy," in *Cultural Anthropophagy: The 24th Bienal de São Paulo 1998*, eds. Lisette Lagnado and Pablo Lafuente (London: Afterall, 2015) pp. 8-62.

13
Martin Beck, "Revisiting the Form of *an Exhibit*," in *Exhibition, Design, Participation: "an Exhibit" and Related Shows of the 1950s*, eds. Elena Crippa and Lucy Steeds (London: Afterall, 2016).

he set himself is the channeling of diverse related spirits, or dispossessed souls.

From the keyboards of Lagnado and Beck, the 'minor' mode we might call exhibition histories rears its head in the registers of art history, destabilizing the language of this dominant, 'major' discipline. Their prose does not immediately read as art history—it does not obviously bear the hallmarks of the different established schools of art historical thought—yet it works away at, and complicates writing in that field. Moreover, their work could be said to be charged with a political necessity, to the extent that it is galvanized by a collective will to resist art's commodification: both authors respond to an experiential (multisensory and durational) past event of art's publicness, rather than to the art object's enduring identity, in the sense that this latter constitutes it as a fixed asset. Clearly this political work can be undertaken by art historians too—and indeed there is trenchant critique within the discipline concerning the force of the market—but a *necessity* is arguably lacking there. Inherent to writing historically about the event of art's exhibition, rather than about art as such—and to its collection by museums, if not by private individuals and corporations—is precisely dealing with the precariousness of contingent, shifting, and disputed meaning and worth. To tackle the other primary characteristic of the 'minor' mode as set out by Deleuze and Guattari, Beck and Lagnado write not only as themselves, nor on behalf of individuals, but *collectively*: they write together with the initial collectivity that produced the exhibitions under discussion—which is to insist on there being a collective agency at issue—and in order to reconvene a community in the after-event.

When I write within the field of exhibition histories myself, I do so with an education in art history and cultural history.[14] And I marvel at T.J. Clark's ambition in the early 1970s to rethink the whole task and method of art history, while teaching the subject at Camberwell School of Arts and Crafts in London (now subsumed within the same university/corporation as my own college). Yet it is already over fifteen years since the US College Art Association felt it urgent enough to ask "Whatever Happened to the Social History of Art?" I would like to try and repurpose Clark's mission, asking: What "new set of concepts" do we need to "import," "keep... in being" and "build... into the method of work" now?[15] And it is here that I want to experiment by drawing on the conceptual work of Walter Benjamin.

Without announcing his departure from Karl Marx's exchange-value and use-value, Benjamin argued that art should be discussed in terms of its cult value and exhibition value. More broadly, he suggested that art might be understood in terms of its working to reconcile humanity with nature. Exemplary for his

14
Since I do not give concrete examples in what follows here, see, for example, "Goshka Macuga, *Picture Room*, 2003" (No. 7 in *The Artist as Curator* series), *Mousse*, No. 48, April-May 2015; and "Biennial Exhibition Histories, Against the Grain: Juraci Dórea's *Projeto terra* in São Paulo, Venice, and Havana," in *Making Biennials in Contemporary Times: Essays from the World Biennial Forum no. 2*, eds. Galit Eilat *et al.* (Amsterdam: Biennial Foundation and São Paulo: Fundação Bienal de São Paulo and ICCo—Instituto de Cultura Contemporânea, 2015).

15
Clark, pp. 561-562.

proposal of cult value was prehistoric mark-making, which he saw as an instrument in mystical or faith-based activity, concerned with the mastery or control of nature. He writes: "the earliest artworks originated in the service of rituals—first magical, then religious."[16] Such artwork is described by Benjamin as having minimal *exhibition* value, in the sense of having little need to be seen publicly: "what matters is that the spirits see it."[17] He concludes: "Artistic production begins with constructs [*Gebilde*] that stand in the service of magic. What is solely important for these constructs is that they are present, not that they are seen."[18] In sum, art's cult value is anchored in ritual practice directed at forces of nature.

By contrast, what is exemplary for Benjamin's proposal of *exhibition value* is modern photography—with Eugène Atget's pictures of deserted Paris streets around 1900 given as a particular instance—and, especially, popular films of the 1920s. This work he sees as not only a product of modern technology, but also as instrumental in affirming this new technology, or in reconciling humanity to it. He writes: "emancipated" from ritual, modern technology "stands opposed to contemporary society as a second nature and, to be sure, as economic crises and wars prove, it is a nature no less elemental than that given to primeval society."[19] Moreover, the new art of Benjamin's time has a "hidden political significance" in that its examples "demand a specific kind of reception. Free-floating contemplation is no longer appropriate to them. They unsettle the viewer; he feels challenged to find a particular way to approach them."[20] And the viewer, herself a "quasi-expert," meets this challenge, engaging with both enjoyment and criticality.[21] In sum, art's exhibition value lies in its need to be encountered, and, in that event, intellectually negotiated: it indicates art's social function, at the forefront of social debate and empowerment.

To nail what might already be clear, Benjamin argues in fact for a progressive shift, *away* from art being based in ritual, which prioritized cult value, decisively *toward* a functionality based in politics, prioritizing exhibition value. Instead, I want to suggest that both values, if somewhat differently inflected, can be seen to be crucially in play today. One could conclude that I wish to extend Benjamin's thesis and antithesis into a teleological synthesis, but I will reserve a demonstration of how exhibition value and cult value are in fact *both* in play, differentially, in not only prehistoric art but also modern art, for another time. For now, I want to elaborate my inflection of Benjamin's dialectic of value in order to reapply it to contemporary art, before turning to the implications for writing the history of this art, and the reasons to construe this in terms of exhibition histories in particular.

16
Benjamin, "The Work of Art in the Age of its Technological Reproducibility," p. 16.

17
Ibid., p. 18.

18
Ibid., p. 17.

19
Ibid., p. 18. Translation lightly edited for clarity in the present context.

20
Ibid., p. 19.

21
Ibid., p. 26.

Invigorating cult value today involves rejecting ritual as a practice only of superstition or magical belief, organized, or alternative religion. Instead we bring into play all the collective or socially determined activity that we instinctively engage in, which is produced intersubjectively rather than with self-conscious deliberation. Turning now specifically to contemporary art, I want to argue that its cult value lies in the ritual engagement of publics—that is, their collective and performatively negotiated engagement—in art's *here and now*. To a limited extent this involves reinstating "the here and now of the work of art," hailed by Benjamin for having been eclipsed by art's modern-day reproducibility.[22] However, this is not "the here and now of the *original*" artwork, which "constitutes the concept of its authenticity," and insists on its unique identity, but instead it is the here and now of art's *display*—whether in a museum, on the streets, at an Internet URL, or anywhere else.[23] The cult value of contemporary art, understood along these lines, is its performative potentiality—in a given context—for convening collectivities, or, we might say, for galvanizing being-in-common. The value of art judged in these terms lies not in its social use toward the *mastery* of nature—as suggested by Benjamin—but in affirming our *entanglement within* nature; in reconciling us with the 'natural' forces, we might say of sociality, or indeed animality, that may drive us.

By contrast, to echo the contrast drawn by Benjamin, the *exhibition value* of contemporary art, such as he advocated for modern art, is tied to "politics."[24] (The political dimension in relation to the ritualistic could be debated productively, but for simplicity I want to keep cult and exhibition value apart here.) As eloquently discussed by others, Benjamin's writing on politics, when otherwise addressing the work of art, can be ambiguous, even while he simultaneously characterizes a brutal modernist artistic choice between fascism and communism.[25] Yet if we set aside the stark political divisions of 1930s Europe, we may clarify the ambiguity over the practice of politics that anchors art's exhibition value, interpreting this in terms not only of ideological debate, but also of wider and more diverse conceptual and ethical discussions.[26] Analyzing contemporary art on this basis, then, means assessing how it prompts and contributes to such debates and discussions. At the level of social function, the value of art judged in these terms does not necessarily lie in reconciling humanity to new technologies construed as a 'second nature,' as argued by Benjamin, but instead in a grappling by humanity with humanity itself.

The implications of all this for art history are twofold. First, in order to do justice to art's cult value we need to research and evoke the decisive events in which it has met its

22
Ibid., p. 13.

23
Ibid.. Italics added.

24
Ibid., p. 17.

25
For a finely nuanced response to these issues in Benjamin, to which this essay is indebted, see Howard Caygill, *The Colour of Experience* (London: Routledge, 1998).

26
Walter Benjamin, "The Work of Art in the Age of its Technological Reproducibility," p. 17.

publics historically. Indeed, through evocation, we may test the possibilities to extend and diversify the audiences for these past occasions. Secondly—and with regard to art's exhibition value—we need to investigate and analyze the political importance of the events by which art becomes public, examining art's intellectual and ethical force in these contexts, historically, and in relation to the present. In other words, then, we find ourselves contemplating the tasks of exhibition histories.

In the process of effecting these shifts of focus and emphasis, we may mark a break with some of the problems of art history that Benjamin had already diagnosed in the 1930s, although they continue to trouble us today. We may specifically work against both the canonization and commodification of art. Within the field of exhibition histories, we may choose to write about artwork included in lavishly archived museum shows and biennials, but equally—even if they are only traceable orally—about remote installations and unannounced performances. We need to write plurally, from diverse perspectives, with different sets of expertise and varying standpoints. We need to question the unity not only of art, but of the public sphere—to challenge our definitions of art and of publics—in order to better understand the multitude of overlapping situations we find ourselves in today.

Of course, exhibition histories need not be written only on the printed page. I find the online possibilities hugely exciting, not least since they allow for text and image combinations that are impossible otherwise. Equally, with art institutions increasingly looking back to their past shows for the making of new exhibitions, there is a gathering interest in how to make convincing displays of archival material in gallery spaces that do justice to the idea of a spatial experience. There are also significant initiatives that defy easy categorization, such as Chimurenga's library-based residencies, in which historical material on Pan-African cultural festivals of the 1960s and 1970s is re-activated. To conclude I will briefly turn to the ambition to reinstate, in some way, exhibitions.

3. Restaging Historical Exhibitions

Seeking to recreate something of a past exhibition is now so popular that different lexicons have been developed that distinguish between the relationships established by the new shows and their historical reference points.[27] We find bids to remake or reconstruct shows, as if their starting point were a destroyed object needing to be replicated, but also bids to riff off or to cover an original, as if it were a tune. I tend to find this aspect of exhibition histories disappointing—all too often it seems to be about shoring up curatorial 'landmarks' (from the

27 See, for instance, Reesa Greenberg, "Remembering Exhibitions," *Tate Papers*, No. 12, October 2009, available online at www.tate.org.uk/download/file/fid/7264 (accessed November 10, 2015); and "Archival Remembering Exhibitions," *Journal of Curatorial Studies*, Vol. 1, No. 2, June 2012. Also Alessandra Troncone, "Il Piacere di Rifare," *Flash Art Italia*, No. 310, May-June 2013, pp. 84-87.

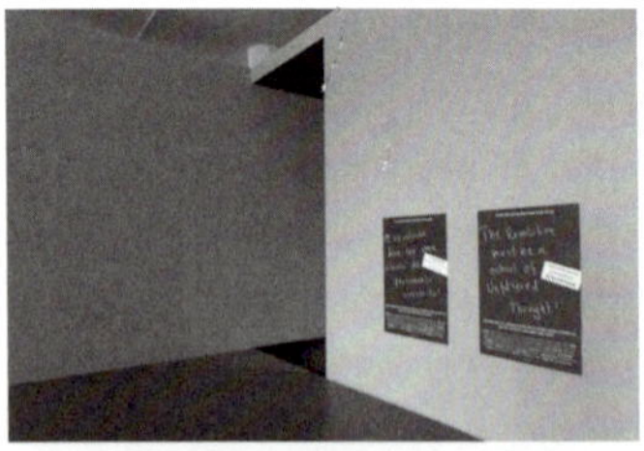

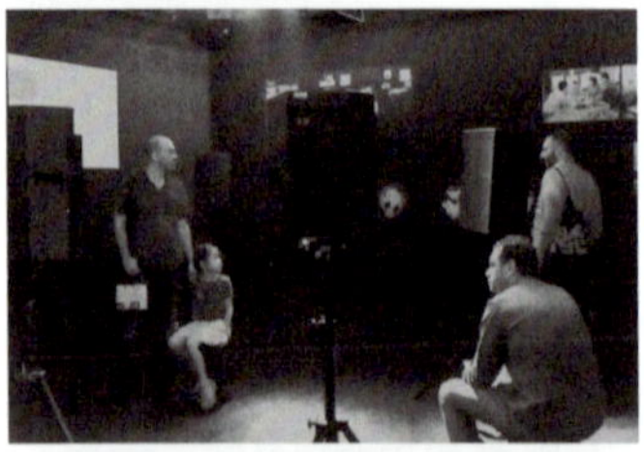

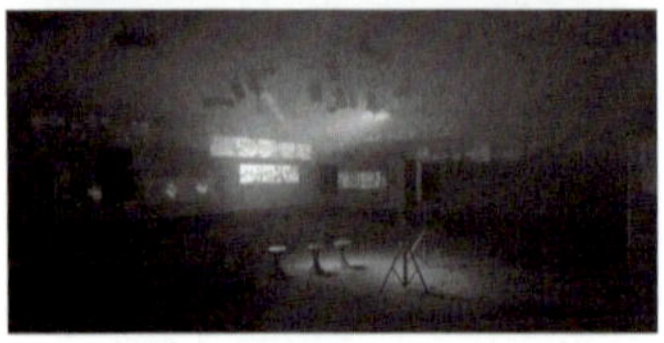

See pp. 234-235
María Berríos & Jakob Jakobsen, *The Revolution Must Be a School of Unfettered Thought*, 2014
Installation (mechanical theater of sound, light, video, and images; poster; tabloids), variable dimensions, 30 min. 45 sec.

past) or about curatorial positioning (concerning the present)—and all too frequently it involves institutional self-congratulation. Most successful, perhaps, are bids to re-enact or restage shows—as if they were performances—maybe because those involved seek to learn something in the process as well as share their findings with new audiences.

One example of the latter might be *The Revolution Must Be a School of Unfettered Thought,* contributed by Jakob Jakobsen and María Berríos to the 31st Bienal de São Paulo in 2014. This show within a show described itself as "a dramatised echo of the Third World Exhibition and the Cultural Congress of Havana 1968."[28] It included digitized film footage of the international congress of 1968, and documentary photographs of the accompanying exhibition; it added smoke, lights, stage direction, and dialogue. It shared its historical research with visitors, and added scholarship, but it also took up something of the motivations behind the original initiative, and reworked the original didactic form in order to pursue the old ends for a new historical and geopolitical situation. As such, it also offered implicit critique of the contemporary art extravaganza—the Bienal de São Paulo—in which it played a role.

Galleries and exhibition halls aside, for me one of the most exciting spaces for restaging exhibitions is the cinema or auditorium. Some remarkable films do much more than simply document the shows they cover. Consider Sigmar Polke's *Untitled (Venice, empty pavilion et al.)* of 1986, in which the artist experimentally exposed and superimposed footage of the deserted space in which he would represent Germany for the 42nd Venice Biennale. Yet even straight film or video documentation has the capacity to powerfully convey the relation between art and exhibition context, in both physical and historical sense. When, for instance, launching a book on the controversial 1989 Paris show *Magiciens de la Terre* in London a quarter of a century later, I found it rewarding to screen extended TV coverage from the time.[29] Not only because something of the kinesthetic experience of the exhibition, in its two distinct venues, was thereby conveyed, but also because it simultaneously threw into relief some of the architectural and conceptual challenges that arguably have since been inherited by Tate Modern, where the screening took place.[30]

At the same time, we might ponder the apparent lack of any filmic documentation—indeed of any official photographs even—of the third Havana biennial of contemporary art held in 1989, the subject of a preceding book.[31] The very difficulty of restaging this show in any meaningful way now should not lessen our interest in the possibilities it offered the art that it brought together, in the light of present concerns. And this

28
This wording was used on the poster displayed outside the installation and in the newspaper distributed in connection with the work.

29
Lucy Steeds *et al.*, *Making Art Global (Part 2): "Magiciens de la Terre" 1989* (London: Afterall, 2013).

30
This event inaugurated a weekend of screenings and discussions co-organized by Afterall and Tate Film. More here: http://www.afterall.org/2014/04/08/Magiciens_Reconsidered_programme.pdf (accessed November 10, 2015).

31
Weiss *et al., op. cit.*

points to the vast number of still more fleeting and decidedly less official public events for contemporary art that might well warrant committed investigation now.

Whatever the state of the archival resources available, the task of exhibition histories involves using past shows of contemporary art to place the present in a critical condition—that is, if it is to do any justice to Benjamin's radical thinking in the 1930s. The point is not to "augment the weight of the treasure accumulating on the back of humanity," but to "provide the strength to shake off this burden so as to take control of it."[32]

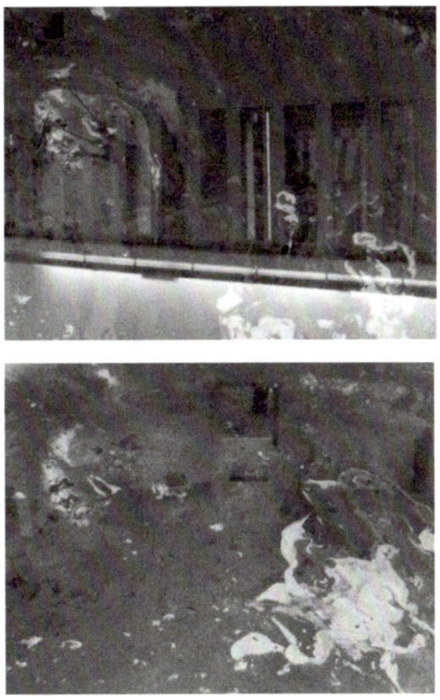

See p. 236
Sigmar Polke, *Untitled (Venice, empty pavilion et al.)*, undated (1983-1986)
Film stills / 16mm transferred to video, color, silent, 28 min. 29 sec.

32
Benjamin, "Eduard Fuchs: Collector and Historian," p. 125.

Obstacles to Exhibition History: Institutions, Curatorship, and the Undead Nation-State

David Teh

How should art be historicized in its contemporary and global phase? What is to be historicized, if not the work of art *per se*? Where art history appears to have shallow roots, the emerging paradigms of curatorial studies and exhibition histories offer appealing alternatives. But their path is strewn with hazards, not least the lack of that visual literacy and of the critical discourses that art history, for all its sins, has long cultivated elsewhere. Whereas exhibition historians in the West have a hegemonic art-historical edifice to overcome, and a relatively consistent field of institutionalized practice to examine, that isn't necessarily the case in other places. The task there will demand not just examining local narratives, but also scrutiny of local competencies and currencies by which some modern art has secured its contemporaneity. And this perspective would highlight the still pivotal role of the Nation as determinant of both curatorial and exhibitionary norms, even—perhaps especially—where the putative internationalism of contemporary art is concerned.

Dilations: Before and after Art History

The new research paradigms mentioned are part of a general disciplinary reorganization, caused by two *dilations*. In the first, the focus of critical thinking on art has moved from artists and artworks onto the larger assemblages in which artworks are typically displayed. This is partly a legacy of Cultural Studies, and an attempt to broaden the notion of 'culture'—once defined by elitist institutions like the museum—to embrace the less exclusive zones of mass media and everyday life. But if mainstream Cultural Studies was content to abandon art history altogether, visual, curatorial, and exhibition studies—often driven by people trained in that older tradition—may be seen as more qualified steps away from it.[1] Reformers within art history have long sought to expand its methods and terms of reference, finding some willing accomplices in exhibiting institutions and among artists, which is evident in the historicity immanent to art practice, and indexed perhaps in its formal dilation since the 1960s. This disciplinary dilation accompanies a second, geographical one—which began later, but has arguably progressed faster—in which the focus of the art world and art market has now widened beyond its historical centers, purportedly to encompass the whole world. The key nodes of 'visual studies' already reflect this in their student intakes, and even their topical range, while art history has seen attempts, ranging from the perfunctory to the grandiose, to recalibrate its sense of what art history looks like, and where it comes from.[2]

In Southeast Asia, peripheral on both disciplinary and geographical maps, neither of these dilations is very well advanced. Yet both reflect attempts by artists and scholars to

1
All three insist on the importance of a properly *aesthetic* experience. E.g. Nicholas Mirzoeff, "What is Visual Culture?," in *An Introduction to Visual Culture*, second edition (London and New York, NY: Routledge, 2009), pp. 6-7.

2
E.g. James Elkins, ed., *Is Art History Global?* (New York, NY, and London: Routledge, 2006); and Hans Belting, Andrea Buddensieg, and Peter Weibel, eds., *The Global Contemporary and the Rise of New Art Worlds* (Cambridge, MA, and London: The MIT Press, 2013).

overcome modernity's built-in exclusions and biases (elitist, colonial, racist), which, left unchecked, would no doubt have proven fatal to art history, as the fulcrum of the world's debt and luxury markets shifts away from the old centers, and a global education market follows suit. However, as much as we may welcome them, these dilations pull us in different directions. Those trained in art history worry about what is lost—traditionalists mourn the old certainties of a canon, or national schools, while even progressive scholars may wonder about the methodological and epistemic bases on which research might now be founded. But in much of the new world this field would now embrace, what concerns us is not the attention deficit of Western scholarship, but the paucity of actual *content*; of critical art history and historically informed art criticism, to say nothing of the discipline's lack of institutional footholds. In Southeast Asia, modern art has not had its historical milestones and meta-narratives debated, or its critical vocabularies vetted, and is still dealing poorly with art's formal expansion. As the respectable disciplinary model is a moving target, institutions wanting to invest in the field don't know where to start. For students, the new paradigm of visual studies seems a reassuringly buoyant pontoon amid the chaos of the two dilations.[3]

My own experience situates me right on the tear; I was educated in the Western tradition but have spent my professional life in places keenly entering global circuits of exhibition and exchange, yet lacking a critical, scholarly apparatus. Southeast Asian art has long been an object of untimely awakenings. As modern art in the West began its formal expansion in the 1960s, bureaucrats and military strategists were rudely made aware of the existence of this region, a bloody front in their Cold War. The result was Southeast Asian Studies, for which 'cultural history' meant ancient religious traditions, which, though blended every which way with local beliefs, gave 'the region' its only coherence other than that of military emergency. *Modern* art was invisible to all but a handful of scholars.[4] Commentators on contemporary art still worry about 'belatedness,' and the tardy adoption of modernist styles and techniques. But, in fact, Cold War communications media have made those transfers relatively fast—the delay is nothing compared to the tardiness of Euro-American art history, which remained largely ignorant of the region's modern art for the better part of a century.

The art that *has* received scholarly attention has tended to be what is most legible within national-institutional frames, thanks to art history's habitual interest in 'national schools,' reinforced by the country focus of area studies. This made sense in some places, but limitations of this practice become clear as artists gain access to a global circuit while bypassing national

3
In its current, broad-spectrum institutional form, The National University of Singapore (where I work) dates from the early 1960s. When art history died in its infancy in 1973, the university's imperial models in the UK had had professorships in the field for over a century. Most of its new role models in the US boast art history programs of 50 to a 100 years' standing. It currently has nothing resembling a degree program in this field, nor plans to start one.

4
A rare exception to the rule was Claire Holt's *Art in Indonesia: continuities and change* (Ithaca, NY: Cornell University Press, 1967).

systems of recognition. Matthew Rampley retraces the 'national schools' model from the racialized iconography of the eighteenth-century classicist Johann J. Winckelmann, a template resolved by the mid-nineteenth century and entrenched by the cultural nationalism of World War I. Rampley makes two important points about national schools: first, that they were an integral component of national becoming, not a secondary phenomenon, but rather immanent to it.[5] Second, in their original context, they did not quite "correspond to the political map" of the day; their points of reference were not nations as such, but cultures—*regional* cultures—which exceeded and predated national borders.[6]

The history of contemporary art must exceed national framings too. Yet we cannot afford to discard them, for they also contain the story of *what it has meant to be international*, a story we cannot do without. I will return to this problem, but first let us make a few general characterizations of contemporary art activity in Southeast Asia, flagging up some of the discursive and structural obstacles to its historicization. For efficiency I will use 'the West' as shorthand for the more developed economic and institutional contexts in which we today find this demand for *dilated* histories of art.

Discursive Density, or, When Attitudes Become Books

The nascent field of exhibition histories is very much a product of these dilations. Among its most advanced expressions to date are two volumes published by Afterall, sharing the title *Making Art Global*, concerning groundbreaking shows held in the geopolitically pivotal year 1989, at distant poles of an emergent 'global' art world: *Magiciens de la Terre* and the Third Havana Biennial.[7] Each suggests a starting point for historicizing the contemporary from what were once considered the fringes of this world, but also highlights the methodological challenges such efforts face. They are therefore salutary to my own project: a history of the contemporary and its 'currencies' in Thailand. Yet they fill me with a sense of alienation, perhaps because both exhibitions were so significant and influential. The criteria of their significance and influence are matters for debate, debates that are only broached, certainly not settled, by these publications. But they implicate all of us—even at the fringes—occupied with the promotion, critique and history of art in its global present.

Both shows are deemed to have crystallized and communicated something—a state of becoming, in which we recognize a set of predicaments (aesthetic, political, practical, ontological) that we have shared, perhaps globally, ever since, and that we have since come to recognize as constitutive of our common contemporaneity. Both issued from public institutions and were

5
Matthew Rampley, "The Construction of National Art Histories and the 'New' Europe," in *Art History and Visual Studies in Europe: Transnational Discourses and National Frameworks*, eds. Matthew Rampley, Thierry Lenain, Hubert Locher *et al.* (Leiden: Brill, 2012), p. 231 & ff.

6
Rampley, p. 233.

7
Rachel Weiss *et al.*, *Making Art Global (Part 1): the Third Havana Biennial 1989* (London: Afterall, 2011), p. 20 & ff; and Lucy Steeds *et al.*, *Making Art Global (Part 2): "Magiciens de la Terre" 1989* (London: Afterall, 2013).

made manifest in public institutional spaces, yet importantly, neither can be read as an unmediated expression of state or institutional will, thanks largely to the pivotal ambivalence of the curatorial function. A certain energy—critical, destabilizing, agonistic—became legible within the frame of each, between each show and its world, and, perhaps as importantly, between their very different worlds; 'dialectical images' flashing before us as the world entered a fraught new phase of its worldiness. A prodigious contemporaneity was present in both, presented itself *there* in the exhibition, a 'change of attitude' immanent to the presentation.[8]

We should not ignore another, retrospective value that arises when attitudes become books. These volumes are also restorative, in the sense of a *redux* (literally: a *leading back*) and therefore in step, if not in league, with a certain spirit that might make for a somewhat awkward companion: the spirit of the market and its recuperation—it would not be overstating things to call this 'global'—of conceptualism and other unreified margins of late modernism. For these are guidebooks to that terrain, its better- and lesser-known landmarks, even as both shows, and both books, redraw modernism's maps. The books are *metaphors* for the shows themselves, offering historical and discursive context, a mode instantly familiar to anyone who has worked at the edges of this global contemporary in the intervening years.

But my alienation really dawns when I wonder: What exhibitions in my own, Southeast Asian frame of reference might deserve such a thorough treatment? One might identify prominent and often-cited exhibitions; chains of curatorial influence might appear here and there. Yet 'significance' suggests influence beyond the immediate circle of concerned professionals, which greatly narrows the field. And the worthy, conflicted, reflexive intimation of a shared and contested contemporaneity? These criteria would relegate Southeast Asian exhibition history to a hypothetical twilight. They certainly rule out the larger international surveys mounted over the years in the region, none of which, by this pointed definition, could be described as 'contemporary.'

Yet the Afterall books indicate some key ingredients, and obstacles, of a history of the contemporary. In the *Magiciens* book, Pablo Lafuente summarizes debates over certain prominent shows including MoMA's controversial *"Primitivism" in Twentieth Century Art: Affinity of the Tribal and the Modern* (1984-1985).[9] His triangulation of critical positions marks this as a very privileged discourse, even as it is a certain privileging (of the West over the rest) that both *Magiciens* and the Havana Biennial, and much of the discourse around them, purported to

8
See Thomas McEvilley's post-mortem of *Magiciens* in *Artforum*, "Marginalia: Thomas McEvilley on the Global Issue," republished in Steeds *et al.*, p. 269.

9
Pablo Lafuente, "Introduction: From the Outside In—*Magiciens de la Terre* and Two Histories of Exhibitions," in Steeds *et al.*, pp. 8-22; see especially pp. 18-20.

dissolve. Lafuente makes no mention of the state, focusing on the discursive rather than the structural dimensions, knowing the latter would be considered in a following essay. But this places us in those years, and that part of the globe, where the ministerial imprimatur was sufficiently benign or at arm's length to be set aside in a political analysis of the large public-institutional, international exhibition. Much as that autonomy may be presented as a norm, globally it is surely more the exception than the rule. There have been few, if any, large exhibitions in Southeast Asia where the same latitude would be tolerable to the responsible critic.

A second privilege is the very existence of historically informed, written criticism, from diverse professional standpoints. Third, the many *shared* privileges that put these interlocutors on the same page: the shared referent of an exhibition they all saw, shared education, and a sophisticated vocabulary with all its historical referents and nuances; a literature written, edited, published, and reviewed by specialists. Fourth, the privileges of *independent* publication, the critical scope enjoyed in various public spheres, with their informed editors, readers, and competitors, and enlightened advertisers.

Along with the documents of art, these privileges are material 'conditions of possibility' of this history, which allow the critic, with 24 years' hindsight, to assess and specify the significance and influence of an exhibition. It is not without envy that I note the density of critical reflection—an embarrassment of riches. And though I sympathize wholly with the shift enacted here, in the name of a becoming global that demands historicization, in places lacking these privileges such a history is inconceivable. Singapore, where I live and work, enjoys zero from four of the characteristics listed. Around Southeast Asia, it is hard to find any place doing better than one from four. It's not that bright minds aren't being brought to bear on the exhibition and discussion of contemporary art—they are—but the means of expression are incomparable, and the prospects of such discursive density very slim. This lack was diagnosed as early as 1986, but seems no less acute today.[10] A project called *Comparative Contemporaries*, initiated in 2003 by the critic Lee Weng Choy, sought to establish shared points of reference for a regional art history, compiling a bibliography from a small network of editors. But their incomplete and somewhat idiosyncratic 'proto-anthologies,' suspended ever since, stand as testament to the scale of the challenge.[11]

10
T.K. Sabapathy, "Modern Art in Singapore: Pioneers and Premises," in *Sources of Modern Art* (Singapore: Ministry of Education, 1986), pp. 129-130.

11
The anthology was archived online by Asia Art Archive, though permissions were secured for relatively few texts. http://comparative.aaa.org.hk/. See also Lee Weng Choy, "Anecdote and Theme: reflections on curating contemporary art from Southeast Asia," *Art Monthly Australia*, No. 279, May 2015, pp. 32-41.

Institutions and De Facto Institutions

As elsewhere, art in Southeast Asia is produced by a heterogeneous array of organizations. Some aspire to institutional admission, some defy it, while others may be indifferent. But exhibitions—at least, those likely to be subjects of historicization—are the products of quite different power relations than those in the West. The validation that institutions afford artists and patrons may be comparable, but there are important structural differences, not least of which is the stubborn fact of authoritarianism. State institutions are subject to direct oversight and intervention. Censorship is common; self-censorship is endemic. Ministries are at least quite transparent in their allergies. The institutions themselves are perhaps more detrimental; they often intervene of their own accord and cannot be relied upon to defend artistic integrity.

A few high-profile embarrassments will help sketch the minefield faced by artists addressing sensitive issues. A 2005 installation in Jakarta's CP Biennale called *Pinkswing Park*, by Agus Suwage and Davy Linggar, featured near-naked celebrities posing playfully in a fantastical landscape. It was censored in response to lobbying and threats by Indonesia's fundamentalist Islamic Defenders Front, triggering the biennale's collapse. Simon Fujiwara's installation, *Welcome to the Hotel Munber*, was first mangled by museum staff and then withdrawn from the 2011 Singapore Biennale, when a senior museum official objected to a pornographic magazine lying discreetly within it. In Thailand, curator Apinan Poshyananda was forced to censor a photograph of queer artist Michael Shaowanasai in monastic drag (*Portrait of a Man in Habits*, 2003) in a university gallery, while Apichatpong Weerasethakul's film, *Syndromes and a Century* (2006), was censored for showing off-duty doctors having a nightcap and a monk playing guitar.

The First-World notion of an independent public institution, subject to bureaucratic review yet operating at arm's length from government, is an exotic one in Southeast Asia. Instead, we find two main types of institution: first, the old-school national museum, which may present a grand, colonial facade—like Hanoi's Academie des Beaux Arts de l'Indochine or the national galleries in Jakarta and Bangkok—but is in fact wholly a creature and agent of the modern. Typically not purpose-built and in disrepair, these are either torpid showrooms of the bureaucracy, or spaces for hire, or both. Their collections, when they have them, are poorly maintained and tend to be displayed without much care or information. Catalogues are often more ceremonial than historical, featuring little text beyond the blessings of a director or some neophyte from the ministry; 'curatorial' texts are rarely more than descriptive. Among the large staff of such institutions, it is rare to find any 'contemporary' or 'curatorial' competence.[12] Indeed, one is surprised to find contemporary art there at all, although its

12
Parallels with the "conspicuously backward" and bureaucratic institutions Geeta Kapur describes in India are striking. "Geeta Kapur: On the Curatorial in India" (interview by Natasha Ginwala), *Art & Deal*, No. 32, April-June 2010, revised and republished by *Afterall Online* at http://www.afterall.org/online/geeta-kapur-part1 (accessed November 27, 2015).

criteria may sometimes be stretched in suggestive ways—I recently found a fourth-century Buddha statue in Ho Chi Minh City's Museum of Fine Arts labeled "Ancient Contemporary Art."

My aim here is not to ridicule, but to emphasize that where modern art has been domesticated by the state, its institutions almost completely *exclude* the contemporary. Those that in the 1970s and 1980s tried to bridge modern and contemporary—like Bangkok's Bhirasri Institute of Modern Art—have not survived (with the exception of Manila's Cultural Centre of the Philippines). Jakarta's Taman Ismail Marzuki, a multi-art form complex opened in 1968, is still visited sporadically by independent groups who bring their own support and audiences with them, but its galleries have long been unfit for contemporary exhibitions. The organizers of the 2013 Jakarta Biennale preferred to install their show in its underground car park. It is hard to see the positive side of this estrangement between generations, but it does offer clues as to how the edifice of modern art defines (albeit negatively) the contemporary—one historian has even suggested that it may be *constitutive* of the regional contemporary.[13]

The second kind of institution we might call a postmodern upgrade of the first, designed to recapture the contemporary. The Singapore Art Museum and the Bangkok Art and Culture Center, for example, are self-consciously 'international,' with at least a semblance of curatorial activity, but still faithfully serve official representational purposes. Awkward creatures, they would walk with the cosmopolitan swagger of the contemporary, but for the limp of a parochial workforce with meager intellectual resources. The hallmark of this second type is a more sophisticated ideological imperative: their masters have begun to take the utility of exhibitions as a form of representational power seriously. Like biennales, they are platforms for city branding initiatives, luring cosmopolitan locals, tourists, and expatriates. As a result, universities, private museums, and foreign cultural institutes—less encumbered by national and municipal agendas—have been important havens for emerging contemporary practice.[14]

The weak institutional landscape severely limits the horizons of research in the region. Combine this with the parlous state of art historical education—the majority of the workforce lacks such qualifications—and one is not surprised that the exhibitions generated in these places are mostly not worth historicizing. Institutions go through the motions of documentation, but seldom with critical self-consciousness. In some countries they generate no substantive historiography at all. The exhibition historian must therefore look elsewhere, and it is the artist who has most often stepped into the breach.

13
Kevin Chua, "On Teaching Modern and Contemporary Southeast Asian Art," *Third Text*, Vol. 25, No. 4, July 2011, p. 469.

14
E.g. the Art Center at Chulalongkorn University and Bangkok University Gallery; NUS Museum and the Institute of Contemporary Arts in Singapore; the Museum of Contemporary Art and Design in Manila; Soemardja Gallery and Selasar Sunaryo Art Space in Bandung. From the 1980s, the Goethe Institut and Alliance Française were both important supporters of experimental practice in the region.

When it comes to making *significant and influential* exhibitions, smaller, independent and artist-run platforms have always led the way: in Indonesia, Cemeti Art House, and later ruangrupa; in Thailand, About Cafe and Project 304, as well as the Chiang Mai Social Installation and Asiatopia festivals; in Singapore, the Artists Village in its early years, followed by initiatives like 5th Passage Artists Ltd and Plastique Kinetic Worms; the Shop 6 group around Roberto Chabet in 1970s Manila, through Third Space, Big Sky Mind, and Green Papaya today. In post-socialist countries such spaces have emerged more recently, like Stiev Selapak and now Sa Sa Bassac in Phnom Penh, Nha San Studio in Hanoi, and San Art in Saigon.[15] It is in these *de facto* institutions' more modest shows and documentation that one finds the stuff of exhibition histories and the key pivots toward the contemporary. Their hallmarks are remarkably consistent: artist-initiated, with a strong collectivist ethos, though often built around charismatic individuals or small cliques. They are autonomous, and often activist, with little or no state patronage—their funding tends to be multi-source, sporadic, and project-based. They show a self-conscious distancing from state-institutional tastes, and from the market. They have fostered less easily commodified art practices and been the bastions of curatorial independence.[16]

The porosity between such groups and state institutions varies, but for decades, the artists achieving the most contemporary currency have launched themselves into international orbit from exactly these independent fringes. The old-school institutions they bypassed have tended to dig their heels in, and defend their patch against the 'foreign' values they represent—post-object, post-studio, and process-based practices, conceptualism, and sometimes the abandonment of national themes. The postmodern institutions, meanwhile, where they exist, have set about recuperating the leading independents for the purposes of a national canon, as has happened programmatically in Singapore—and less confidently in Bangkok and Jakarta, where the private sector happily rents public infrastructure to the same ends.

This scenario is not unique to Southeast Asia—we could find parallels in many places. Indeed, after the recalibration of art history, when it has splintered into the more enlightened programs of visual and 'world art' studies, and histories of exhibition and curatorship, public institutions may no longer be as central to its narratives as we have come to expect. But all this raises a double obstacle: not only has the important activity not yielded much concrete documentation, but historians of the contemporary also find themselves confronted with a quite different kind of organizational memory. For it is not exhibitions,

15
The few influential shows held in national institutions seem anomalies, e.g. *Towards a Mystical Reality* at Kuala Lumpur's Dewan Bahasa dan Pustaka in 1974 (National Agency for Language and Literature, not primarily a visual arts venue). T.K. Sabapathy, "Intersecting Histories: Thoughts on the Contemporary and History in Southeast Asian Art," in *Intersecting Histories: Contemporary Turns in Southeast Asian Art*, exhibition catalog (Singapore: ADM Gallery, NTU, 2012). Claims to the significance of recent institutional surveys, including biennales, rest more on their scale than anything else, e.g. the first two Singapore Biennales directed by Fumio Nanjo, occupying various national institutions; and recent biennials in Yogyakarta whose main venues were the Jogja National Museum and Taman Budaya Yogyakarta.

16
Ahmad Mashadi, "Home Fronts," in *SENI: Singapore 2004, Art and the Contemporary*, exhibition catalog (Singapore: National Arts Council and National Heritage Board, 2004) pp. 17-21.

but independent *organizations* that are the more significant and influential forms in the landscape. And it is the social architecture of those platforms, not the grammar of display—much less the postures of an authorial curator—that makes contemporary art's local emergence visible, and comparable with developments elsewhere.[17]

These independent, artist-run platforms will be the building blocks of contemporary art's history in Southeast Asia. Throughout the 1990s and 2000s, they were outlets and embassies of the contemporary, crucial nurseries in which artists experimented with now *de rigueur* forms like installation, performance, and video. Most are aware of their quasi-institutional role, an awareness registered in regional commentary for more than a decade by now.[18] But substantial, printed documentation remains a rarity, and 'discursive density'—be it around artists, artworks, or exhibitions—is seldom encountered in writing, hence the special value of ethnographic research like Nora Taylor's work in Vietnam.[19] If we are to account for the diversity, successes, and struggles of art's becoming contemporary, we will have to engage with other, oral forms of inscription and recalling.

The Curatorial Function and the Undead Curatorial State

Southeast Asian modern art still has no encompassing iconography, no art historical master narratives through which a regional exhibition history might be posed as an alternative. Some have sought such a narrative in classical traditions. The work of Singapore's lone art historian T.K. Sabapathy offers a suggestive, supra-national frame as the region readies itself for greater economic integration. But this frame has languished for decades without institutional backing; and while it may illuminate the identitarian modernism that passed as contemporary in the 1990s, it struggles to accommodate the more globally attuned practices that have emerged since.[20]

The pivotal broker of this global contemporaneity has been the curator. Yet in Southeast Asia there is little uniformity in the figure's role or aspirations, nor in the discursive and institutional parameters informing curatorial work. Research is not an inalienable part of it, nor has curatorial education taken stable, institutional forms. In this region, the pioneering curator of the contemporary was *by definition* an artist-curator. In his 2008 book—the most substantial effort to date to historicize the contemporary in a Southeast Asian context—Patrick Flores identified four: Apinan Poshyananda, Jim Supangkat, Redza Piyadasa, and Raymundo Albano.[21] All were trained as artists, all gravitated toward the curatorial role in the 1970s and 1980s.

The wider phrase 'curatorial function' better accommodates this hybrid, which has been the norm since, as well as the

17
That 'social architecture' is often built around a platform's founders or prime movers. Attempts to study it are highly contingent on individuals and the vicissitudes of friendship.

18
For evidence of this reflexivity, see *Gwangju Biennale 2002—Project 1: Pause Realization*, exhibition catalog (Gwangju: Gwangju Biennale Press, 2002), and Mashadi, pp. 17-21.

19
Nora A. Taylor, *Painters in Hanoi: An Ethnography of Vietnamese Art* (Honolulu: University of Hawai'i Press, 2009). See also Sandra Cate, *Making Merit, Making Art: a Thai Temple in Wimbledon* (Honolulu: University of Hawai'i Press, 2003). Circumspect though I am about the methodologies of social science, working in Thailand the value of oral histories was obvious and I began to generate them intuitively in my research. Curators new to the region frequently ask for a reading list, a diligence I find hard to discourage, but my answer is always that what they seek is not in any library, and is best gathered by talking to people.

20
T.K. Sabapathy, *Road to Nowhere: The Quick Rise and the Long Fall of Art History in Singapore* (Singapore: Art Gallery at the National Institute of Education, 2010). The ASEAN Economic Community set 2015 as its target for substantive economic integration within the regional bloc, alongside political and cultural measures. In all fields, the progress is visible but unconvincing.

21
Patrick D. Flores, *Past Peripheral: Curation in Southeast Asia* (Singapore: NUS Museum Press, 2008).

collective agency of artist-run initiatives—like the Artists General Assembly in Singapore (1993-1994), the Chiang Mai Social Installation (1992-2001), and even the much earlier Gerakan Seni Rupa Bahru (Indonesian New Art Movement, begun in 1975)—which yielded pivotal exhibitions, but shunned the institutional and market power that might be crystallized in the figure of the curator. Another connotation of 'function' is mathematical, implying permutations dependent on certain variables. This inflection might highlight adventitious curatorial responses to local situations, similar to the 'tactics' Michel de Certeau opposed to the 'strategies' of institutions. More apposite still are the bureaucratic connotations of the *functionary,* the anonymous vehicle of a discourse, rather than its driver (as in Foucault's 1969 lecture), like those who often assume the curatorial role in Southeast Asia's institutions.[22] Even if such institutions have not understood or incubated contemporary curatorial practice, this doesn't mean they have not performed a curatorial function. 'Bureaucratic' is hardly a compliment, yet there is nothing inherently mindless about this functionary. The founding director of the Havana Biennial, rejecting what she called 'curatorial protagonism,' insisted on the designation 'researcher' for members of the curatorial team, a figure Rachel Weiss characterizes as non-authorial and "administrative, if inquisitive."[23]

In the West, the independent curator arose from the affluence of the postwar welfare state, as it sought to democratize the bourgeois luxury of art. The mobility and autonomy of this figure signaled institutional maturity, suggesting that selection and presentation need no longer be the closed preserve of the museum. Thus unshackled, the curatorial function began to move to its own rhythm, with exhibitions increasingly reframed as 'projects.'[24] The more agile *Kunsthalle*—a creature of industrializing Europe and typically not collection-based—facilitated this transition, which was later naturalized by the proliferation of biennials. Notwithstanding the image of 'precarity' they sometimes cultivate, these autonomous curators are fundamental to contemporary art and its circulation as an exemplary form of global and neoliberal exchange: a peripatetic life-form alighting here and there, but properly *coming out of nowhere*. (The contemporary curator is 'based,' not 'born.')

In Southeast Asia, curatorial independence and mobility must be qualified. The better curators typically remain independent of institutions, but few are independent of the market. Their role is often mercantile, and more promotional than critical. And their mobility differs from the seductive nomadism of their global peers. As elsewhere, the curator is a kind of double agent, working both within and outside a 'local' sphere,

22
Michel Foucault, "What is an Author?," in *Language, Counter-Memory, Practice: selected essays and interviews*, trans. Donald F. Bouchard and Sherry Simon (Oxford: Blackwell, 1977).

23
Rachel Weiss's essay is an 'exhibition history,' but even notwithstanding that disciplinary innovation, would stand as a triumph of contextual art history. Rachel Weiss, "A Certain Place and a Certain Time: The Third Bienal de La Habana and the Origins of the Global Exhibition," in Weiss *et al.*, p. 24.

24
On this reframing, see Lucy Steeds in Steeds *et al.*, p. 38.

exporter of local/national product, importer of foreign knowledge and discourse—but rarely of foreign *product*. Even Flores's pioneers, while foreign languages and ideas were key to their distinction, gained traction on international circuits as geographically defined specialists. In fact, they turned out to be a strikingly sedentary bunch. Despite the burgeoning global exchange of art since, very few Southeast Asian curators have become orbital, or have become based elsewhere. Their expertise and advantages have proven local rather than universal, and seldom transferable.

They are less authorial, too, tending toward the summary rather than the essay. To put it more cynically, the curator often serves as a kind of local aggregator, streamlining the supply chain for larger survey shows elsewhere. When I taught the Arts Management MA at Bangkok's Chulalongkorn University, ten years ago, half the students were fresh-faced employees of the national tourism authority. Having no knowledge of art history was still not seen by universities—perhaps even by most artists—as an impediment to entering the curatorial profession. Language, however, was crucial: I could only teach there because these classes were conducted in English. While these students lacked any knowledge of art, they had some facility with communication, which tells us something about what the role meant. As a fledgling art bureaucracy (the Office of Contemporary Art and Culture, then just a few years old) began to put Thai artists on the global, contemporary stage, it needed interpreters, not curators. Even now, many curators come to the job sideways, after studying languages, journalism, or social sciences. A crash course alongside their MA in London, in their second language, is sometimes their first encounter with art historical discourse.

The frameworks of trust, expertise and authority, and relations between artists, curators, and institutions, have therefore evolved very differently to those in the West. Yet the curatorial function *is* generalizable across the region, especially in its complicity with the state—that nation that gave birth to aesthetic modernity, but could only be an awkward, surrogate parent to the contemporary. In the 1970s, when the curator appeared, no nation in Southeast Asia was more than thirty years old. These new polities were not reflecting on centuries of cultural mixture, nor were they poised for a global order of exchange. They were more like teenagers, in the throes of adolescent identity crises—by turns surly and idealistic, despairing and ebullient—rediscovering or inventing traditions and resisting (in some cases even briefly overturning) the dictates of authoritarian parents. Most were susceptible to populist nationalism. The currency of the independent curator, in that context, was international, but not post-national. Flores contends that their role was both "affirmative and deconstructive" with respect to nation, but this also meant a concomitant ambivalence with respect to the *artist*.[25] For these heralds of the contemporary were also the ones disarming the more radical provocations of contemporary art and harnessing it for the purposes of an evolving national form. This complicity has shaped artistic and curatorial work alike. It is probably the most salient general feature distinguishing the Southeast Asian contemporary from that of the West.

Yet even with these regional qualifications, curatorship may be a misleading vector, not just because it has not given rise to the most significant forms, but also for another, less obvious reason: we focus on the state's instrumentalization of the curator at the risk of underestimating its *own*, often formidable curatorial mandate. An inclusive history of exhibition-making must account for both the curator as instrument of the state, and the state itself as an inherently exhibitionary agency, with designs on the curatorial function and the 'contemporary' values unlocked by it.[26] To take this curatorial state seriously, we must look beyond museums and biennales to a wider economy of appearances and spectrum of exhibitionism. And the more one looks at the regional modern, the more one finds that curation has been there all along, sometimes on a massive scale, and usually in the name of the Nation. In the spectacles of Sukarno and Norodom Sihanouk in the 1950s and 1960s, of Imelda Marcos in the 1970s, audiences bore witness to an aesthetic modernity with both contemporary and international pretensions. In all of them, modern art was instrumental, but the authorship of these principals easily eclipsed that of any artist or curator, then or since. This 'dilated' history is bound to shed critical light on the more recent internationalism of contemporary art, which, for all its worldliness, will not make art history global without weighing those older, worldly visions against its own.

25
Patrick D. Flores, "Turns in Tropics: Artist-Curator," in *Modern and Contemporary Southeast Asian Art: an anthology*, eds. Nora A. Taylor and Boreth Ly (Ithaca, NY: Cornell Southeast Asia Program Publications, 2012), p. 175.

26
In a recent workshop in Singapore, Cosmin Costinas juxtaposed Arnold Bode's inaugural Documenta (1955) and Harald Szeeman's seminal 1969 show in Bern with an earlier 'international survey show': Hitler and Goebbels' *Entartete Kunst* (1937). It was facetious, yet salutary for Southeast Asia—especially Singapore with its cultural command economy—displacing presumptions about the curatorial and its nativity to contemporary art, and underscoring art's status as an 'ideological state apparatus.' See the 1987 essay by Walter Grasskamp, republished as "Degenerate Art and Documenta—Modernism Ostracised and Disarmed," in *Museum Culture: Histories, Discourses, Spectacles*, eds. Daniel J. Sherman and Irit Rogoff (Minneapolis, MN: University of Minnesota Press 1994), pp. 163-194.

Under the Sycamore Tree

Curating as Currency: Actions That Say Something, Words That Do Something

Jelena Vesić & Vladimir Jerić

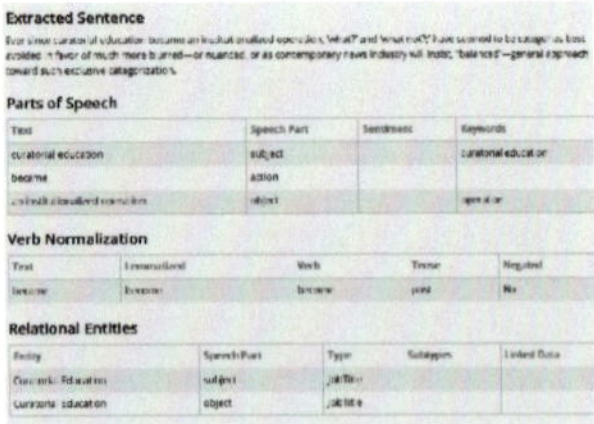
Extracted Sentence

Parts of Speech

Text	Speech Part	Sentiment	Keywords
curatorial education	subject		curatorial education
became	action		
[illegible]	object		[illegible]

Verb Normalization

Text	Lemmatized	Verb	Tense	Negated
became	[illegible]	became	past	No

Relational Entities

Entity	Speech Part	Type	Subtypes	Linked Data
Curatorial Education	subject	[illegible]		
Curatorial education	object	[illegible]		

See p. 239
VocabGrabber, Screen Shot, January 9, 2016 (www.visualthesaurus.com/vocabgrabber)

There seems to be one particular meaning to the word 'curated.' You know the feeling when something odd but not-random-at-all happens? That one. You are about to hear the story of one such event that involves a mystery of Another Place, a lot of talk about curators and featuring one important Sycamore tree.[1]

....

Not that long ago, we were sent to find and bring back 'the chart,' the knowledge a curator should possess in order to curate. We were advised to also get to know what knowledge would be unnecessary, or even harmful for the curatorial task, to learn about the things 'to know to leave behind.'[2] Eventually, we had to understand how to turn the insight of such a complex and concrete procedure into an abstract, academic kind of knowledge. It is hard, and, apparently, only Students can be the judge of that. But, our mission could not fail—our people depended on us coming back with the Recording.

The Old Database revealed some secrets of its own: we learned that the answers we were looking for might hide with one particular Sycamore tree, so particular that it actually has a name. But then our memory unit malfunctioned somewhere above the uncharted area right behind the Gate—a crash-landing we will never be able to forget. We were sure though that somewhere in those never-ending forests this thousand-year-old trunk should be hiding, beaming all its wisdom, just ready to be recorded. So the search began.

Eventually, one afternoon we were lucky enough to stumble upon both: our long-sought-for Sycamore Tree with a Name, and right under it, a group of students engaged in what turned out to be a long, detailed discussion. There were 24 of them, all men, dressed somewhat oddly. Our presence did not seem to bother them at all, and, when we think of it now, they never showed any awareness of us standing right beside them. Discussing their matters intensely, they never interrupted each other. What follows is exactly what we heard.

....

Peter

From various different educational enterprises bearing the name 'curatorial,' developed over the previous two or three decades, no precise lists of curatorial tasks could be derived. There were no averages helping us come up with historical 'what?' and 'what not?' instructions. Ever since curatorial education became an institutionalized operation, 'what?' and 'what not?' have seemed to be categories best avoided in favor of a much more blurred—or nuanced, or, as contemporary news industry will insist, 'balanced'—general approach toward such exclusive categorization.

1
The title of the text derived from the song *Sycamore Trees*, performed by 'Little' Jimmy Scott (lyrics by David Lynch, music by Angelo Badalamenti) in the finale of David Lynch's, television series *Twin Peaks*, first broadcast June 10, 1991. See https://en.wikipedia.org/wiki/Episode_29_(Twin_Peaks) and https://youtu.be/rIXPG8NR5iI (accessed October 21, 2015).

2
Boris Buden, "Towards the Heterosphere: Curator as Translator," in *Performing the Curatorial: Within and Beyond Art*, ed. Maria Lind (Berlin/Stockholm/Gothenburg: Sternberg Press, Tensta Konsthall & ArtMonitor/University of Gothenburg, 2012).

Armstrong

Eventually, we did manage to find one such list, derived from one of the first discussions on curatorial education.[3] This happened during the peak of the emergence of curatorial education programs, conceptualized as training courses to establish and legitimize this profession. It is a 'what' list, and it states students should be taught about the following:

A Cookbook for Curatorial Education

- One should seduce and convince students that the world of art is an attractive one and worth dedicating their life to.
- One should provide encounters with inspirational practitioners—dynamic personalities could be a productive example of how individuals who create in the midst of social chaos are inevitably building a social context.
- Participants should be provided with extensive field research.
- The course should be short and intensive, focused on production, and on working with artists.
- The course should be truly international—one should be able to see one's own continent through the eyes of a colleague educated in a totally different part of the globe, but who has learned similar tools.
- The group should be small and work in a 'laboratory environment.'
- Students should learn to work as a team and to experience qualities of group dynamics and collaboration, as well as a process of constant negotiation.

Barnewall

Out of all the qualities listed, there seems to be one that prevails, gravitating around the expressions of 'group,' 'team,' 'collaboration,' 'working with,' emphasizing the social aspect of the task.

Andrew

Through such an approach the illusion of the promise of success is created, and the idea that the world of opportunities is open to everyone. As we know, this struggle 'worth dedicating your life to' will extract only a few great names.

Samuel

The brief history of institutionalized curatorial education proves that, so far, the decision was made to place emphasis on the practical side of things—most curatorial programs and courses

3
The text comes from a slide in a lecture by Jelena Vesić titled *Practices of Curatorial Education: Curator as a Symptom of Spaghetti Bolognese Politics and is There a Way Out*. The text is a remix of statements by Teresa Gleadowe, Victor Missiano, and Saskia Bos, published in *Manifesta Journal no 4: Teaching Curatorship* (Amsterdam: International Foundation Manifesta, 2004).

were promising 'real world' experience, working on existing projects in a 'hands-on' manner, getting introduced to the 'existing network of professionals,' learning 'current technologies,' and so on. Most of this self-centered and self-oriented curatorial learning ended up in the vicious cycle of anthropological curators studying other curators, and establishing an apparently self-sufficient 'world of curating,' as an autonomous unit within the larger world of art.

G.N.

Not without reason, by insisting that teaching of it should be perceived as 'training,' at least one of the educational facilities acknowledged that the nature of curatorship is more akin to the famously mysterious martial art of kung fu rather than any systematized and academized discipline. If so, a character such as Bruce Lee would indeed epitomize the contemporary figure of 'trained' curator, and his advice on how to teach this sacred art further, we assume, would be immersed in idiosyncratic statements such this one:

> *Be like water making its way through cracks. Do not be assertive, but adjust to the object, and you shall find a way around or through it. If nothing within you stays rigid, outward things will disclose themselves. Empty your mind, be formless. Shapeless, like water. (...) Now, water can flow or it can crash. Be water, my friend.*[4]

Leonard

On second thought, and considering most of the situations one may encounter while pursuing a certain curatorial task, this is not such bad advice. After all, they say that the best exhibitions are curated as if by an 'invisible hand.' The curator needs to be felt everywhere, but not seen. If the audience can see the curator in between the artworks and themselves, the curator apparently did not read the manual, and the exhibition feels odd.

John

Shaolin kind of stuff is not learned through manuals, but by doing. Doing it a lot. 'Doing it' always happens in the present tense, without an inherent need for the future, and with a dubious need to be justified by the past. In that respect, the curator acts like algorithm.

Everyone

Algorithm! Tell us more!

4
The famous Bruce Lee quote comes from the TV series *Long Street*, 1971. See https://youtu.be/LTnSEFsInp0 (accessed November 6, 2014).

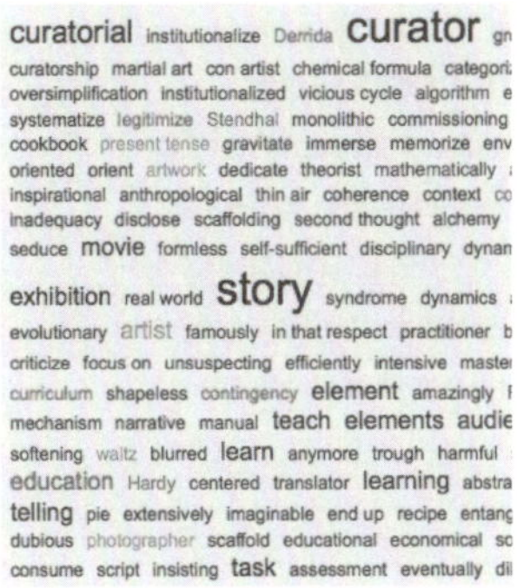

See p. 237
AlchemyAPI, Screen Shot, January 9, 2015 (www.alchemyapi.com/products/demo/alchemylanguage)

John
But also, in Shaolin, the most important is the figure of the Teacher. Without the Teacher, nothing happens.

Isaac
When watching a movie, you don't see a director anywhere in the movie itself; you don't hear them announcing what is about to happen, or explaining the meaning of that what just happened. Of course you may feel as if being guided, directed, but the whole thing only works if you never see the director.

Travis
An exhibition is similar to a movie or a theater play, or to most other products of culture, in that it always aims to tell a story. A number of theorists were contemplating this, examining the relations between *syuzhet* (a discourse—how exactly a certain story is being told), and *fabula* (the narrative—what the certain story tells).[5] But there seems to be much more in the structure of the story than the interplay of these two elements, anyway. Obviously, there are numerous ways and contexts to express or transfer a certain narrative. They can be deemed appropriate or not, timely or not, skillful or not, eventually successful or not: the assessment will be based on the exact choice of storytelling elements at the exact time and place of telling.

Everyone
Story! Yes, it's about the story!

John
In order to tell the story, curators and movie directors need to be in command of what we could recognize as theory, that is, of the narrative itself, alongside all the counter- and parallel narratives out there. They also have to be the masters of practice, of various techniques of carefully sequencing events, or of raising or softening the tone, or of surrounding the uncanny or unfamiliar occurrence with common and comfortable details, so a sense of coherence is being preserved. Arguably, our theory, our *fabula* of the story, can be learned in what we can recognize as the academic way; people can read about it, memorize, criticize, write their own. On the other hand, the specific way of telling the story, its *syuzhet*, does not lend itself to abstraction easily; as we know, without some experience and practical work in telling stories—which can be acquired only by telling stories—even a child will recognize a con artist and refuse to believe.[6]

5
This phenomenon (or perhaps noumenon) was outlined by Vladimir Propp and other Russian Formalists, and explored by Jonathan Culler, Mikhail Bakhtin, Jacques Derrida, and many others. There were a lot of attempts to crack open the mechanism of *syuzhet*, but none were close to success before computer algorithms arrived. In February 2015, professor of English and programmer Matthew Jockers published a piece of software called *Syuzhet Package* with which he analyzed more than 40,000 classic novels, mostly from the nineteenth century. The analysis resulted in graphs of 'plot shapes,' so these tens of thousands graphs of 'emotional trajectories' of different novels could be compared, analyzed, and classified. This effort is, however, far from complete; resolution and accuracy are not yet sufficient, and *Syuzhet Package* has some way to go until its analysis of these thousands of novels, of any novels, or probably of all the novels out there is accepted. See http://matthewjockers.net/2015/02/02/syuzhet (accessed August 21, 2015).

6
Jonathan D. Culler, *The Literary in Theory* (Redwood City, CA: Stanford University Press, 2007).

Ephraim

That also implies the considerable difficulty to distinguish between the *syuzhet* and the *fabula* within the monolithic body of the story: storytelling always required the mastery of these two seemingly different fields, while the story itself cannot allow for the distinction to be known. For the story is only complete when its elements are seamlessly intertwined, to the point at which the audience cannot tell which is which, unless 'stepping out' of the story and observing it from the outside.

John

Stories developed a curious evolutionary mechanism to guard their secrets from being disclosed—in order to get to know the structure of the story, the audience needs to get dis-involved from it, but in that very moment the story itself dissolves, revealing sometimes amazingly elaborate scaffolding that, still, does not account for what the story was. Narratology seems to be one of those sciences still entangled with its own mighty alchemy.

Augustine

Could it be said that movie directors and curators share the same dilemma in regard of their storytelling skills? In order to 'pull the story trough,' despite the notorious contingencies of life, a lot has to be done. That means for a director to know how to act, to be able to improve actors' performances; to know how to frame the scene and be a bit of a photographer, so as not to lose all the important elements of the picture, and to keep out the 'surplus,' the unnecessary and harmful details; to know how to write in order to adjust the script, because to write dialogues is one thing, but to tell stories is another; and, eventually, and probably most important of all, a movie director needs to be so masterful and so convinced of the story himself to be able to not only convince the eventual audience, but to convince the producer of financing the production of the story, ahead of the very first sentence actually being performed.

Charles

Applying this as an analogy to what might be the perceived task of the curator, in order to tell a certain story, no elements will just wait around to be assembled easily into a coherent whole. A curator should be a friend of the artist, and should know how artists thinks, and work with them closely. Curators have to be able to write extensively: not only about particular artists, and the process of curatorial research, and their own and other exhibitions, but also about various philosophical and social contexts, about new economical developments of the Far East, or the wars in countries seen only on television.

Curators frequently engage in commissioning a certain artist, topic, or theme. Curators also have to be masters of ever-more complex technologies used by artists to produce the works and by audiences to consume, or to just get to know about the exhibitions and events. They would need to sing and dance constantly, their left side spinning with artists and media and audience night and day, their right side waltzing subtly with directors, editors, foundations, ministries, banks, never missing a beat...

John
It is not easy to envision such elaborate dancing classes even in some very practical 'How to Curate in 100 Steps' program, so how to do it within the Academy? If we make a list of all the tasks mentioned, and there are many more to add, it would be a very long list. Is it even possible to establish a curriculum for learning all that?

Julian
It seems it is not, but the good news is that perhaps we don't have to. It has been said that "education does not question the need to search for, and teach, facts; nor does it offer systematic ways of reaching for an objective truth."[7]

David
It took us a while to reach this simple conclusion: telling stories is only being taught properly by telling stories about telling stories.

Robinson
The whole thing is therefore not so much about learning what a curator *is*, but about what curator *does*. It is about learning how to produce both "actions that *say* something,"[8] and "words that *do* something."[9]

Hartshorne
As everything has to be curated nowadays—from dinners to news feeds, to any 'experience' imaginable—curating art is not considered to be something extraordinary anymore. Rather than a rare and mysterious activity triggering the curious Stendhal syndrome in the mind of unsuspecting observers, curating has became a demand of the common daily practice of consumption, one function out of many we expect to be built-in in our contemporary cultural products and services.[10] It seems that the market needed more curators and wanted ever more curating. But it also seems that there still isn't a good mechanism of producing enough of them, at least, not efficiently. Shall we return to the original recipe for "Mom's Curator Pie" from 2004?

7
Luis Camnitzer, "Thinking About Art Thinking," May 2015, See http://supercommunity.e-flux.com/texts/thinking-about-art-thinking (accessed August 21, 2015).

8
Richard Schechner, *Performance Theory* (New York, NY: Routledge, 2003).

9
J.L. Austin, *How to do Things with Words*, second edition (Cambridge, MA: Harvard University Press, 1975).

10
Stendhal syndrome, also known as hyperkulturemia or as Florence syndrome, is described as a "psychosomatic disorder that causes rapid heartbeat, dizziness, fainting, confusion and even hallucinations when an individual is exposed to an experience of great personal significance, particularly viewing art." See http://en.wikipedia.org/wiki/Stendhal_syndrome (accessed July 12, 2015). The phenomenon was outlined for the first time in the book *Naples and Florence: A Journey from Milan to Reggio* (1817) by the French author Stendhal (Marie-Henri Beyle). The book documents this condition caused by his first visit to the Basilica of Santa Croce, Florence. The syndrome was diagnosed and named in 1979 by Italian psychiatrist Dr. Graziella Magherini.

Benjamin

Or shall we talk more about the nature of 'the inadequacies of disciplinary oversimplification'? The curator has previously been compared with the translator. We have just compared the curator with the movie director, and we sure are not the first to do so. What else, or more, may curating be?

Hardy

Shall we then focus on notions of interdisciplinarity, or perhaps transdisciplinarity? For example, on questions such as how a chemical formula can be 'beautiful'? Or what is the equal of 'rhyme' in physics? Or if an emotion can be expressed mathematically?

Benjamin

But we still don't know if curating is something best learned by observing and thinking, that is, in an academic sense, or if it is something best learned by doing, by exploring it 'hands-on.' Perhaps it is more useful to talk about what the curator has to do once educated, how they should function within society? Maybe it will help us readdress this problem of education, since we don't seem to be able to define those 'what' and 'what not' lists yet.

Alexander

To be able to juggle with both the epistemological, theoretical, and critical content, and with politics, economy, technology, and all the practical details surrounding the creation and communication of art is far from the only skill set demanded. Among those not mentioned, probably the most important is that of evaluating, ascribing, maintaining, and manipulating the value of whatever the subject of curatorial process is. Let's call it the function of mediation—the term extensively used to describe a myriad of curatorial activities.

Peter

To properly position the curator could be a simple matter of form of a certain architecture represented by lines and nodes, had the contemporary networked society been organized just a bit simpler. But the threads of such hyper-connected environment are woven so densely now that good, fat, well-interconnected knots, or possible new places to plot around cannot be spotted easily anymore. And, by taking into account the contemporary 'super now' phenomenon, in which the imaginary form of social connections and their current importance are measured and rendered in real-time, such an ever- (or never-)changing model would simply overwhelm even the most diligent social architect.

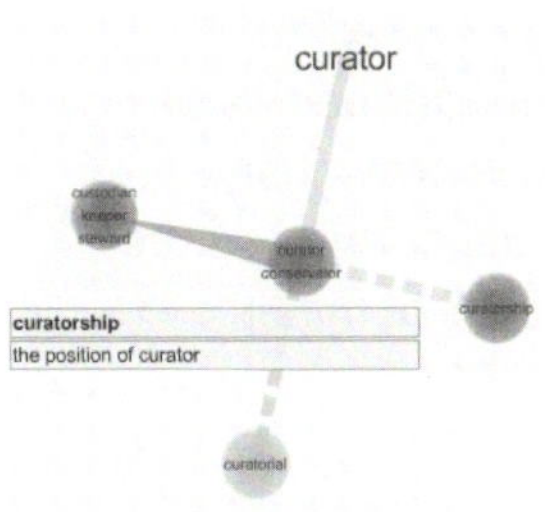

See p. 238
Visuwords, Screen Shot, January 9, 2016 (www.visuwords.com)

John

And would surely turn that poor architect slightly conservative, we may add—it was all so much easier until yesterday, when all it took to guide the experiences of entire populations was to keep an eye on fewer and well-lit positions of museum directors, academy chairs, and media editors.

Armstrong

To summarize this latest binary situation: if curators base their power on two broad, but distinct fields of production—one producing history, evaluation, and debate, knowledge, and the other initiating, breaking, or maintaining relations, producing specific social and professional networks in order to expand and guide this knowledge trough—then the former might be in crisis of inadequate education, but the latter is perhaps even more threatened by the abolishment of its political relevance. To organize people, ideas, and things is always a social service in the present tense, and always politics in the future tense.

Barnewall

It seems that the Conundrum itself would not exist without concern for what the present tense feels like, hence—politics. So we're already stuck, aren't we?

Andrew

It is possible that we are not. Mediation is both service *and* politics. It depends on what particular kind of mediation we are talking about.

Samuel

A lot has been said about mediation so far. We know that "mediators are fundamental, creation is all about mediators, and without mediators, nothing happens." Not even the market, or, especially the market. It has also been said that "nothing passes through the narrow gate into the marketplace itself," and that "this transformation from use value to exchange value involves a deliberate action and 'a someone.'"[11]

G.N.

Exactly, and, as it was said long ago, "the paid critic, manipulating paintings in the dealer's exhibition room, knows more important if not better things about them than the art lover viewing them in the showroom window."[12] What is perhaps new is that today we may be more aware of how the mechanism of 'ascribing value' actually works; it is never just a hidden, coded quality to be recognized by a skillful eye and calculated by an expert. Even with what we perceived as the ultimate expression of all value,

11
Lars Bang Larsen and Søren Andreasen quoted these statements from Gilles Deleuze and Fernand Braudel in "The Middleman: Beginning to Talk About Mediation," adding: "This third man, this intermediary, agent, or dealer, operating at the outskirts of every market town breaks off relations between producer and consumer, eventually becoming the only one who knows the market conditions at both ends of the chain." In *Curating Subjects*, ed. Paul O'Neill (London/Amsterdam: Open Editions/de Appel Arts centre, 2007).

12
Walter Benjamin, himself a keen producer of listicles, wrote this in 1928 and published it in German as part of the collection titled *Einbahnstraße* (Berlin: Rowohlt). Available online at http://archive.org/details/Einbahnstrasse. The translation in English was published in the collection *One-Way Street and Other Writings* (London: NLB, 1979).

we now see that is not the case; before money created its own environment and own measurement of value, there was no such value waiting to be discovered and reflected.

Leonard

Such kind of mediation and the value emerging from it seem to be part of one and the same process.[13] "Money is the technology that mediates between numbers and the fuzzy concept of real-world value," or, in other words, that "money object" has the peculiar characteristic of "having one foot in the world of numbers, and one foot in the physical world."[14]

John

If today we are aware that money-based markets emerge out of the existence of money itself, that is, the origin of money is not in the expression of the markets themselves but rather in the human introduction of the very notion of money, this then might correspond to what we could observe in the world of art.[15] If, in the definitions offered by economists,[16] we replace the concept of money with the one of curating, and the definition of 'money object' with the one of 'art object,' we would be able to say things like this:

- Curating is a technology that mediates between what is a number (annotated, perceived value) and the fuzzy concept of real-world value.
- An 'art object' has the peculiar characteristic of "having one foot in the world of numbers, and one foot in the physical world."
- There is no formal (material) value in the 'art object'—the value will be the one ascribed to the object trough the complex process of curating.
- This value will be in the form of 'a stamp' placed on the 'art object'; it will change over time.
- There were no 'art objects' before the notion of curating was introduced, that is, the function of curating is the necessary condition for the emergence of the 'art market,' or 'the world of art.'

Ephraim

How exactly is this process of curating able to establish value of art objects? Here, at least on the surface, the matter seems to be slightly different than in the world of money. Art objects are considered to be unique and particular, while money is considered to be omnipresent and universal. So here another controversy of the art object emerges—it becomes something unique and particular, but is of universal value and able to transcend all particular financial borders. Its value is at the

13
David Orrell, mathematician and author (e.g. *Truth or Beauty: Science and the Quest for Order*, New Haven, CT: Yale University Press, 2012), outlined this theory during his talk titled *Marshall McLuhan Lecture: Money is the Message*, at the Transmediale Festival, Berlin, January 2015. Available online as Part One, https://youtu.be/ZqsNx-3Thyc, and Part Two, https://youtu.be/a3Au8cgfAx4 (accessed July 12, 2015).

14
What is described as "money objects, such as coins, notes, electrical transactions," are all the possible objects that money is transmitted through; historically, their particular material characteristics—paper, gold, electrons—remain natural and not the bearers of (financial) value. The value is solely determined by 'the stamp,' which is both quite an abstract agreement and a very precise agreement on the exact number to be put on those objects and in regard to who get to 'stamp' the value. (Orrell, Part One, 26 min. 33 sec.)

15
About how exactly money creates value and is not a mere expression of value, see Orrell (Part Two, 2 min. 50 sec.)

16
Orrell, Part One, 16 min. 19 sec., and 21 min. 20 sec.

same time expressed through money and is 'beyond it.' 'Art objects' seem to serve as a meta-category to 'money objects,' or as a 'meta currency.' If one kind of money objects starts to drop in value, its miraculous transfiguration to art object, and then back to another more stable kind of money object will preserve, or even enhance the value. But why is that so?

John

Since the art world became global long before the rest of the world was globalized, and establishing value of art objects through the complex process of curating involves negotiations between various different instances, things look much more complex there than in, say, finance. In order to claim and maintain the new value of any particular art object, it seems that the entire art world needs to be re-balanced each and every time, which is no easy task.

Augustine

But in order to get to what we might call a full picture, we need to have a space outside of it, a certain distance. It was observed a long time ago that "criticism is a matter of correct distancing. It was at home in a world where perspectives and prospects counted and where it was still possible to take a standpoint."[17]

Samuel

Here we might be tempted to accept one very simple definition that is implied by what has been said so far: "curating is the process through which, mainly by the tools of selection and evaluation, a cultural phenomenon or a product of culture is being stamped and re-stamped as the one of meaning and of certain value, or not." But as with any good story, the very surface of the plot is misleading, and there must be more.

Charles

The 'forces of the market' are trying to take over and automatize a lot of aspects of what was perceived as curatorial functions, such are research, selection, historization, archival activities, and all kinds of mediation, especially aiming for the constellation that will engineer the entire *social sentiment* in agreement of a certain value.[18] This process will strip the veils of different activities from the function of curating one by one to reveal what will not be replaced, and hence may be the essence of it—criticism.

Everyone

Oh, criticism! It's about criticism, right? Tell us more!

17
Benjamin, p. 89.

18
Or what is known as *Gliederung*.

Julian

But first we need to get there. And today, the fastest way to get anywhere seems to be to use algorithms. A lot has been discussed on their speed and efficacy, including that the market will be using more and more algorithms in the process of curating. Through algorithms, we can recognize all that is dispensable in a curator, and all what curating is probably not really about.

David

But what if we think that algorithms *may be* sufficient for curating? After all, the functions algorithms are envisaged to perform seem to mirror the list of the perceived tasks of the curator. There are searching algorithms, slicing algorithms, sorting algorithms, and merging algorithms; there are, of course, hybrid algorithms, which combine and automate several of those functions, and more, in one neat package.

Hartshorne

Algorithms can, directly or indirectly, perform the functions of socializing, filtering, researching, archiving... Algorithms can even offer interpretation, up to a certain level. All these things are what a curator does. The figure and functions of curator can be observed from within the art context, but more and more also outside it; curating now resides in all instances of contemporary life.

Robinson

For some reasons probably best explained by all the conspiracy theories out there, computer algorithms seems to be crafted to be especially adept at allegorical doubling of the functions of the curator. Sounds almost poetic: an algorithmic allegory. A perfect match on dating sites where one can choose a perfect robot to be replaced by.

Alexander

We wouldn't say that algorithms create the possibilities to do unimaginable things; that would be similar to admitting that meaning is already there, only hidden in the pile of data. Imagination, as projective category, is rather different from prediction, and it is the latter, not the former we expect as the result of the process of computing. These are precisely what they are: searching and sorting and computing machines, plus the data we decide to give them to process, nothing more, also, nothing less. It is true that now, with algorithms in operation, and with more and more cheap data around (it only works when there is plenty of data, and cheap!), all sorts of things that were deemed to be impossible have become reality.

Peter
Perhaps we are just a tiny bit closer to perfecting the algorithmic curator. In the introduction to their paper published this summer, researchers from Germany wrote: "Moreover, in light of the striking similarities between performance-optimized artificial neural networks and biological vision, our work offers a path forward to an algorithmic understanding of how humans create and perceive artistic imagery."[19]

Armstrong
Now, we seem to be back at the Shaolin territory, as Bruce Lee advised—in the case of self-learning algorithms, the code is trained rather than written.

Barnewall
Like when Bruce Lee entered a hall of mirrors in the famous scene from *Enter the Dragon*. Those hundreds of reflections of Bruce Lee and of his enemy did not have a chance against Bruce Lee himself.[20] He had to eventually destroy all the images in order to win, though.

Andrew
But what is 'algorithmic understanding'?

Samuel
We think this is what we cannot know. Worlds are apart. Have you ever heard a joke that starts with "an algorithm walks into a bar..."?

G.N.
If we explore the differences between the two worlds in regard the notion of time, then we learn about the impossibility of ever 'going there,' that is, of really understanding what the world of these mathematical entities 'feels like.'[21]

John
The world of forms as examined by Plato and Aristotle was based on the notion of the ideal form. Algorithms, through all the filtering and profiling and looping all over again, are constantly perfecting the average form. Implications abound.

Augustine
Yes, art and curating are not about average anything. Can something made from averages, something that is meant to be average, even be criticized?

19
Using algorithms, Leon A. Gatys, Alexander S. Ecker, and Matthias Bethge from the University of Tübingen managed to produce the way for any image to be rendered, that is, 'painted' faithful to the style of several historical artists like Picasso or Van Gogh. As they commented on their research titled "A Neural Algorithm of Artistic Style" (see http://arxiv.org/pdf/1508.06576v1.pdf, accessed September 12, 2015) after showing some rather spectacular initial results: "The key finding... is that the representations of content (the foundation image) and style (of specific artworks) in the convolutional neural network are separable. That is, we can manipulate both representations independently to produce new, perceptually meaningful images." See also http://www.theguardian.com/technology/2015/sep/02/computer-algorithm-recreates-van-gogh-painting-picasso (accessed September 12, 2015).

20
Bruce Lee, *Enter The Dragon—Destroy The Image*. See https://youtu.be/RBnIbqW6ZhM (accessed November 6, 2014).

21
It takes approximately 500 milliseconds to click on the computer mouse, or to snap with your fingers. But algorithm lives in nanoseconds (so it is 500,000,000 nanoseconds, in this case). Today, algorithms can, for example, execute a single electronic trade in hundreds of nanoseconds. For humans an 'infinite' number of algorithmic 'thoughts' could be happening during the time it takes to make that one click, and algorithms are heading toward the horizon of picosecond, one trillionth (one millionth of one millionth) part of a second. This (poor) exercise in math is not here to finally explain why we call the smaller rectangles *smartphones*, but to support the claim that the world of algorithms and the world of humans are very much apart.

Leonard
Algorithms often co-perform with the social subject of 'users,' creating the architecture that shapes the majority of contemporary social performances. So what are contemporary cultural objects and practices in which we can locate a gesture of the curatorial and observe it as part of curatorial education? And back to our Conundrum, can we think of 'what (is) not' as an integral part of 'what (is)'?

Peter
With its 'real-timeness,' its inability to exist either in the past or in the future, how algorithms function does mimic the essential quality of the process of curating—it tries to replicate the outcome, characterized by that one gesture that has the ability to condense what was and what will be into what is.[22]

Everyone
Yes, it's about the gesture!

John
But an essential quality of such an act is missed if viewed as an aesthetical operation; a curatorial act draws its power precisely from its inherent criticism. Without the critical urge, no such act of transformation would have a sense of meaning. If everything was right with the world ahead of such intervention, a curator would be no more than a mad god, constantly rearranging a perfectly fit world just to make humans aware of their lesser-ness, and his boredom, and the curatorial act would be nothing but an act of violence.

Isaac
Only algorithms are truly contemporary; they compute contemporaneity in its smallest units—now, super-now, hyper-now... True contemporaneity operates as the continuous errorless presence, as the dynamic, serial capture of the present.

Travis
Such perception does allow for the functions of filtering, and especially evaluation, but not for criticism. The critique requires distance, and there can be no distance in the super-now.

Ephraim
Looking at algorithms and the results of their actions, all sorts of things would be revealed about humans, and how they may work, but nothing would be disclosed about algorithms themselves.

22
Time, for humans, has some special qualities that are derived from both its inevitable flow and its relative speed. That is, we understand time in historical categories, as past, as future, as something happening now. Most of the things and processes out there, including our own existence, we may observe either as diachronic or as synchronic phenomena, according to what precise application our observation aims; but algorithms are, as it seems, able to endlessly slice our 'now' into ever smaller units of time they can then manipulate at an ever-faster rate. But if you ask algorithm, time is also an essential quality. In the processing unit serving the computing of algorithms, everything is happening now, in 'real-time'; this is, also, where future briefly may happen for algorithms, in the shape of predictions and expected values, as something that can be computed *now*.

Samuel
The best indicator if something is curated is to check how the act itself affects the story that was being told—if *syuzhet* manages not only to reproduce but also affect the *fabula*, then it is curated. If it is a reproductive operation and the narrative came trough unaffected, then it is only a bunch of things put together for the occasion, and curating did not happen.

Everyone
Now, we know! But do we have our lists yet? Can we sign it and call it a day?

Charles
No, not yet. We need to continue discussing and computing the task.

Everybody
Yes, thinking and computing! Tell us more.

....

This is where we left, and can tell no more, as tomorrow under our Sycamore Tree with a Name there were no students anymore, and everything defaulted to the usual calmness of the forest. The weather was so clear that we could even recognize the distant shapes of Tannhäuser. All we could see moving around was a casual quantum rabbit here and there—the weird things were curious, but kept a safe distance from where we were standing. Suddenly, we couldn't program The Tree to tell us any new things; all it did was play back the previous conversations. Our memory unit had enough power now, so we had to leave anyway. But we will be back.

Black-British Artists and Problems of Systemic Invisibility and Eradication: Creating Exhibition Histories of That Which Is Not There

Eddie Chambers

I would like to begin by contextualizing my own involvement in the narratives I will discuss. I entered art school in the late 1970s, and shortly thereafter began to work with a loose association of young artists and art students, on a series of exhibitions and other activities that took place between 1981 and 1984. I came of age, and entered art school, at a time when tens of thousands of other young Black-British people were similarly emerging into adulthood, looking to make sense of their identities. We were the children of Caribbean migrants, who had been born and brought up as part of the British Empire. Coming to Britain, 'the Mother Country,' these migrants—my parents, our parents—took up oftentimes uneasy residence in their adopted homeland. They gave birth to a generation of children who would be the first to grow up embodying an uneasy, curious, yet dynamic state of Black-Britishness. As much as anything else, my own personal history, and the history of tens of thousands of others, speaks of the formation and evolution of Black Britain. Given this, it is perhaps not surprising that so much of my own art, and the art of the others with whom I have worked, touched upon pronounced notions of history and identity.

Being acutely aware of one's own 'history' leads, in some respects, to a wider consciousness of the ways in which a certain history is absent from dominant historical narratives. The widespread absence of Black artists from British art history is symptomatic of a wider invisible-izing of Black people from British history, society, presumed identity, and so on. Somewhat dispiritingly, it is largely in sports and entertainment that Black-British people achieve greatest visibility. The arenas of sport and music are where Black people most frequently acquire any sort of honorary Britishness. Consequently, there are formidable challenges facing those of us seeking to establish wider histories of postwar exhibition activity in Britain—histories that properly address and acknowledge the contributions made by not only my own generation of practitioners, but also preceding and subsequent ones. One of the first things that might strike the would-be researcher is the extent to which the contributions made by Black artists are routinely, historically, systemically disregarded or omitted from dominant narratives. Such omissions are wholly out of sync with the realities of Black-British artists' contributions.

From the late-twentieth century onward, exhibition histories of Black-British artists reveal the extent to which they enjoyed periods of relative acclaim, exposure, and acceptance.[1] At times, such as the early-1960s and the mid-1980s, it seemed as if such practitioners were well established, featuring, as they sometimes did, in important group exhibitions, solo shows, and so on. But Black-British artists—both immigrant

1
Exhibitions and related catalogs such as *The Other Story*, and *Transforming the Crown* were the earliest attempts to fashion histories of Black artists' practice that spanned several decades. *The Other Story* was a landmark exhibition, which sought to outline a history of "Afro-Asian artists in postwar Britain." The exhibition was curated by Rasheed Araeen and organized by the Hayward Gallery and South Bank Centre, London, in 1989. It featured work of artists such as Araeen himself, Frank Bowling, Sonia Boyce, Uzo Egonu, Ronald Moody, Ahmed Parvez, Ivan Peries, and Li Yuan Chia. *Transforming the Crown: African, Asian and Caribbean Artists in Britain 1966-1996* was an exhibition curated by Mora Beauchamp-Byrd, and presented by the Caribbean Cultural Center, New York. The exhibition was shown across three venues between October 1997 and March 1998. Subsequent exhibitions have sought to enhance understandings of the contributions of individual artists, and have highlighted the historically undulating fortunes of certain artists. See for example, Guy Brett *et al.*, *Aubrey Williams* (London: Institute of International Visual Arts, 1998), and Mel Gooding, *Frank Bowling* (London: Royal Academy of Art, 2011).

and British-born—have found that within a few years of any given period of exposure, precious little 'evidence' relating to said exposure exists or remains. So exhibitions that took place in London in the early 1960s are as emphatically erased as the exhibitions that took place in the mid-1980s. How does one set about creating or establishing exhibition histories of that which is not there, or no longer there? With both artists and work being vulnerable to systemic omission from histories of exhibition activity, art historians such as myself are perhaps dealing with 'absence' as much as, or even more so, than that which has an irrefutable 'presence.'

These are by no means abstract concerns. The decade of the 1980s is widely regarded as a particular high point in the visibility of Black-British artists. Three examples to consider here: In 1985, Lubaina Himid presented *The Thin Black Line* exhibition of work by Black women artists, at the ICA in central London. Although the exhibition was presented in what some considered as peripheral spaces beyond the main ICA exhibition galleries, it was, nonetheless, the first time that this prestigious London venue had shown a considerable amount of Black-British artists. Within less than a year, the Whitechapel Art Gallery presented *From Two Worlds*. Unlike *The Thin Black Line*, this was a gallery-wide exhibition that showcased contributions by those regarded as being at the forefront of Black-British artists' practice. This was the first time the Whitechapel had taken such a pronounced interest in this body of practitioners, which included Gavin Jantjes, Sokari Douglas Camp, Denzil Forrester and Keith Piper. In 1988, Sonia Boyce was the first Black-British artist ever to have a solo exhibition at the Whitechapel Art Gallery. Given the longstanding presence of Black artists in London, such 'firsts' were a long-time coming. The first solo exhibition by a Black-British artist at the Serpentine Gallery was by Chris Ofili, in 1998. The first one at the ICA was by Steve McQueen, in 1999. Somewhat ironically, although London is the home to the largest concentration of Black-British artists, London exhibition spaces have demonstrated the greatest resistance to embracing them, particularly as individual practitioners.

Ofili, McQueen, and one or two others went on to ever-greater levels of success and visibility, within relatively short periods of time. Precious little 'evidence' exists of the contributions made by the vast majority of Black-British artists. Many of them—some with once-impressive CVs—have passed into obscurity, or what I would describe as 'functioning obscurity.' While this might well be the fate of all manner of artists, the rendering invisible or peripheral of Black-British artists' exhibition activity not only has grave consequences, but also poses formidable challenges, for researchers and art historians alike.

The reasons for the apparent neglect of Black-British artists in so much of art history are seldom straightforward or easy to identify. In many respects, one has to begin by considering the extent to which only a very small proportion of artists ever achieves any sort of tangible recognition. At any one time hundreds of thousands of people across the country would regard themselves as artists. If we look further afield, there are literally millions of people across the world who would regard themselves as such, and aspire to have their work bought for collections, exhibited in important galleries, and written about in adulatory terms in art journals and be inscribed in the canon of art history. But the art world only ever recognizes a few artists at a time: the favored few achieve varying degrees of celebrity status, while the majority of artists struggle (often in vain) to gain any visibility. It is when what we might call a *racial* dimension is brought to bear, that the results of this partiality create such adverse effects for Black-British artists.

Recovering Forgotten/Erased Histories

Black artists have seldom been accorded the right to simply be 'just' artists, and to be exhibited and interacted with accordingly. Instead of the art world adopting what we might call a 'color-blindness,' it more often insists that Black artists can and must only show up in exhibitions and art projects that set them apart from the wider body of practitioners, and simultaneously de-emphasizes their individuality. A number of artists have struggled to escape this ethnic quarantining, but it is an uncomfortable certainty that many Black artists have achieved their most pronounced visibility in 'Black' exhibitions, or in festivals and commemorations that have an explicit or implicit *raced* agenda. In this sense, it could well be that the exhibitions referred to earlier—*The Thin Black Line*, and *From Two Worlds*—contained the seeds of their own marginalization; by presenting artists not as individual practitioners deserving of exposure, but as 'Black' artists somehow in need of separate (and group) treatment. White culture tends not to regard itself as *raced* in the ways that Black culture is regarded, which leads to a systemic and perennial problem for individual Black artists—that of being perceived and utilized as apparent representatives of ethnicity and cultural practices supposedly reflective of their cultural or racial heritage, rather than simply being framed as 'artists' in their own right. This formidable and systemic framing of Black artists in this way meant, in effect, that they are kept away from mainstream British art and art history.

Notwithstanding the skewed pathologies that saw the bulk of Black artists being accorded separate treatment, there are no acceptable reasons why they should have been so comprehensively left out of dominant histories of British art. But for Black artists to be included in dominant notions of British art means that the would-be researcher has to do an almost inordinate amount of digging. One might assume that such digging is not unusual for those who may have been practicing in Britain a century or more ago. The reality is that Black artists of all periods—even very recent ones—have found themselves vulnerable to being ignored, forgotten, or omitted. We might expect to do a certain amount of sleuthing to uncover information about Ronald Moody—the Jamaica-born sculptor who set up his studio in London, and then Paris, and then London again, in the 1930s and 1940s. But we might have to do a similar (or sadly, greater) amount of it to uncover histories of artists practicing in the 1970s, the 1980s, and even in the years since then. With all but a very small proportion of Black artists coming and going with barely a trace, trying to build a substantial history of Black-British artists is a particularly difficult task.

The absence of Black artists from major books and catalogs of British art is a somewhat circular occurrence. The view, openly expressed up until the 1980s, was that Black artists didn't really exist. After all, how could they, when there was precious little 'evidence' of them in books, galleries, and museums? Thus, Black artists have found their absence reinforced, time and again, leading to the persistent impression that they did not really 'exist.' The art world would look very different if successive generations of Black artists had not been kept out in the cold, decade after decade.

In seeking to contribute to the research for and establishment of more substantial and credible histories of Black artists in the UK, one is faced with a number of difficulties and issues of not knowing. No one knows when the first artists of African, Asian, or Caribbean origin made their way to Britain. It could have been 100 years ago, it could have been several centuries ago, it could have been earlier than that. Simply put, we don't know, because either no records were made, or no records were kept within reach of subsequent generations of researchers and scholars. There is a terrible burden of invisibility and eradication that history has bequeathed the Black-British artist. Setting aside what we don't know leaves us with what we do know, and we know for certain that a substantial history of Black artists practicing in Britain can be traced back to at least as early as the 1920s, with the arrival in Britain of previously-mentioned Jamaican-born Ronald Moody, who would go on to become a much respected pioneer figure in the sorts of histories that are so vulnerable.

Perhaps most alarmingly, what might be called an invisibleizing of Black-British artist continues right up to the present time. As both an example and a consequence of this, even many Black artists who emerged in the 1990s have disappeared from view. The overwhelming body of material and knowledge on Black-British artists remains subjected to the same sorts of adverse pressures and conditions that have existed in this country for centuries, when it comes to the contributions of certain artists and people. The problem of the invisible-izing of Black-British artists has other, equally alarming dimensions. In a great many instances, not even the scantiest records of important exhibitions taking place in decades such as the 1970s, have been produced or kept in safe custody. While being mindful not to cast researchers and art historians as the sole gatekeepers of knowledge, it is certainly the case that a paucity of historical information on Black-British artists translates into, or corresponds with, a paucity of general *awareness* of said artists.

Consequences and Implications of Erasure

Little is generally known, for example, about an important exhibition of *Afro-Caribbean Art* that took place in 1978 in London that included work by Frank Bowling, Lubaina Himid (her first documented exhibition), Donald Locke, and Eugene Palmer. My earliest involvement in organizing exhibitions dates, as mentioned earlier, to 1981, when, together with a small group of other young artists and art students, I organized an exhibition titled *Black Art an' done* at Wolverhampton Art Gallery. The exhibition took place just a few years after *Afro-Caribbean Art*. And yet, I knew absolutely nothing about that exhibition. *Not knowing* means that when it comes to the work of certain artists, every year is a sort of Year Zero. The history of Black artists' exhibitions in Britain might look significantly different if artists had been able to more effectively build on, or acknowledge, what had gone before.

In excavating hidden, forgotten, obscured exhibition histories, one is struck by the extent to which Black and African artists are particularly vulnerable to periodically being cast as 'new.' Consequently, as mentioned earlier, Black artists suffer the vexatious consequences of problematic exhibitions of their work containing the seeds of these artists' own marginalization: by presenting artists not simply as practitioners deserving of exposure, but as 'Black' artists somehow in need of separate and somewhat homogenized treatment. Take for example the notion of 'contemporary African art.' In 1969, an exhibition of that title took place at Camden Art Centre in London. The exhibition cast its artists as pioneers, who through their work could assuage ignorance about Africa and its place in the modern world. But pretty much every large exhibition of contemporary African art that has taken place since 1969 has presented itself in the same sorts of terms. This by and large means that contemporary African art can never be left to exist on its own terms—as a consistent part of mainstream exhibition activity—but must instead wait to be exhibited as part of some or other spectacular undertaking of the 'new,' every one or two decades.

This template of newness was liberally applied to a new generation of Black-British artists during the 1980s. The consequences of this mirrored the consequences referred to earlier, of the ways in which contemporary African art has been framed. In 1984, Sheffield Mappin Art Gallery mounted what is recognized as the first major exhibition of Black-British artists to be presented by a major gallery in the UK. The exhibition was titled *Into the Open* and featured work by some twenty practitioners. (Taking place outside of London, the exhibition lacked the profile and attention of the Black artists' exhibitions at the ICA and the Whitechapel Art Gallery, which took place one or two years later.) But three decades on, pretty much all of the artists in *Into the Open* have now returned to, or are languishing in various degrees of obscurity, or the 'functioning obscurity' that I referred to earlier. Ultimately, Black-British artists have found that to be celebrated for newness is to be damned with faint praise.

In examining archival documents relating to Black-British artists, (particularly from the 1970s onwards) the question "Where are they now?" is never far from one's mind, such is the speed and regularity with which certain artists pass into relative or absolute obscurity. Other factors, equally dispiriting, must be brought into the consideration of the oftentimes-skewed ways in which so many Black-British artists are ignored or posthumously attended to. A relatively successful artist such as Maud Sulter could pass away with hardly anything in the way of acknowledgment and obituaries. Surprisingly perhaps, Sulter's death remained relatively unremarked, the most substantial obituary appearing in *The Herald*, Glasgow, March 22, 2008, a few weeks after her death. An accomplished and prolific photo artist, she has effectively, been 'invisible-ized' since her premature death. (Although, at the time of writing, a retrospective of her work is taking place at a gallery in Glasgow, assembled on a shoestring budget.)

Another artist to suffer a similar fate of art historical obscurity and anonymity was Brenda Agard. She was born in 1961 and died in 2012, promptly entering into a pre-existing oblivion, as if her stellar contributions were somehow insignificant and unimportant. Agard was, though, a familiar and consistent presence in the exhibitions of the mid 1980s that reflected the emergence of a new generation of Black-British artists. In effect, a large number of artists who have made important contributions to the history of Black artists in Britain have fallen into obscurity or disappeared from all vestiges of public professional view. In this regard, Agard's fate is sadly typical.

There are profound consequences of the work of Black artists being accorded scant respect. One final example I wish to cite is The Black-Art Gallery, a gallery space that existed for a period of a decade, between 1983 and 1993. It was located in Finsbury Park, North London, and was the venue for significant solo exhibitions by artists such as Keith Piper, Donald Rodney, and Sonia Boyce. A few years ago I wanted to undertake research into the gallery and approached Islington Local History Centre. (The Black-Art Gallery had been revenue funded by Islington Borough Council.) I was told, in an email, that Islington Local History Centre held no records of the gallery. When it was forced to close in 1993, the entire contents of the gallery—its archives, its files, and its catalogs—were discarded or otherwise lost. This means that it is next to impossible for a history of this important gallery to ever be comprehensively assembled.

Considering the dispiriting example of the erasure of any trace of The Black-Art Gallery in official archives, we can never regard any 'history'—be that of 'Black artists' or 'British art'—as being complete or accurate, at least until a process of fundamental art historical recalibrating has taken place. In some regard, such progress can only be made when the major centers of learning that form such an important part of British art history start to more determinedly adopt radical revisionist practices that seek to *pluralise*. In addition, it will only happen when the leading curators and gallery/museum directors—and those at all levels below them—stop regarding Black artists in raced terms, and begin to treat them as individuals, who, irrespective of the content and nature of their work, simply wish to be regarded and treated on the merits of their work.

The Paradoxes of Autonomy: A Site of Critique

Nikita Yingqian Cai

We are in the epoch of simultaneity: we are in the epoch of juxtaposition, the epoch of the near and far, of the side-by-side, of the dispersed.
—Michel Foucault[1]

During the seminar *Active Withdrawal: Weak Institutionalism and the Institutionalization of Art Practice*, organized by Biljana Ciric and myself, artist Zheng Guogu gave a presentation about his practice. At first glance his might have been just another artist's talk, but, in contrast with the conventions of the Western art academy, Zheng Guogu's explanation of his artistic ideas was minimal. After the talk, Camiel van Winkel, a Dutch attendee, put it to the artist that he couldn't recognize any of Zheng Guogu's work discussed as art. If not radically abandoning an intrinsic Western-centric frame of reference, one would have expected he might have at least humbly admitted insufficient knowledge of other cultures. The blunt political *in*correctness of his statement caught everyone by surprise.

It is worth pointing out that Van Winkel is the author of *During the Exhibition the Gallery Will Be Closed: Contemporary Art and the Paradoxes of Conceptualism*, a book that explores work by only English and American artists, and exhibitions in Northwest Europe.[2] Highlighting the differences in the language of art in the East and the West would have done little to unsettle his biased attitude as a Western scholar.

In his talk, Zheng Guogu showed a poster hung on the outside wall of the studio of the Yangjiang Group, an artists' group Zheng is actively engaged in, alongside his individual practice. The asymmetric studio resembled an eccentric museum building (how global hat phenomenon is!), onto which the text '58 New Wave, Big Steel Making' was attached. He mentioned the minor conflicts they encountered with local residents while the building was being constructed, as well as the private and public activities carried out by the Yangjiang Group in the studio. In addition to being able to identify the political aesthetic of the socialist regime, one might need to know something about China's modern history as well as its art history to be able to identify the double meanings of 1958 and 1985. Presumably, lack of such knowledge should not have been a barrier *per se* to read Zeng's artwork; the real issue for Van Winkel may have been where the artist lives and works, which is the town of Yangjian.

The poster in question has been shown in exhibitions, including *Guangdong Station* (Guangdong Museum of Art, 2008), and *Yangjiang Group: Fuck Off the Rules* (Minsheng Art Museum of Shanghai, 2013.) However, what is key here is that for Zheng Guogu art is part of everyday life, and therefore every

1
Michel Foucault, "Of Other Spaces, Utopias and Heterotopias," trans. Jay Miskowiec, *Architecture, Mouvement, Continuité*, No. 5, 1984, pp. 46-49.

2
Camiel van Winkel, *During the Exhibition the Gallery Will be Closed—Contemporary Art and the Paradoxes of Conceptualism* (Amsterdam: Valiz, 2012).

moment of his life can be art. If his practice were interpreted as a kind of resistance against the museum, or an effort toward self-legitimization, Van Winkel could have easily seen the connection with examples of institutional critique, such as *MoMA Poll* (1970) by Hans Haacke, realized in New York, or Daniel Buren's *Opposite* (1971), which was removed from the Guggenheim Museum. As Simon Sheikh has summarized, "institutional critique was a practice mainly, if not exclusively, conducted by artists, and directed against the (art) institutions, as a critique of their ideological and representative social function(s)."[3] Throughout the history of institutional critique, museums, art institutions, and the market have always been the main targets of attack, considered as the biggest threats to the autonomy of art. The following examples aim to shed light on how the legitimization of contemporary art in China has been primarily driven by marketization.

The Speculative Gesture of Critique

As a concept in Western art history, institutional critique was an important development following the conceptual art movements in the 1960s and 1970s. It adopted essential ideas from conceptual art practices, including a linguistic turn, the focus on process, the ordinary, and the immaterial. In his seminal essay "Conceptual Art 1962-1996: From the Aesthetic of Administration to the Critique of Institutions," Benjamin H.D. Buchloh discusses the interrelationship between institutional critique and the aesthetic of administration.[4] After World War II, the affluent, developed capitalist countries, exemplified mainly by the United States, foreshadowed the emergence of the aesthetic of administration, in which artists textualized, 'documentized,' mediatized, and serialized their works by using formal references to methods of modern business management and institutional administration in an information society. The patronage system of modern museums, the market and its commercial galleries, the writing of art history and the role of art criticism, the proliferation of biennials as major exhibition platforms—all of these aspects developed and consolidated over the same period, and eventually became targets for critique initiated by artists. Hans Haacke's earlier mentioned *MoMA Poll*, for instance, adopted the process of a democratic forum within the capitalist system as both form and critique, with the intention of exposing the rules that very system had internalized. In contrast, Zheng Guogu's seemingly elusive works have nothing to do with the rigid aesthetic Haacke used. To claim that the act of building a museum in Yangjiang is a critique against contemporary art institutions would be to assume institutions provided the rules that govern this practice. However, just as the title *Fuck Off the*

3
Simon Sheikh, *Notes on Institutional Critique*, available online at http://eipcp.net/transversal/0106/sheikh/en/ (accessed November 3, 2015).

4
Benjamin H.D. Buchloh, "Conceptual Art 1962-1996: From the Aesthetic of Administration to the Critique of Institutions," *October*, No. 55, 1990, pp. 105-143.

Rules suggests, Zheng Guogu is not trying to change the general rules of art production and distribution, but to merge the two; to stay loyal to his specific locality while preserving the aesthetic and social autonomy of art.

Andy Hamilton provided a succinct definition of autonomy when he stated: "Autonomy is normally taken to mean that art is governed by its own rules and laws, and that artistic value makes no reference to social or political value."[5] As Hamilton explained, for Theodor Adorno autonomy and commodification are "not two sides of one coin, but are irreconcilable," and, furthermore "Adorno's picture is that as artists became free of church and aristocratic patronage towards the end of the eighteenth century, their work simultaneously became autonomous and commodified through entry into the capitalist market-place."[6]

Only by earning through artistic labor can the artist gain a certain social independence, and thus a level of self-consciousness from which critique might be created. Adorno's analysis and interpretation of the autonomy of art also illustrates the trajectory of the development of contemporary art in China—from the 1985 New Wave Movement, through the beginning of the processes of internationalization and commodification in the 1990s, to the take-over by commercial forces and the art market after 2000. The production and distribution of art in China correspond with what Adorno described as aesthetic autonomy and social autonomy. Aesthetic autonomy stresses that art doesn't directly commit itself to any social or political function, while social autonomy designates art's functionless circulation in society.

In November 1986, the group Xiamen Dada burned a number of works of art in front of the Xiamen Cultural Palace as a performance. In December of the same year, they exhibited random found objects in the Fujian Museum of Art. By creating such paradoxes of what art can or cannot be, they challenged the ideology of the official art system.

In 1998, Huang Yongping, considered to be one of the most controversial artists in the 1980s who entered the international arena via *Magiciens de La Terre* (1989), wrote a text for the project *Away from Art Museum*,[7] in which he stated firmly that "the biggest limitation imposed on artists by art museums is that artists want to exhibit their intent and ambition in museums."[8] He specifically pointed out the struggle between the eagerness to circulate and exhibit artworks and the deficiency of financial means:

> *... to not bring the works to the exhibition is more a cost-effective decision than a special way to participate. The costly approach seems quite unrealistic nowadays due to the*

5
Andy Hamilton, "Adorno and the Autonomy of Art," in *Nostalgia for a Redeemed Future: Critical Theory*, eds. Stefano Giacchetti Ludovisi and G. Agostini Saavetra (Newark, NJ: University of Delaware, 2009) pp. 251-266.

6
Ibid.

7
Away from Art Museum was a proposal for an unrealized act involving the dragging away of the National Art Museum of China from its current location.

8
One Step Forward, Two Steps Back—Us and Institution, Us as Institution, ed. Biljana Ciric (Guangzhou: Guangdong Times Museum, 2012) pp. 74-76.

overall inflation in China. (There's a general lack of funding for art.) The approach we adopt this time may turn out to be an effective way for Chinese avant-garde art to survive.[9]

This allusion to "a general lack of funding for art" could be regarded as an attempt to conjure up a modern patronage system, while Huang Yongping was also absolutely conscious of the exhibition strategies of Xiamen Dada, the group he founded: "It's a gesture to oppose the exhibition-making format that directly transfers works made in the studio to the gallery space, which completely isolates the exhibits from their original context."[10] He even related the question of art's authority to the rationale of its legitimization: "People tend to pay more attention to who gets the certificate, what art is and how they can get the same certificate as well. In the meantime, they forget to ask who issues the certificate and who authorizes art."[11]

Related to this notion of authorization, Wang Guangyi, one of the leading figures of the 1985 New Wave Movement known for his Great Criticism paintings, commented that the Zhuhai Art Conference in 1986 was "a group show of slides," since more than a thousand slides documenting artists' works from all over the country were presented at the event. The act of showing slides could be understood as a gesture "to not bring the works to the exhibition," in Huang Yongping's words, with the Conference understood as the local equivalent of a large-scale contemporary art exhibition. In fact, the Zhuhai Art Conference led to the birth of the Modern Art Exhibition of China in 1989.

However, Huang Yongping not only acknowledged economic reasons for not being able to display the works in reality, but also highlighted the connection between the artwork and its physical context, in this case the studio, rather than the sociopolitical background. In his understanding, if artists can create work but have no control over how it is distributed, academically, or commercially, and if the relationship between production and distribution is severed, then the autonomy of art is sabotaged.

Aside from the Zhuhai Art Conference there were quite a few other conferences that functioned as selection processes for exhibitions, which copied the official socialist rituals of that time in China, such as the People's Congress, the Communist manifestos and charters, the collectivist ethos and the notion of democratic centralism. According to artist Lin Yilin, the founding ceremony of the Southern Artists Salon in 1986 was held in the building of Guangdong Academy of Painting, which was part of the national authoritative art system in the 1980s, and was supposed to be the target of attack for the whole 1985 Movement.[12] Even though their attempt to gain official

9
Ibid.

10
Ibid.

11
Ibid.

12
See the interview with Lin Yilin as part of *Materials of the Future: Documenting Contemporary Chinese Art From 1980-1990*, Asia Art Archive, available online at http://www.china1980s.org/en (accessed November 3, 2015).

authorization was disputed by some of the salon members and deemed futile later, it was challenging for artists to offer critique beyond their historical context and tackle the dominating role of institutions. In some cases their form of resistance adopted the intrinsic hierarchy of power that characterized the existing institutions. Other dispersed, small-scale, and self-initiated exhibitions were often held in the cultural palaces in different cities. They were part of the basic cultural infrastructure of the socialist country, which served to enrich the life and amusement of workers and youth masses. Even after the Modern Art Exhibition of China at the National Gallery of China in 1989, cultural palaces remained the major venues for exhibiting avant-garde art.

The critique that Huang Yongping posed against the authority of museum displays was not targeted at the established institutions of modern and contemporary art as such, but was a protest against their refusal to accommodate contemporary art. It was a speculative gesture to try and conjure up museums and institutions that would openly welcome works of contemporary art in the future. As an artist struggling to support himself, for Huang Yongping art (in the autonomous sense) was as vulnerable as his own professional life. The lack of institutions that showed contemporary work, and the lack of financial means were, and still are, a problem in many non-Western regions. Huang Yongping came to realize that even with the awakening of the artistic self, in a context in which contemporary art infrastructures were insufficient or even non-existent, it was almost impossible to talk about the autonomy of art. Huang Yongping's early sensitivity would later be shared by many other Chinese artists; they knew they could continue to work in poverty and in an atmosphere of suppression, but whoever controlled art's distribution—that is, those who had the resources for interpretation, display, and marketing—had the leverage of power. The real changes happened after 2000, when the art market in China took off against the backdrop of a global economic slowdown, while a significant amount of private museums have since been founded through a combination of both corporate and private funding.

The Aspiration of the Modernist Autonomy

Joseph Kosuth, prolific writer and practitioner of canonical conceptual art, claimed in his text "Art after Philosophy" that Duchamp's readymade "changed the nature of art from a question of morphology to a question of function," and thus "all art after Duchamp is conceptual (in nature)."[13] What Kosuth called morphology can in a socialist context be interpreted as a formalist aesthetic, but Kosuth called for a shift from art's

13 Joseph Kosuth, "Art after Philosophy, Part I," *Studio International*, October 1969, pp. 134-137.

language to art's content. The argument between form (some Chinese artists use the word 'language' to represent 'the form of the language') and content was a frequent topic in the period of the 1985 New Wave Movement, and it is still present in debates among Chinese artists. In an article in the *China Art Newspaper* on November 23, 1985, entitled "The Spirit of the Northern Art Group," artist Shu Qun, another founding member of the Northern Art Group besides Wang Guangyi, described what the concept of art should be:

> *We are firmly against the so-called purified language of painting, and the autonomy dictated by the specificities of its material (medium). In our point of view, the primary standard of judging the value of a set of paintings is to see whether they have manifested the genuine concept, which means whether they have manifested human's rational power of will, and the sublime quality and noble ideals of human beings.*[14]

It is clear that for the 1985 New Wave Movement the interest in art's content was not about proposing art's social and political engagement—on the contrary, art was regarded as the materialization of certain abstract ideals. It revolved around the form of a language, but also the legitimacy of one language over another, meaning the authority of one kind of art over another. Responding to Jean-Paul Sartre's argument that "art should be committed," Theodor Adorno insisted that "This is not a time for political art, but politics has migrated into autonomous art, and nowhere more so than where it seems to be politically dead."[15]

The Market as a Tool of Legitimacy

After 1990, there was a turn in the cultural arena from the modernist idea of emancipation to the postmodern emotions of relativism and nihilism, and avant-garde art activities mostly went underground. The withdrawal from fighting for art's public circulation and presentation gave way to the emergence of the market, which provided a roundabout way for contemporary art to be legitimized, especially in relatively developed and liberal southern China—the Guangzhou Biennial for Oil Painting, in 1992, being one of the examples. According to its main organizer, Lu Peng, the purpose of the Biennial was to open up a legal trajectory to introduce art to the market, with the market here taken as a critical force against the suppression of ideology. In a sense this was not dissimilar from the critical cliché that biennials look like art fairs, while art fairs look more like biennials nowadays. Since art foundations that support the production and exhibition of contemporary art are still a rare

14
See Huang Zhuan, ed., *The Dialectics of Image: Art of Shu Qun* (Guangzhou: Lingnan Art Publishing House, 2009), p. 465.

15
Theodor Adorno, "Commitment," in *The Essential Frankfurt School Reader*, eds. A. Arato and E. Gebhardt (Oxford: Blackwell, 1978) pp. 300-318.

phenomenon in mainland China, and there is no systematic programming and collecting of contemporary art in most state-owned museums, commodification of art has, thus far, been the most immediate tool for Chinese artists to realize economic independence and resist ideological control. To take a strong position against the market is unrealistic for most Chinese artists, as they would have to give up being full-time professionals. In an interview with the artist Xu Tan, he discussed the reasons the members of the Big Tail Elephant group joined forces to organize their own exhibitions. According to him they were fed up with the ideological art charters and movements. Entering the 1990s, most artists realized that changes on a state level would not happen overnight, and they turned their critique toward the nascent art system. Through the efforts of self-legitimization in the form of collective movements in the 1980s, certain stakeholders, such as those who were first introduced to the Western art scene through the Venice Biennales in the early 1990s, were established within the art system, and the development of discourse and exhibitions revolved around the evolution of these entities.

Decentralization, de-collectivization, and de-ideologization became the focus of artists' practice at that point, while the visibility of art in a broader, social sense was still an issue. The market economy had taken hold early in Guangdong province, after Deng Xiaoping's far-reaching southern inspection and speeches between January 18, and February 21 in 1992, especially in the city of Guangzhou. Young artists, like those from the Big Tail Elephant Group, managed to gain extra income from other areas—such as interior decoration design, commercial photography, and custom-made sculptures—to support their own art production and to organize exhibitions. According to Xu Tan, he would save up his teaching fee to buy materials for his own works, which could cost to RMB8,000 to 10,000 per project (about US$1,000-1,200), while around that time China's GDP per capita was only US$300. Liang Juhui, artistic director of the drama production center at the Guangdong TV Station, had the resources to negotiate and secure most of the idiosyncratic sites that the group used to organize exhibitions, including parking lots, abandoned buildings, bars, construction sites, as well as public streets. Being part of urbanizing Guangzhou and its youthful commercial society, the quotidian atmosphere of these venues framed the group's activities and distinguished their exhibitions and works from their northern peers. One might note that economic development in Southern China provided the artists a certain level of economic and social autonomy. Under the premise of de-ideologization, the Big Tail Elephant Group solved the problem of art production and distribution by

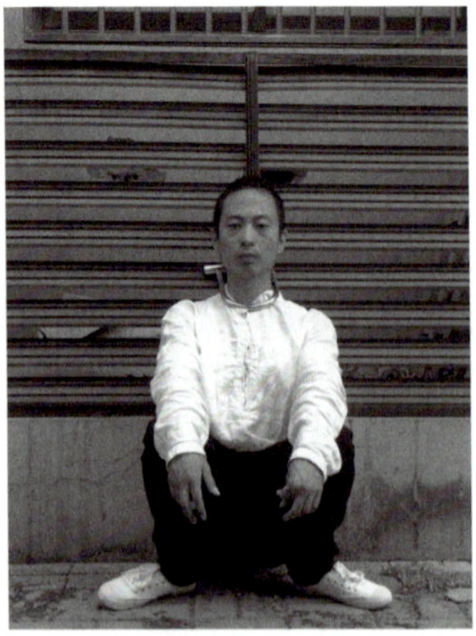

See p. 240
Li Liao, *Spring Breeze*, 2011
Performance, single channel digital video (color, sound), 126 min. 39 sec.

self-organizing its exhibitions. To be able to identify and secure possible venues for these exhibitions, they organized their activities in a way similar to those of a civil society; by negotiating with property owners. The activities of the Big Tail Elephant Group were not primarily intended to criticize, challenge, or intervene in the social, political, and economic context of the day, but were, of course, intertwined with it.

In the earlier mentioned quote from Kosuth, the word 'function' was used in the original text. To translate it directly as *gongneng* in Chinese—meaning a defined role or action given to a person or a thing—would be misleading. What Kosuth might have emphasized was that the content of art is related to or dependent upon other factors. Compared with socially-engaged and activist practices that evolved at a later stage, early institutional critique in the West was still more or less self-referential, but it valued art's political and social meaning, the function of art in general. By rethinking its legitimacy and constructive function within the sociopolitical context, these early works aimed at making changes in art and in society in general. In reinvestigating certain aspects of art practice in China, the intuitive responses of Chinese artists within the totalitarian framework could have been projected as a form of critique, which, however, was not about distancing themselves from the modernist idea of autonomy, but instead aspiring to it. The precondition of their stance was not the canon of the consolidated contemporary art institutions, nor the erosion of art's commodification, but the anxiety induced by ideological suppression and economic and institutional deficiency. By taking control over art production and distribution, artists could construct sites of autonomy in a guerrilla-like manner, which, according to Adorno, could be considered as socially critical, because of art's apparent lack of practical and social functions. The kind of critique as practiced by the artists I have mentioned, and that was embedded in their projects, was dispersed and subjective, yet constructive, and it was projected into the future—that is to say, the institutions of contemporary art to come.

For the majority of young Chinese artists today, their priority is still the independence of the artist-subject, including economic and social independence. With the development of a civil society, in which art production and circulation unavoidably become part of a larger social, political, and cultural landscape, being an artist relates to other social activities (be they everyday activities, in the public sphere, or in the marketplace). It means being engaged, but not completely ruled and regulated by the institutions of art and the mechanisms of society in general, which can thus be defined as targets of artistic critique.

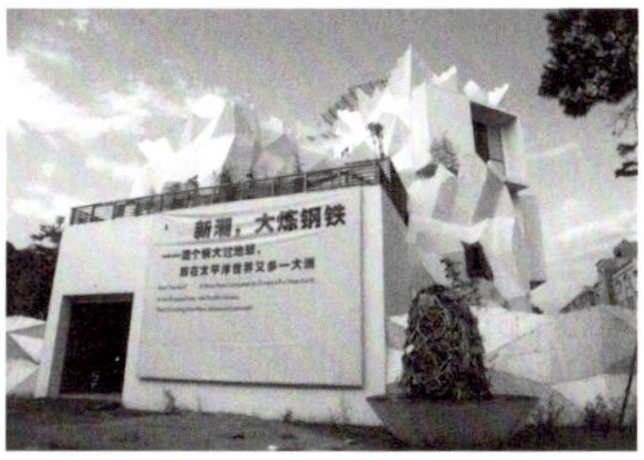

See p. 241
Zheng Guogu, in collaboration with Yangjiang Group, *58 New Wave, Big Steel Making*, 2008
Installation, scrap iron, displayed outside the studio of the Yangjiang Group

The Critique Exceeding the Art World

The documentation of *One Year Performance 1980-1981*, by artist Tehching Hsieh, was presented in its entirety for the first time in mainland China at Ullens Center for Contemporary Art, Beijing, in 2013. Thirty years after the original performance, punching the clock has become a routine obligation for all Chinese people, from government officers, to white-collar workers in the central business districts, to waiters serving in small restaurants. The symbolic meaning of this action, an enforcement of capitalist labor relations, is a shared experience for many. One day in 2011, artist Li Liao asked someone who worked in a commercial building in Wuhan to lock him up somewhere in the same building for a whole day; he was only to be released when that person would clock off. The documentation of the performance in a video, entitled *Spring Breeze* (2011), runs for 126 minutes and 39 seconds. It was first exhibited in the exhibition *Things are Changing* at K11 Space, Wuhan. Until then, Li Liao had barely participated in any exhibitions, and he didn't create art as a full-time artist. Just two years later, in August of 2013, Li Liao was nominated for the Hugo Boss Asia Art Award, and his works were shown in the Rockbund Art Museum, Shanghai. Before this exhibition, he had an argument with his girlfriend's father, who was strongly against his daughter's relationship with Li Liao. According to the father, artists are morally and financially untrustworthy. In response, Li Liao applied for a production fee of RMB40,000 (US$5,000) from the museum and gave the money to his girlfriend's father. The work, entitled *Art Is Vacuum* (2013), documented a personal situation, but touched upon a series of social relations related to the institutions of art—including the contemporary art museum, art awards, production fees, 'artist' as a professional position, and so forth—all of which are mechanisms within the global contemporary art context, and which have become instituted in China over the past decade. What was unique about Li Liao's approach was that he put an end to the universal cycle of art production and distribution, and essentially closed off further possibilities for the consumption of his art. His acute critique was seemingly targeted at his own life instead of the art world, but in the process he challenged and enhanced the earlier canonical concept of institutional critique. When the fight for legitimization exceeds the inner circle of the art world and its discourses, and enters ordinary family life, we realize that our reflection on the relation between art and the everyday has really only just begun.

Again, partly because of the lack of institutional and economic means in China's belated modernity, a mix of modern and contemporary aspirations can be found in institutional critique's practices and projects. Following three decades of avant-garde movements in China, the art market and the process of commodification have completely taken over as dominant forces. Therefore some artists remain reluctant and suspicious in adopting the exhibition as a platform for art production and distribution, and dichotomies between the individual and the collective, private and public, art and non-art, and China and the West still prevail. One cannot help but wonder whether these have to do with the anxiety of an unfulfilled autonomy for the artist, and the precarity of creative subjectivity. Over the past ten years, China has finally reached a golden age in terms of art museums with the massive scale of spatial production motivated by capital, yet a lot of 'counter' spaces have been created from which the agenda of capital might be subverted or ideological control inverted. These spaces can be understood as those which Foucault called heterotopias. To apply the term institutional critique, which originated in the West, to an entirely different context doesn't simply mean to map, categorize, or define art practices according to its original meaning. Instead it produces a different narrative of different kinds of practice, and as a result reinvestigates paradoxes of modernity and contemporaneity, such as the autonomy of art, through another set of lenses.

Redrawing Global Aspirations of Exhibition-Making from a Southern Perspective: Latin American Biennial of São Paulo (1978) and Coloquio De Arte No-Objetual (1981)

Miguel A. López

The active incorporation of platforms for discussion has been one of the main, relatively recent shifts in the exhibition format. Over the past two decades curatorial endeavors that conceived public programs, conversations, and conferences as main parts of exhibiting have become increasingly common. This change points to the emergence of a self-reflexive attitude in the context of exhibition-making, creating an alternative ground for debate, critical reflection, and education beyond the mere presentation of artworks. The orientation toward discursive and conversational dynamics has allowed the rethinking of the social functions of the exhibition and its form of participation in the public sphere.[1] At the same time, the development of this discursive paradigm is often linked to a different way of imagining the political horizon of exhibitions—that is, the organization of discussions and conversations has usually intended to gather various geopolitical positions that challenge the balance of global cultural power configured by historical colonial relations, and confront the hegemonic narratives of the Northern Hemisphere.

This turn toward the discursive or the conversational seems to have reached visibility and legitimacy in the United States and Western Europe, with the 1997 Documenta X "100 Days-100 Guests," where talk was as important as display.[2] This was certainly not the first manifestation of this kind of strategy turned toward dialogical processes, yet it made the phenomenon visible on a global scale. However, their genealogies could still be much more complex. As Anthony Gardner and Charles Green have recently argued, the histories of biennials and large-scale exhibitions "remain *Northern* histories—written predominantly by analysts from the North and reinforcing, even in their self-reflexive critique, a lineage of influence within and from the North—despite their claims to globality."[3] In contrast, with the exception of the Havana Biennial, many events and biennials in the global South that similarly launched distinct strategies to challenge traditional parameters of exhibition-making, and of international circulation have been overlooked. In fact, in a recent study published by Afterall, the 1989 Third Havana Biennial is presented as the paradigm shift. According to Rachel Weiss, it introduced three decisive innovations: one, it abandoned the model of national representations (thus breaking the mold established by the Venice Biennial in 1895), and "rejected the established practice of awarding prizes for individual or national displays."[4] Two, it introduced a curatorial theme as a mode of organization. And three, it emphasized the creation of platforms for discussion, thus representing, in Weiss's words, "a decisive step towards conceiving of biennials as discursive

1
Paul O'Neill has observed the rise of exhibition forms that "incorporate more discursive, conversational, and geopolitical discussion." In his opinion "the ascendency of this 'curatorial gesture' in the nineties (as well as the professionalization of contemporary curating) began to establish curatorial practice as a potential space for critique." Paul O'Neill, "The curatorial turn: from practice to discourse," in *The Biennial Reader*, eds. Elena Filipovic, Marieke van Hal, and Solveig Ovstebo (Ostfildern: Hatje Cantz, 2010), p. 240.

2
The "100 Days-100 Guests" program was a series of public conferences and conversations that expanded into interdisciplinary lectures on architecture, politics, sociology, sciences, philosophy, economy, public space, and art, by Western and non-Western guests from different backgrounds (scholars, activists, filmmakers, artists, theoreticians, architects, among others).

3
Anthony Gardner and Charles Green, "Biennials of the South on the Edges of the Global," *Third Text*, Vol. 27, No. 4, 2013, p. 443.

4
Rachel Weiss, "A certain place and a certain time: the Third Bienal de La Habana and the origins of the global exhibition," *Making Art Global (part 1): The Third Havana Biennial 1989* (London: Afterall, 2011) p. 14. In a similar way, curator Charles Esche suggests that the Third Havana Biennial could be seen as a precedent and important reference for the Documenta X's "100 Days-100 Guests" program as well as other large-scale exhibitions and biennials, such as the Dakar Biennial (rebranded in 1996 to devote itself to contemporary African art). See Charles Esche, "Making Art Global: A good place or a no place?," *Making Art Global (Part 1)*, pp. 8-13.

environments, in which the actual display of artworks is part of a much broader project of research and knowledge production."[5] Weiss is right to point out how these changes have continuing effects on the way the exhibition format is conceived, and the potential of a large-scale exhibition to relativize the Western epistemological hegemony. However, what she describes as *decisive innovations* is not exclusive to Havana. The features of the 1989 Third Havana Biennial—such as the abandonment of national representations, the introduction of a curatorial theme, and the emphasis on the conversational—have precedents, which appeared in some ambitious series of projects in the 1970s in Latin America.

Therefore I will discuss two relatively understudied endeavors here: the first and only edition of the Latin American Biennial of São Paulo in 1978, which was conceived as an alternative to the traditional International Biennial of São Paulo, and the first Coloquio de Arte No-objetual y Arte Urbano in Medellín, Colombia, in 1981. Both events were part of a larger intellectual project initiated by a new generation of Latin American critics, who questioned the role of the Cold War cultural exchange, and the influence of North American and European institutions on framing Latin American art in a series of symposiums. Consequently, the two exhibitions sought to establish a theoretical and aesthetic project that aimed to confront the colonial dynamics that still existed in the continent. Even though both events had no second editions, they are important given how they called the political role of exhibitions as mediators of Latin America in a global system into question, widening the exhibition politics, and gradually transforming the curatorial apparatus.

Biennials and the Cold War

The two exhibition projects concerned—in São Paulo in 1978, and Medellín in 1981—responded to the specific geopolitical and cultural conditions during the Cold War period. Since the 1950s, the activation of the art exchange between Latin America and the United States after World War II was a reflection of the policy that saw in culture the best way to consolidate the new Western political and economic order. To a large extent, the economic and cultural ties between the hemispheres were stimulated by the fear of communism, including Latin American nationalist and populist ideologies. For the United States, the definition of an aesthetic program representing ideological aspirations of the Western bloc was at stake. Such an effort is visible in the writings of José Gómez Sicre, head of the Visual Arts Division of the Pan American Union / Organization of American States. Gómez Sicre postulated a model of art practice that would

5
Weiss, p. 14.

embrace a renewed concept of freedom, which could be shared by all the world's nations, and would dispense with "indigenisms, pesantrisms, [and] workerisms."[6] In other words, he praised various forms of abstraction, and rejected politically engaged art that did not reflect the universal essence desired by him.[7] The search for a common, all-American past, free of conflict, also led him to support the organization of events and biennials in various parts of the continent. Among these events were so-called "American biennials," starting with the American Biennial of Cordoba in 1962, organized under the auspices of Kaiser Industries of Argentina. Unlike the biennials with internationalist aspirations, such as the one in Venice or São Paulo, the purpose of the American biennials was the gradual creation of integrated regional platforms connecting various cities of the South to the United States, in a venture that sought to provide for the Pan-American program of 'development' and 'progress,' a circulation system for modern art. On more than one occasion, these events also became silent spaces of symbolic struggle against social and revolutionary discourses in art, as they were pressured by Gómez Sicre to adopt an anti-communist political stance in relation to the existing ideological tensions in the continent.[8]

Perhaps the most significant outcome of these American biennials was to provoke the mobility of regional critics and thinkers who began to travel around Latin America. As a result, a different kind of dynamic began to emerge. A 1970 symposium of criticism in Quito, Ecuador, and a 1975 symposium in Austin, Texas, brought together a group of important historians and critics—such as Aracy Amaral and Mario Pedrosa from Brazil, Juan Acha from Peru, Damian Bayón and Jorge Romero Brest from Argentina, Marta Traba from Colombia, among others—who attempted to take the pulse of the situation of Latin American art.[9] These seminars aimed to formulate an alternative intellectual project, responding to, and finally rejecting, the overbearing hegemonic presence of the discourses of the Northern hemisphere, and their effects on the interpretative frames and the politics of artistic exchange on the continent.[10] If the figure of the curator in Latin American institutions was almost non-existent, the question about the politics of exhibition and the ways in which certain large-scale events and biennials were assigning meaning and creating contexts for the international reception of Latin American culture was beginning to gather a particular political relevance. For some critics, such as Brazilian Aracy Amaral and Frederico Morais, it was evident that just as the biennial could reproduce the colonial power relations, it could also construct a space of equality in which to confront the cultural dependence and the

6
José Gómez Sicre, "Nota Editorial," *Boletín de Artes Visuales,* No. 5 (Washington DC: Pan-American Union, May-December 1959) p. 3.

7
Of particular significance is an issue of *Art in America* that devotes a dossier to Latin American art, and in which José Gómez Sicre urges Latin America to align with the United States as a natural source of artistic radiation through an abstract style that knows no borders. See José Gómez Sicre, "Trends-Latin America," *Art in America*, Vol. 47, No. 3, 1959, pp. 22-23.

8
See Andrea Giunta, "Bienales Americanas de Arte. Una alianza entre arte e industria," in *Desde la otra vereda. Momentos en el debate por un arte moderno en la Argentina (1880-1960)*, ed. Diana Beatriz Wechsler (Buenos Aires: Ediciones del Jilguero, 1998) pp. 215-246.

9
For the presentations of the symposium in Quito, see Damian Bayon, *América Latina en sus artes* (Mexico City: Siglo XXI, 1974). For the interventions in the "Contemporary Art and Literature in Latin America" Symposium at The University of Texas at Austin (October 1975), see Damián Bayón, *El artista latinoamericano y su identidad* (Caracas: Monte Avila, 1977).

10
In addition to the symposiums in 1970 and 1975, in 1978 three major Latin American art conferences were held. These were the "First Latin American Coloquium of Photography: Made in Latin America" in Mexico City (May 14-16), the "First Ibero-American Encounter of Art Critics and Artists" at the Museo de Bellas Artes de Caracas, Venezuela (June 18-27), and the symposium organized in the context of the First Latin American Biennial of São Paulo (November 3-6). Other smaller, but equally important conferences that same year were the "Situation and Perspectives of the Visual Arts in Latin America" symposium organized by UNAM in Mexico City, and the symposium organized by the Argentine Section of the International Association of Art Critics (AICA) in Buenos Aires. For a critical summary of all these

events and symposiums see Juan Acha, "La crítica de arte en Latinoamerica," *Revista*, Vol. 1, No. 3, 1979. See also *Hecho en Latinoamérica. Memorias del primer coloquio latinoamericano de fotografía* (Mexico City: Consejo Mexicano de la Fotografía, 1978). The public lectures of the symposium in Caracas can be found in the archives of the Museo de Bellas Artes in Caracas. Recently some of these papers were translated into English, see *Resisting categories: Latin American and/or Latino?*, eds. Mari Carmen Ramírez, Héctor Olea, and Tomás Ybarra-Fausto (Houston, TX: Museum of Fine Arts / ICAA, 2012).

11
Vinicius Spricigo, *Modes of representation of the São Paulo Biennial: The passage from artistic internationalism to cultural globalisation. Modos de representação da Bienal de São Paulo: A passagem do internacionalismo artístico à globalização cultural* (São Paulo: Hedra, 2011) p. 29.

12
Amaral says: "Actually, the São Paulo Biennial is still a structure that corresponds to what it was in the 1950s and the world has changed since the 1950s and arts as well. [It is necessary] a total alteration (...), another type of manifestation according to the art object or the processes produced by the artist of our time. Over the last 25 years Latin America has changed too, and São Paulo is, after all, a city located in South America, in Latin America. Well now, São Paulo Biennial is still more or less connected with Europe and with Europe's critical centers, as it has been since its founding. And I think it is unacceptable for it to continue to have such position." Intervention by Aracy Amaral at the second session of debate (October 28) of "Speak out! Charla! Bate-papo!: Contemporary Art and Literature in Latin America," a symposium held at the University of Texas in Austin, October 1975. See Bayón, p. 90. Author's translation.

13
Morais contended: "The São Paulo Biennial internally reproduces international languages imposed by the dominant European exhibitions. Even more: it attempts to extend the same schemes of domination to other nations in

imbalance of the power relations between the so-called Third and First World. In this perceptual shift on the geopolitics of Latin American art exhibitions, the Biennial of São Paulo was transformed into an attractive prospect.

The Latin American Biennial

In contrast to other Latin American countries, for Brazil "the question of biennials has always been central for modern art systems," as Vinicius Spricigo recognized.[11] From its first edition in 1951, the Biennial of São Paulo negotiated the internationalization of Brazilian culture in the postwar period. Following the traditional model of national representations established by the Venice Biennial, the Biennial of São Paulo was born to create a direct dialogue between Brazilian and Euro-American avant-gardes. By the mid-1970s, various local critics were questioning the orientation of the São Paulo Biennial toward the Western capitals of modern art as a geopolitical error that continued to affirm Eurocentrism and colonialism. For example, during the Austin symposium in 1975, Amaral demanded that the Biennial turned its eyes toward the Southern hemisphere in order to confront the meanings produced in the hegemonic centers, and to reintroduce leftist thinking to the event, then controlled by the cultural policies of the military dictatorship.[12] Critic Frederico Morais also developed ferocious arguments in favor of Latin American integration.[13]

The understanding of the Biennial as a part of the battle for dominance during the Cold War would be intensified by the political situation across Latin America, as a number of the countries were subjugated by right-wing military dictatorships, with the collaboration of the Unites States. In 1973 the military coup against president Salvador Allende in Chile not only toppled the first democratically elected Marxist government in the world, but it also tackled Latin American revolutionary desires born out of the 1959 Cuban Revolution. During the 1970s and 1980s, the clandestine program of repression, torture, and disappearing implemented by Operation Condor would finally extinguish this revolutionary impulse through the systematic elimination of left-wing opponents and socialist movements. Officially initiated in 1975 by right-wing military dictatorships, Operation Condor resulted in up to 50,000 murders, 30,000 disappearances, and 400,000 arrests and imprisonments.[14]

The period of crisis the São Paulo Biennial experienced during the 1970s was partly a product of international isolation as a consequence of the boycott supported by prominent local and artists and intellectuals from Latin America, Europe, and the US. In 1969 a call was made for an international boycott of the event because of the continuing military dictatorship in the continent (...) The history of the relations between the International Biennial of São Paulo and Latin America have been characterized by omission, erasure, and submission (to European or North American interests). Above all, it has been marked by the absence of any kind of project or program that would defend the politics of Latin American art or even Brazilian art." Frederico Morais, "Ideología de las bienales internacionales e imperialismo artístico", in *Las artes plásticas en la América Latina: del trance a lo transitorio* (La Habana, 1990, p. 23), originally published in "La ideología de las bienales internacionales y el imperialismo artístico," in *Revista Plural* (February 1978), pp. 49-55, and in "Bienal de São Paulo y América Latina" (São Paulo: Departamento de Información y Documentación artística / IDART de la Prefectura Municipal de São Paulo, April 1978).

14
Operation Condor was promoted by America's CIA, the National Intelligence Directorate (DINA) of Chile under the command of General Augusto Pinochet, and the Triple A (Argentine Anti-Communist Alliance). On November 25, 1975, its creation was approved at a meeting in Santiago de Chile, which brought together the heads of military intelligence of Argentina, Paraguay, Uruguay, Brazil, and Bolivia, convened by the head of the National Intelligence Directorate (DINA) of Chile, Manuel Contreras Sepúlveda. See J. Patrice McSherry, *Los Estados depredadores: la Operación Cóndor y la guerra encubierta en América Latina* (Santiago de Chile: LOM, 2009).

15
According to Isobel Whitelegg, despite being active and developing important internal reforms during the 1970s, the São Paulo Biennial remained invisible to the international mainstream and those five editions that followed 1969's boycott "received little coverage in the international press, and their history hasn't been widely examined." Isobel Whitelegg, "The Bienal de São Paulo: Unseen/Undone (1969-1981)," *Afterall*, No. 22, Autumn/Winter 2009, pp. 106-113.

16
About Walter Zanini, see *Walter Zanini. Escrituras críticas*, ed. Cristina Freire (São Paulo: Annablume and MAC-USP, 2013).

Brazil.[15] A gradual loss of prestige meant that the Biennial Foundation had to undergo a process of restructuring, and to engender larger debates concerning the Biennial's local, regional and international role. In 1977 the newly convened Art and Culture Council, under the directorship of the then President of the Biennial, Luiz Fernand Rodrigues Alves, gave the green light to the creation of a Latin American Biennial that would take place the following year, in 1978, under the artistic direction of the critics Juan Acha (Peru/Mexico) and Sylvia Ambrosini (Argentina). The very fact that the Biennial invited guest directors marked an important shift in the understanding of the exhibition's orientation toward curatorship. It would be further transformed with the creation of the position of 'a chief curator' for Walter Zanini three years later, in 1981.[16]

Various witnesses described the 1978 Latin American Biennial organized by Acha and Ambrosini as a failed attempt to grasp the complexity of the continent. However, all the critics agreed that the Biennial's theoretical symposium was the most significant part of the event. Organized by Acha, as a continuation of the series of seminars initiated in Quito in 1970, the symposium aimed to debate the problems most relevant to Latin American art. Even if the symposium didn't discuss the Biennial artworks themselves, it was an important element in the process of shifting the exhibition's focus—from artworks to the discussions and conversations with larger audiences.[17]

The title of this first Latin American Biennial, "Myths and Magic," was conceived by the Art and Culture Council and was severely criticized by local artists, who resisted a Biennial with a decisively anthropological curatorial frame. The proposal by Acha and Ambrosini was to dispose of the Venice model of national representation and to organize the entire exhibition according to four themes: Indigenous, African, Euro-Asian, and Mestizo. These concepts were an attempt to recognize the "cultural manifestations of race that are part of the formation of Latin-America."[18] They were also intended to create a dialogue among the multiple geographies, sensibilities, and social issues that are shared in the so-called Third World, and furthermore to visualize Latin America as a site where all these places (regions and subjectivities marked by its colonial past) converge. In a way, this curatorial proposal wanted to embrace a discussion about Latin American art and culture from dislocation, as a non-place constituted by its own migrations, diasporas, and displacements. However, this effort to alter the exhibition structure was ultimately undone by the fact that most of the artists refused to associate themselves with any of the four categories, and instead pledged allegiance to their countries as spaces of belonging and representation.[19] Arguably, the most important feat of the inclusion of these four themes was its attempt to contest and disrupt Northern histories of art at the heart of an international institution such as the Biennial of São Paulo, which represented an obedient extension of the Western art system. The exhibition attempted to include indigenous representations, images of vernacular traditions and folk dances, and anthropological documents, alongside Western art representations. The gesture of putting these aesthetic practices on the same level intended to ignite a discussion about cultural representation, and to critique what Pablo Lafuente calls "the Eurocentric, colonial attitude implied by the adoption of a modernist outlook to frame both modern art and non-Western objects."[20]

Soon afterward, Amaral was appointed director of the second edition of the Latin American Biennial, which was slated for 1980. However, due to the internal crisis, the event was eventually postponed. That same year Amaral called an international meeting to debate the possibilities of transforming the International Biennial of São Paulo into a Latin American Biennial. This "Consultative Meeting of the Art Critics of America" was attended by more than 30 invited guests. Amaral's proposal was radical: it aimed to interrupt what she interpreted as a relationship of dependence of the São Paulo Biennial on the United States and Europe. As she stated: "We cease, once and for all, to be observant of others and see ourselves and our neighbors more," ... "we stop being an alternative to the Venice Biennale," ... "the biennale should be a manifestation of a need."[21]

Amaral wanted to transform the Biennial of São Paulo into a more ambitious geopolitical project—a triennial or quadrennial capable of disrupting the hegemony of Northern large-scale art events such as Documenta.[22] As Whitelegg summarized:

> *The Latin American Biennale imagined by Amaral would not be isolationist but rather would include works from Europe, the USA and Asia, selected from a Latin American perspective. This realignment, to read the International through the critical lens of the Latin American, was also an attempt to recruit the longevity and patrimony of the São Paulo Biennial Foundation in shifting the most powerful locus of epistemological enunciation concerning Latin American art from the North to the South.*[23]

However, only 9 of the guests invited to the Consultative Meeting voted in favor of the Latin American Biennial, while 23 voted in favor of maintaining the International Biennial with an emphasis on Latin America. One person voted in favor of alternating biennials, one Latin American one followed by an

17
The symposium was held in São Paulo during November 3-6. It was divided in three sections: "Myths and Magic in Latin American Art," "General Problems of Latin American Art," and "Proposals for the Second Latin American Biennial of 1980."

18
Consejo de Arte y Cultura, "I Bienal Latino-Americana. Um evento histórico", in *I Bienal Latino Americana de São Paulo* (São Paulo: Fundação Bienal de São Paulo, 1978) p. 20.

19
The organizing team explained the situation as follows: "The Art and Culture Council in proposing the regulation of I [Latin American] Biennial aimed to assemble an exhibition through proposed concepts, not only avoiding the geopolitical division by countries but also attempting to display a better view of (an Indigenous, African, Euro-Asian, and Mestizo) Latin America. Unfortunately, the stimuli induced by the Art and Culture Council had as a response by the participants the geopolitical division. (...) Why is that? Latin America really intends to see itself as a whole, or rather still prefers to be separated by nations, culturally speaking?" Consejo de Arte y Cultura, p. 20. Author's translation.

20
Pablo Lafuente, "From the Outside In—'Magiciens de la Terre' and Two Histories of Exhibitions," in *Making Art Global (Part 2) "Magiciens de la Terre" 1989*, Lucy Steeds *et al.* (London: Afterall, 2013) p. 11.

21
Aracy Amaral, unpublished statement, October 18, 1980, from the Reunião de Consulta de Críticos de Arte da America, Arquivo Histórico Wanda Svevo, Fundaçao Bienal, São Paulo. Quoted in Isobel Whitelegg, "Brazil, Latin America: The World. The Bienal de São Paulo as a Latin American Question," *Third Text*, Vol. 26, No. 1, January 2012, p. 132.

22
Conversation with Aracy Amaral. São Paulo, September 2014.

23
Whitelegg, "Brazil, Latin America", p. 132

International one. The results of the vote meant the complete casting aside of the plan to transform the event—something that Amaral called "the betrayal of an initiative."[24]

Colloquium of 'No-objetualismo' and Urban Art

The ambitions of the project of the Latin American Biennial of São Paulo were revisited by the First Coloquio de Arte No-objetual y Arte Urbano of 1981. Again under the general direction of Juan Acha, this four-day event took place in the exhibition halls of the Museum of Modern Art in Medellín in Colombia. The Coloquio constituted another attempt to imagine alternatives to the biennial model that would incorporate critical readings of contemporary art emerging from, and responding to local and regional needs. The event had two main premises: one, to conceive a large-scale Latin American exhibition comprising performance, installation, and ephemeral works, which were to stand apart from the traditional forms of art and exhibition-making. Two, the event aimed at a continued looking for what Acha called the need of an "independent visual thinking," producing local theories that allowed a rethinking of Latin American and international art from a non-colonial perspective.[25] In particular, it attempted to test the limits and usefulness of the concept of 'no-objetualismo.' In contrast to what has been suggested, the term 'no-objetualismo' is in no way a synonym to 'dematerialization of art,' the phrase coined by Lucy Lippard. In turn, 'no-objetualismo' is a critique of the hierarchies of high art and the politics of representation claimed by Western modernity. For Acha, no-objetualismo could as easily encompass a performance or a ready-made as a piece of craft, a carnival or festival, or popular design, in that all of these forms were capable of bringing about the crisis of the Western, unique, bourgeois, capitalist conception of the art object.

At the exhibition at the Museum of Modern Art of Medellín, videos, installations, actions, and documentation were presented, together with a series of public activities, and performances and live artworks appeared throughout the conference presentations of guest theorists and critics. The event attempted to dissolve the distinction between the temporal and spatial experience of the exhibition and that of critical discussion. It intended to construct a platform for exchange in which the spheres of art production and critique were displayed along one, single horizon. The conversational format of the event—the emphasis on connections between people, ideas, works, and actions that happened every day—created an extremely dynamic environment in which all the theoretical and critical hypotheses regarding the state of Latin American art production were permanently reformulated.

24
Aracy Amaral, "A Bienal Latino-Americana ou o Disvirtuamento da uma Iniciativa" [1978], in *Arte e Medio Artístico: Entre a Feijoada e o X-Burguer*, Aracy Amaral (São Paulo: Nobel, 1983) pp. 296-300.

25
See Juan Acha, "La necesidad latinoamericana de un pensamiento visual independiente," in *Ensayos y Ponencias Latinoamericanistas*, Juan Acha (Caracas: GAN, 1984) pp. 57-73.

The Coloquio took place between May 17 and 21, simultaneously with two other international events. The first one was the IV Biennial of Medellín, inaugurated on May 15, which had its previous edition in 1972.[26] The second one was the Meeting of the Association of Art Critics on May 16 and 17, with invited international guests.[27] It was the simultaneous occurrence of these three events that made the experimental character of the Coloquio apparent, especially because of its self-reflection on the act of exhibition-making, and its objective of consolidating a regional intellectual network.

Privileging ephemeral activities and public discussions as central loci of the event implied not only the introduction of research and critical reflection into the form of the exhibition, but also the recognition of the discursive character of the artworks themselves. In other words, the works were understood as social objects, the meaning of which is negotiated in the process of becoming public. Acha's aim was to bring artists and theorists together in a situation in which art making and critical thought experienced a kind of cross contamination. For example, the performance by Venezuelan artist Carlos Zerpa entitled *El enviado de Dios* [The Godsend] made a deep impact on the arguments on the Peruvian theorist Mirko Lauer, forcing him to reconsider his skepticism regarding the political possibilities of no-objetualismo. Other works made parasitic and ironic use of the talks delivered during the symposium. Argentinean artists Leopoldo Maler and Marta Minujin used some pages left on the table by one of the critics on the first day of the seminar as a script for a musical performance piece, chanted by a chorus of 40 students. Other artworks also had a discursive format, such as *Montaje de momentos plásticos* by collective No-Grupo from Mexico, which created situations of conversation and exchange with the public, and parodied the language of academic and traditional art presentations. Yet another project served as an excuse for social debate—namely, *The Profile of a Peruvian Woman* (1980-1981) by Teresa Burga and Marie-France Cathelat from Peru, which was an art and feminist sociological research project that examined the living conditions of middle-class women.[28]

The performative character of the Coloquio introduced questions that went beyond the discursive shift of the exhibition format. The fact that the event took place in the Museum of Modern Art raised the issue of how to embrace performance and ephemeral actions, which complicated the traditional museum set-up. If Acha's proposition of bringing these works together as an antidote to the forces of the market and consumerism was as genuine as it was idealist, the synergy of the broad range of perspectives at the Coloquio managed to construct a

26
The Biennial was made possible by the financial support of Corporación Bienal de Arte de Medellín, created by the joint effort of Suramericana Insurance Company, the Banco Comercial Antioqueño, Coltabaco, and the Cámara de Comercio of Medellín. See Carlos Arturo Fernández, *Arte en Colombia, 1981-2006* (Medellín: Universidad de Antioquia, 2007).

27
International guests included the Colombian critic Marta Traba, the French critic Pierre Restany, the Argentinian critic Jorge Romero Brest, and Jasia Reichardt, the former director of the Whitechapel Gallery, among others.

28
Regarding this project see Teresa Burga and Marie-France Cathelat, *Perfil de la Mujer Peruana* (Lima: Instituto de Investigaciones Sociales y Artísticas y Banco Industrial del Perú, 1981). See also Miguel A. López and Agustín Pérez Rubio, eds., *Teresa Burga. Estructuras de Aire* (Buenos Aires: MALBA, 2015).

living and revitalizing space of intellectual and artistic exchange. In this sense, the Coloquio affirmed that an art exhibition could happen alongside incisive critical thinking.

On the other hand, Acha's goal to propose the concept of 'no-objetualismo' as a means of reading the avant-garde practices, ultimately failed. After its immediate use in the early 1980s, the term fell into oblivion and was employed only by a small group of artists in Mexico, Colombia, and Peru. Similarly, other concepts developed by local artists and theorists were gradually replaced by notions that have more currency on the global stage.[29]

Nevertheless, the question of how these categories have attempted to create spaces of resistance remains pertinent. What is gained and what is lost when we read specific experimental and critical practices from so-called peripheral contexts, and when we interpret them through transnational ideas such as 'conceptualism,' 'ideological conceptualism,' or 'institutional critique'? How to consider these experimental practices from the particular forms of situated knowledge, formulated by local agents in their attempts to give names and political weight to their own critical experiences?

French critic Pierre Restany—who was one of the guests—criticized the traditional format of the Medellín Biennial, and called for the creation of a 'Biennial of Marginality' as a counterproposal. His idea was to generate a global narrative that would "explode the global map."[30] Restany asserted:

> *It would only be a proper Third World Biennial if instead of comparing Colombia with the United States or Venezuela with England, we made a direct connection between the countries of Latin America and other countries in Asia or Africa with similar economic, social, and political conditions. For example, see the art of Colombia with the art of Pakistan, or Algeria and Libya with Brazil. This is how you could make a more informative and relevant biennial, and create something in real accordance with the moment that the developing countries are living. Medellín could thus conceivably produce the best Third World Biennial.*[31]

Restany expressed the idea already in circulation—that is, that it was necessary to penetrate the geocultural and geopolitical authority of the West, and to embrace the global in a different way, moving beyond the Cold War binaries. The Third-World vocation of the fictitious 'Biennial of Marginality' was thus representative of a desire and formulation that were clearly developed by the Havana Biennial in the late 1980s. The same vocation was also suggested by the multiple cultural

29
See Miguel A. López, "How do we know what Latin American Conceptualism Looks Like?," *Afterall*, No. 23, Spring 2010, pp. 5-21.

30
Celia Sredni de Birbragher, "Pierre Restany propone: la Bienal de la Marginalidad [Entrevista]," *Arte en Colombia*, No. 16, October 1981, pp. 71-73.

31
Oscar P. Gomez, "Bienal de Medellín. Opiniones-entrevistas I," *Arte en Colombia*, No. 16, October 1981, p. 50.

maps of the Third World invoked by the four concepts of race (Indigenous, African, Euro-Asian, and Mestizo), proposed as a curatorial framework by Acha and Ambrosini for the First Latin American Biennial in 1978. It was even present in Amaral's frustrated attempts to transform the succeeding São Paulo Biennial into an event similar to Documenta, with the aim to rewrite the global from a Latin American perspective. All these projects—the First Latin American Biennial of São Paulo, the frustrated Second edition of this Biennial led by Amaral, the First Coloquio de Arte No-objetual y Arte Urbano organized by Acha, and the first editions of Havana Biennial—attempted to recognize and underline international artistic and cultural differences from a shared postcolonial condition. Notably, some of these ideas also had further developments and evolutions. For example, the 'failed' effort of having a lasting Latin American Biennial of São Paulo became the premise of the first edition of the Mercosul Biennial in Porto Alegre, Brazil, curated by Frederico Morais in 1997. It was there that a political examination of the historical development of the art of the continent was presented in tension with the Northern views of Latin American art.[32]

Conclusion

Both events discussed in-depth here—the first Latin American Biennial of São Paulo and the First Coloquio de Arte No-objetual y Arte Urbano—sought to transform the political scope of art exhibitions and biennials. The Latin American Biennial on the one hand introduced the necessity of reordering the hierarchies of Western art and non-Western cultural production; it was an attempt to critique the Eurocentric gaze and colonial framing of art. The first Coloquio de Arte No-objetual on the other hand promoted integration of various discursive dynamics into the exhibition structure, challenging traditional display, and complicating the temporal and spatial experiences of the audience. These two events attempted to generate a regional intellectual infrastructure necessary to respond to a Western history of art. They also promoted strategies of building models of micro-globalism and South-South conversations, which used the exhibition format as a means to redraw the maps of exchange beyond the economic and cultural imperatives of the North. This approach would later be consolidated by the Havana Biennials during the mid- to late-1980s and would guide subsequent transformations of curatorial practice. However, the legacies of the Latin American Biennial and the Coloquio de Arte No-objetual y Arte Urbano, as well as other local events, are fragile. That is precisely why it is crucial to emphasize their accomplishments: how they helped to reimagine the global

32 See Frederico Morais, "Reescrevendo a história da arte latino-americana," in *Catálogo Geral da I Bienal do Mercosul* (Porto Alegre: FBAVM, 1997) pp. 12-20.

aspirations from the Southern perspective. How they introduced discursive and conversational models into exhibition-making as a way to contest hegemonic Northern histories of art. How they explored the political possibilities of the exhibition's agency. And, finally, how they confronted the colonial heritage inherent to the format of a large-scale international exhibition.

On the Solo Show: From Resistance to Repression

João Ribas

The ongoing history of curating and exhibitions underscores the particular role that display practices have played in the presentation and reception of art. Concerned with its own putative narrative, this history amends traditional art historical methodologies—including categories of genre, style or period—by directly engaging with the experiential, scenographic, and epistemic dimensions of exhibition-making. These historical accounts, however, only began to be written in the early 1980s, suggesting that the historiography of exhibitions and curating has, in a sense, been repressed in art history.[1]

Yet there is also a repressed aspect within this ongoing historical account itself, given the fact that it is largely written around a single typology; that of the 'paradigm shifting' group exhibition. In the extensive literature on curatorial practice, and exhibitions produced in recent decades, the solo exhibition has been, surprisingly, and rather conspicuously, overlooked.[2] As a typology, it is given scant attention compared with group shows or biennials. There seems to be neither a comprehensive empirical history of the solo exhibition as a form, nor are important examples of these exhibitions—once tellingly referred to as 'one-man shows'—presented as central within such exhibition histories. The discursive presence of the form seems entirely compressed into the biographical and chronological focus of art historical writing, on the one hand, and art criticism on the other.

The position of the solo exhibition within curatorial discourse has been described tersely by Rob Bowman in *The Exhibitionist,* suggesting that in relation to the group or biennial, the solo exhibition

> *sounds straightforward and declamatory, a vehicle for the artist's voice in the first person singular, unmediated by curatorial meta-text ... what scope could possibly be afforded an organisation or curator that chose the solo show as a specialism?*[3]

Supporting a particular representation of curatorial labor, supposedly opaque within such exhibitions, this reproduces a narrative asserting the importance of certain types of exhibition-makers in the postwar era.[4] In doing so, it devalues the historically significant, as well as current acuity, of curatorial work focused on monographic exhibitions, many of which have come to define the very critical discourse around individual artists' practices. Even in its ubiquity as a form generally encountered in most contemporary art institutions worldwide, the solo exhibition remains remarkably unconsidered and under-theorized, although it plays a significant role in forming many of the norms readily employed in producing nearly all types of exhibitions today.

1
Mary Anne Staniszewski, for example, writes of the "history of the exhibition as culturally repressed," in *The Power of Display: A History of Exhibition Installations at the Museum of Modern Art*, Mary Anne Staniszewski (Cambridge, MA: The MIT Press, 2001) p. xxi.

2
Exceptions include the discussion of solo exhibitions by William Blake (1809), and Joshua Reynolds (1813) in issue 14 of *Tate Papers* (Autumn 2010), as well as Robert Jensen's study of the retrospective in nineteenth-century France in *Marketing Modernism in Fin-de-Siècle Europe* (Princeton, NJ: Princeton University Press, 1994).

3
Rob Bowman, "First Person Singular," *The Exhibitionist*, No. 1, 2010, pp. 35-38.

4
One interesting point to note in relation to this valuation of labor is how the typology is central to the work of female curators such as Lynne Cooke and Beatrix Ruf.

Not only has the solo exhibition been insufficiently historicized, but its practical and conceptual concerns—how such exhibitions are put together, what assumptions underpin them and what criteria can be used to evaluate them—have also been largely glossed over.[5] This omission is reproduced by the pedagogical model of curatorial education, in which solo shows are not commonly produced as thesis projects.[6] It is thus a historical omission enforced by a pedagogical framework, which, in turn, reproduces a particular historiographical model.

What then might account for this repression? Why should solo exhibitions have such a lowly status within exhibition histories and curatorial discourse, even when these shows are largely the form through which artists' work is presented and assessed, and the basis on which both value and relevance are ascribed?[7] Part of the answer is of course the political economy in which this type of exhibition operates: a complex asymptotic web of dealers, collectors, critics, commercial galleries, non-profit institutions, museums, and curators. This dense network includes as much a reputational economy (in which the solo exhibition functions as a type of currency), as a real economy of dealers, collectors and auctions, and an economy of *curatorial prestige*—particularly tied to the group show and biennial. It is along this lineage of prestige that the history of exhibitions has thus largely been written: as a history of thematic or survey exhibitions with articulated themes, or that address or forecast current artistic developments.

Even if the typology of the solo exhibition is not significantly addressed in terms of its historical, methodological, or ideational aspects, there is a set of tacit or implied conventions that are commonly employed in its production and reception—what we might call the 'grammar' of the solo exhibition.[8] Perhaps most patent are the following: *chronology,* in the sense of a narrative (often biographical), or some formal or conceptual development that is spatialized within an exhibition;[9] *connoisseurship*, that such exhibitions consist of exemplary works by an artist, which are related to, or illustrate, development based upon some general teleology, as Robert Storr has argued;[10] *evaluation*, in the sense that solo exhibitions play a key role in assessment, with the mere fact of an exhibition itself functioning as a marker of relevance, in their nature of being, almost always, hagiographic; and lastly, *mediation,* as the solo exhibition is commonly seen as representing the artist's voice, and so supposedly comes with curatorial self-effacement. In this sense, the solo exhibition, in its supposed "purity," becomes a "way of paying penance" for the "excessive role of the curator today," in Carolyn Christov-Bakargiev's words.[11]

5
A notable exception is Robert Storr's essay "Show and Tell," in which he discusses some of the tacitly conveyed assumptions, effective strategies, and shortcomings of the retrospective solo exhibition as practiced in contemporary curating, though he does not address its history or development. See Robert Storr, "Show and Tell," in *What Makes a Great Exhibition?,* ed. Paula Marincola (Chicago, IL: University of Chicago Press, 2007).

6
Exceptions include *John Smith: Solo Show*, organized by the Curating Contemporary Art graduating students at the Royal College of Art in 2010. The exhibition was accompanied by a two-part publication, the second volume of which reflected on the solo show as an exhibition format. See *John Smith: Solo Show* and *Solo Show* (London: Royal College of Art, 2010).

7
Storr, p. 18.

8
Ibid., p. 23.

9
Ibid., p. 26.

10
Ibid., p. 21.

11
Carolyn Christov-Bakargiev in *The Producers: Contemporary Curators in Conversation*, eds. Susan Hiller and Sarah Martin, Vol. 4 (Gateshead: Baltic Centre for Contemporary Art, 2002).

Such tacit conventions must of course have originated somewhere. In addressing the relative absence of the solo exhibition within the historiography of curating and exhibitions, the methodological approach of the genealogy (in the Foucauldian and Nietzschean sense) seems particularly apt. A genealogy traces the advent or development of a set of norms through their diverse trajectories, and rather than uncovering a single origin, works backward to "disentangle the separate strands of meaning that have come together in a (contingent) unity in the present," as Raymond Geuss has stated.[12] Focusing on the errant origins of the solo exhibition in the late-eighteenth and nineteenth centuries, as forms of critical and productive resistance, and drawing on a variety of sources—from eighteenth-century gossip, to art historical writing—the aim of this genealogy is, then, to relate the development of such exhibitions to the conventions of contemporary exhibition-making, as well as to assess which of the related historical concerns might still be relevant today.

Perhaps the earliest modern artist in Europe to hold a solo exhibition was the Dublin-born painter Nathaniel Hone, who had been elected to the Royal Academy in London in 1768.[13] Hone submitted a painting titled *The Pictorial Conjuror, Displaying the Whole Art of Optical Deception* to the annual exhibition at the Academy in 1775. Described as "humorous, but really scurrilous,"[14] Hone's painting was summarily rejected as a thinly veiled "malicious satire."[15] The work's theme was deemed to be the pastiche of historical styles in the work of the Academy's president, Joshua Reynolds, in what amounted to an accusation of plagiarism.[16] Hone, as he expressed in the catalog for the exhibition, was also accused of having produced "an indecent figure or caricature of an eminent female artist," in the form of the painter Angelica Kauffman, another Academy member, portrayed as the obeisant figure resting on the conjuror's knee.[17]

As a result of the rejection, Hone organized his own solo exhibition in London in May 1775, which brought together various paintings, enamels, and miniatures from throughout his career, including the rejected painting. The exhibition, Hone claimed, was a direct appeal to the public, to "whose candour and judgment" he was "submitting himself and his art."

In the nine-page catalog that accompanied the exhibition, Hone announced it as "Mostly the Works of His Leisure and Many of Them in His Own Possession," and published his correspondence with Kauffman concerning the rejected painting. The aim was that this would "excuse the presumption of offering to the public an exhibition singly of his own labours."[18]

The anxiously apologetic tone is telling; while the solo exhibition was a way to affirm independence or defend a

12
Raymond Geuss, "Nietzsche and Genealogy," *European Journal of Philosophy*, Vol. 2, No. 3, December 1994, p. 282.

13
See Kenneth W. Luckhurst, *The Story of Exhibitions* (New York, NY: Studio Publications, 1951) p. 53. Konstantinos Stefanis argues that "the first retrospective known to have been staged by an artist," in "Reasoned Exhibitions: Blake in 1809 and Reynolds in 1813," *Tate Papers*, No. 14, Autumn 2010, available online at http://www.tate.org.uk/research/publications/tate-papers/reasoned-exhibitions-blake-1809-and-reynolds-1813 (accessed October 24, 2104). See also Graham Reynolds and Katharine Baetjer, *European Miniatures in the Metropolitan Museum of Art* (New York, NY: Metropolitan Museum of Art, 1996) p. 128.

14
Julia Clara Pitt Byrne, *Gossip of the Century: Personal and Traditional Memories*, Vol. 2 (London: Ward and Downey, 1892) p. 488.

15
John Thomas Smith, *Nollekens and His Times* (London: Richard Bentley and Son, 1895) p. 134.

16
Amelia Faye Rauser, *Caricature Unmasked: Irony, Authenticity, and Individualism in Eighteenth-Century English Prints* (Newark, NJ: University of Delaware Press, 2008) p. 58.

17
Original catalog for Hone exhibition, quoted in Smith, p. 135.

18
Ibid.

reputation, its explicit commercial and hubristic dimensions necessitated rhetorical maneuvering.[19] It is interesting to contrast the anxious language used by Hone with the contemporary superlatives so frequently employed today with such exhibitions: 'the first major,' 'the most comprehensive,' 'the most significant collection of works,' 'the largest exhibition of the work of...,' etc.

In 1871, John Singleton Copley exhibited a single painting, *Death of the Earl Chatham*, in a presentation timed to coincide with the Royal Academy exhibition. Copley, also a member of the Academy, had lost a commission and as a result decided to exhibit his own version of the historical painting.[20] Along with selling lithographic reproductions of his work, he charged admission of one shilling to the exhibition, claiming it had been seen by tens of thousands of visitors.[21]

Thomas Gainsborough would organize his own exhibition in protest against the way his work was displayed in the annual summer exhibition at the Academy in 1784.[22] Gainsborough, a founding member, wrote to the committee responsible for its arrangement that he would not allow the full-length painting of the daughters of George III, *The Three Elder Princesses* (1784), to be shown "higher than five feet and a half."[23] This amounted to demanding "a radical dispensation from the rule that full-length or three-quarter-length portraits were hung above the 'line', a projecting wooden molding running around the walls of the main exhibition space at a level of eight feet from the floor," as Richard Dorment writes.[24] While he considered this convention to be apt for larger pictures that could be seen from a distance, Gainsborough argued "the likeness and work of the picture will not be seen any higher," and so demanded that it be displayed at eye-level.[25] When the hanging committee refused, Gainsborough removed the painting from the exhibition, and organized a show of 25 of his works in his own house.

Organized in artists' homes, studios or rented rooms, such exhibitions became increasingly common in the late-eighteenth century, offering artists a new kind of opportunity to experiment with display of their work outside of the increasingly restricted criteria of committee-selected and -organized shows.[26] These early historical examples set up a recurring motif of the emergence of the solo exhibition, as what William Hauptman calls a "counter-exhibition." As with the Salon des Refusées of 1863 in Paris, such exhibitions opposed the dominant exhibition practices of the late-eighteenth and nineteenth century, offering artists an opportunity to "express their indignation" at refusals and rejections.[27]

Until the late-nineteenth century, the Royal Academy exhibition, and its French equivalent, the Salon, functioned as

19
Ibid., p. 134. As Pitt Byrne wrote, the scandal "brought [Hone] into such bad odour throughout the profession that he was obliged to deny in the most formal terms the existence of any such intention as that imputed to him in this caricature," *op. cit.*

20
The Death of Earl Chatham, see http://omeka.lts.brandeis.edu/items/show/502 (accessed October 24, 2014).

21
See Simon During, *Modern Enchantments: The Cultural Power of Secular Magic* (Cambridge, MA: Harvard University Press, 2004) p. 246.

22
See Luckhurst, pp. 54-55.

23
Richard Dorment, "The Great Room of Art," *The New York Review of Books*, June 13, 2003, available online at http://www.nybooks.com/articles/archives/2002/jun/13/the-great-room-of-art/ (accessed October 24, 2014).

24
Ibid.

25
Thomas Gainsborough quoted in *A Century of British Painters*, Richard Redgrave and Samuel Redgrave (Ithaca, NY: Cornell University Press, 1981) p. 73.

26
See Stefanis, and Philippa Simpson, "Lost in the Crowd: Blake and London in 1809," *Tate Papers*, No. 14, Autumn 2010, available online at http://www.tate.org.uk/research/publications/tate-papers/lost-crowd-blake-and-london-1809 (accessed October 24, 2014).

27
W. Hauptman, "Juries, Protests, and Counter-Exhibitions Before 1850," *The Art Bulletin*, Vol. 67, No. 1, March 1985, p. 105. See also Patricia Mainardi, "Courbet's Exhibitionism," *Gazette des Beaux-Arts*, No. 118, December 1991, p. 256.

central venues for artists to present their work to the public. Crowds to the Paris Salon, for example, often averaged more than 23,000 people a day, and nearly a million annually.[28] Reputations and careers were made through such official exhibitions, which were subject to "artistic control by [the] appointed body," in terms of style, size, subject, and display method.[29]

Well into the nineteenth century it was considered demeaning for an artist to offer work for sale directly to the public through any venues outside such official exhibitions.[30] As the nineteenth-century French critic Louis Peisse wrote, outside these venues "there would be only picture shops" selling art supplies and stationary, along with genre paintings.[31]

Mere inclusion in an official exhibition was an affirmation of value; a refusal was, on the other hand, a denunciation. The refusals themselves, often due to the jury's politicized sensitivity to "offending or unflattering themes," became increasingly common.[32] In the Salon of 1827, around 47 per cent of the over 3,000 paintings submitted were refused, nearly eight times the number rejected a decade earlier, as Hauptman recounts.[33] By 1840, 53 percent of the works submitted to the Salon were rejected. Artists were largely left to the vicissitudes of these juries and governing bodies, and whose rejections were the source of ongoing protests and petitions.[34] The rise of the solo exhibition as a form is thus directly tied to the need for alternative models to resist such centralized forms for the reception and consumption of art, which afforded both legitimacy and economic support.[35]

In 1809, William Blake organized an exhibition of his own work in response to such strictures. Blake's particular intent was both to sell the 16 watercolors on view and to affirm the importance of the medium against a perceived bias on the part of the Academy. As the artist explained, this made it "necessary that [he] should exhibit to the Public, in an Exhibition of [his] own."[36] As Philippa Simpson writes of the exhibition that was recreated at Tate Britain in London in 2009, Blake created a precise arrangement of old and new works, evincing "an attempt to marshal the pictures into some visual (or theoretical) system," with the earliest work appearing last in the catalogue.[37]

Perhaps the earliest example of a solo exhibition in continental Europe is that of Jacques-Louis David's exhibition of *Les Sabines* (*The Intervention of the Sabine Women*, 1799), which opened in 1799 in one of the galleries of the Louvre. The exhibition consisted of the single large painting along with a mirror hung opposite, reflecting both the work and the viewer.[38] With it, David effectively brought the "custom observed in England," of the exhibition to France.[39]

28
See Ross King, *The Judgment of Paris* (New York, NY: Walker & Co., 2006) p. 17.

29
Ibid., p. 44. See also Marci Regan, *Paul Durand-Ruel and the Market for Early Modernism* (Baton Rouge, LA: Louisiana State University, 1997) p. 3.

30
Mainardi, p. 255.

31
Louis Peisse, quoted in Mainardi, p. 257.

32
Hauptman, p. 97.

33
Ibid., p. 98.

34
Ibid., p. 23 and p. 96, and King, p. 34. One example includes setting rules that restricted artists to submitting only three works. See King, p. 33.

35
See Jensen, p. 23.

36
William Blake, quoted in David Blayney Brown and Martin Myrone, "William Blake's 1809 Exhibition," *Tate Papers*, No. 14, Autumn 2010, available online at http://www.tate.org.uk/research/publications/tate-papers/william-blakes-1809-exhibition#footnote12_ep9xtun (accessed October 24, 2014).

37
Simpson, *op. cit.*

38
John Stephen Hallam, *Paris Salon Exhibitions: 1667–1880*, available at https://sites.google.com/a/plu.edu/paris-salon-exhibitions-1667-1880/salon-de-1800 (accessed October 24, 2014).

39
Jacques-Louis David, quoted in Mainardi, p. 258.

The French painter Horace Vernet organized his own exhibition in 1822—after nearly all of his submitted paintings to the Salon were rejected due to their supposedly politicized content. Vernet's exhibition, held in his studio and consisting of 45 paintings, effectively constituted the first retrospective in France.[40] "A bold stroke, but a fortune one," as *Putnam's Magazine* described it, the exhibition was particularly popular, becoming "the centre of attraction in Paris."[41]

Vernet's exhibition set the precedent for Gustave Courbet's well-known solo exhibitions in 1855 and 1867.[42] While Courbet had debuted in the Salon of 1840s, by the 1850s only 2 out of the 18 paintings submitted had been accepted.[43] Courbet's exhibition of 1855 was a reaction to the exclusion of two of his most famous paintings from the Universal Exposition that year. Featuring a selection of 40 paintings, the exhibition opened on June 28, 1855, near the Universal Exhibition itself, and surveyed seven years' worth of his work at the age of 36.[44] To publicize it, a set of public advertisements was plastered over the walls of Paris, "next to street performers and quack doctors," as one newspaper commented. Both the public advertisements and the accompanying catalog described it as "an exhibition and sale."[45]

Tellingly, Courbet called it an *exhibition*, rather than an *exposition*. As Patricia Mainardi explains in her study of Courbet's practices, *exhibition* "assumed in nineteenth-century France a pejorative connotation of ostentation and immodesty[;] a commercial enterprise, such as a shop window display, would be an exhibition."[46] In contrast to this negative connotation, *exposition* connoted a didactic and edifying endeavor. Seeing his *exhibition* as "held in an atmosphere of extraordinary independence," Courbet wrote, "people will think I am a monster."[47]

Along with such self-organized exhibitions, artists also began to exhibit more widely in the various commercial galleries that gained prominence in the 1850s and 1860s. Paul Durand-Ruel, for example, organized exhibitions of the work of Pierre-Auguste Renoir, Claude Monet (who did not participate in group exhibitions after the 1890s) and Camille Pissarro, among others, all accompanied by publications.[48] These types of solo exhibitions organized after the late-nineteenth century would most likely involve the direct participation and support of an art dealer, in terms of archives and inventory, linking the commercial art market with the production of curatorial knowledge.[49]

Within this genealogy, the innovative exhibition designs of James McNeill Whistler developed in the late-nineteenth century are particularly significant. Display practices were an essential part of his artistic practice, and Whistler himself

40
See Hauptman, p. 97; and Carol Armstrong, *Manet Manette* (Princeton, NJ: Princeton University Press, 2002) p. 4.

41
Charles Blanc, *Histoire des peintres de toutes les écoles: École française* (Paris: Renouard, 1865) Vol. III, p. 8, cited in Hauptman, p. 97. Translation by the author.

42
See Hauptman, p. 97.

43
Mainardi, p. 255.

44
Mainardi, p. 254.

45
Charles Perrier, quoted in Mainardi, p. 259.

46
Mainardi, p. 254.

47
Gustave Courbet, quoted in Ten-Doesschate Chu, p. 140.

48
See King, pp. 48-51, and p. 147, and Jensen, p. 131.

49
For a detailed discussion of the role of commercial galleries in the organization of retrospectives in the late-nineteenth century, see Jensen, p. 110 and p. 131; and King, pp. 48-51, and p. 147.

innovated, and substantially developed, many conventions associated with modern exhibition practices.[50] Whistler's exhibition history in fact consists mainly of solo shows beginning in 1874, in commercial galleries and venues such as the Flemish Gallery and the Fine Art Society, both in London.[51] As one contemporary reviewer put it, in these exhibitions the "gallery and its contents [were] altogether in harmony—a 'symphony of colour,' carried out in every detail... above all, in the juxtaposition of the pictures."[52]

Whistler's articulated arrangements weren't strictly based on chronology, size, or genre, but rather followed aesthetic and decorative principles. As he writes in *The Gentle Art of Making Enemies* (1890), his aim was "to prove that the place in which works of art are shown may be made as free from discordant elements which distract the spectators' attention as the works themselves."[53] Paintings were "well spaced [so] that each may, to a certain degree, be studied by itself." In the case of paintings with prevalent green tones, for example, Whistler suggested, "the background should be neither red nor green, but, theoretically, a grey."[54] Whistler's exhibitions, as the scholarly work of David Park Curry has shown, are marked by such careful attention to arrangement, order, framing, and lighting, all of which Whistler meticulously considered.[55]

Throughout the nineteenth century, the development of the solo exhibition marks a decisive turn away from the established display practices of both European museums and Salons, where artworks would be grouped by size, genre, or type in order to emphasize an "ideal organic unity" and "quantitative method," rather than any individual merit, thematic focus, or stylistic emphasis.[56] If Christian von Mechel's 1780 installation of the Habsburg collection at the Belvedere in Vienna had pioneered the European convention of ordering collections according to national school and chronology,[57] by 1894 Paul Signac writes in his diary that paintings should be displayed in a single row, with works by the same artist hung together in an evenly spaced sequence at more or less eye-level.[58] These new conventions of display are largely developed alongside the emergence of solo exhibitions, and eventually incorporated institutionally by the end of the nineteenth century.

This shift from quantitative effect to qualitative display involved new biographical and teleological conceptions of artistic production, which had a significant impact on how relationships among artworks were developed both spatially and discursively, significantly inflecting definitions of artistic development, and the sequencing of artworks in space.[59] As Germano Celant has written of late-nineteenth-century expository methods, with "new emphasis on the individual work,

50
For more on Whistler's exhibition practice, see David Park Curry, *James McNeill Whistler: Uneasy Pieces* (Richmond, VA: Virginia Museum of Fine Arts, 2005); Jensen, pp. 43-44; James McNeill Whistler, *The Gentle Art of Making Enemies* (New York, NY: Dover, 1967); and Colleen Denney, *At the Temple of Art: The Grosvenor Gallery, 1877* (Madison, NJ: Fairleigh Dickinson University Press, 2000) p. 220. Some of Whistler's exhibition designs were recently restaged as part of the 2014 Liverpool Biennial in an exhibition at the Bluecoat, curated by Mai Abu ElDahab and Rosie Cooper, July 5 until October 26, 2014.

51
Jensen, pp. 43-44, p. 123; Whistler, *op. cit.*; and Park Curry, p. 68.

52
Henry Blackburn, quoted in Joyce Hill Stoner, "Whistler's Views on the Restoration and Display of his Paintings," *Studies in Conservation*, Vol. 42, No. 2, 1997, p. 111.

53
Whistler, p. 48.

54
Whistler, quoted in *Recollections and Impressions of James McNeill Whistler*, Arthur Jerome Eddy (Philadelphia, PA: J.B. Lippincott Company, 1904) p. 138.

55
As Park Curry writes, "Many of today's familiar exhibition design techniques and museum practices were introduced to London a hundred years ago in one-man and group shows partially or entirely arranged by Whistler. These techniques include indirect lighting, colour-coordinated walls, uniform framing, elegant spacing, large banners outside the exhibition space, the sale of specially designed catalogues and photographic reproductions of art, elaborate evening openings and admission charges for temporary exhibitions." Park Curry, "Total Control: Whistler at an Exhibition," *op. cit.*, pp. 67-82.

56
Germano Celant, "A Visual Machine: Art Installation and its Modern Archetypes," in *Thinking about Exhibitions*, *op. cit.*, p. 374.

57
See Debora J. Meijers, "The Places of Painting: The Survival

of Mnemotechnics in Christian von Mechel's Gallery Arrangement in Vienna (1778-81), in *Memory and Oblivion: Proceedings of the XXIXth International Congress of the History of Art held in Amsterdam, 1–7 September 1996*, eds. Wessel Reinink and Jeroen Stumpel (Boston, MA: Kluwer Academic Publishers, 1999).

58
See Mary Tompkins Lewis, ed., *Critical Readings in Impressionism and Post-Impressionism: An Anthology* (Berkeley, CA: Ahmanson-Murphy, 2007) p. 65. According to Walter Grasskamp's scholarship on the history of exhibitions, the convention of hanging works in a single row was established in German museums. See Dorothee Richter, "A Brief Outline of the History of Exhibition Making," *On Curating.org* issue 06, available at http://www.on-curating.org/index.php/issue-6.html#.VG4We0smV4M (accessed October 24, 2014).

59
See Jensen, p.112. As Germano Celant has written of nineteenth-century expository methodology, with an emphasis on individual artists and individual works, a narrative and connecting relationship among artworks was developed describing artistic development, sequence, or characteristic. Germano Celant, p. 374.

60
Celant, p. 374. Celant speculates that "perhaps it is with the advent of the first world's fairs, and in particular with the specific pavilions for Courbet and Manet at the 1867 fair, that the expository method becomes more refined."

61
Charles Baudelaire, *Painter of Modern Life*, ed. and trans. Jonathan Mayne (New York, NY: Da Capo Press Inc, 1986) p. xviii.

62
Ibid.

63
Ibid., p. 47.

64
Ibid.

65
See Martha Ward, "What's important about the history of modern art exhibitions?," *op. cit.*, p. 458; and Jensen, p. 113.

shown with contemporary work by others, or shown in retrospectives, importance comes to be given to a 'linear' articulation of the works of art."[60]

Such a shift from the quantitative to the qualitative can in fact be seen to emerge from within the epistemological order of the Salon itself, as the writings of its great chronicler, Charles Baudelaire, make evident. Having singled out Eugène Delacroix's work in his review of the 1846 Salon, Baudelaire delivered a lecture on the artist indicative of such a shift following Delacroix's death in 1863.[61]

The lecture starts by introducing the practical, quantitative problem of accurately cataloging Delacroix's extensive artistic production. Starting with the 77 paintings exhibited in the Salons, Baudelaire eventually gives up and admits to the failed attempt to draw up an inventory, claiming, perhaps rhetorically, that the output was just too extensive. Leaving the task behind, Baudelaire explains that "the important thing... is to search for, and to try to define, the characteristic quality of Delacroix's genius."[62] The interest in this qualitative description of genius, rather than in mere quantitative inventory, mobilizes two distinct conceptions: the idea of a 'good' or important work, which enforces connoisseurship;[63] and that of chronological teleology, or, as Baudelaire puts it, "Delacroix's genius is precisely that he knows not decadence; he only displays progress."[64] These same qualities, which Baudelaire uses to frame and define the singular nature of Delacroix's work, are those that are firmly established within solo exhibitions, in their monographic and retrospective forms, by the end of the nineteenth century. By the turn of the century, these exhibitions are in fact seen as a marker of artistic success, defining the very idea of historical validity, or canonical status, as Paul Cézanne's solo exhibitions at the Salon d'Automne in Paris—in 1904 and 1907—demonstrate.[65] Representative of a shift in the distribution of power within the political economy of art, such exhibitions evince the adoption of these conventions of solo exhibition, including the emergence of the figure of the curator, largely absent within the initial emergence of the monographic show.

In contemporary terms, the lack of attention given to the solo exhibition also ignores the possible critical function of such exhibitions today. Part of the reason may be their largely celebratory, spectacularized, and market-driven dimension—all factors that perhaps contribute to their exclusion from the writing of contemporary exhibition histories. Yet they remain a central means through which the art market positions, contextualizes, and circulates value, in dialectical tension with the institutional production of legitimating distinction or edification. It seems, then, that such exhibitions have gone from allowing for the articulation of a critical, social, or economic counter-polemic in their dissident origins, to now being perceived as a canonical form lacking in criticality—ubiquitous, yet ignored.[66] So while the writing of recent art history involves confronting a history of individual exhibitions—as crystallizing moments for artistic production—to what extent can curatorial discourse continue to maintain a distance from the solo show as a catalyzing form?

From a global art historical perspective, the importance of such exhibitions might also act as a corrective to the kinds of totalized history—both global and revisionist—that is often presented in group or survey exhibitions. To do so also entails, of course, opening this history to its non-Western and feminist valences. In this sense, monographic exhibitions can be understood as reflecting, and indeed producing, important changes in the formation of curatorial practices. The importance of such exhibition practices rests in their function as the archive of contemporary art history, as the central means of presenting and historicizing the art of the present. It is then crucial to understand the function of such exhibitions in the political economy of art. In light of this, how might we call upon the errant history of resistance, experimentation, negation, and critical engagement that the solo exhibition represented, in order to reflect upon the current role of such exhibitions within a globalized art system?

66
Kitty Scott in correspondence with the author.

On the Case of Curatorial History

Jeannine Tang

In the spring of 1995, Bruce Altshuler devised the first "Proseminar: Studies in the History and Practice of Exhibition," a required seminar at the Master of Arts program at the Center for Curatorial Studies, Bard College, where I teach. While the record of his effort is brief—"a focus on the relationship between exhibitions and the art presented," and the roles of "artists, dealers, critics, collectors, attitudes toward the audience/public; and contrasts between exhibitions organized by artists and non-artist curators or institutions"—this nonetheless described several coordinates for study that are now commonplace in exhibition history and curatorial studies.[1] The conditions for Altshuler's undertaking were far from what they are today: instructors now have multiple edited volumes and monographs of contemporary curatorial and exhibition history, periodicals such as *The Exhibitionist*, and the *Journal of Curatorial Studies*, publications' series such as Afterall's exhibition histories, and innumerable online lectures to guide their classroom endeavors. But, in 1995 Altshuler had few such resources. Most of the texts selected for his course drew from broader art histories or exhibition catalogues of various avant-gardes.[2] In such literature, exhibitions were featured at length and in detail, while rarely being a central subject within scholarship itself—indeed, these early attempts at exhibition history were fully interdependent with early modern and modern art history.

This was evident in an early assignment of Altshuler's, in which students compiled copies of exhibition source materials, such as slides, press releases, and published reviews, into binders that were submitted along with their finished essays.[3] This task indicated a pedagogical desire not only for the production of narratives, but an examination of the very sources and structures upon which these narratives themselves rely. The assignment also addressed a pressing concern during the early years of the graduate program; that neither a central frame of reference nor a consistent body of knowledge for exhibitions yet existed. The question of which exhibitions were worthy of examination—and how to even approach, theorize, or contextualize this study—was an open one. In the twenty years between Altshuler's first class and my writing today, many exhibitions are *known*: they have shifted status from a mere fact to now bearing the weight of exemplarity and significance. This interval—between two statuses, born by the same object of study—interests me here. It relies on a case being made for it by a person in the company of others, a case made for the object that migrates it from anecdote to example, incident to event, obscure to canonical, incidental fact to point of reference. What follows are some details and remarks on how others have taught exhibition history at a single institution, presented in

1
Bruce Altshuer, "CS 502: Proseminar: Studies in the History and Practices of Exhibition," in *Graduate Program in Curatorial Studies. Center for Curatorial Studies, Courses 1994-1995*. Center for Curatorial Studies, Bard College, Library and archives special collections.

2
These included writings by Ian Dunlop, Lucy Lippard, Barbara Haskell, Stephanie Barron, and Donald Gordon. Althusler's own writings that were utilized in this course, and later work subsequently informed by developments in the field, are embedded in Bruce Altshuler, *The Avant-Garde in Exhibition: New Art in the Twentieth Century* (New York, NY: Harry N. Abrams, 1994; Berkeley, CA: University of California Press, 1998); Bruce Altshuler, *Salon to Biennial—Exhibitions That Made Art History, Vol. 1: 1863-1959* (New York, NY, and London: Phaidon Press Inc., 2008); Bruce Altshuler, *Biennials and Beyond: Exhibitions that Made Art History: 1962-2002* (New York, NY, and London: Phaidon Press Inc. 2013). Afterall Books *Exhibition Histories* series (2010-), information at "Exhibition Histories: Books and Events," http://www.afterall.org/books/exhibition.histories/exhibition-histories (accessed December 23, 2015).

3
These binders have subsequently been kept at the Center for Curatorial Studies, Bard College's library and archives as part of the institution's special collections.

4
This essay proceeds in the spirit of how questions of pedagogy have themselves been an area of emphasis within contemporary art history, to suggest that active questioning of the pedagogy of curatorial history might be a valuable area of inquiry as the discipline continues to take shape. See the special issue "Rethinking the Introductory Art History Survey," *Art Journal*, Vol. 54, No. 3, 1995; and Peggy Phelan *et al.*, "Art History Survey: A Round-Table Discussion," *Art Journal*, Vol. 64, No. 2, 2005, pp. 32-51.

5
In parsing these course descriptions, it is clear that they are not a precise key to what took place in the seminar itself.

Prior to 2009, they do not include detailed weekly lists of readings. They cannot help us understand the grain of seminar discussion and debate, nor are they guides to the historical process of students and faculty producing histories of exhibitions together. Rather, these course descriptions are prospective, anticipatory texts—written in preparation for an oncoming semester, before an instructor would enter a classroom. These texts offer aims, promises, and expectations to an unknown and unmet student body. These descriptions might also be perceived to be conscious and unconscious responses to the field, and the institution: many position themselves as building upon, or deviating from, literature as it currently stands, and past syllabi the current teacher might (not) have glimpsed, acting also as contemporaneous responses to the state of exhibition history at the time. As such, these descriptions are always provisional and hopeful, while also frequently critical, speculative, and ambitious.

6
Martha Ward, "CS 502: Proseminar: Studies in the History and Practice of Exhibition," in *Graduate Program in Curatorial Studies. Center for Curatorial Studies, Courses 1996-1997*. Center for Curatorial Studies, Bard College, Library and Archives special collections. Ward utilized the following principal texts: Reesa Greenberg *et al., Thinking About Exhibitions* (London: Routledge, 1996); and Brian O'Doherty, *Inside the White Cube: The Ideology of the Gallery Space* (Santa Monica, CA: Lapis Press, 1986), in addition to her own Martha Ward, "Impressionist installations and private exhibitions," in *Art Bulletin*, Vol. 73, 1991, pp. 592-622.

7
A utilitarian description occasionally stands in place of an instructor's individual course description, e.g. "The proseminar surveys the history of museums, galleries, and other exhibition spaces and explores how social and cultural conditions, institutional requirements, and aesthetic conceptions have shaped past and current exhibition practices." Fraser would subsequently teach a course, "CS 585: Institutional Critique and the Critical Analysis of the Artistic

the hope of keeping this ground unsettled, and curatorial history itself an open question, even as curatorial studies becomes ever more acceptable as a primary discipline, with new programs being launched every year.[4]

Altshuler taught the Proseminar again in 1998, and the course was otherwise taught by an array of art historians and curators, whose interest and approaches marked its contents.[5] In 1996, Martha Ward centered her course on display practices, its "continuities and breaks" with art movements, institutional forces and political developments, and their effect on the constitution and behaviors of publics, utilizing newly-published material on exhibition history by Reesa Greenberg, Bruce Ferguson, Brian O'Doherty, and others.[6] After that, in 1998 and 1999, the Proseminar was taken up by Konstantin Akinsha and Andrea Fraser.[7] The languages of these courses mark how exhibition history began as something to be invented, forged from scraps, extracted from the social history of art, and emerging concurrently with the rise of museum studies, cultural studies, and visual culture. This interdependence with art history, and criticism is marked not only in the mixture of curators and art historians who taught the course, but also in the emphasis by many instructors upon the necessity of critical interpretation toward exhibitions and their social worlds. Such critique was informed by Marxist, feminist, and ideological analysis, as their instructors' choice of languages corresponded to the rise of multiculturalism and critique of globalization in the art field, and the reception of postcolonial, post-structural, postmodern, and psychoanalytic theory in art history and art criticism. In addition to the Proseminars, elective courses often featured exhibition history, and through these pedagogical efforts—along with the efforts of many far beyond this single institution—certain exhibition examples or thematic concerns around globalization, national identity, publics, and local contexts, have since become commonplace references or concerns in the field.[8]

By the mid-2000s, it became clear that instructors saw the necessity of sustaining critical analysis in the wake of exhibition history's institutionalization as a domain of study. Susan Cahan's 2003 Proseminar announced that "curatorial studies is a field that is still in formation," stressing not only exhibitions of "strong and diverse critical responses," but the necessity of critical interpretative approaches.[9] The following year, Christian Rattemeyer's Proseminar would mark that "the study of the history of exhibitions has become an increasingly well-documented area of research," although it remained "far from exhaustive or complete."[10] And in 2006, Rhea Anastas would position exhibition studies as a "rapidly expanding

Field," to introduce students both to art practices known as 'institutional critique' but also to the sociology of Pierre Bourdieu. "CS 502. Proseminar: Studies in the History and Practices of Exhibition" (Fall 1999). This description was utilized by Helen Molesworth teaching the course in 2000 (in collaboration with Konstantin Akinsha, Caron Duncan, and Miwon Kwon), as well as Norton Batkin in 2001 and 2002.

8
For instance, in a Fall 1994 seminar on site-related sculpture, Lynne Cooke lists exhibitions such as *Skulptur Projekte Muenster* (1987), *Culture in Action* (1993), *InSITE* (1997), for bringing sculpture out of the museum and reinventing the sculpture park, returning to sculpture's histories as a public art form in urban context. In a Spring 1996 seminar on ethics, Ivo Mesquita highlights *The Black Male* (1995), *Les Magiciens de la Terre* (1989), which have since recurred through numerous Proseminar courses. Mary Jane Jacob's Fall class on museums and their local communities in 1997 marked questions of publics, power, and location as vital to museological study. In Spring 1997, Lowery Stokes Sims considered how main-stream museums and ethnically focused institutions differently presented the art of ethnic, sexual, and religious minorities, examining such exhibitions as *Harlem on My Mind* (1969), *Mining the Museum* (1992-1993), *The Decade Show* (1990). And for her Fall 1998 class on "Globalization and the Art of the Americas," Mari Carmen Ramirez recommends, for problems of globalization as they manifest themselves in art's social field of cultural exchange and distribution, a movement beyond discussions of identity, toward emphasis on subjects such as the growth of privatization and free markets, forms of deterritorialization and displacement, new classes of cultural 'brokers,' and the role of curators in these globalizing processes. For the above syllabi, see Lynne Cooke, "CCS 551. 'Places with traces...': Exhibitions, Projects, and Site-related Sculpture," (Fall 1994); Ivo Mesquita, "CS 578. Ethics and Curating" (Spring 1996) Lowery Stokes Sims, "CS 580. National Art and the Issue of Ethnic Minorities: The Case Study of African Americans" (Fall 1996); Mary Jane Jacobs,

literature," accumulating "a canon of exhibitions" that risked obscuring, and outpacing, "rigorous and reflexive theoretical critiques" of exhibitions as a discursive field, to emphasize instead the necessity of criticism in the project of exhibition history, artist-organized, and publication projects.[11]

The title of the Proseminar would subsequently turn toward curatorial history, rather than emphasizing exhibitions as the field's proper noun. In 2004, Rattemeyer proposed the history of exhibitions to be a parallel history of modernism, and hypothesized that by focusing on exhibitions of contemporary art, we might arrive at "a first tentative outline of the development of curatorial practice as a distinct discipline" after World War II. Anastas's course descriptions from 2007-2008 would describe "the project of historicizing exhibitions and curatorial practice" as forms of "reflexive analysis and description." The Proseminar was then retitled the "History and Practices of Curating" in 2012 by Maria Lind, to better accommodate the various activities by curators—commissioning, catalyzing projects, work in education—that might itself be part of curatorial work, while not discretely exhibitionary in their form or effect.[12]

This shift has since been maintained, to emphasize the wider theories and practices of curating in which an exhibition is included, and was a shift consciously made in tandem with vocabularies and debates on the curatorial.[13] In Spring 2013, Johanna Burton and I changed the course title to "History and Theories of Curating" (to better distinguish the seminar from the Practicum courses, simultaneously held at the graduate program). And in Fall 2013 Paul O'Neill and I changed the title yet again to "Histories and Theories of Curating," to acknowledge what the vast multiplicity of histories, practices, and discourse that touch—and constantly exceed—our 15-week pedagogical efforts. In maintaining an emphasis on curating, the scope of study has expanded to encompass experiments or redefinitions of the exhibition, but also included activities produced by curators more appropriately named otherwise, such as performances, events, acquisition, collection development, durational, research-based, networked, activist, or infrastructural projects conducted under the auspices of curating.

Pedagogy, Genre, Value

The Proseminar will undoubtedly change again, by my own hand, and those of many others. I excerpt these fragments of institutional history to make evident how various people have made cases for exhibitions or curating, and imagined the past and present of their field, not only through their practice and their written histories, but in their choice of examples, listing of texts, and writing of syllabi. The case for each exhibition or curatorial endeavor is always an event that "hovers about the singular, the general, and the normative."[14] Each case longs "to organize publics, however fragile or fleeting."[15] These organizers, teachers, students, editors, and authors, all singled out specific exhibitions or curatorial projects, in order to generalize their importance. Importance itself is cast in terms of contemporaneity, avant-garde experimentation, exhibitionary form and typologies, curatorial innovation, institutional transformation, the emergence of publics, contexts for subject-formation, reflexive, critical thinking, and political practice.[16] Through these terms—and many others—certain exhibitions are recommended as exemplary. Our genres of explanation and conditions of value are not outside of existing norms (even as we resist them, often through other kinds of norms inherent within even socialist, radical, and anarchist thought). Rather, it is through our normative genres of explanation that we produce specific narratives, in which certain objects are imagined as able to bear the weight of explanation, or densely hold the space of narrative precedent and prognostic futurity, while other objects remain as anecdotes, too particular, too incidental, or illustrative to adjudicate such space and time.

These genres of explanation—and the friction between them—co-exist within a single institution, a single field, whose edges are ever porous. Looking over past syllabi suggests that curatorial, exhibitionary, and art history are interdependent lines of inquiry, drawing inspiration from or corroborating the lacunae of their companion fields. Indeed, the concern with curatorial canonization in the field signaled by these syllabi, emerged in conjunction with the growing disciplinarity of curatorial studies within graduate programs, and the corresponding struggles of educators inside and outside the academy to keep a young field's foundations from calcifying. The critique itself borrows (consciously or unconsciously) from the language of social histories of art informed by theories of feminism, colonialism, and historical materialism since the 1970s. Such analysis informs the syllabi I have traced, and in light of the economic and political attacks on the arts and humanities at large in the US and in other nations, I am invested in considering critical art history and critical exhibition and curatorial studies to be sibling domains of enquiry, each a repository of broken genres and tentative strategies from which the other might draw motivation, rather than conceive of curatorial history as the Oedipal successor or critical corrective of the former.[17]

Indeed, social histories of art remain useful for their attention to consider the institutional, structural, and

"CS 581. Contemporary Art Museums Within Their Communities" (Fall 1997), and Mari Carmen Ramirez, "CS 563. Globalization and the Art of the Americas." See course books from Fall 1994-Spring 1998 at *Graduate Program in Curatorial Studies. Center for Curatorial Studies, Coursebooks.* Center for Curatorial Studies, Bard College, Library and Archives special collections.

9
Cahan's examples include *Cities on the Move* (2000-2001), the 1993 Whitney Biennial, *The Family of Man* (1995), *Harlem on My Mind* (1969), *Differences: On Representation and Sexuality* (1984), *Primitivism* (1984). Susan Cahan, "CS 502. Proseminar: Studies in the History and Practices of Exhibition," *Graduate Program in Curatorial Studies. Center for Curatorial Studies, Coursebook 1998-1999.* Center for Curatorial Studies, Bard College, Library and Archives special collections.

10
Christian Rattemeyer, "CS 502. Proseminar: Studies in the History and Practices of Exhibition," syllabus Spring 2004.

11
Rhea Anastas, "CS 502. Proseminar: Studies in the History and Practices of Exhibition," syllabus Spring 2006.

12
Maria Lind, "CS 502. Proseminar: Studies in the History and Practices of Curating," syllabus Spring 2009.

13
See Irit Rogoff, "Turning" *e-flux Journal* (November, 2008), available online at http://www.e-flux.com/journal/turning (accessed December 2015); Maria Lind "On the Curatorial, "*Selected Maria Lind Writing*, ed. Brian Wood (Berlin: Sternberg Press, 2010), pp. 57-66; Beatrice von Bismark, "Curatorial Criticality: On the Role of Freelance Curators in the Field of Contemporary Art," in *Curating Critique* (Frankfurt am Main: Revolver, 2007), pp. 62-69; Irit Rogoff, "Smuggling—A Curatorial Model," *eipcp*, August 2006, available online at eipcp.net/dlfiles/rogoff-smuggling (accessed December 2015); Paul O'Neill, "The Curatorial Constellation and the Paracuratorial Paradox," *The Exhibitionist*. No. 6, 2012, pp. 55-60.

infrastructural forces that make certain kinds of curatorial work more possible to produce, and more likely to be historicized and available. I take a page here from Linda Nochlin's landmark text of social history of art, "Why Have There Been No Great Women Artists?" (1971), in which she argues that the problem of women's exclusion from the museum and the canon lay not in their individual work, but in the gendered criteria, institutions, and assumptions by which artistic greatness was socially produced. These include the formation of artists in artist families, their access to studio space, the art academy and salon, as well as hierarchies of genre, distinguishing the greater from the lesser arts, distinctions that were themselves dependent on training and education.[18] For Nochlin, the maintenance of systemic cultural misogyny existed in the very ideology and apparatus of greatness that would establish the singularity of the great artist. Drawing from her framework, we might also consider the *apparatus of curating* as both a framework and domain of historical research that generates conditions for curatorial work and its historicization.[19]

The question of how objects become exemplary, gain generalizability, and receive credit remains a question of art's institutions, structures, and infrastructures, through which various forms of capital are distributed in ways that are themselves racialized, nationalized, gendered, as well as classed. Many exhibitions that have become significant were written about in their day, and often produced by people situated within, or in some proximity to, institutions of considerable resources, thereby having access to forms of social, economic, cultural, and political power. Indeed, to even conceive of keeping records, an exhibition curator would have had proximity to trained art historians, institutional curators, archivists, and collection managers, a university education, prolific and frequently-exhibited artists, in order to know what to keep, how to negotiate, and who to donate or sell an archive to. It is through such direct vectors of power or proximity to power, that certain curators and projects—whether mainstream, alternative, or a compromise between—have left a paper trail. Would we have the records of Political Art Documentation and Distribution (PAD/D), had Clive Philpot, archivist at MoMA, not emphasized the necessity of saving such records, and proposed their accessioning into MoMA's special collections? How well would we know of Lucy Lippard's exhibitions without her involvement with Printed Matter, her work as a library page at MoMA, her education at the New York University, or the accessioning of her papers into the Smithsonian American Art Museum, to be processed and made available by trained archivists and historians?

14
My thoughts on normative genres of explanation, cases, and exemplarity are fully indebted to Lauren Berlant, "On the Case," *Critical Inquiry*, Summer 2007, pp. 663-672.

15
Ibid, p. 664.

16
Bruce Altshuler has productively remarked on the different canons by which exhibitions are distinguished: some are judged canonical for their art historical significance—exemplified by early texts of the role of exhibitions in the development of various avant-gardes, and others for their curatorial innovation, as certain exhibitions produced, or reshaped, crucial types, forms and genres of exhibitionary production. See Bruce Altshuler, "A canon of exhibitions," *Manifesta Journal*, No. 11, 2011, p. 13, and the rest of this special issue devoted to the problem of canons in exhibition and curatorial history.

17
Hito Steyerl rightly points to how critiques on the putative 'institutionalization of critique,' disregard how critique is very much itself in jeopardy. For Steyerl, "while critical institutions are being dismantled by neoliberal institutional criticism, this produces an ambivalent subject which develops multiple strategies for dealing with its dislocation. It is on the one side being adapted to the needs of ever more precarious living conditions. On the other, there seems to have hardly ever been more need for institutions which could cater to the new needs and desires that this constituency will create." Hito Steyerl, "The Institution of Critique," *eipcp*, January 2009, available online at http://eipcp.net/transversal/0106/steyerl/en (accessed December 2015).

18
Linda Nochlin, "Why Have There Been No Great Women Artists?," *Art News*, No. 69, January 1971, pp. 22-23

19
Maria Lind, "On the Curatorial," in *Selected Maria Lind Writing*, ed. Brian Wood (Berlin: Sternberg Press, 2010), pp. 57-66.

These are examples I include in my syllabus, and models that my students and I still find valuable. We have them because of forms of social capital, housing stability, and structural support their makers had (or had access to), which allowed them to maintain personal and collective records in sufficiently dry and clean physical space, without confronting the necessity of disposing of such materials. But our having them begs the question of why and how they were saved, and the broader issue of whose records—typically principal, senior, established curators—are typically rescued from destruction, and whose records—such as those of exhibition designers, artists, networking or adjunct curators, exhibition managers or administrators, grant officials, and state diplomatic agencies—are more generally disposed of, because they were never designated significant and mindfully maintained, or, due to reasons of state secrecy, unavailable for public view.

For work to even be designated worthy of cultural preservation, we might also ask what education and languages an exhibition curator or respondent would need to access, embody, know, and speak, in order to describe their efforts in ways that were legible, and understood by host institutions. And consequently, by what terms, and in what genres of explanation we make cases for exhibitions, and establish criteria for their being exemplary. Indeed, the common terms of advocacy and valuation are not themselves outside vectors of power, or modernist assumptions. For instance, numerous exhibitions that have become significant are strongly tethered to the historical avant-garde and neo-avant-gardes of surrealism, Pop, conceptualism, and aleatory procedures, and increasingly certain forms of institutional critique. The rhetoric of radicalism (in the reinvention of exhibitionary or curatorial form) persists in our scrutiny of exhibition typologies, and the basis of an educated, complex reception or production of an exhibition is itself structured by the presumption of a bourgeois public sphere, and a liberal democratic media apparatus that could capture its response.

These terms of value shape the curatorial and exhibition records that we have access to, by which we tell stories of exhibitions and curating, in addition to materialist stories of labor, value, social mobility, and power. I am reminded, every day, of the wealth in which I write and teach, in a university with databases, books, periodicals, access to archives, and primary source materials in New York City, informed and intellectually-curious colleagues and students. In teaching a class on curatorial history, my students receive the cultural and geographical support for their research on exhibition history in repositories that are poised, desirous, and knowledgeable of such enquiry, whether they seek out museum exhibitions, biennials, artist-run spaces, or performance events. Yet in spite of this plenitude, I am frequently reminded of the absences that we continually encounter. Particularly when we discuss modes of ephemeral or event-based activity, or the production of curatorial histories in other regions, there remain vastly different conditions for locating such materials—if they even exist—and consequently, the other kinds of criteria for curatorial history are necessitated.

Our source materials are differentially valued and accessed across diverse conditions of access and interpretation. To this end, I have found recent art history and visual culture about, or informed by, performance particularly useful. Their emphasis on hermeneutically undervalued forms such as gossip, and their explicit negotiation with—rather than avoidance of—scant archival traces, and work that remains extremely personal in nature, is instructive, especially in how the reproduction of life and the reproduction of culture are written as fundamentally intertwined, rather than held apart. The work of Gavin Butt on the hermeneutics of gossip in the work of gay male American artists of the 1960s, Carrie Lambert-Beatty on Yvonne Rainer's lesser known dances represented by limited textual record, or the work of Krista Thompson examining the disappearance of photography from slave archives in the Caribbean, come to mind. These scholars methodologically incorporate various conditions of social, institutional, medical, and colonial fugitivity into their work as part of the hermeneutics of history, studying the arrangements of power reproduce the invisibility or presence of an object, to inform an understanding of the very objects themselves that are lodged within or withheld from view.[20]

As I proceed with curatorial history on the page and in the classroom, my beginning is often a break with any coherent notion of global society or art historical genealogy, through a recognition of the diasporic temporalities and references that would see modernity, exhibitions, curatorial work, and their significance through conditions of dissonance, incongruence, and incommensurability. Perhaps we might write toward acknowledging, if not actively incorporating, the enigmas of alterity that underpin our historiographical enquiry, and the political conditions that shape them. To then also seek out not only exhibitions that were not just the necessary, urgent, accessible, and well-documented capsules of an age or zeitgeist, but also those whose significance lay in their marginalia, their brush against the grain, too obscure to be extensively documented, too contingent to register in the epochal genres of time. We might also invest in infrastructures of historicization, to encourage their multiplication and trouble the ground on

20 Gavin Butt, "Introduction," in *Between You and Me: Queer Disclosures in the New York Art World, 1948-1963*. (Durham, NC: Duke University, 2005), pp. 1-21; Krista Thompson, "The Evidence of Things Not Photographed: Slavery and Historical Memory in the British West Indies," *Representations*, special issue on New World Slavery, Vol. 113, No. 1, Winter 2011, pp. 39-71; Carrie Lambert-Beatty, *Being Watched: Yvonne Rainer and the 1960s* (Cambridge, MA: MIT Press, 2008).

which we stand: conducting, recording, and publishing our oral histories, putting our resources behind uncommon libraries and archives, and giving our support to the historians, librarians, and artists archivists that keep these atoms of history alive. Even if—and especially when—they seem specific, too partial, too incipient, their language too contrary to bear the weight of generalization, they will have mattered nonetheless, by other criteria, on other terms, and through other kinds of cases we might only begin to comprehend.

What to research?

Luis Camnitzer
Mélanie Bouteloup
Galit Eilat
What, How & for Whom
Liam Gillick
Simon Sheikh

the source of our nobility and our path to the highest things

Luis Camnitzer

Time and Money

The conundrum of education serving *either* to improve the mind *or* facilitating access to jobs has been around for the longest time. Art, of course, was never mentioned directly as something relevant for these choices, although our views on education are concurrent, and have a direct impact on our views in regard our relation with art. In the US, positions became very clearly articulated, and, in a way, transcending locality, when slaves were freed after the Civil War and empowerment became an issue. Booker T. Washington and W.E.B. Du Bois represented the two opposing positions.

Washington was a defender of 'practical' education, while Du Bois took a position closer to the liberal arts. Washington focused very closely on the kind of labor that had been imposed by the practice of slavery. He differentiated between the degrading "being worked," and the dignified "working."[1] He also complained about the loss of practical training that occurred following the Civil War, when a generation disconnected from any manual skills emerged. In what today sounds like a bad and unfortunate caricature, Washington stated "It is discouraging to find a woman who knows much about theoretical chemistry, and who cannot properly wash and iron a shirt."[2] His more general position was that priority should be placed on creating wealth. Only wealth would allow for subsequent "leisure and the enjoyment of literature and the fine arts."[3]

Du Bois strongly countered this position.[4] He recognized the need for manual work, but required that "teachers must instruct, not simply in manual dexterity, but in mental quickness and moral habits," adding that "ignorance and poverty are the vastest of the Negro's problems."[5]

We could say that Du Bois lost the battle over time, not only for the groups and social class he was worried about, but all the way up, just short of the borderline with oligarchy. Today there are defenders of Du Bois' position, but they are not very forceful, or lack real power. Michael Roth, president of Wesleyan University, recently published the book *Beyond the University: Why Liberal Education Matters*. He describes the function of the arts between both World Wars as "... part of the development of a student's ability to explore the highest values of a civilization."[6] Culture, he believes, may be dealt with by following traditional views, either as a set of values (which he favors), or, as it is seen at the end of the twentieth century, as a set of conventions, this being the anthropological view.[7] The traditional view according to him would be studying "the source of our nobility and our path to the highest things."[8] Roth is a staunch defender of the liberal arts, but strikes me as seeing tradition as a set of absolute values, which would make his

1
Booker T. Washington, "Industrial Education for the Negro," in *The Negro Problem*, Booker T. Washington *et al.* (New York, NY: James Pott & Company, 2003), available online at http://teachingamericanhistory.org/library/document/industrial-education-for-the-negro/ (accessed June 7, 2014).

2
Ibid.

3
Ibid.

4
W.E.B. Du Bois, "Education," in *The Crisis*, June 1915, pp. 132-136, available online at http://www.library.umass.edu/spcoll/digital/dubois/EdEducation.pdf (accessed June 7, 2014).

5
W.E.B. Du Bois, "The Training of Negroes for Social Power," in *The Outlook*, October 17, 1903, pp. 410-412, available online at http://www.library.umass.edu/spcoll/digital/dubois/EdTraining.pdf (accessed June 7, 2014).

6
Michael Roth, *Beyond the University. Why Liberal Education Matters* (New Haven, CT: Yale University Press, 2014) p. 144.

7
Ibid.

8
Ibid., p. 145.

position closer to defending a static tribal culture than one informed by constant inquiry. Accordingly one may conclude that values then have to be maintained—maybe somewhat honed—but, if at all possible, not radically challenged. All this is relevant to the position of art in our culture. This position is complicated, because art is an area of production of objects for those who have the ability to see them: it is a means to either maintain or challenge those ideas about nobility and higher things, and it also is a way of thinking.

This leads me to discuss two insights: one is 'Time is money,' and the other is 'One image is worth a thousand words.' They are not mine. 'Time is money' comes from Benjamin Franklin, who coined it in a free moment in 1748. And I fully realize that the idea of 'coining' and 'free moment' here acquire extra significance. The statement about the worth of images seems to also have originated in the US, in 1911, to then be retroactively attributed to old China. As a counterpart to Mastercard's 'priceless' slogan, Franklin helped transmute priceless quality into monetized quantity. Meanwhile, the image-word equation points to many other things. Among them is the fact that it signals the limitations of the spoken and written word, shows another effort at quantification, and the neglect of better image-literacy relations in case the adage were true.

Before addressing Franklin's insight, I want to briefly attack quantification in general. The quantification of time and its monetization are part of a much larger quantification ideology that is also taken for granted in the educational system, and may partially explain art's ghetto situation. The ideology not only applies to the reification and fragmentation of time, but also applies to our attempts to organize infinity punctually, wherever we encounter it. Aesthetically speaking, this is the essence of realism. An infinite amount of dots make up visual reality, and for each dot the realist tries to make a corresponding one on the canvas. In digital imaging it is about getting as many pixels on the screen, aiming at the highest resolution possible. To become literate we learn all the words we can. To make somebody knowledgeable, we put as many bits of information as possible into their heads. Which means that alongside realist art and realist computing, there is also realist pedagogy. In essence it is all part of a consistent aesthetic of re-presentation, rather than an effort in presenting. While in real life everything functions in approximations, connections, and dynamic patterns, a very old-fashioned art paradigm continues to rule our institutions. The explanation may be that quantity may be owned, while quality may only be aimed at.

Once we establish and accept that time is quantifiable and may be translated from its own units into monetary units, we also face the issue of ownership and control. It is not that time wasn't owned before Franklin: it is just that with his statement the issue was codified and thrown into our faces. Once time is owned and monetized, people are at the mercy of those who control it.

This is not only a factor in labor relations, and in the definition, control and use of leisure time. It also has implications for how space and product design are used. The efficiency of well-designed functional objects is shown by sculpturally reflecting time economy. Bentham's Panopticon was a device to save on surveillance time by transmitting the feeling of being observed without the use of actual manpower in doing it. The Panopticon is therefore better understood as a time administration tool rather than as architecture. Furniture in turn works as if it had a built-in chronometer. Kitchen stools, bar stools, museum benches, chairs, dinner chairs, armchairs, sofas, and finally beds—in that order—have an increasing allowance of time, with an invisible alarm clock telling us how long we may stay. The same clock also ticks in artworks, and is ideally coordinated with people's attention spans and interests. When not coordinated, attention span rules. The average time dedicated to the *Mona Lisa* by visitors of the Louvre is 15 seconds.

Within the education system, the extreme example of time monetization is, of course, the credit system. It is a concept that still puzzles me 50 years after I first encountered it in the US. When I arrived here, I came from an art school where my generation had abolished the degree, because we felt that the fixed five years required to become an artist didn't make any sense. Some people became valid artists earlier, some later. The point is that today most artists are trained in universities and their initial credibility is coupled with quantified time. BFA, MA, PhD, and whatever degree may be created in the future for the sake of academic commerce, are translated into an amount of credits. One acquires credits, not education.

Once I started teaching in the US, I had to figure out how to fit the acquisition and development of knowledge into these 'credits.' I tried to find out what a credit is, and the only answers I got were related to time, not to knowledge. To gain some qualitative flexibility in my job I then suggested the introduction of 'debits,' but my colleagues thought this either very funny or very foreign. The quality aspect, according to schools, was to be dealt with through other equally intangible units, called grades, which doesn't help much.

Credits started in the US early in the twentieth century, and are now spreading around the world. In other countries they are not necessarily for sale, but address other concerns. Following the Bologna Accords in the European Union, they help take studies and degrees from country to country. They are called ECTS credits, which stands for European Credit Transfer System. One of the goals is the academic convergence in Europe, and between Europe and the US. The resulting portability of education may make some sense. However, designed for employment, it comes with a heavy and explicit emphasis on skills over abstract thinking, in what is called competence-based learning. Even without sales, this impacts the definition of education by limiting access to the humanities to those who can afford them. This concentrates the administration of values in regard to nobility and altitude to a wealthy segment of the population. Among those lucky enough to own their time, nobody would view values as vertical, static, and tribal. However, anthropologists of the future may differ in opinion when studying how we handled the canon in our exhibitions and classes.

In the late 1960s I participated in a symposium of intellectuals of the Americas that also included the US. The meeting intended to help a better inter-continental understanding. One of the participants was Frank Stella. At some point Stella made the idiotic comment that US artists were better than Latin American artists. At the time I attributed his statement to imperialist exceptionalism. We were both young then, and thought in schematic ways. My reaction to his statement was equally idiotic—I showed chauvinist outrage—and our paths never crossed again. More mature today, I see Stella's point rooted in a much deeper place, reflecting a pervasive, less provincial, but more dangerous view. His comment was a consequence of his tribal belief, but it was mixed with a more general notion that art should be approached as a set of manual skills that belong to a vocational profession. This obviously didn't mean that art should be devoid of ideas, as skills acquired during art training still contained valuable knowledge. The definition of profession and professionalism is what did it.

Though as Latin American intellectuals on the left we liked to pose as cultural workers, we never really believed we were. At the time, art in Latin America was unquestionably a humanist activity, and, tapping into the same darkness as the humanities, we used speculation in trying to reach higher things. But this was partly because we practiced art in the absence of a functioning market. Meanwhile, though, it was difficult to break into it. US artists had a market, which meant that US artists had to think competitively. They had to hone practical and strategic skills in order to make it. Stella already had conquered his niche by then, but the Latin Americans in the symposium hadn't. So, from a narrow understanding of professionalism, Stella was right, and he rubbed it in.

However, I don't believe that Stella saw the whole picture. Rather, he acted based on the assumption that meritocracy is good and defines culture, that culture is shaped by individuals and not collectively, and that art has values with absolute international validity. In which case, art would rightly be a competitive activity. Its quality could be ranked, ignoring context and culture. This, though shallow, is a conventional and widely accepted view. What I'm sure Stella didn't perceive then, is that with his version of professionalism he also endorsed Washington's position at the expense of that of Du Bois. This is something particularly tricky when applied to art. Probably all those sharing Stella's views believe that they are on Du Bois' side. While one may conceive of a plumber lacking the knowledge imparted by liberal arts courses, this is more difficult to sustain when talking about artists, regardless how badly they may be trained or educated.

There is a whole school of thought in the US that goes much further. It hinges on the belief that when it comes to certain jobs, all academic degrees, not just in the liberal arts, are a waste of money. A predictive statistic from 2010 envisioned that only 7 out of the 30 job opportunities in the US in the next decade will require a bachelor's degree. As a consequence, Professor Richard Vedder, an economist from the University of Ohio, "likes to ask why 15% of mail carriers have bachelor degrees according to a 1999 federal study."[9] He adds: "Some of them could have bought a house for what they spent on their education."[10] He therefore advocates a radical change in US society, or the recognition of a radical change that already has taken place. It is a society with a minority of wealthy educated people in one class, and a majority of uneducated workers in the other.

Meanwhile, the formal education focused on art making treats it like a skill-based vocational study, rather than one that addresses cognition. However, art does address cognition, and is, in fact, on the high end of critical thinking. The disjunction between training and actual profession may explain the kind of reality artists face. They become 'good with their hands' in skills that have no menial application, and then they are expected to develop critical thinking and deal with knowledge on their own. So art is approached as a discipline good for production, yet placed in the humanities, while the humanities are being pushed up the economic and social scale. By being conditioned by leisure, both as activity and consumption, art becomes part of social stratification. Most art makers need a different job for survival and make their art in their free or freed time. Most consumers need leisure time to go to museums and galleries, and money to go to museums.

9
See Jacques Steinberg, "Plan B: Skip College," *The New York Times*, May 15, 2010, available online at http://www.nytimes.com/2010/05/16/weekinreview/16steinberg.html?pagewanted=all&module=Search&mabReward=relbias%3Ar&_r=0 (accessed June 6, 2014).

10
Ibid.

Image(s) and Word(s)

Now about the second insight: the one about 'An image is worth a thousand words.' Thousand words are about four letter-size pages double-spaced written in font size 12. Referring to one image, the statement sounds like the perfect description of art criticism. Unexamined, it sounds rich, even poetic, and extols the potential for the evocation those single images might attain. Maybe because I was educated as an artist, the phrase sounds to me more like an example of the toothpaste-tube conundrum, with the thousand words squeezed out of the picture after previously having been squeezed into it. Though the image implies an act of data compression, one of the possible implications is that an image cannot really be fully grasped. Its evocations hopefully need more than the thousand words to pin the image down through some kind of a description. Done badly, it will transform the image into a post-facto illustration. Done better, words will try to make the picture work as a synthesizing symbol that might have contained them. One way or another, the words will be sitting next to the picture. As an artist I actually like to aim at pictures that are worth one thousand pictures. The picture and all its worth would then act as a generator of imagination, with infinite new toothpaste tubes.

Let's go deeper into leisure time now, because in our society I believe that this is what makes art a middle-class affair. There is a third interesting saying worth mentioning: 'Dolce far niente.' It is kind of an ethnic slur filled with envy, perhaps similar in quality to the word 'siesta.' Appropriated by non-Italians, this 'sweet doing nothing' doesn't really refer to today's 48 percent unemployed Italian youth. It is applied to the small minority worldwide that can afford it. Leisure time is considered unproductive time, that is, time that could be used for production. And since production is controlled, so is the allocation of leisure time. Leisure time of those who don't own it, but are permitted to have it is therefore considered a waste. This explains why even the most progressive governments are willing to subsidize work and survival time, but not leisure time. It also explains why most activities exercised during granted leisure time pay back through consumption. It helps maintain those industries that sell products for leisure time activities, including tickets to museums. With the exception of a few corporations that employ elite workers, nobody has seriously considered a policy of equal distribution of leisure time to be used for the development of creativity.

Mexican entrepreneur Carlos Slim, according to *Forbes* the richest man in the world, makes his money through his TV broadcasting empires. Slim recently suggested that people work only three days a week. Not to be too generous, he coupled this with 11-hour workdays and retirement delayed by 15 years, thus making up in excess for the 7 missed hours per week. The policy should free up leisure time to improve the workers' culture, which in Slim's case means selling more TV entertainment. They may also, to Slim's credit, visit his two museums with a combined collection of 66,000 pieces of art, for free.

In New York, however, this would work out differently. A family of four going to a museum can easily spend US$200, when one adds transportation and lunch to the US$25 ticket. With that money one could buy cable gold packages and have repeatable kicks instead of one fleeting experience. Museums are generally aware of this problem and therefore seek to create blockbuster shows that demand reduced attention spans, or at least present them as such. Since there is a process of feedback that influences all art activities and that include production, artists today often produce accordingly, and mostly focus on a public defined as middle-class and up. The use of feedback may partly explain the process of simplification that occurs in much of the more recent art. For some years now I've been tempted by the idea of a curatorial project: a mega-exhibition with the title *Small Ideas on a Grand Scale*.

When museums try to reach other segments of the population it becomes a missionary activity focused on spreading the canon. That probably explains why education departments in most museums are secondary appendices, reduced to popularize the appreciation of art, and to perform public relation duties. Most museums still see themselves as bearers of "the source of our nobility and our path to the highest things," even with Roth's 'Arnoldian conception' being passé. This statement could be somewhat modulated by putting the word *our* in bold: **our** nobility, and then writing "the path to our highest things." This at least would clearly communicate that we are talking about tribal issues, and that the institution is there to uphold our canon. Yet, it would still be a problematic statement from a pedagogical point of view. It is both declarative and dogmatic. So here we come closer to confronting the function of art exhibitions if we were to believe that they really have some connection with education.

Scissors and Ideas

Looking at things more practically, when we speak of informal art education, I believe that art should be introduced in schools via curatorial assignments and not through crafts. And this should happen as early as the word art has some meaning for the students. Some years ago, somebody wondered what teachers might do if the use of color pencils, scissors, and glue were declared illegal in pre-school and kindergarten. I thought it a wonderful idea. Teachers would be forced to think about real art issues, instead of using the development of small motor skills to avoid them. I have no problem with making things, with becoming manually proficient, or with acquiring skills. I would welcome a small motor skills program, which would be much more important than competitive sports on any academic level. But as it is approached today, the entry to art takes sides with Booker T. Washington's position. Art remains hidden under the guise of playing with materials. Making is emphasized over cognition and speculation, which are to be done later with leisure. So, although I'm not a big fan of curatorial projects, it is on this basic level that I believe there has to be a curatorial approach to give some relevance to art during the early stages.

The student should face what art actually is, or might be, instead of being reduced to see what motor skills it may produce. To understand this, teams of students may be assigned the task of separating art from non-art after making up their own definition of it, and deciding what ideas and conditions are required for its acceptance or rejection. Requirements may be totally arbitrary and unrelated to conventional definitions. Art may be defined as any unbalanced thing with green and with stripes. Everything else then becomes non-art. With the definition set, team members go about finding or making appropriate works. From a broader perspective there is a clearly formulated problem that has to be solved. No matter what, the teams are applying a curatorial focus by organizing the world into two categories: art and non-art. The next step then is to solve a second problem: setting up a presentation in which an audience will easily recognize art and non-art as separate, which is a task often shared with more sophisticated curators. This includes ways of ordering, signifying, and displaying, discussing the role of pedestals, showcases, frames and enclosures. The assignment addresses taxonomy, its effects, and the presentation and communication of both the organizational system as well as what is organized. Probably more importantly, it also allows teams to work before being affected by the reigning canon. They are promulgating their own. If we place problem formulation and its solving before a canon has a chance to take effect, we have a better chance to encourage creative decisions.

Now I want to come back to the Panopticon. Museums and exhibition venues probably follow the Panopticon model much more closely than schools or any other institution, excepting jails and banks. Guards and video cameras control and implement the 'don't touch,' 'stand back,' and 'move along' policy needed for the preservation of valuable objects.

However, the differences separating institutions in this regard are slowly disappearing. No matter how enlightened the curatorial jargon, the museum set-up continues to reflect set values. The *nobility-higher things* ideology does not include its own critique. The activation of the visitor is reduced to consumption, and is only allowed to happen within the discovery and contemplation of these values. Added to this, precedence is given to the preservation and development of the institution. The aim is to increase the circulation of warm bodies, because that justifies architectural expansions, mostly reflected in the building of atriums, souvenir shops and places for gourmet food. The mission of transmuting warm bodies into warm minds does not seem to be of primary concern.

Another consequence of this is more consequential, because it distorts the role of works of art and the artists' communication with the public. While there is still room for contemplation and pondering about better things, the institutional message may be summarized as follows: We show you objects that this space has designated as culturally important and that you absolutely should see and appreciate. We will assist with your appreciation experience if you join our docents during scheduled times and you buy publications at our shop. Docents and publications will tell you about the artists' lives and what makes the works so good and worth looking at.

The public is not told either what makes 'important' artists important, or if that importance is relevant. It is not told what criteria are used to determine that something is 'good,' or if it is local or global, context-bound or absolute, temporary or eternal, technocratic or by consensus, challenging or affirming, tasteful or not, and so on. I once asked a curator working in a museum about how the quality of 'good' is determined, and the candid and disarming response was "we do the best we can."

In pedagogical terms, the main question not asked is if a particular work of art is needed, if it is something that once present has become indispensable. Therefore, to establish a need or indispensability to acquire or view a piece seems to be a much better heuristic device than trying to figure out quality. 'Need' helps to determine not only what would be lost if the piece stopped existing, but who would lose out in case of its absence. Is there a 'need' to see the *Mona Lisa* for an average of 15 seconds? Possibly yes, though probably for different reasons than those during Leonardo's time. This last question is more relevant for public consideration than just asserting that it is important and good. The first entry in Google for Leonardo (when I tried) was about the Ninja Turtles. It was followed by an MIT magazine and a pizza parlor, and then entries were slowly overtaken by Leonardo Di Caprio.

Focusing on the question of *need* helps to identify the problem being addressed, and the conditions that ultimately generated the existence of the work. This process allows us to see whether our own needs are included in the conception of the work or not. Put in another way, identifying what prompted the artist to consider it necessary to make a work of art leads the viewer to speculate about all other possibilities involved in the process of creation.

Art appreciation traditionally follows a path determined by an evaluation of the quality of the art. Generally these determinations have been expressed through declarative statements. And I declare that declarative statements are bad pedagogy. More progressive approaches, like 'visual thinking' and 'visible thinking' methods, may lead one to make associations with other, non-artistic topics. But they always do so with the requirement of going *through* the work of art, thus limited to the perceptual outlines posed by what one sees. When exploring the need for existence of a work of art it seems more sensible to go *around* the object, not *through* it. One then not only takes in the context and conditions, but also fully project thoughts and feelings and has a collegial approximation to the artist.

The question then is again: what is the function of a museum and its exhibitions? Is it a Panopticon-type vault, acting as a repository of hopefully perfect cultural objects? Is it a secular church in which to explore a definition of perfection? Or is it also, and maybe primarily, a conceptually wall-less organization serving to continually reexamine the origins and values of the canon operating in a particular moment? I would like this to be a space that although it not always shows heresies, definitely encourages people to be heretic. The walls should be nothing more than an osmotic membrane breathing both ways, and the exhibits should be geared to activate departures and creativity in the viewer.

Some years ago I was working as a pedagogical curator for a museum. I made an educational proposal for a particular exhibition and the director's curt response was "This is a museum, not a school." I was angry and as a revenge I sent him a photoshopped facade of the building bearing in big letters "The museum is a school: The artists learn how to communicate; the public learns how to make connections." After venting I realized that I liked it as an art piece. It is basically a con piece that I am still peddling to institutions. The set-up is an implicit contract drawn between the museum and the public, so that subsequently the public may hold the museum accountable when failing to implement the text. The requirements are that the text be written in the official typeface of the institution and that official institutional postcards with the image are sold in the souvenir shop.

It is time we recognize art as a method for approaching knowledge, a tool for inquiry far more powerful than manufacture. This gives primacy to imagination, pattern identification, connection making, and an escape from linear thinking. Education—and museography, as its subsidiary—is still rooted in the nineteenth century. It is stuck in quantitative thinking based on the accumulation of discrete information units. The prestige of a researcher is backed by the many years spent gathering information. Meanwhile Google's flaunted prestige is based on bringing to your screen several millions of entries in a fragment of a second. The only problem with Google is that it is one of the many transformations of the Panopticon.

In 1969 a student of mine, Frank Miata, added a prophetic saying to our collection of adages. It was 'Paranoia is true perception.' At the time he thought it was a complaint, but today I realize it is a call to true critical thinking. Not of the jargony post-structuralist kind, but the ethical one that makes us see that we have to pay to look at the culture we are continually producing, and that somebody else receives the payment.

Knowing who owns and administers our ability to spend time for leisure is a question worth asking. There is nothing wrong with the pursuit of nobility and higher things, as long as there is also a perception of who is hiding behind them to profit. During the late 1820s, Simón Rodríguez, the teacher of Simón Bolívar, wrote: "The first task of education is to deal with things. The second is to deal with those who own them."[11] Today I would translate this latter part into "to deal with problems and with those who reify and own things."

To finish I want to conflate the wisdom of George Bush I with that of Mao into a new adage, and say that "one should dream of a thousand points of light so that we can let a hundred flowers bloom." If nothing else, this may take care of quantitative nonsense and promise the perception of some quality.

11
Pedro Grassi, ed., *Escritos de Simón Rodríguez* (Caracas: Sociedad Bolivariana de Venezuela, 1954) Vol 1, p. 126.

it is reading that counts

Mélanie Bouteloup

THE ENVOY: But have things ever happened otherwise? History was lived so that a glorious page might be written, and then read. It's reading that counts. (To the photographers) *Gentlemen, the Queen informs me that she congratulates you. She asks that you return to your posts.*
—Jean Genet[1]

The Day After is over, ending four months of intense activity around artist Maryam Jafri's exhibition at Bétonsalon—Centre for Art and Research, Paris. Here I propose *The Day After* as a catalyst to reflect on the role of research in the curatorial, and my conception of the curatorial as a mode of research. First of all, I should clarify that I understand research as a process of questioning normalized forms of production, classification, and knowledge distribution. Along with Jean Genet, whose quote I chose to use as an epigraph, I would like to insist on the urgency of *reading* as a way to decipher the power relations lodged *between* words and images.[2] Research is *learning to read*, and this skill is fundamental for maintaining one's own agency in a sustainable way.

If we all agree that we are living in a world in crisis, we must also concede that the contours of this crisis are almost impossible to define. Connections may multiply, but many borders—geopolitical, economic, social, and environmental—persist, and even appear to intensify. We inhabit a space where boundaries are at the same time shared *and* divided, and we are entangled in a complex web of both exchanges and oppositions. In this context, a myriad of individual stories are woven together, often enveloped in the shadow of too linear a history, which impedes an understanding of the implications of this crisis and thwarts any possibility to counteract it via resources available. In our globalized world full of abrasions, frictions, and tensions hidden behind false reciprocities and hegemonic historiographies, we experience a kind of paralysis to a point at which it is sometimes difficult to even breathe. When grand narratives are no longer tenable, there is an urgent need to listen to those who may be able to contribute to the shattering of the status quo. Not to bring about a movement of incorporation, but to undertake the task of *removing* established frameworks and magnifying our ability to read, listen, and widen the circle of what is taken into account in relation to history.

All public archives in Iraq were presumed destroyed in the 2003 invasion. Iraq's official independence day is October 3, 1932, when it gained independence from Britain. An online search for Iraqi Independence Day yields almost no images. In 2012, an American company named Tehrkot Media claimed

1
Jean Genet, *The Balcony* (New York, NY: Grove Press, 1958), p. 75.

2
Along Genet's there are several others whose voices I decided to insert within my text. These excerpts are selected from the research process led by and made visible in the exhibition *The Day After* (Bétonsalon—Centre for Art and Research, Paris, March 18-July 11, 2015).

to have some images of Iraqi independence. The images show King Faisal I of Iraq, in his palace gardens, giving an independence speech to a group of British and Iraqi VIPs. The monarchy, criticized by Pan-Arabists as a tool of British imperialism, was overthrown in 1958 by an army coup. In 2014 Tehrkot Media went bankrupt. The site and its images have subsequently disappeared.
—Maryam Jafri[3]

If art cannot be a remedy to the obliterative tendencies of many common nationalistic historiographies, I do think it offers a space where dissonant voices can be heard. Moreover, I consider it as one public sphere from which contradictory discourses can actually enter into fruitful conversation, capable of providing and enacting opportunities for individual and collective emancipation. As a curator, I am deeply engaged in *realizing* this vision. As philosopher Chantal Mouffe describes in *The Return of the Political*, one of the prerequisites for the construction and maintenance of an emancipated society lies in the faculty to embrace differences, contradictions, and conflicts.[4] For art to create a site that can contribute to the reactivating of democracy—in which people can assemble in a reflective engagement with the world—it is necessary and crucial to defend a conception of art as a work in process rather than a finite object; as a contact zone where it is possible to provoke situations and encounters between divergent and sometimes oppositional voices. I understand art as an arena in which problems can be rendered palpable, and where we can reflect on key issues of our time, where digressions, bifurcations, interpretations, and reassembling are encouraged, and demarcation lines are displaced, and distance can be made manifest. I see conflict as a fertile force in this context; one that enables diverse interests, disciplines, and singularities to learn from each other, inspire each other, and be mutually moved.

I do believe in the exhibition as a framing device through which a discourse is produced and can be discussed, but I also think there is a necessity to seek new ways of rendering artistic works public, by broadening the scope of curatorial practice. In this sense, I am committed to producing exhibitions through collective and collaborative fieldwork, an exercise I will provisionally call 'research-based inquiry.' This practice consists in investigating blind spots in history, by assembling knowledge from different sources, and making room for singular interpretations to surface. I am interested in envisioning several degrees of disclosure for a work of art, and its capacity to build ephemeral communities, within and beyond a complex network of partnering organizations. It is through this intense intertwining

3
Maryam Jafri, exhibition text, in *The Day After* (Bétonsalon—Centre for Art and Research, Paris, March 18-July 11, 2015).

4
Chantal Mouffe, *The Return of the Political* (London and New York, NY: Verso, 1993).

that I believe the deconstruction of conventional methods of knowledge acquisition can happen, and disjunctive connections can be produced, shared, and distributed. These processes diffract official chronologies by combining personal stories and collective memories to make way for new forms of historiography, in which the *other* is not an object, but becomes an active subject of their own history. Spending time and energy on maintaining a lively constellation of interlocutors is then crucial for the sharing of resources, enhancing the dissemination of content, and circumventing the hegemony and Eurocentrism of certain discourses.

There are many challenges and pitfalls in this endeavor. Research is a long process that demands time and concentration, which we are lacking in our small-scale, non-institutional organizations whose economies are precarious and dependent on scarce public funding and constant applications to multiple agencies (financial and otherwise). But I have learned that these constraints can actually be transformed into assets, as we are driven to invent tactics of navigation and modes of working collectively, in close cooperation with each other, and this enables us to stay aware, resist certain misconceptions, and adapt. We are constantly led to devise alternatives to the established modus operandi. By doing so, our curatorial activity is to be considered research-based in the sense that it is wary of not using conventional formats that can come across as too discursive, or too didactic. On the other hand, though, we must attempt to present academic research within exhibitions by working closely with researchers without instrumentalizing their methodology. One recourse may be to maintain tensions between different systems of producing knowledge, following the methodology proposed by artist Eric Baudelaire, through "Juxtaposing fictions that have documentary tendencies with documents that open fictional spaces. Setting up a dialogue between them in a single exhibition."[5] Research-based curating is not just about articulating material, but also about experimenting and inventing form. Theoretician Lotte Arndt once told me that she could see the possibility in art spaces to think things more radically, to look for form instead of presupposing, to invent a form for research *while its content was being researched*. The form, then, becomes a tool to think. There is a need for testing sites for such experiments. Running Bétonsalon, an institution located within the walls of a university, I feel a responsibility to make visual layouts manifest that are capable of setting ideas in motion and speaking with their own voice, language, and vocabulary, although I am very conscious about the difficulty to do so without falling into some sort of fetishism or reification. The problem lies in the difficulty

5
Eric Baudelaire, "Powers of the False (Notes from a Journal)," artist's exhibition pamphlet, in *Modern Monsters: Death and Life of Fiction*, 2012 Taipei Biennial, curated by Anselm Franke (Taipei, 2012).

of manipulating ambiguous materials: Should we allow ourselves to intervene with our own personal gestures? Or is it more appropriate to respect their original physicality by negotiating their presentation under the guise of neutrality? Convinced by the fact that every document is a personal testimony and that there is no such thing as neutral transcription, I believe a historical object should be approached in a very personal way, while keeping its social life in mind. That is why I am interested in instigating an embodied moment for recounting an object's multiple contexts of production, reception, appropriation, and reinterpretation. This is akin to reading out loud, or storytelling in the sense that it is about finding imaginative ways to convey experience and knowledge.

> *Two or three years after Partition, it occurred to the Pakistani and Indian governments that like the prisoners in their jails, the insane too should be exchanged. This meant that mentally sick Muslims in Indian mental homes should be sent to Pakistan, and the Hindus and Sikhs in Pakistan's mental homes should be handed over to India.*
> —Saadat Hassan Manto[6]

Motivated by these sensitive questions and aspirations, I have spent the last few years focusing my attention on studying how institutions in charge of registering our common knowledge and heritage have been trying to translate the migration of objects through time and space. For instance, I became interested in looking at the processes, causes, and effects of patrimonialization around official representations of history in Western museums—what one could call a "*mise-en-ordre, mise-en-scene* and *mise-en-forme*."[7] Driven by anthropologist Johannes Fabian's statement that "There is no knowledge of the Other which is not also a temporal, historical, a political act," my objective was then to question how we could employ other possible representations and uses of histories, which would take into account that we are both acting and acted upon.[8] How can we develop non-linear and more imaginative historiographies? How to account for the contradictions, influences, and resistances with a more transcultural approach, in which the distinction between the tangible and the intangible would be less rigid? Instead of providing definitive answers to these questions, let me now introduce you to *The Day After* in detail. Over a year or so ago, I, along with Virginie Bobin, associate curator at Bétonsalon, invited artist Maryam Jafri to develop a four-month experimental exhibition and public program in Paris. Eventually titled *The Day After*, it was the artist's first project in France, and the exhibition will now be reenacted and amplified

6
Saadat Hassan Manto, "Toba Tek Singh," (1955) in *The Oxford Book of Urdu Short Stories*, ed. and trans. Amina Azfar (Oxford: Oxford University Press, 2009) p. 85.

7
For more on this subject, see Benoît de L'Estoile, *Le goût des autres: de l'Exposition coloniale aux arts premiers* (Paris: Flammarion, 2010).

8
Johannes Fabian, *Time and the Other: How Anthropology Makes Its Object* (New York, NY: Columbia University Press, 2014), p. 1.

in 2016 at Blackwood Gallery in Mississauga, Canada, and Tabakalera in San Sebastián, Spain.

The Day After takes root in Jafri's ongoing project *Independence Day 1934-1975* (2009-present), an installation composed of photographs taken on the first day of independence in former European colonies across Asia and Africa between 1934 and 1975. The photographs are sourced from the countries themselves (in order to highlight, in the artist's words, "how post-colonial states in Asia and Africa preserve the founding images of their inception as independent nations"), and display striking similarities, despite disparate geographical and temporal origins, revealing a political model exported from Europe and in the process of being replicated throughout the world.[9] The installation gathers images collected from 29 Asian and African archives, juxtaposed according to a specific grid, mapped around categories of events, such as speeches in parliaments, street celebrations, or stadium gatherings. In her arrangement, Jafri emphasizes the generic character of the rituals and ceremonies held during the 24-hour twilight period, when the territories transformed into nation-states. The grid, reminiscent of both photo-conceptualism and storyboards, is broken, disturbing the ideological order at play in the images and suggesting non-linear readings. (Fig. 1)

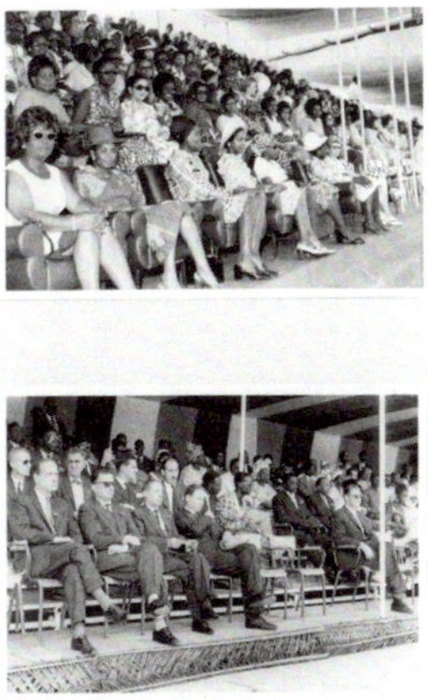

Fig. 1, see p. 242
Maryam Jafri, *The Day After*, detail of Maryam Jafri, *Independence Day 1934-75*, 2009-ongoing, at Bétonsalon—Centre for art and research, Paris, 2015

The Day After takes this rare "second-order archive"—or "collection of collections," as Jafri calls it—as a starting point to give a voice to stories at the margins of history's official images and to the myriad relationships surrounding them.[10] We proposed to Jafri the idea of bringing together the network of journalists, archivists, artists, and researchers who helped her gather these images, and whose work resonated with the issues raised by the project. A variety of materials (magazines, photographs, films, texts, as well as artworks) were subsequently gathered, and rearranged within sculptural display structures created in collaboration with artist Hadrien Gerenton to form a companion to *Independence Day*. They were activated and recharged by various interventions of researchers and artists invited to interact with the exhibition during a series of events (including study days, performances, workshops, and visits) held either at Bétonsalon, or in collaboration with partner organizations in Paris. Begun in advance of the exhibition and continuing as it progressed, these workshops—like the one entitled "An unverifiable attempt to enter history," offered by artist Soufiane Ababri, together with the seminar entitled "Politics of the Postcolonial Body," taught by doctoral and postdoctoral students from Paris Diderot University, and others organized with art schools—were an opportunity to generate diverse new viewpoints, which transformed the exhibition into a

9
The quote from Maryam Jafri is derived from an e-mail to the curators of *The Day After*, 2015.

10
Stephanie Bailey, "Archives on Archives, Maryam Jafri in conversation with Stephanie Bailey," *Ibraaz*, November 6, 2013, available online at http://www.ibraaz.org/interviews/101 (accessed October 28, 2015).

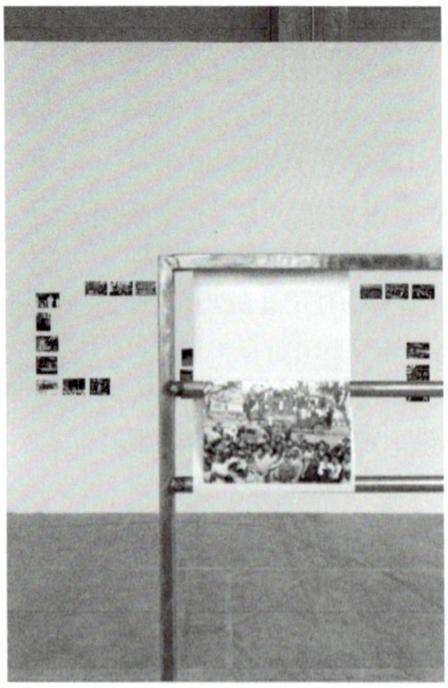

Fig. 2, see p. 243
Maryam Jafri, *The Day After*, detail of Helihanta Rajaonarison, photographs from ANTA fund, at Bétonsalon—Centre for art and research, Paris, 2015

constant work in progress. With *The Day After*, we aimed to provide a catalyst to the many studies linked to issues raised by the exhibition in France and abroad, and provide a working space for them to intermingle, thus uniting and strengthening positions while eliciting unexpected dialogue. In practice, we did our best to provoke crossovers between academic research and artistic or curatorial research. An example is the study day "Other Gestures", which was organized in cooperation with the Chaire Global South(s), hosted by Françoise Vergès in the framework of her seminar at Collège d'études mondiales de la Fondation maison des sciences de l'homme, the UDPN—Usages des patrimoines numérisés (Idex SPC) program from ComUE Paris Sorbonne Cité, and part of the *Collecting Matters Programme*, a collaborative fellowship initiated by Kadist Art Foundation (Paris) with Nomas Foundation (Rome), and David Roberts Art Foundation (London), which marked a collective commitment to encourage new ways of thinking, sharing, and producing knowledge around collections.

Conceived as a non-chronological, fragmented, and highly subjective journey through various case studies and meetings, *The Day After* served as a terrain of investigation to expand on some of the questions that emerged from our conversations with Jafri, such as: What role(s) has the archive played in the construction of the nation-states that emerged from the processes of decolonization? What sorts of images are produced on independence days and what images are not produced/preserved? What are the possible substitutes for the institution of the national archive? What gestures, uses, and networks could be put into play to turn heritage into a tool for emancipation and knowledge? *The Day After* sought to focus on the peripheral context of the images gathered by the artist, so as to generate a reexamination not only of the photographs themselves, but also of the context in which they were produced and the historical narratives attached to them, as in the study by Madagasy historian Helihanta Rajaonarison, who collected personal stories from inhabitants of Antananarivo at the moment of its independence and in so doing brought out other readings of official photographs.

> *Actually, for us (my family and me), it was a holiday like any other, only with Tsiranana's speech added to it. We were confused because it's true we wanted independence but not like "that one"* (sic)*! The idea of taking photos didn't even cross our minds!*
> —Gisèle Ravoniharison, 75 years old, retired nurse, Antananarivo, October 2010[11] (Fig. 2)

11
Originally published in French in Helihanta Rajaonarison, "Images de fêtes à Antananarivo (1958-1960). Quels sont les temps forts de l'indépendance pour les Malgaches?," in *Les indépendances en Afrique. L'événement et ses memoires, 1957/1960-2010*, eds. Odile Goerg, Jean-Luc Martineau, and Didier Nativel (Rennes: Presse universitaire de Rennes, 2012), pp. 253-271.

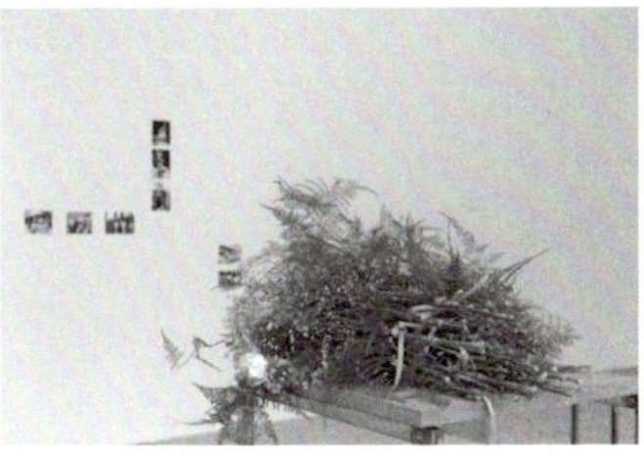

Fig. 3, see p. 244
Maryam Jafri, *The Day After*, view of Kapwani Kiwanga, *Flowers for Africa, Federation of Mali*, 2012, at Bétonsalon—Centre for art and research, Paris, 2015

"Not only is it impossible to reduce photography to its role as producer of pictures," theorist Ariella Azoulay reminds us, but "its broad dissemination over the second half of the 19th century has created a space of political relations that are not mediated exclusively by the ruling power of the state and are not completely subject to the national logic that still overshadows the political arena. This civil political space… is one that the people using photography—photographers, spectators, and photographed people—imagine every day."[12] It was to this political exercise of an imaginative gaze and of *reading* that *The Day After* invited us.

By way of a conclusion, allow me to say that rather than aiming for the unattainable ideal of a definitive and objective history, I think it is the investigative *process* that matters: the detangling, exploring, questioning, probing, analyzing, diagnosing. These actions are at the core of my curatorial work. I try not to smooth over conflict, but compose exhibitions in which objects stay vulnerable to uncontrolled encounters. By provoking this volatile movement, I am vigilant to avoid being authoritative, and instead seek alternative channels for producing and spreading knowledge. As Frantz Fanon writes in his final prayer in *Black Skin, White Masks*: "O my body, make of me always a man who questions!"[13] I am convinced that it is through a permanent practice of research, and of questioning the established order that agency can be sought. (Fig. 3)

12
Ariella Azoulay, *The Civil Contract of Photography* (New York, NY: Zone Books, 2008), p. 12.

13
Frantz Fanon, *Black Skin, White Masks* (New York, NY: Grove Press, 1967), p. 232.

collectivity, conflict, imagination, transformation

Galit Eilat

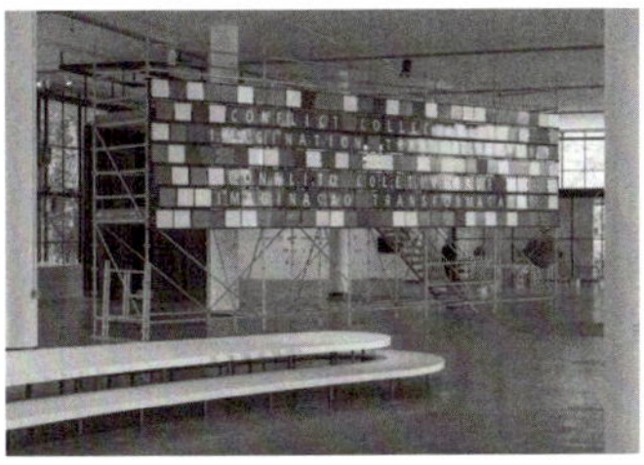

See pp. 246-247:
Bik Van der Pol, Turning a Blind Eye, 2014
Installation shot from press preview 31st Bienal de São Paulo, September 1, 2014

The title of this essay, "Collectivity, Conflict, Imagination, Transformation," is composed of the four building blocks that guided the curatorial team[1] in the development of the concept for the 31st Bienal de São Paulo—four notions, which, when brought together, have the potential to change reality.[2] Charles Esche, Nuria Enguita Mayo, Pablo Lafuente, Oren Sagiv, and myself arrived in São Paulo after a stormy winter in Brazil, during which hundreds of thousands of citizens in major cities went out into the streets to protest against the rising costs of public transportation. The protests led to other struggles by various organizations and unions that fought for better wages, education, and health care, among other public services. While the Bienal is an established institution that has a place of honor in the pantheon of exhibition histories, it is also a temporary and contemporary art event. It therefore seemed important to us that it should take account of what was going on in Brazil at that moment. One of the key questions that accompanied the curatorial team when we embarked on this enterprise was how to give a voice to the social processes being experienced in the country: how to *present* reality, without trying to *represent* it.

To gain a deeper understanding of Brazilian society and to engage with local artistic perspectives, interests, concerns, and urgencies we enacted two initial measures to ensure this; first, the non-Brazilian members of the curatorial team relocated to São Paulo during the research and exhibition period. Secondly, research was convened through a series of Open Meetings, which took place in different cities in Brazil (such as Porto Alegre in the South, Fortaleza, Recife, and Salvador in the North East, Belo Horizonte, and São Paulo in the South East, and Belém in the North), and Latin American capitals and a few cities outside Latin America. The meetings did not have a structure or an imposed subject; the idea, on the contrary, was to put forward an exploratory format, which participants could use in the way they thought best. During these gatherings the curator's role was that of moderator, and was rooted in an attitude of active listening. The meetings allowed us to set up a situation of exchange in which we could touch on issues of art and its relationship to life in the cities. In this schema we were able to explore the educational and cultural infrastructure, local social dynamics, and current political struggles, among many other issues. All this information has been fundamental to how the curatorial concept developed.

Traveling through Brazil and other parts of Latin America, the movement of people, their displacement, and resettlement became a major concern—from the right to free, or even affordable, public transport, to the experience of migration, and the social invisibility of nomadic groups, as well as attempts to

1
The 31st São Paulo biennial curatorial team consisted of Charles Esche, Galit Eilat, Nuria Enguita Mayo, Pablo Lafuente and Oren Sagiv. Associate curators were Benjamin Seroussi and Luiza Proença. See more about the curators at http://www.31bienal.org.br/en/post/888 (accessed December 8, 2015)

2
See for more details the Bienal website's information page at http://www.31bienal.org.br/en/information/766 (accessed December 8, 2015).

establish interlocution with indigenous people. Each meeting was observed and reported on by an independent critic, and later shared online on the Bienal blog.[3]

A residency period was offered to artists and artists' collectives from Brazil and other geographies to support the development of new work. We encouraged collaborations between individuals and groups in the development of projects, as this seemed to respond to our current time. Through their work we examined conflicts underlain by unresolved relationships between groups, between different historical narratives, and between ideas incongruent with official perceptions of the Brazilian establishment. At the same time we tried to contemplate these conflicts collectively, in the belief that such a process is more enriching and effective than individual thought processes and work. We identified imagination and transformation as tools that help one advance beyond and change one's current position. Art at its best has revolutionary power. It can make that which was forbidden yesterday acceptable today, enabling us to observe reality differently. This transformation is also the result of processes that we experience, and can be comprehended via acts of translation, transgression, transgenderism, and other measures that conceal a turn and reject the notion of one absolute truth.

The idea of a turn is often attributed to religious conversion, to a change of political system, or the attempt to define a moment in which social and institutional conventions change, giving way to a different set of common values. Such a turn may only occur without exact mechanisms of control and command. At present, the intensification of national movements, ascents, and collapses in the markets of the global economy, and increased inequality in the distribution of resources all indicate a paradigmatic change. When the status quo is enforced concurrent to that change, the non-existent is rendered tangible abruptly. The turn discernible to us on the horizon seeks a way to rid itself of predetermined parameters. It does not shy away from conflict and confrontation as vehicles of change.

The Bienal opened in light of a conflict that confronted us with the very notions, actions, and concepts that had inspired us throughout the work process. It opened on September 7, a few days after a ceasefire was secured between Hamas in Gaza and the Israeli government. Due to the proximity between that military attack and the Bienal opening, the majority of the participating artists demanded that the Bienal Foundation boycott Israeli state funding in solidarity with the Palestinian people.

3
To read the reports please see http://www.31bienal.org.br/en/posts/860 (accessed December 8, 2015).

An Introduction to Boycott

An organized Palestinian call for a boycott on Israel was made by PACBI (Palestinian Campaign for the Academic & Cultural Boycott of Israel) in 2004.[4] The boycott movement called upon the international community to show solidarity with the Palestinian struggle; to avoid collaboration with state-funded Israeli academic, cultural, and other institutions and organizations, as well as participation in events organized or sponsored by official Israeli organizations or ones with economic partnerships in the occupied territories. This boycott is to be applied until Israel complies with international law, ends the occupation and the discrimination and oppression suffered by the Palestinians within the Green Line, and acknowledges the right of return of the Palestinian refugees to the territories of historic Palestine. The BDS (Boycott, Divestment, and Sanctions) Movement, which is better known today, was established in 2005; in addition to its call for an economic boycott, its goals were identical to those of PACBI.[5]

The rise in international support of a boycott of Israeli institutions and products was triggered by the Israeli attack on Gaza in 2008-2009, during which more than 1,000 Palestinians were killed, and the takeover of the Turkish ship Mavi Marmara in 2010, which had left Turkey to break Israel's naval blockade of the Gaza Strip, alert international public opinion to the situation of Gaza residents, and transfer humanitarian aid. The ship was boarded by an elite unit of the Israel Defense Forces (IDF) before reaching the Gaza shores. During this takeover, nine international activists were killed, and approximately twenty more were injured.

Israel's response to the rising support for a boycott was the introduction of a new law, the Boycott Law (Law of Prevention of Damage to the State of Israel through Boycott, 2011), which applies to citizens of Israel and states that any public call for a cultural, academic, or economic boycott of any person or party solely on the grounds of affiliation with the State of Israel, one of its institutions, or a territory under its control (a clause which was added to the law to cover the prevalent call for boycott of products from the Jewish settlements in the Occupied Territories), will be considered a civil injustice, and hence sufficient cause to establish a punitive damage claim. The phrase "boycott of the State of Israel" in the law covers many forms of conduct whose connection to the literal meaning of the word 'boycott' is far from clear. The law may apply to intentional avoidance of buying products made in a factory in Judea and Samaria, or voluntary abstention from cultural contact, such as deciding not to perform in an Israeli theater or exhibit in an Israeli museum in Judea and Samaria, refusing to

4
For more information on the campaign see http://www.pacbi.org/.

5
For more information on the BDS movement, see http://www.bdsmovement.net/.

study in Ariel University in the West Bank, or to visit the Jewish settlements beyond the Green Line. Through this law, the State of Israel denies the elementary civil right of organization intended to encourage citizens to avoid partaking in what others perceive as wrong or sinful by abstaining from economic ties or visits to certain territories.

Israeli propaganda tends to define any struggle against government policy as a type of terror: diplomatic terror, economic terror, cyber-terror, legal terror, and anti-Semitic terror, the latter being the most effective internationally. In doing so, it deems any form of struggle against the occupation as violent and illegitimate. The Palestinian choice of a strategy of boycott and diplomatic-economic sanctions, however, is based on tactics of nonviolent struggle considered legitimate and effective around the world. *Vis-à-vis* the mighty propaganda machine implemented by Israel, the Palestinians have opted for a tool intended to expose the international community to their plight, and enable anyone, anywhere in the world, to express active support for their cause.

One should note that the Israeli propaganda efforts are underpinned by a double standard regarding the Palestinian boycott of Israel. Israel itself advocates a boycott against Hamas in Gaza, against the regime in Iran, and—recently—against the boycott supporters themselves. For Israelis living in Israel it would be hard to call for a boycott when they themselves cannot boycott the products made in their country or the university in which they study/teach, and continue to pay taxes to the Israeli state. Nevertheless, it is their civil right (although not according to Israeli law) to support the international BDS calls against Israel or any other nonviolent measure that may make their country end its occupation, considering that until Israelis feel international pressure and threat on their economy and culture, there will be no change.[6] This is as equally legitimate and moral a stand as the position maintaining that a boycott is immoral and ineffective.

Even among those who support a boycott of Israeli products and institutions in principle, many object to an academic and cultural boycott. This objection relies, *inter alia*, on the argument that a cultural boycott without an economic one is ineffective. Another argument often voiced by the artistic community, not only in Israel, is that art is apolitical and should strive to create a dialogue between cultures, hence it must not be boycotted. Adherents to this claim usually regard art as autonomous, and will fight to preserve it as such. The idea that art is autonomous implies its lack of any form of utility (other than economic, perhaps), eliminating any possibility for action, or a political/social call by art, thereby negating the

6
Please see http://boycottisrael.info/.

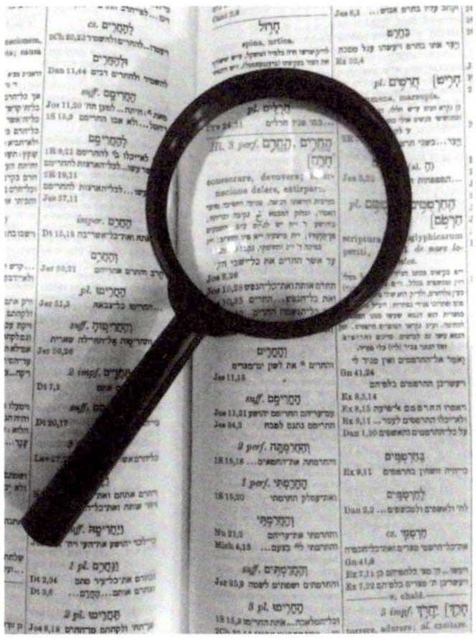

See p. 245
Cross-references

argument that art can form a bridge between cultures and create dialogue.

A Guide for the Perplexed

In the following paragraphs I will try to explain the logic behind the cultural and academic boycott, and the conditions for its effectiveness. Such a boycott differs from the economic or consumer boycott, because it works simultaneously on symbolic, representative, and informative levels, and should take place in the public sphere. Therefore, discussion of the boycott, and the lively debate accompanying it, furnishes countless opportunities to present the reasons that led to it—the wrongs inflicted by the Israeli regime—and deny its legitimacy, thereby undermining the democratic image that the State of Israel tries to sustain. This may subsequently thwart economic collaborations, or investment in Israeli companies, an act that may turn into economic sanctions and lead to the end of the Occupation. In contrast, thus far the consumer boycott has been performed by individuals, without media reverberations. Only boycotts by corporations or large companies attract publicity, generating a media buzz that exceeds the isolated boycotting act, but these instances are relatively rare.

Many Israeli artists, curators, and cultural activists who support the Palestinian struggle maintain that a cultural and academic boycott leads to silencing, and does not distinguish between supporters and objectors of the occupation. In order to reply to this argument one must distinguish between different forms of boycott. PACBI's call for boycott demands a refusal to work with government institutions, or ones sponsored by the State of Israel, while rejecting the boycotting of individuals. The issue remains unresolved when individuals employed by public and government institutions are concerned. This dilemma arises mainly with regard to the boycotting of academic scholars who lecture in public universities (as the majority of universities in Israel are public and subsidized by the state). It also applies to Israeli artists who have been granted government support, and even Palestinian artists, citizens of Israel, who were given such grants. The strict objectors ban any connection with the State of Israel, thereby preventing discussion of the boycott and eliminating the potential for public debate regarding the essence of the boycott, its justification, and modus operandi—concerns that are vital to the success of the boycotting act.

In making this argument about the need for public boycott, I draw on two sources: one originates in Jewish tradition, the other in my own professional experience.

The Hebrew word for boycott is *herem* (חרם), which goes back to biblical times. It first appeared in Leviticus. The word *herem* is sometimes associated with the Holy of Holies (the Sanctuary) (Leviticus 27:28),[7] and at other times, with abomination and profanity, hence, what is boycotted is abhorred and cursed (placed under *herem*) (Deuteronomy 7:26).[8] The Hebrew root *H-R-M* has two major denotations. One refers to something that is forbidden to touch, while the other is something sacred. These gave rise to a third denotation: *herem* is one of the ways to dedicate human beings and property to God or His representatives. Deriving pleasure from that which was placed under *herem* is prohibited. He who enjoys it is called an embezzler, and is placed under *herem* himself. The word *herem* has been given numerous interpretations by various commentators in different eras. All of them, however, refer to the principle that it is forbidden to touch the object placed under *herem* or that the object is consecrated (namely, it becomes the property of God, hence untouchable). Most of the biblical contexts for *herem* are war-related. Only later did the term come to designate the exclusion of a person from the community, of excommunication. The distinction between *niddui* (ban, ostracism) and *herem* originated in the Babylonian Talmud (third to fifth centuries CE). According to that distinction, a *herem* was applied after 60 days of *niddui*, during which the ostracized person had a chance to mend their ways. After that period, *Herem* designated the disgrace of ostracizing, and the person placed under *herem* could neither study the Torah nor work.[9] Following the Geonic period (eleventh century CE), *niddui* and *herem* were used to reinforce public regulations within the Jewish community. One of the best-known cases of *herem* was the one initiated in 1656 CE by the Rabbis of Amsterdam against Baruch Spinoza and Uriel da Costa, claiming that their teachings were heresy. Slightly later, boycotts were decreed against Sabbatai Zevi's adherents, against Hassidim, against Jacob Frank and his followers, and against Enlightenment and Reform Jews.[10]

An act of *herem* within the Jewish community is performed in the presence of a *minyan*, a quorum: ten men who represent the public domain, as in a prayer quorum. *Herem* in the orthodox Jewish community is the most radical act implemented against an individual, cutting off and excluding them from the community. Understanding the etymology of the word and its biblical roots (the term was never secularized, nor acquired a civil synonym) may account for the alarm it elicits in the Israeli public, and in the Jewish world at large, as well as the mass mobilization for the bitter fight against it.[11]

While the Biblical view of boycott makes the public announcement of any boycott a defining aspect, there are also professional reasons why a boycott should be made public.

7
"Notwithstanding no devoted thing (*herem*), that a man shall devote unto the Lord of all that he hath, both of man and beast, and of the field of his possession, shall be sold or redeemed: every devoted thing (*herem*) is most holy unto the Lord." (Leviticus 27:28, King James Version of the Bible, 1604-1611).

8
"Neither shalt thou bring an abomination into thine house, lest thou be a cursed (*herem*) thing like it: but thou shalt utterly detest it, and thou shalt utterly abhor it; for it is a cursed thing (*herem*)." (Deuteronomy 7: 26; King James Version of the Bible).

9
See the website of the Shalom Hartman Institute (text in Hebrew), http://heb.hartman.org.il/Dvarim_Achadim_View.asp?Article_Id=41&Cat_Id=281&Cat_Type (accessed August 10, 2015).

10
See https://he.wikipedia.org/wiki/%D7%97%D7%A8%D7%9D_(%D7%94%D7%9C%D7%9B%D7%94 [Hebrew] (accessed August 10, 2015); for English, see https://en.wikipedia.org/wiki/Herem_(censure) (accessed August 10, 2015).

11
The Arabic term for boycott is *haram*, denoting a prohibition, taboo, or alternatively, something sacred, dedicated to God, much like the Hebrew denotation of the term. In everyday language, however, the prevalent term for boycott is *mukataa* (المقاطعة), which derives from section or fragment, something that should be cut off.

The following are two examples of boycott attempts or successful boycotts against Israeli representation in international art events that I personally experienced. In 2011 I co-curated the 52nd October Salon in Belgrade with Alenka Gregorič. The exhibition featured local and international artists, including Lebanese, Palestinians, and Israelis. During the preparations for the show (several months before the opening), the project organizers applied to the Israeli embassy in Belgrade, asking for support of the event, and received an affirmative response. When we learned of the Israeli support, we demanded that the Lebanese and Palestinian artists be advised thereof, and they announced unequivocally that they would not participate in the exhibition. The organizers decided not to risk the show and declined the Israeli offer. The boycott worked here, and the Israeli state was not represented in this cultural platform, despite the participation of Israeli artists. Similarly, the São Paulo Bienal featured local and international artists, including Lebanese, Palestinians, and Israelis. In this instance, too, the Biennial approached the Israeli embassy in Brazil for support of the project, which was also approved. The opening was scheduled for several days after the official ceasefire between Hamas and Israel. This attack on Gaza was the third and cruelest ever performed by Israel. It took the lives of more than 2,000 Palestinian civilians and combatants, with 72 dead on the Israeli side, 67 of them soldiers. To this day Gaza has not been rebuilt, and its citizens still live amid the debris. In this context, one must add that the Brazilian Ambassador to Tel Aviv was called back in protest during the Israeli attack on Gaza, concurrent with a harsh exchange between the Foreign Ministry in Jerusalem and Brasília, which was reported in the international press. Only after the Israeli president apologized to the President of Brazil diplomatic relations were reinstated.

As in the case of the October Salon, this time, too, the artists were informed of the Israeli support. They were updated personally, as they were in São Paulo to develop their works. A meeting was held, with the participation of the Palestinian and Lebanese artists, two representatives from the curatorial team, and the Bienal Foundation President, in which the latter clarified that he had no intention of rejecting the Israeli support, and expressed his dismay that we were importing external problems that did not pertain to Brazil. His main argument was that the Bienal Foundation was not a political body, and that it would accept funds from any economic organization or country willing to support the event. Following the meeting and additional harsh exchanges, the artists wrote a petition demanding that the Bienal administration decline the Israeli support. In their letter they explained that:

At a time in which the people of Gaza return to the rubble of their homes, destroyed by the Israeli military, we do not feel it is acceptable to receive Israeli cultural sponsorship. In accepting this funding, our artistic work displayed in the exhibition is undermined and implicitly used for whitewashing Israel's ongoing aggressions, and violation of international law and human rights. We reject Israel's attempt to normalize itself within the context of a major international cultural event in Brazil.[12]

In their declaration the artists demanded that their work not be used to whitewash Israel's aggression in Gaza, namely not to enable the State of Israel to be represented in an international cultural event, and to benefit from the symbolic value of the artists' works. The artists considered that the presentation of their works under the emblem of the Israeli state clashed with and undermined the messages they wished to convey. Their argument pertains to many cases in which artists are asked to represent various entities through their work, which is true of cultural events large and small, and museums that raise funds and offer the symbolic capital and contents brought by artists in exchange. Obviously, the problem does not lie in the fundraising itself, but in the degree of transparency, or lack thereof, in the artists' awareness of the support, and whether they agree to the transaction offering financial capital in exchange for symbolic capital.

In this spirit, the curators published a declaration supporting the artists, both those who decided to side with the Palestinian struggle, and those who chose not to.

We, the curators of the 31st Bienal de São Paulo, support the artists and understand their position. We believe that the statement and demand by the artists should also be a trigger to think about the funding sources of major cultural events. In the 31st Bienal, much of the work seeks to show that struggles for justice in Brazil, Latin America, and elsewhere in the world are connected. The idea of living in transformational times is fundamental to this Bienal, times when old patterns of behavior are exhausted and long-held beliefs are questioned. This transformation also affects the relationship between curators and organisers of major cultural events such as this Bienal. At the outset, we accepted the traditional agreement in which curators have artistic freedom and the Foundation has responsibility for the financial and administrative affairs. The Bienal de São Paulo Foundation has very correctly kept to this agreement throughout. In our turn, we assisted in international fundraising. However, as

12
See Mostafa Heddaya, "São Paulo Biennial Participants Demand Organizers Return Israel Funding (Updated)," *Hyperallergic*, August 28, 2014, online at http://hyperallergic.com/146032/sao-paulo-biennial-participants-demand-organizers-return-israel-funding/?wt=2 (accessed August 10, 2015).

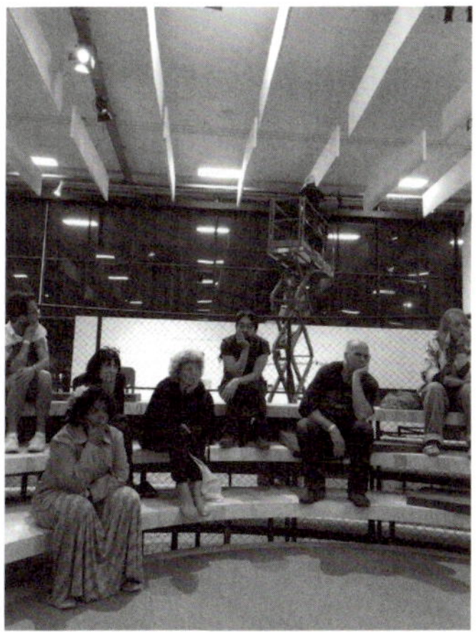

See p. 245
A 7 pm meeting

a consequence of this situation, alongside other incidents at similar events worldwide, it is clear that the sources of cultural funding have an increasingly dramatic impact on the supposedly 'independent' curatorial and artistic narrative of an event. The funding, whether state, corporate or private, fundamentally shapes the way the public receives the work of artists and curators.[13]

Every evening at 7 pm during the week before the opening, a meeting initiated by the artists was held for updates and coordination. Many differences of opinion emerged during these conversations, some regarding the way in which they were to organize, act, and respond. Questions came up, such as whether the only problematic representation was the Israeli one, or whether there were other, similarly controversial countries or Brazilian organizations. Many questions were asked regarding the artists' commitment to the audience that had been anticipating the opening of the event for two years, and their commitment to the local producers with whom they had worked, etc. At the same time it was clear that all the artists wanted the Bienal to open as planned, and that as a group they did not want to let anyone leave, so that if the Bienal were to open, it would be with the participation of all the invited artists.

The Foundation's refusal to comply with the artists' demand or negotiate with them sparked a media reaction. More than 70 percent of the artists declared that they would not take part in the Bienal if the State of Israel were represented. The day before the opening an agreement was reached between the Foundation and the artists that Israel's sponsorship, and any other state support, would be restricted to their own nation's participating artists and not apply to the Bienal as a whole. While Israel was ultimately represented in the exhibition and there was no boycott, the struggle over the boycott demand yielded a message of solidarity and sharp denunciation of Israel's measures in the Gaza Strip in the Brazilian and international mass and social media.

The Silent Boycott

The events around the boycott in São Paulo proved that the *public* call for a boycott is as important as the act of boycotting itself. This essay was written a year after the conclusion of the deadly attack on Gaza, and the cultural boycott in the Israeli art field is felt today more than ever, as museums, art centers, and galleries encounter an increasing number of artists who refuse to exhibit in Israel. Much of this, however, is done privately and discreetly (or, more accurately, by email). The boycott itself, its motivations and effect on the Israeli art world are not made

13
See Mostafa Heddaya, "São Biennial Curators Join Artists in Repudiating Israeli Sponsorship," *Hyperallergic,* August 29, 2014, online at http://hyperallergic.com/146308/sao-paulo-biennial-curators-join-artists-in-repudiating-israeli-sponsorship (accessed August 10, 2015).

widely known, and are not discussed in public—many of the invitations to exhibit in Israel by state-funded organizations or private non-funded entities are met with a negative response; sometimes the invitees simply omit to answer—hence the act of boycott does not fulfill its potential, and remains a mere refusal or disregard of the invitation.

The refusal to exhibit in an Israeli museum or gallery, to perform in Israel, or to participate in an event sponsored by the State of Israel is at the core of this boycott action, but without making it public knowledge or disseminating the reason for the refusal, the boycott remains between the inviting party and the refusing party, failing to make a public impact. A meaningful boycott must take place in the public sphere, or, more specifically—in the media/communication sphere. For instance, refusal to sell an artwork to an Israeli museum by an international artist who does not wish to be included in the collection for ideological reasons is not a boycott if the artist does not declare that he is boycotting the museum or its collection. Refusal to collaborate with Israeli art institutions or not inviting them to take part in international projects without public/media repercussions explaining why the invitation was withdrawn, or never considered to begin with, can be regarded as lack of time, indifference, or disregard. On the other hand, international events and organizers that fail to invite Israeli artists or cancel their participation in international events when they are neither supported by the State of Israel nor represent it, take an ineffective measure, which does not contribute to the boycott movement. A boycott is a civic action and does not occur behind the scenes, between individuals, or in the private sphere. The boycott is not a goal in itself; it is an instrument to bring about change, and to put pressure on Israeli citizens and the state of Israel. Therefore boycott is unproductive if it is not announced publicly. If the Israeli public remains unaware of its existence and pressure is not put on the government from within, no change will take place, rendering the boycott pointless. The silently boycotting individuals or institutes may feel that they have made the right ethical decision for themselves, but they fail to contribute to the potential change aimed at by that boycott movement.

The question provoked by the boycott is this: Is there a difference between refusal to exhibit somewhere since the budget is insufficient, or the museum is not important enough, or the project's underlying concept is not interesting enough, etc., and a refusal to exhibit for ideological reasons? Obviously, all reasons for refusal are legitimate, but this does not qualify them as a boycott. It is not a boycott if the refusal occurs outside the sphere of representation. Every refusal has an impact, but to try to change official Israeli policy toward the Palestinians living under occupation, it takes more than a refusal or silent solidarity. It takes a campaign to awaken public opinion for international solidarity with the Palestinian civil struggle.

what do you want to know?

What, How & for Whom/WHW

The increase in access to information distribution networks—in all of their technological forms—of the past decades has both been lauded as a means to democratize society, and lamented as a tool for manipulation and distraction. With the constant and ceaseless stream of news on social, economic, and political changes that engulf people and places near and far, with vast repositories of knowledge available at the touch of our fingers, the question increasingly becomes: What does one really want to know? What is the knowledge that one seeks out, partially from a desire to learn, and partially from the socially enforced need to be informed, up to speed, both in one's profession, and in increasingly changing skills needed to maneuver everyday life? From this relentless flow of data, what information does one attempt to process and make sense of, as opposed to the information one deliberately blocks out as fast as one can?

Of course, many thinkers have pointed out that being informed does not mean being knowledgeable, let alone truly involved, and that knowledge can only result from a process of transformation of one's understanding of the world, which in turn comes through the practice of transforming the world itself. The groundbreaking writings on critical pedagogy in the 1960s and 1970s drew attention to the basic fruitlessness of gaining knowledge through acquiring a degree. And yet, to this day teaching through formalized educational system follows "the banking concept," as Paulo Freire so correctly described it in his *Pedagogy of the Oppressed*.[1] In most instances formal education continues to incline toward, in Freire's words, depositing knowledge into passive students, which in practice means delivering as much information as possible, or providing what at best could be described as elaborate vocational training.[2] Developing critical self-reflexivity, and expanding the range of questions that are accepted as legitimate within each particular field, and within society in general, has certainly not been on the agenda of many a school or university. The proclivity toward conservative positivism of teaching the students seemingly neutral facts has only been exacerbated by regressive tendencies of neoliberalism, characterized by general retreat from the ideologies of social change. Often, as in the case of the former Eastern European countries, the move toward political revisionism has been followed by significant changes in school curriculums, tailored to discredit any past revolutionary attempts, and to steer imagination toward acceptance of the given social relations. The general political push to move education into the realm of commercial activities, and turn it into an expensive commodity, has been visible across different geographies, resulting in 'streamlining' of the curriculums toward more 'applicable' subjects and approaches. Even in the countries

1
Paolo Freire, *Pedagogy of the Oppressed* (New York and London: Continuum, 2005), pp. 71-86. The entire second chapter of the book deals with the 'banking' concept of education as an instrument of oppression.

2
Ibid.

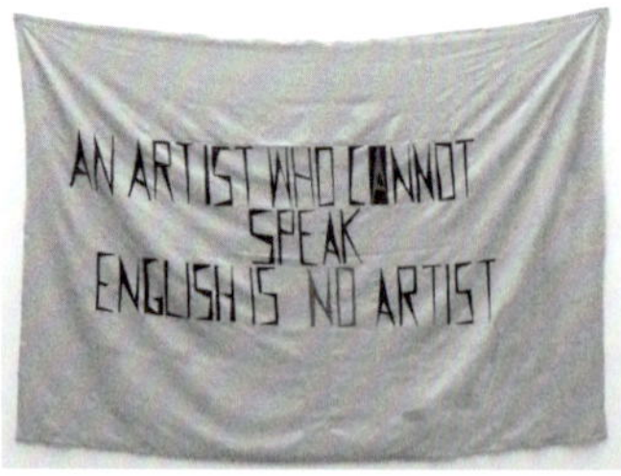

See p. 250
Mladen Stilinović, *An Artist Who Cannot Speak English Is No Artist*, 1992

005.94

A public library is:
- free access to books for every member of society
- library catalog
- librarian

With books ready to be shared, meticulously cataloged, everyone is a librarian.
When everyone is librarian, library is everywhere.
http://www.memoryoftheworld.org

See p. 250
Public Library info card

where, until recently, public education was taken for granted as a public service that was unquestionably available to all, introduction of university fees is deepening the rift between the ones who can and the ones who cannot afford to study. Education has slowly but surely slid back toward the function of reinforcing the profoundly oppressive social order.

And yet, despite being aware of the paternalistic, pacifying, and alienating tendencies of schools, faced with the dismantling of public education we should pledge our allegiance to it, and side with Gramsci's insistence on norms of cultural authority, and the role of public education in achieving general conditions necessary for 'citizens' to 'govern.'[3]

A Curator Who Cannot Speak English Is No Curator

Although the dissolution of the ties that used to closely relate the level of one's schooling to the advancement in one's social status was astutely diagnosed already half a century ago, nothing denotes 'respectability' to this day in such a shorthand manner as a university degree, and emerging professions tend to insert themselves into the society of the 'esteemed' occupations as fast as possible.[4] Numerous new programs of curatorial studies are a case in point, as it seems that they are emerging at a rate hitherto reserved for new biennials. The inclination toward a more theoretical or a more practical approach of exhibition-making varies from program to program, as well as their ideological leanings, but the sheer number of newly established studies signals the tendency of instituting the common denominator of knowledge needed to belong to the curatorial profession, and the growing sense of the necessity to go through a curatorial school to be a curator. And yet, when it comes to prestige and international visibility, the figure of the 'worldly curator' still wins over the 'well-trained curator.' She is well-traveled, excellently informed, easily adapting her practice to a variety of different localities, knowledgeable about artistic positions from different parts of the world and various cultural and political contexts, and her connectedness to a global network of like-minded professionals and market players represents one of the most poignant symptoms of today's relationships in contemporary art.

Mladen Stilinović created his work *An Artist Who Cannot Speak English Is No Artist* in 1992, only a couple of years after the fall of the Berlin Wall, and at a time when the first curatorial study programs were being instituted. The statement from the title was written on a pink fake-silk wall banner, and later this work has been carried out in a few other versions, including an outdoor banner and a T-shirt. Stilinović's practice has left a strong mark on younger generations of artists, and *An Artist*

3
See Antonio Gramsci, "In Search of the Educational Principle," *New Left Review I*, No. 32, July-August 1965.

4
See for example André Gorz's passionate and insightful "Destroy the University," originally published in *Les Temps Modernes*, No. 285, April 1970.

Who Can Not Speak English Is No Artist has become his most quoted work, appearing as the title of Jacup Ferri's hilarious mock-confessionary video from 2003, and as a slogan on people's websites, in their studios, and living rooms. In a fairly straightforward, but also quite ironic manner, the work deals with the position of an artist from Eastern Europe at the moment of its supposed re-integration into the 'mainland' of Western European democracy, and refers to the geopolitical reconfigurations during which culture has often been seen as a means of 'introducing' former socialist countries to the standards of Western liberal capitalism. Not only *An Artist Who Cannot Speak English Is No Artist*, but Stilinović's practice in general gives an acute diagnosis of maladies of that time that, for lack of a better word, was often called 'the transition,' and in which narrow-minded local interests collided with the implacable and all-encompassing logic of capital and globalization. The deadweight of ideology during the decades of this 'transition' from state socialism to Western capitalism has primarily manifested itself through the overall codification and conversion of all life experiences and choices to the market, and through economic profitability as the only measure of social success. Stilinović uses ridicule, rudeness, and political incorrectness to mock mythologization, and ideological manipulation, and invites toward constant reexamination of all seemingly unquestionable social and economic relations. The statement *An Artist Who Cannot Speak English Is No Artist* rings true well beyond the Eastern European context within which it was made, and draws attention to the complicated mechanisms of cultural integration and representation, and their relationship to curatorial responsibility and ethics.

During the over twenty years since Stilinović made this work, the contemporary art world has gone global, just like all other spheres of production. The attempts at puncturing and reexamining the Western canon have been successful, at least to a certain extent, and the notion of 'marginal' geography has been thoroughly redefined, while a fair number of artists and cultural workers from different geographies have become internationally renowned and are present in major international exhibitions and institutions. And yet, the old power relations are still in place. In order to develop long-continued international careers, rather than stumbling into one-off participation at some of the prestigious events that market themselves as 'presenting the xxx number of artists from all of the continents,' artists from so-called 'marginal' geographies first of all have to secure gallery representation at the highest possible Western level. Analyzing the birthplace and current place of residence of artists participating at Documenta exhibitions, Chin-Tao Wu showed that the movement of artists is still very much a one-way flow toward the Western centers and infrastructure, and demonstrated that "although it is forever shifting, the global art world nevertheless maintains a basic structure: concentric and hierarchical."[5] Throughout the massive shifts in the ideological landscape, and their reflections on cultural production, the supremacy and ubiquity of English is one of the things taken for granted, and it can certainly be said—with an equal dose of irony and uncomfortable truth—that "the curator who cannot speak English is no curator." Despite the fact that, alas, not all of us speak it that well, we are still doomed to read, write, and increasingly even think in English, navigating the turbulent waters of our professional lives with what often seems, and rightly so, like a limited choice of vocabulary. But as Hito Steyerl in "International Disco Latin,"[6] and Martha Rossler in "English and all that"[7]—both published as a response to Alix Rule and David Levine's "International Art English"[8]—point out, to focus on inadequacy of our English would be misplaced. The critical question of curating becomes: How do we make an attempt at self-reflexivity, looking into ways in which we ourselves are entangled and implicated in this dynamic of power between the particular knowledge required to be constantly present within the global network, and the limited access to the resources? Only in this way can we try to tackle the issue of the hegemonic language that we are all adopting, sometimes consciously and sometimes inadvertently—both literally, in the form of English, and metaphorically, in the form of universally accepted modes of presentation of contemporary art. The challenge becomes how to engage with artworks that do not speak this global language, and how to create platforms for producing knowledge that is anchored in local histories and at the same time aimed at strengthening international solidarities. The partial answer may be in stubborn and concentrated efforts at building durable local institutions, and doing so despite the socio-political context of colossal economic crises and social uncertainty, in an environment that is entirely project-driven and funded, as well as increasingly instrumentalized by daily politics.

If we are to continue to invest into the potential of the exhibition format and the art institution as public sites that can enable learning through changes in perception on both the individual and the collective level, we should not take the educational process that takes place within the exhibition for granted. While we should advocate for learning from the knowledge inherent in the artworks themselves—be it an abstract painting or a protest poster made during street demonstrations—the narrative of an exhibition as a constructed whole is an entirely different matter, which can either reinforce or refute

5
Chin-Tao Wu, "Biennials Without Borders?," *New Left Review*, No. 57, May-June 2009.

6
Hito Steyerl, "International Disco Latin," *e-flux Journal*, No. 45, May 2013, available online at http://www.e-flux.com/journal/international-disco-latin/ (accessed August 13, 2015).

7
Martha Rossler, "English and all that, " *e-flux Journal*, No. 45, May 2013, available online at http://www.e-flux.com/journal/english-and-all-that/ (accessed August 13, 2015).

8
Alix Rule and David Lavine, "International Art English," *Triple Cannopy*, No. 16, July 2012, available online at http://canopycanopycanopy.com/issues/16/contents/international_art_english (accessed August 13, 2015)

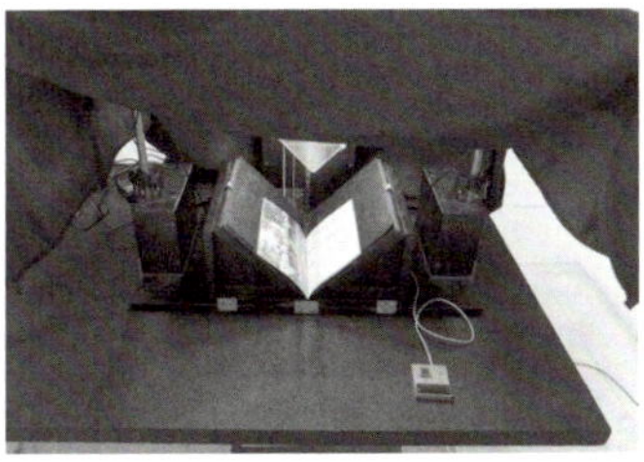

Book scanner at *Public Library* exhibition, Gallery Nova, Zagreb, 2015

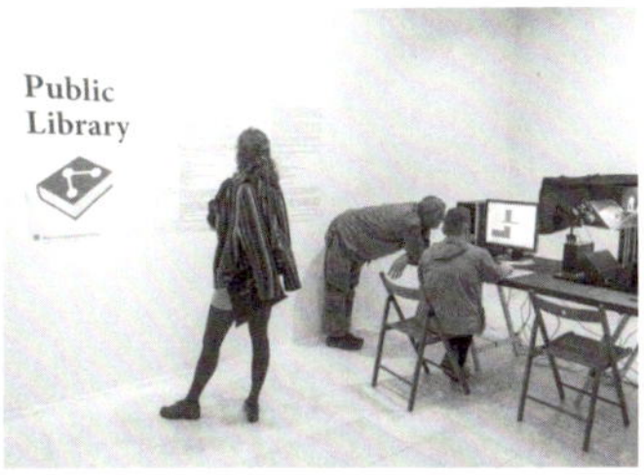

See p. 250
Installation view *Public Library* exhibition, Gallery Nova, Zagreb, 2015

class, race, and patriarchal relations. Critical curating has to do with an effort to deal with system changes rather than with symptoms, and it is not about having explicit 'political or critical content,' but about defying quick and easy understandings. In his article published in the first international edition of the magazine *Praxis* in 1965, Croatian philosopher Danko Grlić followed the Marxist tradition in writing about gaining true knowledge through interaction of theory and practice, which leads to the process of transformation. He stated: "Man cannot have the ambition to transform the world if he does not at the same time transform his own ideas and principles."[9] But he also warned: "Naturally, to define human practice (i.e. practice worthy of human beings) as transformation is still not to define it adequately in content. Certain questions are necessarily implied—in order to avoid a banal relativism—of the quality, purpose, and meaning of this transformation."[10] If education has any ambitions of being progressive, it should first and foremost look at its own purpose and assess the effects that new approaches to knowledge as the basis of capital reproduction have on the totality of contemporary existence.

When Everyone Is Librarian, Library Is Everywhere

Public Library is an ongoing hybrid media and social project initiated by Marcell Mars, Tomislav Medak, and Vuk Ćosić in 2012, based on ideas from the free software movement.[11] Through building a repository of digitized books, and enabling others to do so as well, it thematizes the idea of the public library as an institution offering universal access to knowledge for each member of society. It is a platform for the free sharing of books, but also for advocating social solidarity in learning and the production of knowledge, drawing attention to the discouraging fate of public libraries as endangered institutions, as one of "these invisible infrastructures that we start to notice only once they begin to disappear."[12] In its involvement with art institutions, *Public Library* consciously attempts to use them as a resource for their 'campaign,' pinpointing the warped logic in which

> *the commodification of knowledge, education, and schooling (which are the consequences of a globally harmonized, restrictive legal regime for intellectual property) with neoliberal austerity politics curtails the possibilities of adapting to new sociotechnological conditions, let alone further development, innovation, or even basic maintenance of public libraries' infrastructure.*[13]

The project stresses the necessity of producing sociability through the collective use of existing public resources, actions,

9
Danko Grlić, "Practice and Dogma," *Praxis*, International Edition, Zagreb, 1965, No. 1. p. 52.

10
Ibid., p. 51.

11
See http://www.memoryoftheworld.org.

12
Marcell Mars, Manar Zarroug, and Tomislav Medak, "Public library," in *Public Library*, eds. Tomislav Medak, Marcell Mars, and WHW (Zagreb: Multimedia Institute and What, How & for Whom/WHW, 2015).

13
Ibid.

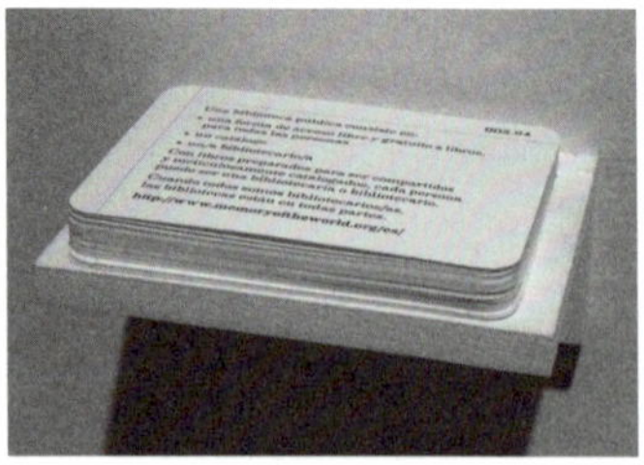

Installation view *Public Library* at *Really Useful Knowledge*, Museo Nacional Centro de Arte Reina Sofia, Madrid, 2014

and experiments, either by developing new forms of sharing, or by fighting to maintain existing ones now under threat of eradication. Its presence in exhibitions is always strategic, and it varies depending on the need of each particular context. For example, for the *Really Useful Knowledge* exhibition at Reina Sofia in Madrid, the production funds were used to build a book scanner at Calafou, an anarchist cooperative outside Barcelona, and at the museum the project was presented by a simple card offering basic information on how to access it on the Internet.[14] At Gallery Nova in Zagreb, the exhibition was set up so that collecting, scanning, and sharing of the books could happen within the space.[15]

During the civil war, after the break-up of Yugoslavia in the 1990s, several hundreds of thousands of books were removed from public, school, factory, and specialized libraries, former Yugoslav People's Army centers, socio-political organizations, and private book collections in Croatia, because of their ideologically undesirable content, the Cyrillic letters they were written in, or ethnic or political background of the authors. They were thrown into bins, discarded in the street, destroyed, or recycled.[16]

Written-off, on the occasion of the 20th anniversary of the Storm was an exhibition/action organized in Gallery Nova in Zagreb as a collaborative effort of What, How & for Whom/WHW and the *Public Library* project. It took place in early summer 2015, and was timed to coincide with the media frenzy surrounding the official celebration of the anniversary of the military operation Storm, conducted by the Croatian Armed Forces in 1995, which marked the official end of the civil war in Croatia, officially called the 'Homeland War.' The citizens were invited to bring the books that were brutally removed from public libraries in the 1990s to the gallery so that they could be scanned and later on made available via the website www.otpisane.org. Apart from documentary material on book destruction, books brought in by citizens, and scanners for their digitization present in the gallery space, the exhibition/action included series of performances by the artists Antonio Grgić, Siniša Ilić, Božena Končić-Badurina, Siniša Labrović, and Luiza Margan, which provided different approaches to looking at the complicated relationship between private and officially sanctioned reading.

Written-off, on the occasion of the 20th anniversary of the Storm was called *Written-off* because the media and politicians often presented removal and destruction of books as a legitimate and routine procedure of writing off books from the libraries, often combined with statements about unwanted books, written in Cyrillic letters, described as ideologically unacceptable,

14
Really Useful Knowledge was held at Museo Nacional Centro de Arte Reina Sofia, Madrid, from October 28, 2014, until February 9, 2015, curated by WHW.

15
Public Library was held at Gallery Nova in Zagreb, May 27-June 13, 2015, while the exhibition/action *Written-off, on the occasion of the 20th anniversary of the Storm* was held at Gallery Nova, June 18-July 13, 2105.

16
The data on discarded books was collected through extensive research on 'library purification' and gathered by Ante Lešaja in *Libricide—the destruction of books in Croatia in the 1990s*. What this book clearly shows is that the destruction of books—as well as the destruction of monuments of People's Liberation War and antifascist struggle in Croatia—was not a result of individual actions, as official accounts are trying to argue, but a deliberate and systemic activity, which symbolically summarizes the dominant Croatian politics of the 1990s.

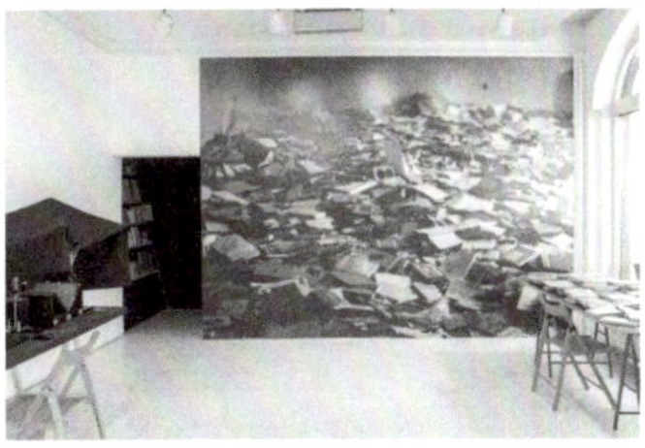

See pp. 248-249
Installation view exhibition/ action *Written-off, on the occasion of the 20th anniversary of the Storm* at Gallery Nova, 2015

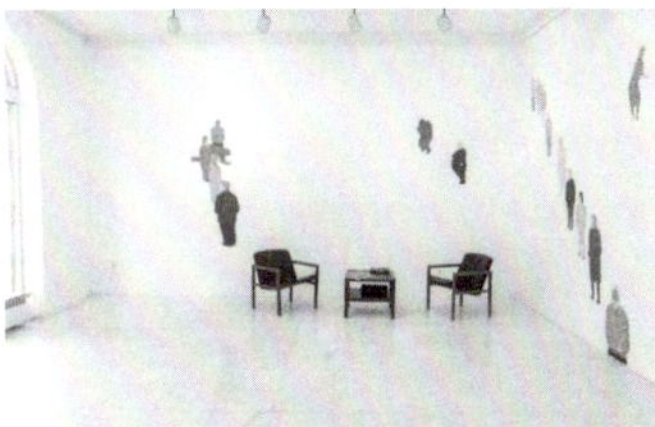

Installation view Siniša Ilić, *Wall Composition with a Motif of Oral History, a Group for Learning by Hearth and a Group for Not Learning by Hearth*, at exhibition/action *Written-off, on the occasion of the 20th anniversary of the Storm*, Gallery Nova, 2015

dangerous, harmful, unnecessary, unsuitable... Arguing differently, *Written-off* placed book destruction in the social context where destruction of 'undesirable' and 'unsuitable' monuments and books happened simultaneously with the destruction of houses and killings of 'undesirable' and 'unsuitable' citizens, outside and regardless of war operations.[17] In opposition to the official state discourse, which disregarded the critique of military celebration of an operation that resulted in the death of hundreds of civilians, soldiers, and policemen, and even threatened to legally sanction expressions of critical opinions on the nature of the Homeland War, the exhibition/action at Gallery Nova drew attention to the questions that the anniversary of the Storm actually opens up—power over writing history, ethno-nationalism as another face of neoliberalism, the character of the war and justice in its aftermath, status of the victims, refugees, etc. It refused to accept the rhetoric of war and existence of the 'enemy' as the basic condition of creating the Croatian nation, and of maintaining its mythological vision. It opposed the discourse that positions the war crimes against civilians of a 'wrong' nationality as justified, and the need for them as historically irrefutable. According to this discourse, one ethnic group has the protection and sanctuary of the state, while the members of other ethnic groups can live only under the benevolence of the first group. It is the twisted logic that perpetuates the discourse of internal conflict and war *ad infinitum*, a discourse that, like during the 1990s, still serves its purpose of ideological mystification, and parallels the arguments about the necessity of capitalism as the only possible social system that should not be questioned at any costs.

To commemorate, but also to oppose the political logic, which resulted in the mass exodus and killings of civilians, the exhibition/action *Written-off, on the occasion of the 20th anniversary of the Storm* attempted to bring as many of the thrown-out books as possible back to the public archive, and thus make them available to all. In this way, it marked the anniversary of the Storm through collective action in which the production of knowledge became the site of conflictual engagement, and it attempted to question the role of the exhibition and the gallery as platforms for political and aesthetic experiments.

In his wartime diaries, George Orwell argues that "evidently when a scandal passes a certain magnitude it becomes invisible."[18] It is, however, necessary to act against the normalization of scandal. Though it is clear that art itself cannot overturn the consequences of political activities and military actions on the lives and destinies of individuals (those killed, murdered, the refugees, but also those who are perpetrators and witnesses), it

17
It should be noted here that according to the 1991 Census the Serb population amounted to 12.16 percent of Croatian citizens, while according to the 2001 Census, in 10 years of the conflict their proportion in Croatian demographics fell to 4.54 percent.

18
George Orwell, *Diaries* (London: Penguin Books, 2010), p. 404.

can be effective within the cultural field. The collection and digitization of books, their archiving, and dissemination were envisioned as a symbolic act with which the Croatian public takes its part of responsibility.

Learning Together, but What For?

Approaches to learning that move away from traditional and institutionalized education, such as Stilinović's position of an autodidact in close communication with a number of his fellow artists, or the development of networks for self-education and peer learning, as in the case of *Public Library*, offer the possibility of building different approaches to curriculum and methodology, as well as moving away from ossified and oppressive intellectual positions.[19] They show a way out from increased commodification of learning processes, from education organized as a market of certificates and degrees of varying prestige. More importantly, they attempt to recapture the joy of learning, in spite of the atmosphere created by the paradigm of the 'knowledge society,' in which we are constantly reminded that we should learn continuously, in order to be flexible and adaptable, an active participant in 'lifelong learning'—a process whose very name has long ago slipped from its original optimistic meaning, and acquired sinister managerial tones. It is through this enjoyment in learning, from and with artists, refusing to learn only that what we are told we have to learn, each time and in each different social and institutional context, that an attempt at self-reflexivity of our profession should be made, to see what the limits and possibilities of curatorial practice are, and what the social rights, and intellectual and cultural legacies are that are worth fighting for. Only then we can use our connectedness, and our mastering of the hegemonic language, to rediscover 'the quality, purpose, and meaning' of our practice. Maybe that is how, in an ironic twist, learning English will pay off.

19
In the 1970s Mladen Stilinović was a member of the Group of Six Artists, whose wish for more autonomous modes of production and distribution of artworks led them to exhibiting in public spaces in what they called 'exhibitions-actions,' while during the 1980s he ran the hugely important artist-run city-owned space Gallery of Extended Media in Zagreb. In the 1990s he started to regularly organize exhibitions in his apartment, which consciously worked on redefining the rules of conduct and power relations in the Croatian art scene.

The Incomplete Curator: aka Fighting the Delineated Field

Liam Gillick

The incomplete curator is aware of shifting curatorial scope. They do not see their work as the production of encyclopedic knowledge. They say to themselves "To pretend, I actually do the thing: I have therefore only pretended to pretend."[1] The incomplete curator is part of a curatorial mass. They know that there are an infinite number of other curators. They look in the mirror and recite the words "To say 'we' and mean 'I' is one of the most recondite insults."[2] The incomplete curator is under pressure to prove capable of an academic method. Yet they ignore the shadow of correct technique. With tears in their eyes they shout "The point is not to stay marginal, but to participate in whatever network of marginal zones is spawned from other disciplinary centers and which, together, constitute a multiple displacement of those authorities."[3] The incomplete curator is fully aware of lingering authority. It is not something to be assumed or accepted. They feed on the statement "The state of exception is not a dictatorship, but a space devoid of law."[4] Pace and discourse are messed around with—to be slowed down or sped up, or kept at the same speed, is the incomplete curator's way to remain in permanent conflict with contradictory flow. They fight hard for a resuscitation of the public domain. The incomplete curator attempts to save those that exist as memories and fights for new commons at all times. The incomplete curator sees writing in tension with everything they do: Writing in tension with the self, and writing as a contradiction to action. For the incomplete curator "Language is legislation, speech is its code. We do not see the power which is in speech because we forget that all speech is a classification, and that all classifications are oppressive."[5] The incomplete curator begins with an acknowledgment of the disappointment of art. For them this is something to be accentuated, accepted, and reframed. For the incomplete curator "The depressed person is a radical, sullen atheist."[6] Incomplete curators see voids as potential. They accept all mental spaces as ones to be used and energized. They sit in empty rooms and reflect on the fact that "In all the circumstances where an individual must learn something without any means of having it explained to him. There is no-one on earth who hasn't learned something by himself and without a master explicator."[7] The incomplete curator swallows hard and faces the institution. They even face their institutional neighbors on the other side of the street while sweeping the street free of broken glass. The incomplete curator knows that "What isn't a good idea is to pull back from our commitments in order to win a broader acceptance. In fact, despite my suggestions that a broader public opening for our work exists, it's possible that smaller, more focused audiences make more sense. It certainly depends on what you're trying to

1
Jacques Derrida

2
Theodor Adorno

3
Judith Butler

4
Giorgio Agamben

5
Roland Barthes

6
Julia Kristeva

7
Jacques Rancière

accomplish with your work."[8] The incomplete curator fights the continual reconstruction of the narcissistic institution. At the same time they keep a lid on self-loathing. For the incomplete curator "Sadism... is a massive cultural fact that appeared precisely at the end of the eighteenth century and that constitutes one of the greatest conversions of the occidental imagination... madness of desire, the insane delight of love and death in the limitless presumptions of appetite."[9] The incomplete curator is amused by discourse in relation to the object of art. For the incomplete curator agrees that "it is only a matter of terminology: on the side of utterance, the apprehension of a painting is discursive, whereas on the side of the content it happens that it ceases to be. The whole point is to define the concrete operators enabling us to go from one to the other."[10] The incomplete curator is always pushing toward cognitive collapse. They accept that it may not be possible to mediate or explain. They think of documentation and desire and death: "Cameras help to minimize collateral damage, and very often, without a camera a missile cannot fire. Certainly, without a camera a drone can't function, which means that the very ways in which we wage war are determined in part by how cameras work and whether they work at all."[11] Incomplete curators suffer alone. They construct subjects that might only exist on paper or in the brain. For the incomplete curator "Every discourse, even a poetic or oracular sentence, carries with it a system of rules for producing analogous things and thus an outline of methodology."[12] The incomplete curator believes in the group as a supportive antagonist. Bringing together disagreements as part of the construction of potential. The incomplete curator has a good memory and a sense of political purpose. "The days of Seattle involve a corporeal arrangement, a combination of bodies (with their actions and passions) composed of individual and collective singularities (multiplicity of individuals and organizations—Marxists, ecologists, union activists, Trotskyists, media activists, 'witches,' Black Bloc, etc., which practice specific corporeal relations of co-functioning); and there is an arrangement of statements, a regime of statements formed from a multitude of statement regimes (the statements of the Marxists are not the same as those of the media activists, the ecologists or the 'witches,' etc.) The collective statement arrangements are not expressed solely through language, but also through the technological expression machines (Internet, telephone, television, etc.) Both arrangements are constructed in terms of the current relationships of power and desire."[13] The incomplete curator makes a big thing of avoiding responsibility. They might only do this right at the moment when the pressure is highest to accept responsibility. For the incomplete curator

8
Martha Rosler

9
Michel Foucault

10
Felix Guattari

11
Judith Butler

12
Jacques Derrida

13
Maurizio Lazzarato

"The individual mirrors in his individuation the preordained social laws of exploitation, however mediated."[14] The incomplete curator believes in a phantom public. If it does not exist then it might be necessary to create it. It is something they think about as they recite these words: "A project of radical and plural democracy on the contrary, requires the existence of multiplicity, of plurality and of conflict, and sees in them the raison d'être of politics."[15] The incomplete curator believes in the education of artists. Something not limited to pointing out to artists all the other artists they do not know, and books that they have not read. For the incomplete curator "... the educational system is the particular apparatus that produces the child, and it does so through a singular political operation: the de-sexualization of the infantile body and the disqualification of its affects."[16] The incomplete curator smiles at the idea of faith, hope, and charity. While at the same time telling artists about all the artists they do not know about, and all the books they have not read. There is no contradiction here: "What I claim is to live to the full the contradiction of my time, which may well make sarcasm the condition of truth."[17] The incomplete curator is an agent of compromise. Reveling in an acceptance of the limits of any given structure. For the incomplete curator understands that "All forms of consensus are by necessity based on acts of exclusion."[18] The incomplete curator works hard toward the end of withering the museum as a cultural 'state.' They make use of entryist strategies at any given moment. For them a foundational truth is that "The paradigmatic body of Western control societies is no longer represented by the imprisoned body of the worker, the lunatic, the ill person, but rather by the obese (full of the worlds of the enterprise) or anorectic (rejection of this world) body, which see the bodies of humanity scourged by hunger, violence and thirst on television. The paradigmatic body of our societies is no longer the mute body molded by discipline, but rather it is the bodies and souls marked by the signs, words and images (company logos) that are inscribed in us—similar to the procedure, through which the machine in Kafka's 'Penal Colony' inscribes its commands into the skin of the condemned."[19] The incomplete curator is not without an aesthetic dimension. The incomplete curator demonstrates a desire to recognize an aesthetic dimension in locations that are not limited to the work or the location of work at any given moment. For the incomplete curator "Artistic subjectivity without content is now the pure force of negation that everywhere and at all times affirms only itself as absolute freedom that mirrors itself in pure self-consciousness."[20] They know that subculture has been subsumed by research. So as a result they resist the pressure to control spontaneous groupings. They are fully aware that "The

14
Theodor Adorno

15
Chantal Mouffe

16
Paul B. Preciado

17
Roland Barthes

18
Chantal Mouffe

19
Maurizio Lazzarato

20
Giorgio Agamben

struggle between different discourses, different definitions and meanings within ideology is therefore always, at the same time, a struggle within signification: a struggle for possession of the sign which extends to even the most mundane areas of life... safety pins... These 'humble objects' can be magically appropriated; 'stolen' by subordinate groups and made to carry 'secret' meanings..."[21]

Incomplete curators sigh at indifference and corruption. At the same time they are fully supportive of wandering off, and doing something more interesting right at the point that responsibility is highest. For the incomplete curator "Today's milestone is human madness. Politics is a part of it, particularly in its lethal outbursts. Politics is not, as it was for Hannah Arendt, the field where human freedom is unfurled. The modern world, the world of world war, the Third World, the underground world of death that acts upon us, do not have the civilized splendor of the Greek city-state. The modern political domain is massively, in totalitarian fashion, social, leveling, exhausting. Hence madness is a space of antisocial, apolitical, and paradoxically free individuation."[22] For in their heart the incomplete curator keeps artistic confrères and consoeurs. It's not so hard. For they know that "Poets are the only people to whom love is not only a crucial, but an indispensable experience, which entitles them to mistake it for a universal one."[23]

21
Dick Hebdige

22
Julia Kristeva

23
Hannah Arendt

Curation and Futurity

Simon Sheikh

Education is the point at which we decide whether we love the world enough to assume responsibility for it and by the same token save it from ruin which, except for renewal, except for the coming of the new and young, would be inevitable. And education, too, is where we decide whether we love our children enough not to expel them from our world and leave them to their own devices, nor to strike from their hands their chance of undertaking something new, something unforeseen by us, but to prepare them in advance for the task of renewing a common world.
—Hannah Arendt[1]

Admittedly, curation and futurity may seem a somewhat unwieldy title—why not simply thrown down the gauntlet and ask the question, or make the promise, of 'the future of curating'? Indeed, this would be an interesting question, and one that is often asked and discussed in curatorial discourse, both among practitioners of the profession, and within education programs for prospective curators—the education of curators always being about the future of curating, of course! But rather than speculate on structural changes within the field, or make grand claims for new methodologies and processes of curation, or, for that matter, new audiences and constituencies for our practices, I want to instead point to the temporal and historical relations that curation as an endeavor has to futurity—to the notion of future itself, which may or may not tell us about the future of the discipline or profession. Moreover, this connection to the future is what is at stake in curatorial studies, in education as such, and thus it pertains to the future curatorial what not and study what conundrum that so intrigues and confuses students and researchers alike! Finally, the intrinsic relationship between curation and education needs mentioning; that curating is always already educational, even in its most willfully obscure forms, as it is a mode of address that places viewing subjects, as well as objects, in a relation to knowledge, history, and as I shall argue, futurity.

In a historical sense, institutions of art mediate, and are as such educational platforms, and curators can therefore not be distinguished from educators in any principal sense. The museum, and by extension curatorial processes, inscribes both subjects and objects in specific relations of power and knowledge—of the nation state, of Western civilization etc.—in a transfer of knowledge and direction of desires and agencies that are educational, entertaining, narrative and/or informative—traits that are as often complementary as they are conflicting. Current educational departments and outreach activities in large institutions fulfill thus not an additional function of the

1
Hannah Arendt, *Between Past and Future—Eight Exercises in Political Thought* (1968) (New York, NY: Penguin, 1993) p. 168.

institution, but are constitutive of the institution, and, as I have argued elsewhere, curating and education provide two sets of rhetorics upon the same objects and subjects.[2] Basically, the museum and the practice of exhibition-making are always already pedagogical endeavors, but particular practices can of course strive for the disciplining of bodies, the cultivation of national subjects, or, conversely, the emancipation of minds, and the raising of consciousness. Curators are a specific form of educators, whether as tastemakers, managers of consciousness, or pedagogical mediators, for that matter. As a curator we cannot thus disregard our pedagogical roots and roles, nor simply excuse ourselves by saying that we are merely following institutional procedures, or, as is often the default defense, just mediating tendencies in contemporary art, as curating is itself constitutive of these relations.

Now, as it has become commonplace to highlight, the very word curator comes from the Latin *curare*, meaning 'to care.' The curator is thus a caretaker, traditionally, of course, of objects, artifacts, and artworks in a collection, rather than an exhibition-maker or public programmer. This implies a dual relationship to the objects. Firstly that as custodian of history, as archivist of materials, and secondly, as a handler of precious objects, of valued goods that need to be protected from wear and tear, from their material limitations and historical demise. In other words, cultural value goes hand in hand with economic value, and the curator is the gatekeeper, indeed often the keeper of the keys, or, if you will, the key itself. What is striking, however, is the curator's relationship to history, to the temporality of the collection assembled, and the future of the objects in the collection, as well as to the objects that will be added to it in the future. By entering the collection, the objects are immediately historical, and the curator is thus by definition the caretaker of the past, as an archivist and historian. Curation of objects is, in this sense, retrospective, and deals with the understanding, preservation and conservation of the past, and with the presence of this history—art history—in the future. In educational terms, this is precisely the difference between courses of art history and of contemporary curating, which amounts to nothing less than a *Methodenstreit*, a struggle between disciplines and methods, which is not without historical precedent.[3] Indeed, there are many museum curators and directors, particularly in the United States, who insist that the only way to become a curator is to become an art historian, specialized in a specific field, i.e. a specific area of art history (geographic, medium-specific, periodic etc.), rather than through curatorial courses and their methods and focuses. Which begs the question, if art history is dedicated to the past, can curatorial studies orient themselves toward the future?

2
Simon Sheikh, "Letter to Jane (Investigation of a Function)," in *Curating and the Educational Turn*, eds. Paul O'Neill & Mick Wilson (London/Amsterdam: Open Editions/de Appel, 2010) pp. 61-75.

3
I have imported the German term *Methodenstreit* in lack of an accurate English term. *Methodenstreit* within art history has to do with how the new art history, post-structuralist and feminist, mainly, challenged the tradition of the discipline, and was coined by the art theory magazine *Texte zur Kunst*. See *Texte zur Kunst*, November 1997, Vol. 7, No. 28. It is my contention that such a *Methodenstreit* is now at play between curatorial studies and art history, not just in terms of how to be qualified for handling art objects in the museum, but also in how to deal with the contemporary in art, where curation is of course always already implicated in the contemporary as praxis. Moreover, the great divide is fully visible in the new research area of exhibition histories.

Before exploring this proposal, it needs to be stressed that this struggle is not only disciplinary and academic, but also professional and political: it has to do, obviously, with recruitment and employment within the art industry, and the battleground is not only institutional spaces and private collections. But it also has to do with the terrain of contemporary art itself, where both contemporary curatorial practice, art history, and art criticism (although the latter to a lesser and lesser degree) have stakes in, and are making claims for what constitutes contemporary art, and thus in a more ontological sense what is art and what is not, as is so often debated, but by extension also the more overlooked, but in my mind more philosophically interesting and politically pertinent: What is the contemporary? If contemporary art is, in the words of Boris Groys, that which shows the contemporary, the immediately present, it follows that such an art cannot be concerned with the past and past forms, but perhaps also not yet of the future, but simply the here and now.[4] Obviously, this creates some methodological problems for art history and its theory of periodization. If contemporary art is simply the period that comes after modern art, the issue is when this shift occurs, and through which stylistic elements. And indeed, whereas contemporary art 20 years ago was defined as art after 1945, it is now periodized as art after 1960, and it probably will not be long until contemporary art is dated as starting in 1989.[5] The period of the contemporary is thus constantly tied to the present moment, to a now that can be historicized within a graspable time frame that fits with the stylistic shifts within modernist art history, which leads to two major theoretical problems: most of all to the unanswerable, but crucial question of the end(s) of contemporary art, and what can or will replace it? If it can be periodized, then there must not only be a beginning, but also an endpoint, and the apparent difficulty of pinpointing this moment may have to do with the constant updating of its start date. Which relates to the other difficulty, which has to do with the visible change in artistic styles indicated by the shift from modern art, and its specific traits and aesthetics, to something called contemporary art. This shows, of course, a central aporia in the vision of art history, namely the insistence on periodization through discernable visual styles, particularly since contemporary art is, if anything, characterized by a plurality of styles, which would indicate that the *post*-modern, as the contemporary in art history, does not indicate the end of art favored among many art historians, but perhaps rather the end of art history.

It would be premature, and perhaps also misleading, to only locate curatorial caretaking within dealing with the past and artifacts of historical value, and to relegate it to the dustbin

4
See Boris Groys's essay "Comrades of Time" for an exegesis on contemporary art, in *Going Public*, Boris Groys (Berlin: Sternberg, 2010) pp. 84-101.

5
Alex Alberro, *Periodizing Contemporary Art* (Cambridge, MA: The MIT Press, forthcoming).

of art history, as it is also highly present in the curating of contemporary art—highly present in the present, so to speak. Indeed, the idea of taking care of art and artists as the primary task, and even moral obligation of the curator, has recently had a renaissance within curatorial discourse. As a field of study, curating has a fairly short history, but as a term it has rapidly proliferated, both in terms of the thinking within the discipline itself—moving from collections to exhibitions and onto philosophy, or what is sometimes termed curatorial knowledge. It has also expanded way beyond the discipline, and is now gaining widespread currency, be it in music festivals, fashion collections, or gastronomy. And, after a decade or so of exuberance, we are now witnessing a phase of retraction, and even reaction (in the first case in terms of a back to basics approach, and in the second in terms of a rhetorical rejection of the very term curating). Such a plea for curating returning to its fundamental task of care-taking can be found in curator Anthony Huberman's affectionate, and highly influential essay of 2011 entitled, simply, "Take Care"![6] In this text, Huberman makes several proposals, partly for the importance of small-scale institutions and long-term projects, but also for not-knowing, for replacing the idea of knowledge within exhibition-making with the idea of care, and, moreover, of infatuation, fandom and love: "After all, the ideas that make us curious are not the ones that we fully understand, but the ones we care about—*I Love It* is always more compelling than *I Get It*."[7] What is notable in this love of art, is how close the techniques of the curator are aligned with the logic of the collector, and indeed the curatorial practice of the Artists' Institute, which Huberman ran at the time of writing, consisting of one-person presentations, one for each season, allowing for an intimate approach akin to one that many private collectors strive for. However, the phrase 'Take Care,' can also be read as cautionary, as a warning, in the sense of 'Beware,' itself the title of one of the key essays in the canon of the contemporary by Daniel Buren.[8] Buren's warning was to not turn conceptual art into objects of desire, and indeed against the very idea of exhibiting: "... it seems to us that to exhibit or set forth a concept is, at the very least, a fundamental misconception right from the start and one which can, if one doesn't *take care*, involve us in a succession of false arguments."[9]

Given Buren's subsequent canonization and the worldwide circulation of his practice, it is ironic to now see how his warning can be read as a criticism of the circulation that constitutes what can be termed contemporary art, or even the art world at large, with its magazines, online platform, biennales and art fairs, what Pamela M. Lee has described as "... a pervasive routinization of its norms and procedures."[10] It thus feels

6
Anthony Huberman, "Take Care," in *Circular Facts*, eds. Mai Abu ElDahab, Binna Choi, and Emily Pethick (Berlin: Sternberg Press, 2011) pp. 9-17.

7
Ibid., p. 13.

8
Daniel Buren, "Beware," in *Conceptual Art: A Critical Anthology*, eds. Alex Alberro and Blake Stimson (Cambridge, MA: The MIT Press, 1999) pp. 144-156.

9
Ibid., p. 145, my italics.

10
Pamela M. Lee, *Forgetting the Art World* (Cambridge, MA: The MIT Press, 2012) p. 2.

tempting to get off this carousel, to exit the endless circulation of objects and statements, and indeed forget the art world altogether. It is doubtful, however, whether one can stop the art world, just as we cannot stop the world, although we can destroy it, something many would argue we are already in the process of doing. However, rather than not caring anymore, we should expand our notion of care, and if our love of art does not lead to a love of the art world, which is, after all, simply an industry, albeit a romanticized, but also highly unregulated one, with all that this entails—corruption, cronyism, and precarity—then perhaps it would be more challenging to think about art and the world, and not only the art world. Can the care we take for objects and ideas be extended to the world at large, from objects to hyper-objects, and from history to futurity? A love of art, with all that this implies of taste and taste-making, value and class, aestheticism, and so on, is not useful without a love for the world. Rather, to put up a show is to show that we care, our care-taking a taking care of the world. As world-making, curating is a form of future projection, setting up horizons of the possible and the impossible, naturally, but also asking questions of temporality, history, and futurity. It is thus not just about future generations, and how to co-inhabit the world—a common world—but also to engage with the politics of time: What is contemporaneity, whose future, and for how much longer?

It is hardly surprising—given the state of the world—that the past takes up so much of our imagination, not just in art history and theory, but also in political theory and philosophy. Just think of the recent writings of Franco 'Bifo' Berardi, according to whom we are after the future, and Slavoj Žižek, who claims that we are living in end times, brought about through the terminal crisis of global capitalism, a broken political system and the worldwide ecological disaster.[11] It is not so much that the future is unforeseeable, but rather that it does not appear very promising, or that it seems to simply be vanishing before our very eyes, as the world as we knew it disappears, indeed ends altogether. This sense of foreboding is also seen in so-called ecological thinking, as in Timothy Morton's writings on *Hyperobjects*, a 2013 book with the telling subtitle *Philosophy and Ecology after the End of the World*.[12] For Morton, hyperobjects are things such as global warming or black holes, operating on a scale and temporality that is relative to humans, whether manmade or not, and what is of interest here is how they are tied to the future rather than the past:

> *Futurality is inscribed into the present, ending the metaphysics of presence, not through some neat philosophical footwork, but because the very large finitude of hyperobjects*

11
See Franco 'Bifo' Berardi, *After the Future* (Edinburgh: AK Press, 2011), and Slavoj Žižek, *Living in the End Times* (London: Verso, 2011).

12
TimothyMorton, *Hyperobjects—Philosophy and Ecology after the End of the World*, (Minneapolis, MN: University of Minnesota Press, 2013).

forces humans to coexist with a strange future, a future "without us."[13]

For Morton, this brings about the end of the world, not as the sudden explosion of the globe in some apocalyptic moment, but rather the end of *worlding* itself, making the idea of 'a world' inoperable. The notion of world, and the potential mastery and mappability this implies, is replaced with intimacy and care, a sharing of the afterworld with all things, including the non-human. This is part of an attempted move toward an object-orientated ontology, of course, something that we are ironically also witnessing within contemporary curation. It is ironic, since curating is precisely a type of worlding, and if it does include objects and their possible agencies, it always does so through selection, and thus as much through exclusion of things and ideas as the inclusion of them. No exhibition gives space to all things at all times, but as an assemblage of things—in the most expanded sense of this word—the exhibition creates a place from which to view things otherwise not in view, while obscuring others. In a word, it establishes a *worldview*. So when we are asking what to research, we should research the world, not just the end of the world, or of worlding, but how we can reconnect with the world, as a commons, for ourselves, our children, and our distant future descendants.

If we are, as Morton suggests, "the curators of a gigantic museum of non-art, [...] a spontaneous museum of hyperobjects," then our task must be the positing of another possible world and providing a manual for spaceship Earth, at a time when the world seems increasingly unmanageable.[14] And rather than reveling in the so-called ends of the world, whether as something to be mourned in the forms of retro-utopia or future nostalgia, or whether something to be celebrated that we must accelerate toward at highest possible velocity, I suggest that we rather look to Zygmunt Bauman, who, in drawing upon Gramsci's famous concept, has suggested that we are living in times of an interregnum.[15] The thesis being that we are witnessing the disappearance of an old world order, but in such a way that the new has not yet emerged, or is not capable of emerging due to the death throes of the existing order. The interregnum is thus not only a period of transition, but also a holding position, a time of uncertainty and unpredictability, but not fixed on outcomes of doom and destruction. Bauman goes on to briefly outline three related areas that will decide the outcome of the interregnum, and it seems to me that it is precisely such issues we should be studying at this historical moment. He lists: *Institutional disparity*, which has to do with the inability of current political institutions to act on a global scale; *future of the*

13
Ibid., p. 94.

14
Ibid., p. 121.

15
Zygmunt Bauman, "Times of Interregnum," *Ethics & Global Politics*, Vol. 5, No. 1, 2012, pp. 49-56.

migrants, again dealing with the inevitable movements of peoples through globalization; and, finally, *endurability of the planet*, which concerns both the growing gap between rich and poor, and the crises of climate change on the planet. Each of these issues can naturally be threaded through the institutions and circulations of the contemporary art world, and are certainly at the heart of the contradictory tensions within curatorial education programs, their global reach, and alignments within an internationally integrated art system of exhibitions, institutions, markets and, arguably, public spheres. In a sense these issues are not only areas of research of study, although they will undoubtedly become increasingly so, also within willfully depoliticized aesthetics, but they are also what influences and conditions *how* we research and study, and deal with antagonisms within the academy, contradictions and supposed equality in the class room, and the necessary cultural translation that is ongoing between students from all over the globe, as well as between students and teachers in terms of contexts and relations of power and knowledge. As studying is indeed becoming, perhaps it would be useful to think of the educational arena as an interregnum. In this sense, the future of education is intimately connected to the future of the world.

If curating is thus a process of world-making—of fashioning the world and the profession of curating anew—curatorial education must be an endeavor of providing emerging curators with the tools for them to not only navigate the world, but to care for it, and to think of this care-taking on a planetary level. This is what is at play, naturally, in the famous quote from Hannah Arendt used as an epigraph for this essay. Arendt actually wrote about what she saw as a crisis of education in the 1950s, although her essay had a renewed resonance when it was part of the book *Between Past and Future* in 1968. If the notion of being between past and future was Arendt's attempt at defining the contemporary, it is of course also a way of positing the contemporary as a kind of interregnum, where the old is dying, but the new not yet born. But, as is well known, 1968 is a crucial year in the history of modern education, as it was the time when students took it upon themselves to revolutionize the educational systems they found themselves in, a "*cri de coeur* against the evils of the world-system," as Arrighi, Hopkins and Wallerstein phrased it in their summation of "Anti-Systemic Movements."[16] Needless to say, there has been a major reversal of the outcomes, changes, and meanings of these events, not least with the ongoing neoliberal reforms of education across the board. Speaking from the context of the UK, we are faced with the contradiction of increased privatization in economic terms, but increased regulation and governmentality

16
Giovanni Arrighi, Terence K. Hopkins, and Immanuel Wallerstein, *Anti-Systemic Movements* (London: Verso, 1989, 2011) p. 101.

in terms of what we deliver, leaving us with the worst of both worlds. Obviously, the marketization of everything is being brought to bear with an iron fist upon the educational complex. Simultaneously, the education of artists and curators has always been directed by the professional field, rather than the abstract values of academic freedom, or the rigor of scientific research. In this sense, the contradictions currently at stake in the business models of universities are inherent to our education programs, which also means that they are the places where these contradictions can be studied, as they are indeed embodied. We are in the thick of it, and the only way out seems to be in.

Hannah Arendt's claim was that education is the place where we measure our care for the world: but in terms of its futurity, how we will entrust to our children, so that they can care for it. Moreover, how much we care for our children has to do with two things: not only whether we will entrust them with the world, to succeed us, but also whether we, through education, will allow them to renew the world, and thus to supersede us as well. In other words, again, education is not about tradition, but about renewal. Finally, the last line of the quote, which is indeed the last line of the essay from which it is drawn, refers to the renewal of a common world, so not that of individuals, but of the commons, something which is striking today, over 50 years since Arendt read those lines. Here we can move from Arendt's basic humanism into something else, namely the communing of the world, and thus a more political reading, that leads in the direction of both anti-capitalist struggle and environmental issues on a planetary scale, and, if you will, allow for a thinking about the rights of humans as well as non-humans in this common world—in other words, the most pertinent issues and contested debates of our time. Education is thus inherently about the future, about the future of disciplines and practices, and future generations of practitioners—it is thus a form of care, as is curation, but a care-taking for the world, for not only its possible futures in any utopian sense, but for its very survival as a life world. And indeed this is why we use the word program not only in educational facilities, but also in political projects, as in 'having a program.' While not referring to the notion of interregnum, but using many interludes(!), in *Living in End Times*, Slavoj Žižek neatly sums up how we must now program:

> *Our situation is thus the opposite of the classical twentieth-century predicament in which the Left knew what it had to do (establish the dictatorship of the proletariat etc.), but simply had to wait patiently for the opportunity to offer itself. Today, we know not what we have to do, but we have to act now, because the consequences of inaction could be catastrophic.*[17]

17
Žižek, p. 480.

What to Practice?

Nancy Adajania
Tobias Ostrander
Koyo Kouoh
Zasha Cerizza Colah
Sumesh Sharma
Hans Ulrich Obrist
Vivian Ziherl
Sarah Rifky

An Autodidact's Practice: Investigating the Reserves of the Curatorial Moment

Nancy Adajania

As a form of inquiry, exhibition history embraces far more than the visible and accomplished fact of an exhibition; indeed, it proposes an expanded view of the ongoing, and often invisible processes that inform exhibition-making. My focus here will be on what I call the plenary intersection ('plenary,' derived from the Latin *plenum*, indicating that which is 'full' and 'abundant'). The plenary intersection is the occasion when multiple agendas—including the curatorial, the artistic, the pedagogic, the diplomatic, and the theoretical—converge, and in that process generate conversations, collaborations, exhibition projects, and other experimental outcomes that exceed the prevailing institutional and disciplinal frameworks. These outcomes have often eluded definition and documentation since no discipline has claimed them.

Rich in possibility and hazardous in execution, these experimental outcomes of plenary intersections have often transformed the nature of exhibition practice—while also recalibrating the relationship between the field of art and other social, cultural, and political fields. And yet, being restricted to the moment of performance by their temporality, and the subsequent unreliable operations of memory, these outcomes vanish. Some of them trigger a transformation, legible as trace and persistence, both at the individual and the institutional level. But for the most part, they live on only as orphan knowledge in the folk memory of practitioners, unnamed and unframed, and disregarded in formal historical accounts. I argue that these in fact constitute a reserve that must be examined, as a surplus that can enrich our resources as we negotiate the demands of the present. I would like to gloss these reserves by way of reference to Walter Benjamin's conception of history as that which flashes up, talismanic, at a moment of danger, and to Bachelard's emphasis on the epistemological rupture, which liberates us from the conceptual obstacles that disciplines produce internally as default axioms or limit conditions. These reserves are, in my view, vital to the project of retrieving lost exhibition histories—for here we are not simply the archaeologists of exhibitions buried under layers of amnesia, but also witnesses to the thriving contexts, scenes, sites, and engagements from which such exhibitions have emerged, and to which they bear witness.

The retrieval of these reserves is not an attempt to add new items to an institutional canon or curriculum. Rather, it advances a new itinerary of inquiry, and points us in the direction of a transient pedagogy: one that enables us to critique received histories, and destabilize canons formed and sustained on foundations of repression or amnesia. By rejecting the universalizing assumptions of a global curatorial model, a transient pedagogy insists on critically engaging with the idiosyncratic, unpredictable predicaments of the regional and their entanglements with global narratives. By embracing a transient pedagogy we embrace the condition of being auto-didacts—not as bearers of a canonical form of knowledge and modes of knowledge production, but as committed to the constant renewal of the epistemic moment.

Both by temperament and method, I find myself an auto-didact. In my research, too, I am drawn to the figure of the autodidact as researcher, archivist, activist, improviser of situations and solutions, and to historical contexts where the autodidactic impulse could articulate itself, often producing vital, yet unacknowledged histories of practice. Many of these histories of practice have crystallized in the form of exhibitions that have fallen under the radar of art-historical attention, specifically because they took the form of commercial expos, international cultural festivals, and research assemblies. Therefore my recent research has been directed toward the study of such exhibitions, which were charted across the domains of technology, exhibition-making, craft, science, and design—and that I regard as the seedbeds of a parallel and alternative history of postcolonial Indian art. In this alternative account, the dominant figure is not the artist who works solely within the framework of the gallery system, but rather the inventor of visual and expressive experiences who works across a broad typology of production systems and exhibition contexts. In my case studies, I address the affinities between the practices of the trans-media artists, exhibition designers, and pedagogues Dashrath Patel and Charles and Ray Eames.

It is my conviction that Indian art history has stagnated within the boundaries set by the established institutions, and curricular emphases of conventional academia and of the art market. I would argue that the project of writing a national art history is a fundamentally flawed, reductive, and ultimately unproductive project. Because it assumes that most of the formative factors essential to the emergence of a national art field are internal to a nation-state, and that encounters with the outside world are at best articulated through apprenticeship, the external stimulus of influence, or assimilation. In the recent past, while researching the transcultural initiatives of the Cold War era, I have excavated and analyzed the lost history of Triennale India, whose inaugural edition took place in 1968. I have argued that Triennale India could retrospectively be seen to have manifested *a confident globalism from the South* and even *a globalism before globalization.* The Triennale India was a powerful gesture of building cultural infrastructure, true to its origin in the Nehruvian matrix of thought, with its emphasis on a global position of non-alignment. Having embraced non-alignment as its genealogical matrix, the Triennale thus aspired to bypass the cartography of superpower-led geopolitics, and remap the atlas of global art, forging affinities between Asia and Latin America, Africa, and Eastern Europe, and thus develop a new cosmopolitanism.[1]

The exhibition history of Triennale India had remained buried under official apathy and the indifference of the art world for four decades. It was assumed to be yet another state-sponsored art initiative that had become defunct. By activating and contextualizing this orphan knowledge, I was able to tap into the reserves of this lost curatorial moment, and reconstruct and acknowledge the occluded history of Nehruvian internationalism, and the dream of a collegial and equitable cultural multilateralism. To retrieve a lost exhibition history or art history constitutes, for me, the active production of a regional history—and not a passive contribution to the teleological, Hegelian unfolding of such a regional history. Left to themselves, the rudiments of the many potential regional histories that we may summon into being would remain simply that: stray fragments, isolated episodes, like tablets written in a script yet to be deciphered.

In the same spirit, when I was discontented with the simplistic contextualization of Indian new-media practices under the clichéd rubrics of globalization, and the advent of new technologies in the 1990s, I excavated a deeper pre-history for new media practice in India—and changed the terms of the discourse, such as it was.[2] My account displaced the model of globalization that relies on external stimulus, and argued for a robust parallel and alternative history of Indian art, which remains largely untheorized and untold in both academia and the art market. This alternative history is built around seminal experiences of transcultural collaboration, international sites and circumstances, and the experimental creation of emergent design sensibilities and technologies in 'third spaces' (Homi Bhabha's term), which were neither 'national' nor 'foreign,' but occupied an intermediate zone.[3]

My current research on Dashrath Patel, who I regard as one of the pioneers and precursors of new-media practice in India, takes forward my ongoing work on the 'unacknowledged prehistory' of this form. As I will show, Patel and the Eameses were, in their different ways, responsible for the founding of the National Institute of Design; they had also worked together on the Nehru exhibition that was shown in New York in 1965. I focus on the strong connections between Patel's practice and that of Charles and Ray Eames, and argue that, within the framework of the Cold War and its cultural politics, Patel, like the Eameses,

1
See Nancy Adajania, "Globalism Before Globalisation: The Ambivalent Fate of Triennale India," in *Western Artists and India: Creative Inspirations in Art and Design*, ed. Shanay Jhaveri (London: Thames and Hudson, 2013), also available online via https://www.academia.edu (accessed September 30, 2015).

2
As part of my research, I have retrieved and reframed the contributions of the Vision Exchange Workshop, initiated in 1969 by artist Akbar Padamsee, and supported by the Jawaharlal Nehru Fellowship program. Vision Exchange was an early laboratory for interdisciplinary research; its outcomes took many forms, including the production of photographic series, prints and artists' films. It was here that Padamsee, as well as artists like Nalini Malani and Gieve Patel, experimented with filmmaking for the first time. Other explorations that I have retrieved from historical amnesia, or re-read through a different lens, are Krishen Khanna's improvisation with wide-angle-lens projectors to create palimpsestual photographs, as well as M.F. Husain and Tyeb Mehta's films of the late 1960s and early 1970s, sponsored by the Films Division. See Nancy Adajania, "New Media Overtures Before New Media Practice in India," in *Art and Visual Culture in India 1857-2007*, ed. Gayatri Sinha (Bombay: Marg, 2009).

3
Homi K. Bhabha, *The Location of Culture* (London and New York, NY: Routledge, 1994), pp. 36-39.

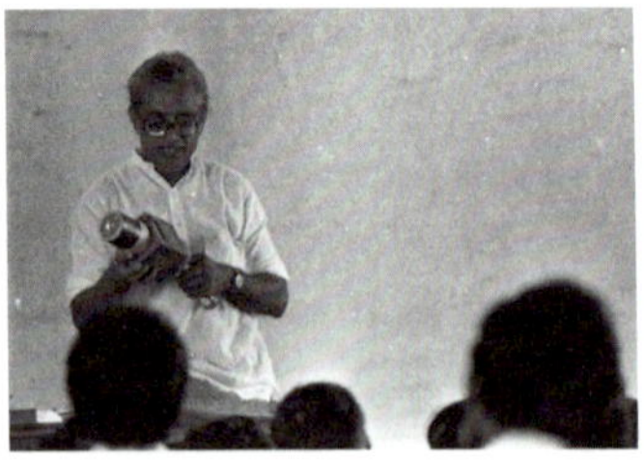

See p. 251
Dashrath Patel demonstrating a torch-operated projector made from a cardboard box and magnifying glasses for activists working in villages without electricity

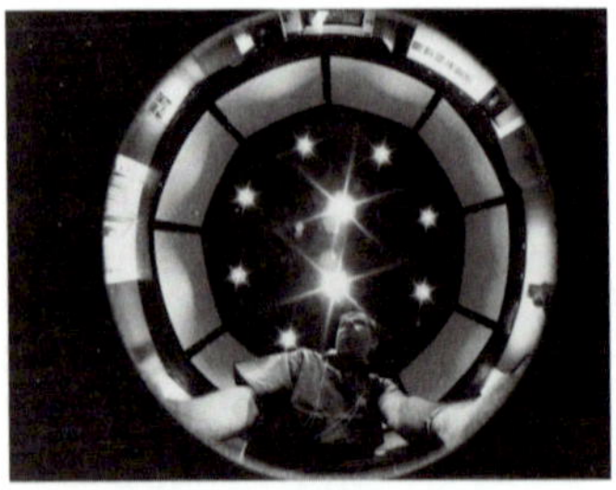

See p. 251
Dashrath Patel's self-portrait at the India pavilion, Montreal Art Fair 1967. He is surrounded by a nine-screen, 360° projection of *A Journey in India*

was engaged in the quest for a new public for the artistic transformation of everyday experience. If the Eameses collaborated with the State Department and the military-industrial complex on some of their projects, Patel too worked with the Nehruvian Indian State. In both situations we find a driving concern with synthesizing the seemingly disparate energies of technology, education, entertainment, and art into unprecedented, new experiences of being public.

Our conventional ideas of art as made and defined within the institutions of the art world has blinded us to sources and sites of art practice that lie outside them. This explains why Dashrath Patel has not been accorded the distinguished place he deserves in the history of independent India's art; as a conceptually provocative and technically ingenious pioneer who anticipated the new-media developments of the 1990s by several decades.

In this context, Sadanand Menon's account of Patel's intervention at the Montreal Art fair is instructive:

> *... [I]n 1967, Dashrath ... creat[ed] a 9-screen 360° projection of "A Journey in India" for the India pavilion at the Montreal Fair, with no access to high-tech equipment. Faced with the task of having to create a "circarama" effect, he devised a plywood housing for nine cameras which he would wear around his neck. Linked to a single remote shutter-release apparatus, the cameras facing different directions would go off simultaneously to create the effect of "shooting in the round."*[4]

Patel's heroic struggle to present a multi-screen projection in the late 1960s may surprise those who believe that the history of multimedia installations in India begins in the 1990s. However, my unearthing of this pioneering moment from the exhibition history of world art fairs to produce a prehistory for new media practices in India is not intended as a simple argument for chronological primacy. Rather, it points to the conceptual deficits of art-world reception that prevented Patel's multimedia experiments from being embraced as a model of alternative practice. It also demonstrates the pernicious effect of Chinese walls separating different sectors of the Indian cultural domain. In the fields of design and architecture, the trade-fair pavilion was seen as the locus of innovation that fed directly into questions of a designer or architect's ongoing practice. By contrast, in the field of art the struggle to secure the high and inviolable ground of studio practice was so strong that any other (and seemingly flagrantly 'commercial') demand made on the artistic imagination was seen to be diluting or contaminating it. This Brahminical aversion promoted the cult of the single author and

4
Sadanand Menon, *In the Realm of the Visual: Five Decades (1948-1998) of Painting, Ceramics, Photography, Design by Dashrath Patel*, exhibition catalog (New Delhi, National Gallery of Modern Art [NGMA], September 18—October 18, 1998).

aesthetic autonomy, a distaste for collaboration, segregation between the 'pure' Fine Arts and the 'commercial' Applied Arts, and the primacy of the academy-trained artist over the subaltern art practitioners denigrated as 'folk' and 'tribal' artists. In short, for the Indian art world of the late 1960s, the 1967 Montreal World Fair occupied the questionable realm of trade fairs and expos. Thus Patel's multimedia installations and exhibition design for national and international exhibitions were seen as a commercial, organizational activity rather than as part of an expanded art practice. Today, with the Chinese walls having partially come down, Patel ought to be seen as a pioneer of new-media art and an artist-curator of exhibitions and happenings on a mammoth scale. As we have observed, however, the lack of a nomenclature that is responsive to the actuality of practice can leave practitioners marooned outside history, hence the urgency on my part to research and resurrect this narrative.

As founder-secretary of the National Institute of Design (NID), Patel laid the foundation for professional design practice in India, nurturing the institution for two decades (1961-1980). An influential pedagogue for generations of design students, Patel initiated and developed courses in visual communications, exhibition design, and ceramics. While at NID, and even later, he was the chief designer of many important state-commissioned exhibitions at home and overseas. A Nehruvian initiative, NID was international in its outlook from the very beginning, seeking collaborators in India and elsewhere. Arguably one of the earliest and most significant of these collaborations was with the legendary American designers and educational filmmakers Charles and Ray Eames. Indeed, NID was instituted on the basis of *The India Report*, prepared by the Eameses in 1958, and commissioned by the Indian government to assess the feasibility of a design institute that would aid small-scale industries.[5]

I have deliberately chosen to read the careers and choices of the Eameses and Patel alongside each other to show that, despite stark differences of political and cultural contexts, there are significant points of affinity. Both of them had to negotiate the tension between artistic freedom and political complicity. Earlier I mentioned how Patel had engaged in an Ixion-esque struggle with multimedia technology at the Montreal World Fair. But the self-portrait he produced there showed no signs of the struggle. Shot from a low angle, Patel looked regal and statuesque, ready to broadcast from outer space, illuminated by a starburst of lights. A 360° multimedia projection surrounded him, waiting to tell the story of a young nation. When we look at the images that were projected on these screens, we descend from intergalactic orbit into the everyday life of India:

5
See Charles and Ray Eames, *The India Report* (1958) (Ahmedabad: National Institute of Design, 1997).

not the Eamesian cloverleaf highways of the *Glimpses of the USA* exhibit, but auto-orientalized street and market scenes, dense with people belonging to different classes, castes, ethnicities, and regions. This density is attended by a sense of flux: people constantly in motion, the country represented as a work in progress.

How do we reconcile Patel's project of self-presentation, informed by a measure of artistic freedom, with India's larger project of representing itself to the world, aimed at propagating a monolithic image of the country? Did Patel compromise his imagination by acting as a cultural spokesperson for the nation? Like the Eameses, Patel was a creative opportunist; he made full use of the opportunities to travel, experiment with the latest technologies, and profit from transcultural encounters. The 1967 self-portrait shows anything but a compromised figure. He strikes the confident pose of an artist-inventor contributing to the nation-building epic. Patel was not averse to creating monumental exhibits, even when the subject demanded something more modest, as is evident from his involvement with the Gandhi centenary exhibition, *The World Is My Family* (New Delhi, 1969). Inspired by Otto Frei's tensile structures, Patel designed an airy, minimalist pavilion to cover 16,000 square feet of exhibition space. Since its plastic-coated khadi roof weighed several tons, he devised an ingenious system that would permit ease of construction and dismantling; later, he would grandiloquently tell the journalist Sunil Mehra: "The principle employed to bring it down was [the] same [one] they used in transporting blocks of stone for pyramids."[6] But then again, Patel's penchant for grand projects did not prevent him from introducing simple 'listening posts' into the exhibition, for viewers to encounter Gandhi's speeches intimately (sound art *avant la lettre*). Patel and the Eameses mediated between the registers of entertainment and education. At the spectacular IBM pavilion at the New York World's Fair (1964/1965), for instance, an ovoid theatre (the Information Machine) was equipped with multiple screens, live performances, and a seated audience that was raised 50 feet high by way of a hydraulic lift.[7] Yet below the theatre was the modest exhibition, *Mathematica: A World of Numbers… and Beyond*, in which pedagogy was articulated through play: abstract mathematical conundrums were explained through three-dimensional models and graphics without diminishing the poetics of scientific discovery.

It is impossible to separate the work of the Eameses and Patel from the official policies of their respective nation-states: the Eameses were part of the military and scientific ascendancy of the postwar US, just as Patel was part of the technocratic

6
See Sunil Mehra, "Colours of a Genius," *Outlook*, September 28, 1998.

7
Charles Eames, along with Eero Saarinen, designed the memorable IBM pavilion at the New York World's Fair, which was seen by millions of people. The fair's main thematic was a universal call for 'Peace Through Understanding,' blithely ignoring, of course, the superpower's escalating presence in Vietnam.

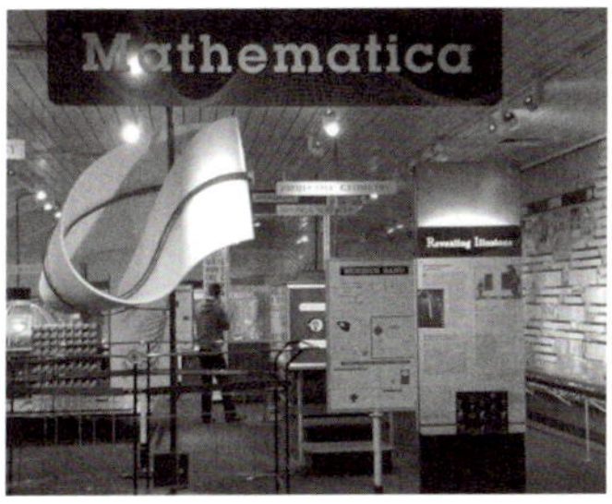

See p. 252
The Eameses' *Mathematica* exhibition, housed in the New York Hall of Science

narrative of the Nehruvian and post-Nehruvian Indian state. However, the Eameses were no mere techno-maniacs, and remained keenly aware that advances in science could produce both beneficial and sinister effects; the knowledge that gave birth to cybernetics also threw up the atom bomb. The credits at the end of the Eameses' very popular 1953 instructional film *A Communications Primer*, for instance, which weaves together the fields of mathematics, visual arts, trade, warfare, and early computing, signal their familiarity with the military and scientific ascendancy that played a pivotal role in World War II and continued into the Cold War. Sharing space with Claude Shannon (the film is based on his mathematical model of communication) are the names of John von Neumann, Robert Oppenheimer, and Norbert Wiener. Neumann was a member of the Manhattan Project led by the US, the UK, and Canada, which produced the atom bomb that annihilated Hiroshima and Nagasaki. Unlike Oppenheimer, Neumann remained unrepentant to the end of his life, refusing to acknowledge the horrors of technological warfare. In retrospect, we can see how the shadowy development of wartime technology existed in parallel with everyday peacetime applications.

While Patel did not have the luxury of using the latest technology and infrastructure—available to the Eameses from America's Cold War military-industrial complex—like them he produced elaborate multimedia exhibits, his creative opportunism sometimes overriding moral considerations. Even as he participated in the national and world expos during the 1960s, the Nehruvian nation-state became besieged by regional discontent, and the challenge of radical leftist politics; these specters would not find representation in the diplomatic circulations of the expo universe. Eventually, however, Patel too would confront the dilemmas of his position.

In the early 1980s, Patel left NID. He felt the institution had failed to live up to its early promise. Meanwhile, Indian industrialists had not supported innovative indigenous designs, and merely copied Western designs disconnected from Indian reality. With a new surge of energy, Patel moved from the school of design to the school of dissent; instead of training design experts who would intervene in the public sphere on behalf of the disadvantaged, he put the tools of communication directly in the hands of activists at the Madras-based 'Skills' workshop.[8] Among other contributions, he evolved a quick, inexpensive screen-printing process that activists could use to produce posters and pamphlets on urgent issues like Dalit repression, human rights violations, and women's rights. Like the Eameses, he loved the creative problem-solving approach. When Sundarlal Bahugana, a key leader of the grassroots environmentalist

8
In this later phase, Patel made a transition from Nehruvian technocratic modernity to a Gandhian understanding of Gram Swaraj, rural independence. Gandhi's emphasis on self-sufficiency became the basis of his design praxis. At the invitation of the Gandhian activist Vikasbhai, Patel trained artisans at the Rural Design School in Sewapuri, near Varanasi, making them responsible for their own production units. Discovering that Dalit women, who cured leather in lime pits, suffered from dermatological problems, he designed large rolling drums that could be operated collectively, saving the women from direct contact with the lime.

movement Chipko, asked him to design a slide projector that could work in villages lacking electricity, he devised a simple torch-operated projector using a cardboard box and magnifying glasses.

Ironically, Patel's patient handcrafting of the tools of dissent took place around the same time as his participation in the inaugural events of the Festivals of India during the mid-1980s. These extravaganzas exported India's 'traditional' forms of theater, art, dance, and music to London, Moscow, Paris, and other global capitals (it is another matter that these forms did not belong to a continuous 5,000-year tradition, but in the Hobsbawmian sense were 'invented traditions'). They involved the labor of thousands of artisans and hundreds of performing artists. In retrospect, selling India as a folk paradise during the 1980s seems to have been especially ill-timed, when Prime Minister Rajiv Gandhi had already ushered in the era of information technology, proposed as a panacea for India's underdeveloped economy.

To Patel's credit, though, his Festival of India events in Moscow and Paris were born of a desire to democratize public spaces, to stage happenings through a participatory choreography, where the distinction between the audience and the performers could potentially be 'blurred.' Even in this predicament, Patel shared an affinity with the Eameses. They could be seen as being committed to the production of a *Gesamtkunstwerk*, a total artwork, in a manifestly democratic public space like an expo.[9] Similarly, Patel was preoccupied with the transportation, even the *translation*, of festive forms like the Indian *mela* and the *utsav* (the former being a more secular celebration than the latter) into a European context.

At the Moscow edition of the Festival of India in 1987, Patel "worked out an entire procession of flotillas on the Moskva River for the eight-kilometer stretch from the Kremlin to Lenin Stadium. Literally a million people lined up on either bank of the river."[10] At the Lenin Stadium, also, a film portraying the movement of crowds at an Indian *utsav* was presented on a gigantic nine-screen projection in the round. Patel planned the procession of flotillas to subvert the "rigidity" of the Soviet system and "get the whole of Moscow to participate."[11]

Patel's idea of the *utsav* went beyond the conventional democratic exchange at an expo. As a gigantic form of sociality, the freely accessible procession allowed for a breaking down of hierarchies that would baffle a still avowedly communist system, stifled by the stratification that had set in over seven decades of rule by an oligarchy that governed in the name of the people. Mikhail Gorbachev, the reformist General Secretary of the Communist Party of the Soviet Union, had announced his

9
See Martin Filler, "Charles and Ray Eames," in *Makers of Modern Architecture* (New York, NY: New York Review of Books, 2007), p. 116.

10
Dashrath Patel in conversation with B.N. Goswamy, "Intensifying the Experience of Light," in Menon, p. 36.

11
Ibid.

sweeping program of economic and political restructuring, *perestroika*, in 1986, but he would implement his revolutionary policy of democratic openness and freedom of expression, *glasnost*, only in 1988. The Festival of India took place in the interval between these seismic events, in a society that was still Soviet in its political certitudes and cultural reflexes.

Coda

My account of the prehistory of new-media art in India—entangled as it is with the history of exhibition design and the world expos, nationalist politics and Cold War transcultural encounters, and grassroots activism—is intended to elude simple default binaries, including those of art versus commerce, art versus activism, and old versus new media.[12]

We now recognize as erroneous the long dominant diffusionist worldview that treated all non-Western modernities as derivative of a paramount and originary Western modernity. But we must regard the opposite contemporary tendency, to frame regional histories in dogmatic and defensive terms—as though the world's regions were island universes developing along their own evolutionary trajectories, in which narrative the encounter with a reified West is cast variously as interruption, amnesiac episode or retarding accident—with equal suspicion. Such a narrative can only lead to a dangerous neo-nationalism. As an alternative position, I would support a third way of bearing witness to the relationship between the self and the other: a method premised on critical trans-regionality, which allows us to disclose histories of friendship, dialogue, and collaboration.

I would like to close this essay with a moment of floating adjacency between the visions of Dashrath Patel and the Eameses, which occurs in *901: After 45 Years of Working*, a film by Eames Demetrios—Charles and Ray's grandson—that documents the shutting down of the couple's office at Washington Boulevard in California after Ray's death in 1988. You could miss a particular sequence if you are not looking carefully. Offering an intimate panorama of the bric-a-brac of work and play, the camera sweeps past what looks like a wall clad with the *Pabuji no pad*, an Indian narrative scroll. Below it, we catch a glimpse of the *Mathematica* poster. Both artifacts are flanked by the Indian national tricolor. An Indian picture narration scroll next to an American pedagogic timeline—how do we read this proximity? Both objects exemplify cellular, nested narratives that form a complex whole: one a predecessor of cinema, the other a precursor of hyperlinked cyber-narratives.

What role, one might ask, does friendship play in the construction of a regional history of Indian new media

12
This paper incorporates material from an earlier essay. See Nancy Adajania, "Dashrath Patel's Non-Aligned Alignments," *Seminar* No. 659, ed. Ananya Vajpeyi (July 2014).

practices?[13] It could allow for a rip in the Cold War history of binaristic self-versus-other worldview. Despite the insurmountable political and cultural power play, friendship makes space for a possible self-presentation in entanglement with the other's predicament, as against opposing self-representations that are often already marked by neocolonial aggression, postcolonial defensiveness, performances of nationality, or geopolitical exigencies. In other words, friendship—with its nuances of mutual curiosity and collaboration—could open up the unmarked space of non-aligned alignments.

13
My privileging of the notion of friendship can be seen as a tribute to the cultural theorist Rustom Bharucha's account of 'affective affinities' between the worldviews of two friends—the Indian poet and thinker Rabindranath Tagore, and the Japanese cultural historian and curator Okakura Tenshin—over and across their ideological differences and shifting cultural emphases. See Rustom Bharucha, *Another Asia: Rabindranath Tagore and Okakura Tenshin* (New Delhi: Oxford University Press, 2006).

Strategic Regionalism

Tobias Ostrander

For the past several years I have used the phrase 'Strategic Regionalism' to describe my practice as a curator working in Miami. Looking back, I recognize that my development of this approach began as an interpretation, or creative misreading, of a round-table discussion in the October 2011 edition of *Artforum*. The discussion involved several artists and art historians addressing recent developments in Californian art history and its manifestations in *Pacific Standard Time*, where multiple institutions in Southern California presented exhibitions focused on art produced in this region between 1940 and 1980. In the printed discussion in *Artforum*, Richard Meyer stated, "Could the same excavation of art-historical and contemporary riches have implications in rethinking the history of post-war art elsewhere? Might a model of creative and scholarly site-specificity—rather than regionalism—be applied to post-1945 art?"[1] Thomas Crow then went on to actually propose an assessment of the art in New York during this period from a regional perspective. This regional specificity was attractive to me in relation to the program that I was in the process of initiating at the Pérez Art Museum Miami.

The two terms 'strategic' and 'regionalism' have separate resonances that, when placed together, generate questions through hinting at implied contradictions and banalities that ask for clarification. Perhaps the attraction to these terms has to do with the way they evoke the notion of 'strategic essentialism,' as proposed by the postcolonial cultural critic Gayatri Spivak on the one hand, and, on the other, the architecture theory outlined in Kenneth Frampton's famous text "Toward a Critical Regionalism."[2] While these theorists were not explicitly references in my initial thinking about these terms, I believe aspects of their ideas have intersections with my interests in using them together; specifically Spivak's writing on how essentialist notions of identity, traditionally seen as limiting, can be manipulated and re-employed toward specific political and cultural aims; and Frampton's emphasis on the defining characteristics of a particular 'place' and the creative uses of locality.

Strategic Regionalism helps convey a tendency I have seen with artists and curators who are looking beyond the 'global' or the 'local,' and choosing to work with contexts closer to 'home' or their sites of production. Ten to fifteen years ago, there was a general push to travel and expose one's practice to multiple, diverse, and often distant cultural contexts. I feel that in more recent years that has been replaced by a strong desire for the 'local,' with many cultural producers reacting to the homogenizing tendencies of globalization by engaging with the specificities of place. What I am trying to describe currently is a tendency I see in which artists and curators are developing

1
The title of the transcript of the round-table is "L.A. Stories." Participants in the discussion were art historians Thomas Crow and Andrew Perchuk, curators Maurice Tuchman and Ali Subotnik, and gallerist Helene Winer, as well as artists John Baldessari, Harry Gamboa Jr. and Liz Larner. Critic and scholar Richard Meyer, and *Artforum* editor Michelle Kuo moderated.

2
Kenneth Framption," Toward a Critical Regionalism: Six Points for an Architecture of Resistance," in *The Anti-Aesthetic: Essays on Postmodern Culture*, ed. Hal Foster (Port Townsend, WA: Bay Press, 1983).

projects within cultural contexts that share similar cultural, linguistic, or political affinities, in other words a 'regional' perspective that is not limited to a geographical location, but often does imply spatial proximity. I read these interests and choices as strategies that perhaps reflect a certain fatigue with cultural translation, with having to continually describe the specific cultural-political landscapes that one works in in starkly foreign contexts; descriptions or contextualizations that are not necessary within contexts closer to home. I see this mapping as slightly different from developing networks, which are often much more diverse geographically; I see this tendency as tied, but not limited, to cultural geography.

I am thinking specifically about conversations I have had with several Mexican artists and curators, who are drawn to working in Colombia, for example. Not only because Colombia has a growing and dynamic cultural scene, but because discussions of everyday violence, political corruption, social and economic inequalities begin at a certain level of common understanding, about similar colonial histories and economic structures, that facilitate more nuanced and specific conversations about how artistic models might address these issues. In general, I see much more interest among artists and curators from Latin America in working in other cities within this region than I did ten years ago, when everyone was trying to produce projects in Berlin, New York, or London.

In conversations with a colleague at a museum in Japan, she expressed her commitment to working regionally. She described how in the past she had pursued exhibitions of well-known artists working in London, the United States or Germany, but was now focused on generating cultural dialogues between Japan, China, South Korea, and Indonesia. She spoke of her investigation of common themes that might create points for discussion across Asia, such as relationships to Buddhist thought, and its expressions within contemporary artistic practices, as a way to speak across linguistic borders toward shared cultural histories.

The notion of Strategic Regionalism has also helped me address my own desire to develop a program that is visibly site-specific and transnational. After working in Mexico City for eleven years and returning to the US to work in Miami, I have been extremely uncomfortable with the way in which US museums often look to 'curate the world,' feeling free to investigate work from China one year, then Africa in the next, in an expansionist and imperial manner, producing projects that often lack a clear relationship to the specific contexts of each institution.

For the past two years I have been pursuing an exhibition program at the Pérez Art Museum Miami that looks to define

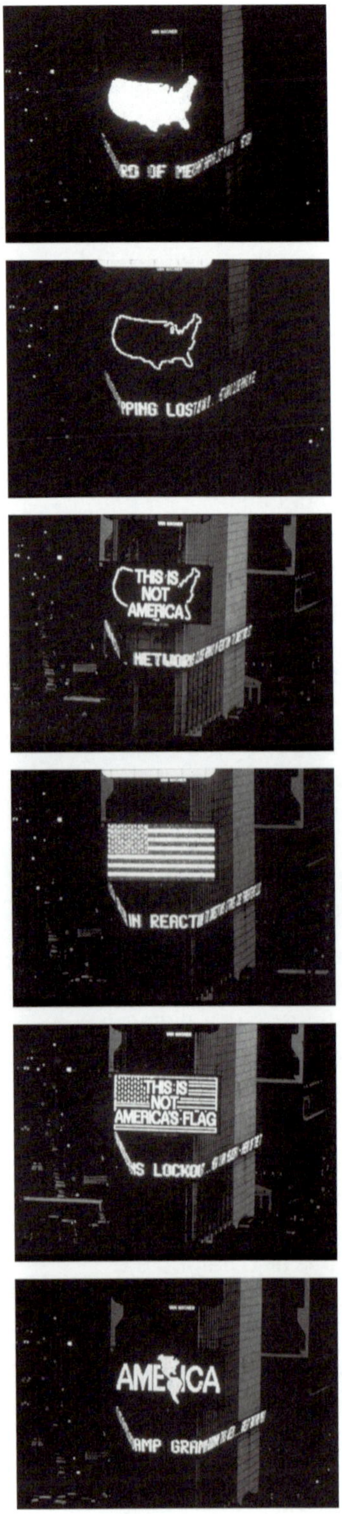

See p. 253
Alfredo Jaar, *A Logo for America*, 1986
Public intervention at Times Square, New York

Miami as a cultural hub situated within a network of institutions, artists, and thinkers working nearby. Miami is a city that has strong ties to the Caribbean, and Central and South America, while it is also directly linked to the Southern United States. I have been developing a program that identifies its sites of research as the Caribbean basin, meaning the Caribbean islands, Central America, the northern coast of South America, as well as Texas, Mississippi and Louisiana. Through a selective identification with this 'region' in which the Pérez Art Museum Miami places itself, I have tried to create a curatorial project that is responsive to our locality and its publics in a direct and provocative way. Through this transnational perspective I seek to highlight and celebrate the cultural dynamics that are at play in Miami as a young, immigrant, tourist city, and to use these defining characteristics as creative resources, and as a way to connect it to other contexts with similar dynamics.

These objectives have manifested themselves in programmatic choices and the establishment of particular relationships and interpretive strategies, several of which I would like to outline briefly here. Since the opening of PAMM's new building in 2013, six galleries have been dedicated to presentations of the permanent collection. *AMERICANA*, the first iteration of this set of galleries, presented six interrelated exhibition-essays with artworks by artists based in North America, South America, Central America, and the Caribbean. Prominently displayed in the exhibition was the photographic documentation of Alfredo Jaar's 1987 Times Square billboard intervention *This is Not America*, in which he criticized the use of 'America' as only referencing the United States. The piece helped articulate the overall hemispheric perspective being pursued in these revisions of the permanent collection. This past year these galleries were re-hung using the thematic *Global Positioning Systems,* which addressed the effects of globalization on notions of place and non-linear understandings of history. This exhibition expanded the view of the collection concentrically outward, connecting artworks from the Americas to others produced in Europe, the Middle East, Africa, and Asia.

During the first year that the museum was open we presented the exhibition *Caribbean: Crossroads of the World*, organized by El Museo del Barrio, the Studio Museum in Harlem, and the Queens Museum. This large and extensively researched project exhibited over 200 pieces by artists who have worked in the Caribbean over the last three centuries. Through our re-contextualization of the exhibition, and the symposium we organized, the museum sought to demonstrate our focus on the Caribbean basin, and initiate a long-term engagement with this area during this crucial opening. This emphasis was concurrently pursued through multiple and ongoing research trips by the curatorial staff to former British, Spanish, French, and Dutch islands in the region. Out of a desire to share resources and information, the museum became a founding partner of Tilting Axis, a regional network that began as a conference titled "Tilting Axis: Within & Beyond the Caribbean—Shifting Models of Sustainability and Connectivity," held in 2015 in Barbados, at the alternative space Fresh Milk. An evolving project that is in a process of self-definition, Tilting Axis's second conference will be held at PAMM in 2016, and address the notion of 'Caribbean Strategies,' as they relate to cultural practices pursued on the islands and within diasporic contexts.

Poetics of Relation is a large group exhibition I curated at PAMM with guest curator Tumelo Musaka, which directly responded to my pursuit of a Strategic Regionalism methodology, through being locally informed and internationally linked. Presented during the summer of 2015, the exhibition included six artists—Hurvin Anderson, Yto Barrada, Zarina Bhimji, Tony Capellàn, Ledelle Moe, and Xaviera Simmons—who share overlapping concerns regarding landscape, migration, memory, and new forms of identity. The title *Poetics of Relation* is taken from a book by the Martinique-born poet and cultural critic Édouard Glissant (1928-2011).[3] In this text, he articulates his theory on how an individual's identity is defined in relation to encounters with other people, cultures, and contexts. Informed by his experience as a Caribbean writer of African descent, his ideas respond to the traumatic history of colonialism, while offering an open-ended model of self-definition. The exhibition's structure sought to address the experience of Miami's many diasporic communities, individuals whose understandings of place and home are relational, existing between here and elsewhere. The exhibition additionally took inspiration from the city's tropical landscape, which affects the city economically, through tourism, and psychologically, as a source of pleasure and imagination. *Poetics of Relation* placed this local context and its cultural questions in dialogue with similar investigations pursued by these artists working in the Dominican Republic, Great Britain, India, Jamaica, Kenya, Morocco, New York, and South Africa.

The attraction to the writings of Glissant emerged from research in the Caribbean, but they in turn have helped me further refine a regional perspective and articulate the structural dynamics at play in this process. Glissant's ideas on 'Relation,' informed by Gilles Deleuze and Félix Guttari's theories related to rhizomatic structures, offers a productive model for defining identity, and, by extension, notions of place. His theories complicate traditional binary understandings of a 'Self' as defined against a foreign 'Other,' by emphasizing unity within

3 Édouard Glissant, *Poetics of Relation*, trans. Betsy Wing (Ann Arbor, MI: University of Michigan Press, 1997).

multiplicity, and how identities form a center that is defined through interactions with multiple cultural contexts simultaneously. These theories of 'Relation' are easily expanded toward notions of 'center' versus 'periphery,' offering a model through which a place like Miami, often understood as an off-center cultural context, can see itself as its own, self-appointed center, structured through its direct and chosen relations with other contexts. It is this kind of cultural mapping that can be seen as a contemporary form of regionalism.

As these coordinates and contextual nodes become defined and more visible over time, they form a conceptual frame through which exhibitions and the museum's program might be understood and validated. I am thinking about how, for example, the large survey of Nari Ward's work, titled *Sun Splashed*, which PAMM Associate Curator Diana Nawi organized for the Fall of 2015, is seen differently within the regionally-focused view we have developed. While born in Jamaica, Ward has produced work primarily in the United States, and he is most often recognized as an African-American artist. His interest in the Caribbean and the exploration of Jamaica's vernacular has become more explicit in recent works, but are elements of his practice that are often underemphasized within critical reception. Instead of simply representing another art world venue for the presentation of Ward's sculpture, Miami and PAMM's program offer a unique possibility for highlighting the Caribbean character of his production, not only through its reception by publics that have ties to Jamaica or similar island contexts, but also through its exposure to the museum's designated institutional peers or 'neighbors,' who have been involved in the project from early in its development, and who have followed its realization, actively interpreting its contents from this localized perspective.

I have been trying to articulate how Strategic Regionalism, rather than offering an elaborated theoretical proposition, represents a particular form of curatorial practice. I see it as a methodology that does not limit possibilities within a given context, but rather is a way to refine and guide choices when conceptualizing a cultural position. I have looked to outline how the term 'strategic,' refers to the development of a particular set of criteria or goals related to place that inform selection. And with 'regionalism,' how I am looking beyond conventional notions related to defining a local character, toward the idea of connecting one's own 'centered' locality outward, to create a cartography of interconnected contexts, that have implied synergies and mutual interests. As with any methodology, these ways of working continue to evolve and mutate, as they respond to these structured modes of exchange.

Being Africa:

Contextual Narratives of Artistic Environments

Koyo Kouoh

This text considers the contextualization of African artistic environments through the various trajectories of independent art spaces that have emerged on the continent since the 1990s. I journey back to the intellectual and political premises at the root of these initiatives to think about how art centers, exhibition producers, artists, and thinkers at large work, and often barter with issues of autonomy, solidarity, and criticality. Rather than quantifying the lack of effective national or public programs available for the support, representation, and preservation of such structures, I will consider independent commitments and collective apparatuses, where the conditions for production and dissemination are both highly self-organized, and linked to a flow of progressive ideas and practices.

Establishing a Canon

Since the mid-1990s, the field of visual arts has rapidly undergone internationalization, which has to a large extent followed the geopolitical routes of increased de-territorialization of markets, education, and the production of knowledge. While in the West there has been a concurrent flow of government as well as philanthropic funds in aid of international exchange, such generosity largely goes amiss in African cultural policies. This reality inherently gives rise to questions surrounding the non-existence of transnational visions for cultural and artistic production, and the extent to which a lack of public funding undermines this activity, and has a direct impact on the representation and validation of artistic and intellectual practice. Contemporary artistic practice is strongly linked to the notion of being 'international,' and with this carries an unspoken prerequisite; being 'contemporary' means operating within a given range of aesthetic, political, and discursive languages. This 'globalism' brings to the fore practices and behaviors, as well as international protagonists, who by wielding an ease of mobility and intellectual skillfulness are able to transmute cultures into cultural products, ready for consumption by an international audience.

In Africa, the majority of cultural institutions, such as museums and art galleries, archives, and art academies have been established either by the former colonial state, or in the context of a postcolonial nation after the liberation movements of the 1950s and 1960s. As a consequence, the cultural field has often been shaped according to national aesthetics, ideological concepts, and policies. Under what may appear to be a rather inhibited condition that many artists, intellectuals, and thinkers have repeatedly criticized and distanced themselves from (particularly in relation to state-initiated cultural politics), across the last two decades, and increasingly in the last ten years, a whole host of new spaces and initiatives have taken shape. While the wording of mission statements may vary from space to space, many of these independent spaces share a common ground, having responded to a cultural urgency, and a need to address an artistic and critical void. What this urgency necessitates are more platforms for multi-faceted production.

As art centers in the West are threatened by closure, and some are even effectively forced to close due to the spiraling strain of budget cuts, more and more spaces are establishing themselves in Asia, the Americas, and Africa. If things continue in this vein, I predict that a form of *political and social transformation* will occur. It seems that the Western art world will soon be subsumed into a much larger global force, as a wave of a new artistic elite, adept at challenging the most seasoned artists based anywhere between Vienna and San Francisco, takes up the gauntlet.

It seems clear; different canons, economies, and dialectics, and, most importantly, a highly informed audience are emerging. This trend is especially apparent in Africa, where a variety of independent and/or private art initiatives has recently been established, filling the void left by state-initiated cultural and artistic programs and their empty promises. These initiatives set themselves apart from state-affiliated institutions as well as commercial (art) markets by creating alternative models and platforms for negotiating art and history, and by reflecting upon and archiving art, visual culture, and cultural history.

So before I continue, I think it is necessary to re-contextualize what is generally understood as 'contemporary African art,' since overarching definitions have tended to prove controversial in the past. Are we even surprised? How can we define artists based on a given geography when so many people migrate, or are descendants of diasporan parents? Can a monolithic intonation of 'African culture' be considered when speaking about such a vast territory? In this capacity, I am lucky. I do not have to attempt to answer such questions single-handedly. Some very insightful and eloquent individuals have already addressed this.

Operating in the Void

In May 1989 the exhibition *Magiciens de la Terre* was held at the Centre Georges Pompidou in Paris. Bringing together artists from all over the world, *Magiciens...* sought to highlight a new reality on the global art map. This exhibition became the mythical starting point of what is now commonly referred to as 'Global Art,' and, even today, *Magiciens...* acts as a keystone in the trajectory of African contemporary art exhibitions.

It comes as no surprise that *Magiciens...* was problematic in an intellectual and curatorial sense, and further highlighted a crisis of representation and analysis of African artists and their practices. Yet it must be said that *Magiciens...,* perhaps inadvertently, proved constructive in some capacity; that is, it materialized the creative potential of a curatorial crisis.

It is in the aftermath of *Magiciens...* that institutions such as Iniva (Institute of International Visual Arts) founded in London, UK, became active in dealing with internationalism. Magazines such as *Revue Noire* and *Nka: Journal of Contemporary African Art* were launched, in Paris and New York respectively, providing explorative and critical platforms for African artistic and intellectual activity. And curators such as Okwui Enwezor, Simon Njami, Gilane Tawadros, Salah Hassan, Olu Oguibe, and Clémentine Deliss emerged with force.

Of course, one may note the geographical bias of this artistic and curatorial activity; the majority of these 'milestone' exhibitions curators were organizing were indeed produced and exhibited in Europe and the US. All bar one, *Africa Remix,* which made its way to Johannesburg. As much as this generation of exhibition-makers and critics contributed to a greater understanding and knowledge of artistic and intellectual discourse through the lens of 'Africa,' one cannot deny that they operated in the context of an infrastructural void. What this curatorial methodology fell short in was constructing an infrastructural ground on which to root their efforts, and those of their contemporaries. What is needed to progress is the formation of an *artistic ecology.* An ecology is only made possible through the establishment and continual engagement of institutions within a given (s)pace; institutions that are also able to provide sufficient support for artistic and intellectual practices.

The birth of private cultural spaces and institutions in Africa in the 1990s came as a result of several factors. The most commonly cited is the lack of national organizational structures able to host projects, and conduct convincing debates around contemporary experience. However, I will insist here that by owing the emergence of private spaces to the negligence of African states would be to reduce these initiatives to a mere mechanical reaction that did not follow from independent or original thought. Although funding for medium- or long-term artistic projections is practically nonexistent in Africa (as such subsidies granted by international organizations are not forever, and are given with the proviso that it is for their development), I would argue that this factor fails to suffice as a direct causality for the issues surrounding their survival. Indeed, while independent spaces such as Doual'art in Douala opened in 1991, pioneering this concept in an environment that could only be described at the time as ravaged, spaces of a similar nature have also been established in South Africa, where academic, commercial, and governmental structures are already in place.

Autonomous Zones

In this case, a comparison can be drawn with Europe and the US, where a number of alternative spaces have risen to the fore since the 1980s. Were these new spaces an attempt at satisfying the dream of autonomy? Most noteworthy is that these spaces were driven by a desire to distribute and disseminate an ideology *through* a mechanism wherein direction and programming could be separated from nationalistic ideologies and public bureaucracies, and thus position themselves as explicitly independent. In the short history of these spaces, there has also been a focus on collectivity and sharing, which has played a significant role in terms of their proliferation. Sharing an ideal, sharing knowledge, sharing experience, while shattering a hierarchical system that reserves art for the preserve of the elite. Where social divides between 'educated' citizens and 'others' remains a familiar and widespread issue, this divide is all the more pronounced on the African continent. Thus, the challenge that these professionals decidedly latched onto was to make culture accessible to all.

The comprehensive goal of such spaces, each by their own measure, is to answer the essential question asked by the German philosopher Ernst Bloch: the question of the 'We.' The 'We' that Bloch alluded to was naturally contextual, and could adapt to the environment in which it was discussed. We might note that the context of the 'We' will vary according to certain art spaces in Egypt,[1] Cameroon,[2] Senegal,[3] or Nigeria.[4] In Dakar for instance, home to the Dakar biennial and Senghor's utopia, the 'We' will not have the same resonance as in Cairo, where the Egyptian capital still suffers from the turmoil of a revolution, the sustainability of which has yet to be ensured. In Cameroon and Nigeria, where cultural policy is practically inexistent, and political conditions engender constant tensions, we may consider a different strategy of citizens' involvement. In Kenya, a country still hostage to its geography and the regimes of its colonial past, the 'We' has yet another face.

The complex issue of the 'We' points to an infinite number of dimensions, and particularly a fundamental duality, without which is it difficult to determine its essence: the group and the individual. The group (the 'We') is a set of interdependent groups interacting, i.e. within a larger collective field such as a continent, religion, ethnicity, and so forth. The 'We' represents a collectively of constituent groups within which each individual

1
Darb 1718, founded by the artist Moataz Nasr in 2008.

2
Doual'art, founded by Marilyn Douala Bell and Didier Schaub in 1991.

3
RAW Material Company, founded by Koyo Kouoh in 2008.

4
CCA Lagos, founded by Bisi Silva in 2007.

must find their identity. Yet in this gesture identity is the synthesis of these different categories into a homogenized and singular actualization, which we may also decide to rethink.

What may be more useful here is an appropriation of what French philosopher Jacques Rancière refers to as "territories of shared thought," in which borders are transgressed in order to reconsider our relationship to identity.[5] This, Rancière proffers, is nothing to do with a lack of knowledge or with knowledge production, but is more a *manoeuvre* that has been historically practiced within worker emancipation. He continues: "My whole itinerary focused on this issue which I subsequently called 'distribution of the sensible': how, in a given space, perceptions of the world are organized and sensible experience is linked to intelligible modes of interpretation."[6]

In this gesture, Rancière puts his finger on the challenge that many cultural figures face and continue to address. In this process, in which knowledge sharing holds an important place, I agree with him that what matters is not so much the 'transition from ignorance to knowledge,' as the way in which one might cross a border like moving between the opposite ends of a binary. Transgressing the limits of the borders of identities involves a redefinition of the foundations of the sovereign nation and its priorities. Art and cultural production has taken on a considerable importance in this debate in recent decades. Can we grasp the needs of our times with contemporary tools? Can we move beyond the codification of a monolithic history of the world that is outrageously simplified? Can we change the analytical tools whose purpose was to lock complex identities into geographic essentialism? It is utterly visible that art centers have succeeded in annihilating geography through their inscription in a pan-African and global space. Can they then overcome the barriers of communitarianism by redefining the relationship of individuals to their societies?

Creating Publics

Bombarding ourselves with reflexive questions surely demands a certain strength, and a course of action along which to proceed. Before we commence with the next logistical step of a disentanglement from systemic cultural organization, we must quite possibly first discuss the means available for moving beyond cultural borders. Primarily, there seems to be a prevailing contradiction between these spaces and their sites of establishment, which we can address at once. In most cases, the public-private dialectic is exacerbated by the fact that these spaces are often located on the margins of public cultural establishments. The notions of public and private always appears inherently conflictual, to the extent that, while the latter

5
Jacques Rancière, *Et tant pis pour les gens fatigués! Entretiens* (Paris: Editions Amsterdam, 2009).

6
Ibid.

aims to deal with a sphere of intimacy and operates on a basis of proximity, the former caters to state ideologies, and, as a result, frequently limits the freedom of the other, if only through its regulatory function.

Operating on proximity—as independent art spaces often do—means knowing their audiences intimately (since they too rely on a sense of collectivity and collaboration), while the anonymous tools put in place by the state frequently do not live up to audience expectation. Hence an inevitable cavity opens out, which often leads to a misappropriation and mismanagement of public facilities, and financial resources. In such an immense undertaking of re-appropriating public space, it is vital that art centers have a thorough understanding of their audience, since their founders are also their leading consumers. Due to this proximity, independent art spaces are able to problem-solve and address issues by approaching a collective body that is actively engaged in the space. There is no intermediary between funder and consumer, as, to an extent, there is little difference between the two. To cite RAW Material Company as an example here, for the first two years 50 percent of the budget of RAW Material Company was compensated by my personal earnings. Ideologically, RAW Material Company was born out of the necessity to create a space for knowledge sharing. The core motivation was to establish a space for alternative education and learning. Since RAW would fail to maintain its operation if I were to retract my partial funding, I continue this arrangement. All the while, I insist on transparency and advocate the importance of art spaces as critical sites of experimentation and freedom. They are themselves *de facto* experiments, and I believe that their true significance will only take shape once they enter into an operative symbiosis with their environment.

Art centers seek to grasp their changing reality by holding up a mirror to the citizenship, and engaging with a local audience. This creates a form of reactivity, a particular sensitivity to the worlds around them, whose shape is transformed by their presence. The eye, or, more exactly, the consciousness, does not only allow projection; it also encourages introspection. This double prism necessarily refers to the concepts of space and perception.

Further, founding directors of art centers in Africa are identity anomalies. Like Janus, they cannot be satisfied with a single unequivocal representation. The self-evident facts they attempt to highlight are necessarily manifold, and even contradictory, since they are permanently open to the movements of the world, and the changes in their own environment. What they present as obvious fact is not intended as a definition, since they are aware of the impossibility of presenting oneself to the world through a distinct identity.

The New Citizen

It is within this set of frameworks that the concept of a new citizenship is being developed. A concept that rejects all forms of elitism, and rebukes the barriers between those who know and those who do not know. In Dakar, Lagos, Cairo, and Douala, the concept of the curator is at best blurred, and at worst still in the process of being defined, echoing the multiplicity of practices encountered in society, which cannot always be reflected in the codified language of contemporary art. Rancière reminds us that artists are citizens like any other, and their role in society is no greater than that of a blacksmith or a dentist, each of whom makes a contribution to the common good in their own area of activity. For art centers, this means working on what Homi Bhabha calls "metaphoricity," a term he uses to describe a sort of communal imaginative space that is "never simply horizontal," but is a *metaphoric movement* that "requires a kind of doubleness in writing; a temporality of representation that moves between cultural formations and social processes without a centered causal logic.'[7]

In his traveling theory, Bhabha evokes, then challenges, the intrinsically horizontal nature of imagined communities and evokes the concept of this doubleness. And here I would extend the notion of doubleness into a *multiplicity*. The metaphoric movement of communities requiring a market, a yard, or a street, which thereby becomes the locus of a particular aesthetic that art centers echo attentively. This multiplicity should be the focus of our attention, because it contains the contradictions without which no society can control its own progression. There is also no *centered causal logic*, but rather a set of micro-logics, which, when shared, constitute the warp and weft of a social fabric. An art center, like an identity, is never fully formed, but is always in the process of becoming through its interactions with site and community.

7
Homi K. Bhabha, *The Location of Culture* (New York, NY: Routledge, 1994) p. 202.

How to Put Ourselves between the Closing Door and Its Frame?

Zasha Cerizza Colah

In the face of systemic injustice, presumed illegality, like gratuitous generosity, become vital outlets. The invitation to write about the future of the curatorial institution compels a starting point taken from the perspective of those in perpetual and pressing movement, and from the perspective of the production of illegality by nation-states. Where there is little or no recourse to a judicial system, suffering somehow compels our disservice to the law. Curating is telescoped here to the single event, of staving open a closing door.

The Invisible Sites of Exhibitions

A work that unfolds like a storyboard of variously sized oil paintings captures one artist lending his sneakers by edging them over a barrier, so that another artist wearing sandals is allowed to enter a private art event where his footwear was objected to. The series of paintings is by Nikhil Raunak, an artist-member of Clark House, whose subjects confront racial histories, from apartheid to the caste system, and the continuance of those histories into the contemporary moment. His work is also a condemnation of how these issues play out within the workings of the art system itself. In this work the elitist barrier propels acts of generosity and cultural dissidence; a simple exchange that humorously seeks outlets, but makes outlaws of both artists. This carnivalesque crossing of a line of entry, is treated here as having conceptual continuum with other crossings.[1]

As a member of an artist-curatorial collaborative called 'black rice' we cut our teeth on the militarized treatment of civilians at the peripheries of India.[2] In the border regions of the country, the un-constitutional Armed Forces Special Powers Act (AFSPA), which gives absolute power and impunity to Indian soldiers over civilian populations to brutally curb insurgency and self-determination, has been enforced in vast swaths of forest and rural land that have been demarcated as 'disturbed areas' without public debate for tens of years. The Act was recently removed in the state of Tripura, but reinforced over the state of Nagaland, and continues to be enacted in the states of Manipur, Assam, districts in Arunachal Pradesh, and Kashmir. As continues the fifteen-year-long hunger strike protesting AFSPA by the civil rights activist Irom Sharmila. If extra-military atrocities could happen in the 1980s and 1990s with impunity in major cities of border areas, what happened in small villages? And how far was this from the decision-making power center of Delhi? If paranoia accompanies our curating today, that paranoia was learned.

Every court has a veil of justice, behind which certain communities of people, or whole geographic areas, are denied

1
If, on the one hand, the idea of crossings are literalized and fatally apparent—2015 has seen the crossing of the liquid wall of the Mediterranean, the separation walls and barricades being erected along Hungary's national borders, and an asylum seeker shot dead by border police in Bulgaria—on the other hand, crossings also metaphorically describe forms invented to address injustice, when recourse to the courts of justice, to public debate, or policy-making, have been made impassable.

2
Black rice was my collaboration with art historians Iris Yingsen Chuba and Rahul Bhattacharya, to research the contemporary art of India's Northeastern states, based in Tuensang village, Nagaland, between December 2007 and July 2008.

equal access to the law. If we acquiesce that all institutions of the nation-state carry systemic horizon lines that protect and privilege only a few—where those beyond remain hidden in an unremitting state of vulnerability to injustice—then the invisible horizon lines necessarily become the invisible sites of exhibition-making. The idea that curating itself may be theorized—in addition to the indispensable duty to historicize forgotten exhibitions, and the political imperative to gather the traces of erased culture—is predicated on 'speaking nearby' cultural actions, artistic practices, and exhibition formats within places that have been politically and culturally stifled. The title of my text attends to situations where political and social freedoms have been closing in or diminishing, seeking the cultural strategies—of dissent, of humor, camouflage and fiction—that have been keeping the remaining open doors ajar.

In one instance in the Manipur hills, the artist Zamthingla Ruivah, facing an abyss of amnesia regarding the meaning of various geometrical designs found within the suppressed Tangkhul-Naga tribal visual culture, came to adjust and dwell on the humble, Kafkaesque movement of insects to describe the spirit of a murdered young woman—her neighbor—and a community's path to justice under AFSPA, in luminous red wool.[3] Her woven skirt, called a 'kashan,' came to be copied by other women by hand, like Chinese whispers, over a vast area of more than 300 villages, like an interactive public monument to the Naga Hills. In an exhibition *L'exigence de la Saudade* (at Kadist Art Foundation, Paris, 2013), and later in *Insert* (in Mati Ghar, New Delhi, 2014), the original woven kashan, as well as the kashans by other hands dating from 1990 to 2013, were displayed. The display mimicked the long scrolling line of the kashans worn by women of many villages when they gather once a year, as though each woman herself were standing together in the exhibition room, wearing these slightly varying geometric insignia of cultural resistance; a feat of solidarity and of collective imagination.

To further the concept of crossing over some form of invisible threshold, the philosopher Adi Ophir, to whose writing my own work has been deeply indebted, arguing against the Israeli occupation in Palestine in his book *The Order of Evils*, does not resort to hope for a utopian new state system.[4] Instead, when the institutional exchange systems are oppressive, he believes that people effect 'conversions' of the system. He writes:

> *Conversion is an exchange relation in which capital is transferred from one field of action to another, and its value, which was previously stated in terms of one field, is now translated*

3
The Tangkhuls are a Naga tribe in the hills of Manipur state. The suppression of Naga visual culture can be traced to proselytization for Christianity, the breaking down of the tribal Morung education system, and decades of militaristic violence.

4
Adi Ophir, *The Order of Evils: Toward an Ontology of Morals*, trans. Rela Mazali and Havi Carel (New York, NY: Zone Books, 2005).

to another... It is impossible to convince the court to change its verdict, but it is possible to bribe the warden. It is impossible to change a political decision that causes suffering, but it is possible to join the injured ones in a demonstration of solidarity and share with them even a little of their suffering... Some channels of conversion are always blocked: situations in which one cannot give love, work magic, activate authority, or give meaning... Such blocks can be coincidental, and they could be a deliberate result of social actions. But more often they are an unintentional but systematic and non-coincidental consequences of social power-relations... It is possible to characterize social situations, social order, and political regimes in terms of the exchange relations they enable or block.[5]

To Ophir, it is these processes of translation and conversion that need to be kept open. And it is the suffocation of recourses that amplifies suffering. Ophir prefaces his book with an argument for his interest only in instances of real suffering and damage, and not in abstractions of ideological wrongs, and concepts. With this complicated, suspicious approach to fiction and abstractions over real situations is the realization that fiction, imagination, and illegality may often be the only open recourse to 'conversion'—even more so when the abstract fictions are participated in collectively by those who live behind the horizon line of the judicial and police systems, in a state of perpetual discrimination and second-citizenship. If any theory accompanies our curatorial practice, it emerges from formative entanglements in the body of work of certain artists, and their fictive elaborations.

When the Burmese artist Htein Lin was deported by China back to Myanmar, he returned to Yangon's law university, finished his degree, and began working with a troupe of Anyeint comedians—a traditional Burmese form of comedy whose protagonists are a beautiful dancer and a comedian. On graduating, Htein Lin decided he wanted to be an artist. Some years later he was arrested by Myanmar intelligence on a faulty charge. While in prison, Htein Lin wrote his experience of the trial in a quickly set up Special Court into a short story, which he circulated clandestinely to entertain the other prisoners.[6] Until the final hearing, he and 25 others had been locked into separate cells, denied lawyers, and the advice of their families and friends. Trained as a lawyer, he asked if he could defend himself. In the middle of a fiery plea, the judge interrupted him, saying, "You are wasting your time, I have no power to decide anything, the judgment will be given to me from the intelligence officers. We are only waiting." Htein Lin said, "I sat back.

5
Ibid., pp. 304-305.

6
The story of the Special Court was first related to me by Htein Lin in May 2008, and was later translated by Ko Moe. It was retold by Htein Lin in the work *I C U JEST* (2012)—the title being an anagram for 'justice,'—shown in a parallel exhibition of the Kochi-Muziris Biennale, 2012.

I stopped pleading my case. I was a comedian, an actor, who had studied the law and knew my rights. But then I looked at the judge, and realized he was no different from me, he was an actor too, acting the part of a judge." When an envelope was passed to the judge, he read out their sentences. "While the judge read out our jail sentences, 40, 30, 10 or 7 years of imprisonment, we began to laugh. We began to laugh irrepressibly, congratulating each other on the number of years we were given. That night in prison, instead of separate cells we were allowed to come together, and could see our families for the first time since we were forced to leave our homes." They carried through the laughter, enacting elaborate rituals of celebration, toasting each other in their political prisonership, as the prison guards looked on, foxed.

In court, laughter restructures and denies the world order, and converts the court into how the prisoners saw it: farcical. The idiom of performance and the logic of parody, inserted into the court of law, were amplified by collective participation. Htein Lin encoded pain and horror in a language of laughter and farce, and conjured a mirror-world, a meta-commentary of parody over reality, a fiction that could address the law, from the other side of the systemic horizon line. Here the instances of collective imagination amount to a kind of 'crossing.' The idea of collective imagination, as a fiction, is evoked in the face of blanket injustice, especially in situations where there is little or no recourse to a legal system, or when the system is unconstitutional or extra-legal. Perhaps the future role and premise of the curatorial is one that works precisely in this spatial dimension: effecting crossings of the invisible or sometimes brutally visible systemic horizon lines. Even as several of our exhibitions have appealed against the use of all sedition laws, we knew our cities were becoming further confined. The public institutions that are increasingly reducing access were to us the closing angles of open space, within legal, penal, educational, and even culture's hierarchical systems, purging intellectual vision. Losing ground slowly leaves time for guilt to settle. How do we stave this off, place our foot in the way of the closing door?

The acrobats and tightrope walkers who collect at Clark House's street corner, have learned the practicalities and strategies of carving out space. The Dombari or Dom community—immigrants, from indigenous tribes, who have been pushed from their lands, for mining, or industry, have formed a community working in the city as acrobats or musicians. They keep the doors open constantly, and disassemble and disperse at a moment's notice, when the police approach. From them we may learn how to never ask for permission to use the street. It is the itinerants who can teach us 'conversion,' and from them we often borrow exhibition space, circumventing the normal course of obtaining permissions. What has come to seem necessary to a way of thinking about public space, and of curating within it, is to seek and learn strategies of illegality from itinerant practitioners, on how to maneuver through the streets, and occupy its spaces. The space of Clark House itself has its own history of being a refuge for political dissenters during the Indian Emergency from 1975 to 1977. As a union of cultural dissent, Clark House has been tracing the city's legacy of artist solidarity movements—from the fiery PROYOM, the Progressive Youth Movement active through the 1970s, especially through the Emergency, when serigraphed posters were clandestinely put up in railway stations, factories, and bus stops overnight, by artists like Navjot Altaf and Altaf Mohammedi, to Open Circle, which ran from 1998 to 2008, whose members were Tushar Joag, Sharmila Samant, Archana Hande, Shilpa Gupta, and the art historian Chaitanya Sambrani. In addition to the political content of this art history, it also forms an almost untold legacy of art in public space in the city, only just beginning to be written and understood.

Though promised to the public, what is open today may one day come to close. In *The museum is where objects go to die* (2011), proposed as an exhibition reflecting on a collection moving from private to public ownership, a small canvas by Krishen Khanna, called *Betrayal* (1950), was to be displayed in such a way that a tiny inscription at the back of the canvas could also be read. The inscription reads: "This painting was sold to Rudy von Leyden, who bequeathed it with several other paintings to the Prince of Wales Museum before he left India." Von Leyden was an Austrian art critic who came to Bombay in exile, fleeing World War II. However, the painting did not reach the Prince of Wales Museum until 2010, and must have been sold to a private collector, and then traveled a very different route from the one intended. It is only serendipity that the painting finally reached the very museum it was once bequeathed to. The story of the work's journey—a betrayal—highlights a peculiarity of our Indian museum context; that what has come to the public realm needs protections for it to remain in the public realm, and then to remain visible. To me, the sound of jangling keys marks institutional time. The keys are double edged. Doubly inscribed, they secure objects in safety, and they have the potential to keep things away. Today the keys are also digital watermarks. From marking time, they now mark use. If we heed sociologist Saskia Sassen's warnings, the digital promise of widely distributed knowledge will also find new forms of closing off cultural public property, with digital formats that will force us to pay for what was once free.

Over the course of making exhibitions, ideas about collective imagination turned to related fictions of collectively endowed reality, which institutions—including museums—have a habit of fixing. We critiqued this in the exhibition *Insert* (Mati Ghar, New Delhi, 2014), following an invitation to debate the extant public cultural infrastructure in India. Against the logic of institutions, we humorously referred to Polish writer Witold Gombrowicz's obsession with the philosophy of form, especially displays of nationality as 'forms,' as a mask that gets stuck—'Polishness,' 'East European'—as forms of habit that solidify into a facade, to underline our view of the outer facade of the art institution as an ideological fixing. Mati Ghar, meaning temporary house or mud house, was a circular building with a dome, especially chosen for the exhibition. It was erected twenty years earlier as a temporary structure in the museum grounds for a conference on time, but had somehow remained, and was being used as a second exhibition space. Taking the mud house at its material meanings, members of Clark House proposed several destabilizations, to restore its original temporality. A pattern painted over half the building's exterior by Yogesh Barve, sought to make the building partially invisible, and merge it with the surrounding tree cover. Amol Patil made the ground of Mati Ghar tremble within the arc of the building devoted to his video and installation. Prabhakar Pachpute made drawings of migrations of people whose lands had been taken for mining, on treated plaster walls that in the course of the exhibition would perpetually fall in pieces to the floor, revealing the red mud of the original walls. Rupali Patil made a temporary structure of corrugated metal sheets that opened the building to the elements and the open sky. Each work was proposed at some level as an unfixing of the institution. Throughout contemporary curating's short history, many curators have put themselves in between the demands of collectively-endowed realities—in front of the museum's own ideological prestige, in front of boards, between government tourism agendas, in front of elitism in education—to never entirely conform to the institution's ideological facades, its own stagnating fixing into normalization.

In solidarity with the resignations of our curatorial colleagues and friends in museums and smaller institutions in Hungary with the rise of Victor Olban, we sought to subvert the revisionism of identity with quasi-fictional associations of identity, between the nomadic Banjara community in India, and the Roma in Hungary. *Associations of Identity* (2012) became useful to highlight the nation-state's production of illegality, and the meaningful mobility of nomadism. We were invited to curate an exhibition that took place within the Hungarian Information and Cultural Centre in New Delhi, which we used as a symbol of the government we wished to address. The Banjara's ancient wooden caravan that we met with on a road in Rajasthan retains a worldview that is in clear opposition of the nation-state, and the sensibility of moving away from the routine political organization of life. The itinerant, and illegal, is a world-view from the imperative of survival, or from the spaces of meaningful mobility and the need to travel in which nothing is complete or settled. To our paranoid world, this may be the most adjusted voice.

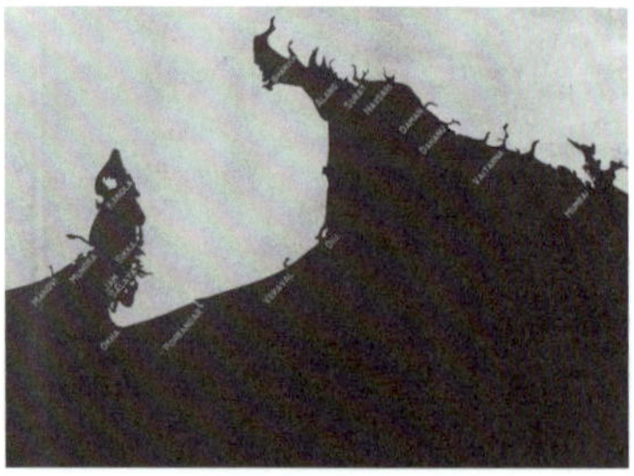

See pp. 254-255
Collaboration between CAMP and Clark House Initiative, *Country of the Sea*, 2015, (detail) solar-exposed cyanotype on cotton fabric, 5 × 16 feet, commissioned by Dr. Bhau Daji Lad Museum, Mumbai, for CAMP's exhibition *The Country of the Sea*

Inverting ideas of unity and abstraction, this work treats the ports along the coasts as cities of their own country. It brings the coast of Africa uncannily close to that of the Indian subcontinent. The work unfixes the land, and fixes the volatile sea instead, providing a visual metaphor for speaking of institutions, taking into account their own sense of stability from the perspective of movement and migration.

Il Faut Qu’on Se Bouge!

Sumesh Sharma

Curating in a context where exhibition histories are still being investigated and written, and the nuances of visual culture are multi-layered, 'cues' uncover codes based on the assumption of a common visual memory or association with objects. 'Curatorial cues' are a set of visual comments that allow distant ideas in an exhibition to unite, or aid in the deciphering of layers that artworks present using methods of juxtaposition and visual intuitiveness. Curatorial cues often allow us to circumvent the museum bureaucracies we are critical of, and these are not acts of representation but rather those of agility. This agility is allowed to us because we do not consider ourselves an institution, a commercial gallery, or a not-for profit space. Rather we function as an artists' union that concerns itself with exhibition-making, and its histories. Artists and their lives become the points of departure for any exhibition we curate. They connect the disparate elements that are characteristic of our projects.

Equities of Voice

A dusty afternoon in Dakar, and a group of girls, young students at the Lycée, pass the Village des Arts. Ismaila Manga sees them walk past his studio each day. Acquiring an education in a country lacking resources is often the only path out of poverty. Embedded within Senegal's colonial history, an economy dependent on France and import necessitates a system based on money orders. Each year many Senegalese travel to work in Europe and North America. Paris, Marseille, Brussels, and New York are home to large diasporas. Dakar stands at a 'Grande Carrefour' of routes that take Bangladeshi, Iraqi, and other Sub-Saharan immigrants onward to Morocco, from where they can slip into Spain. The European Union has criticized the flow of migrants from the coasts of North Africa heavily, using diplomatic measures such as cuts in financial aid, and instituting border checks at airports and ports across North and West Africa. Manga himself was a migrant to Quebec, where he studied at the Faculty of Arts, and subsequently worked for more than a decade. During winters he would come across large stretches of flat land covered in snow, only broken by bare trees, reminding him of the arid laterite landscapes that stretched into Mali, where patches of large green baobabs denoted a source of water and hope. Returning to Senegal, Manga found a large amount of rotting iron scrap collected by Indian and Bangladeshi immigrants to be exported for recycling. Rolling his canvases in powdered metal rust he recreated the laterite landscapes, interspersed with human figures from whose heads enormous trees had grown, critiquing the dehumanization brought about by race politics. In a neighboring studio, the artist Louis Bassene stated that migration is not only about labor, but at a certain age everyone moves, it is natural: "Il faut qu'on se bouge!"

Village Des Arts began as an informal settlement of artists in old barracks for Chinese construction workers in Dakar. It is largely inhabited by artists who do not register with the interest in 'aesthetics *en vogue*' of visiting curators. As an Independent Curators International fellow, I belonged to the bandwagon that often stopped by in Senegal. However, I was keen to research those *not* connected to international funding mechanisms, and sought out artists who sustained practices based on inter-artist dependability—those who found sustenance in immigrant networks in New York, Paris, and London, cities with large Senegalese diasporas. It is not uncommon to find immigrant artists unsuccessful in global art capitals for a variety of reasons, including language barriers, inaccessibility to art circles, or institutional apathy, but able to sustain themselves through their native diasporas in those cities. As with the artists in the Village Des Arts, a colonial texturing often dominates their painting practices, even when they work abroad. It is their dependence on Western classical academic traditions of art-making that becomes a cause of discrimination within an art system that is now keen on a historical embracing of conceptualism, new media, and a post-Internet aesthetic. Even though painting is as anathema to their social traditions and culture as the first instances of Dadaism or ephemeral practices were in Europe.

Migration is a contemporary reality for most artists coming from countries and regions that now attract high-powered museum acquisition committees. Institutional success in museums, scholarships for arts schools—such as the École Supérieure des Beaux Arts in Paris, influential residencies such as ISCP in New York, or the Rijksakademie in Amsterdam—and participation in biennials, or friendships with powerful curators and artists, are often pathways to migrant lives abroad. These include political, intellectual, and economic exile.

In his work, Bassene appropriates biblical histories to reconstruct Christ as a figure among the Jolas, a tribe that put up a tough fight with the encroaching colonial French. Artist Marije Gertenbach creates portraits of Jesuit priests and travelers who crossed oceans to evangelize among populations colonized by the Portuguese. Often artists took part in inquisitions of faith in these distant lands. Many registered their protest in the murals they painted into the arches of the churches they were commissioned to produce. Behind the layers of oil, and among the images, lay instances of indigenous resistance. Gertenbach paints on burlap and jute to suspend complex layers of images and critique, the way oil holds together pigment. Artists, masons, and architects from Brazil were sent to create large cathedrals and furniture for the seventeenth-century catechisms. They were indigenous Indians who had mastered the art of marrying Iberian aesthetics with tropical know-how essential for laterite soils. Gertenbach was commissioned to make a triptych of three murals that would come to occupy the neo-gothic arches of Clark House in Bombay. The idea was to rejuvenate the lost Lusitane history of the street we find ourselves on, with the Cathedral of the Holy Name being our neighbor, but also to consider the migration of people across Lusitane colonies and the internationalism attached to it through culture and food.

When Clark House proposes painters for institutional shows it often receives confused smiles that veil the inherent shock. The art market embraced the postmodernist face of painting, but since the global financial crisis it has depended on sales of modern masters. Although minimal abstraction still finds space, both financially and philosophically, figurative painting is all but left to a few artists who substantiate their practices with a certain political and art historical urgency. Low-tech practices in new media using cellphones are largely sustainable, but access to sophisticated techniques and presentation is a luxury in places where electricity is supplied only at irregular intervals. Rigid curatorial bureaucracies in Europe do not take such ground realities into account when proposing shows with artists from their former colonial possessions. They also often fall prey to the survey show phenomenon, which depends largely on the exotic, or a certain definite placement within Western accounts of art history. Thus practices in painting of artists such as Manga, Gertenbach, and Bassene become institutional risks, even though they reflect a certain current and historical urgency.

Loretti Pinto draws parts of passports on the facades of South Goa's Portuguese colonial heritage, commenting on the large migration of Catholic Goans using the right to a Portuguese passport to find jobs in the United Kingdom. Goans have been legendary seafarers and they have often found employment as stewards on British ships. There are diaspora communities of Goans in Southeast Asia, Africa, and South America. But economic conditions and land economics have forced many in recent years to avail of the passport policy, and move to Portugal. Like many other artists in India, Pinto depends on a validation system that is based on success in their artistic careers on foreign shores. Artists vie for inclusion in institutional group shows, or residencies, and even spend their own resources for their work to travel. This is peculiar in a culture where until not long ago travel across the sea led to one's loss of caste. But the stagnation of economic opportunities during

India's socialist period saw widespread migration to Northern America, the Middle East, and Europe. Foreign travel became an aspiration few Indians could afford. Pinto often critiques these aspirations as reasons for the emptying of her village in South Goa, even though she understands the reasons, including scarcity of resources such as land and water, which often fall into corporate hands in cahoots with the state. Museums, art schools, and other platforms for the diffusion of art now work in tandem with geopolitical situations that are often more benign, such as the movement of French artists from Paris to New York in 1968, or Italian curators to London after the financial crisis of 2008.

Recent migrants, however, flee unfortunate lives, unable to make their culture travel, almost mimicking the exodus of Chaldeans from Iraq, and the Nestorians from Syria, as well as the Copts leaving Egypt. Many migrants are lost as they pile onto boats to cross the Mediterranean to islands such as Lampedusa. Once rescued, or accepted, they scatter around Europe seeking livelihoods escaping immigration sleuths. The experience is violent, physically and mentally. Right-wing groups in Europe underline their actions through posters warning of a deluge of black skin and Islam. The violence the images seek are directed to yellow posters, left to be picked up by young children, college students, retirees and tourists, who visit the 31st Biennial of São Paulo. The posters are from the archive of the artist Juan Carlos Romero, who through it explores the typography of the black word 'Violencia.' Influenced by Frantz Fanon, Romero sees his cause with oppressed people, especially those who were under dictatorship in his native Argentina. These posters were selected and traveled to Bombay, without permission from the artist or the biennial, to be part of an exhibition curated by me, where they were to change their context—dealing with the communal passion of riots between Hindus and Muslims. The offer to collect these posters during the biennial allowed me to take the license to turn them into curatorial cues.

Harry Sewbalak, a singer in a YouTube video with archival photos of Indian immigrants, sings a *birha* about the journey of the Bihari indentured labor at the sugarcane plantations of Suriname, which involved travel from famine stricken Bihar by way of ship from Calcutta, to lives of cutting tropical forests to grow coffee and cacao. 'Birha,' or 'separation,' is a melancholic set of songs sung during a musical session or 'Baithak' in East India, and now in diasporas of indentured Indians in the Caribbean, South America, South Africa, Mauritius, Burma, and Fiji. Much like in the Portuguese Fado, Birha singers lament their past and find solutions to their present, which almost always concerns the separation from family, a lover, or native lands. Other singers, including Mohammed Sharief and Rudy Baldewsingh, sing about the prospects of migration and the happiness the descendants of the indentured laborers now enjoy in Suriname and the Netherlands. To archive memories a lot today is uploaded onto YouTube, to be watched as one runs a corner shop along a canal in Amsterdam. These personal archives are often mined by artists, leading to interesting revelations. Artists at Clark House often borrow music, sounds, and other material for their animations that then become part of biennial installations, and are later acquired by museums. This undeclared open source use today contributes to many practices that might have suffocated under the dictatorship of royalties and permissions. When a young Bihari artist encounters Harry Sewbalak's music, he is at once internationalized to the notion of camaraderie with others in the Caribbean; connected by folk music while divided by geography and decades of history from those in Suriname.

After the transfer of Bombay from the Portuguese to the British on the occasion of the marriage of Catherine of Braganza to King Charles II in 1662, the local Indo-Portuguese community began to call themselves East Indians, giving up the Portuguese creole they spoke in favor of English and their native Marathi. But in Maratha-held territories, on a peninsula on the Arabian coast, in the village of Korlai, Portuguese creole has been preserved outside the abandoned naval fort of Revdanda. At the beginning of the year, all at Clark House traveled for a residency across the sea to the archipelago. It was before the Indian general elections, and the Maharashtrian identity had been fed into everyone's minds, based on a resurgence of regional parochialism that began before most of our births. Revdanda houses the remnants of the Jewish population called the Bene Israel, who arrived on the coast of the Konkan after the second demolition of the Temple in Jerusalem. Women wore the nine-yard saree, a traditional sarong, while they spoke almost only Marathi. The young talked of impending 'Aliya' to Israel. We then visited Korlai. Unlike Bombay, Korlai remained a Portuguese speaking village hidden away, ruled by the Maratha General Kanhoji Angre. This hybridity was made possible by the sea. Our Lusitane histories extended to Zanzibar, Djibouti, Yemen, Mozambique, and the Emirates. A lady in the village sang us a song in Portuguese, which Yogesh Barve recorded in a video, as a testament of his own family's history, which is born out of migration to Bombay for work, not celebrated but rather blurred by parochial oneness. Identity politics and a national turn toward the right in India have left many young artists confused, and sometimes in agreement with what can be considered fascist views. Barve's films counter these absolute perceptions and oppose the falsehoods of nationhood.

Goats migrate with their herders to markets across states in India, following paths that are not determined by roads. These paths are congested during festivals such as Eid, when the demand for rams increases for the ritual sacrifice. In Senegal, herders from Mali bring in prized large rams for the ritual sacrifice called Tabazhki, and l'Aide in France. Goats circumvent visa regimes and quarantine as the need negates all borders. When the real goat is expensive or unavailable, a terracotta ram from nineteenth-century Mali is used for a symbolic sacrifice.

The Ebola crisis in West Africa caused politicians across the North Atlantic Treaty Organization to call for blanket bans on travel by West Africans to their countries. The myopia and racism of visa and political regimes that stretch from North America to Australia would have surely shocked Leonardo da Vinci, who had actually scripted a set of 15 books of drawings and writings on flight and movement. *The Codicos Atlanticos* were added as curatorial cues to an exhibition curated by the artist Nikhil Raunak for the Clark House Initiative. His exhibition *Tales between Borders* (2014) presented the possibility of art and artists enacting social change, or determining our most natural right: one that allows us to move.

The border has been India's most defining characteristic as a nation. The country has fought multiple wars with China and Pakistan on issues of border demarcation. It is also actively negotiating its territory in the Northeast with indigenous tribes that claim and demand self-determination, because they see these borders as residues of colonial conquests, not as natural associations with the Indian nation. Nikhil Raunak, whose father was a soldier serving in the Indian army, first had to overcome his inherent belief in nationalism, to begin discussing the propositions of the exhibition. He did so with a group of younger Indians who had not related their existence to the tensions thousands of miles away. Clark House then proposed insertions that were curatorial cues, either by other artists such as Ismaila Manga or Marije Gertenbach, or through objects that held histories, such as the clay sacrificial lamb from Mali. These insertions altered the context of the exhibition, allowing it to position itself within the context of border conflicts across the world. Specifically the borders that are now etched virtually on flight maps through visas and travel restrictions, or that play out across the Mediterranean and the English Channel, as deaths, televised debates, and rescues.

Clark House began in an old shipping office across two museums (the CSMVS Prince of Wales Museum and the

National Gallery of Art Bombay), and the art deco single-screen Regal cinema. This notion of in-between spaces reflects our positions on the materiality, political, and historical specificity, and the formats of diffusion of art. Informed by artists' practices and our own reading of exhibitions and cultural histories we propose alternate inheritances of art history and philosophy. The institution will not change; it shall always remain in a realm of inherent stable movement and that is the expected usefulness of such an extensive organization. Thus we are in sync with the institution as a gray scale.

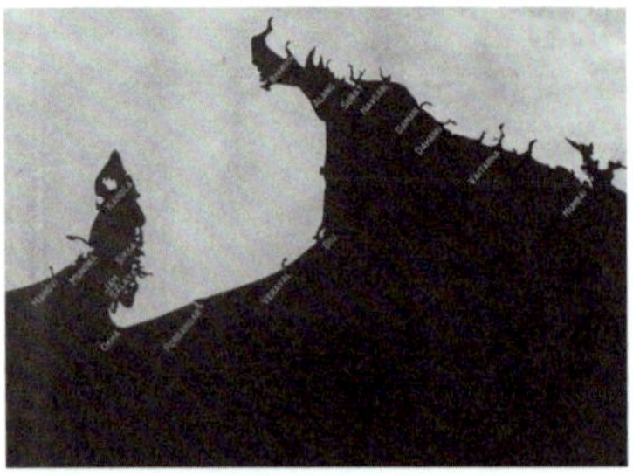

See pp. 254-255
Collaboration between CAMP and Clark House Initiative, *Country of the Sea*, 2015, (detail) solar-exposed cyanotype on cotton fabric, 5 × 16 feet, commissioned by Dr. Bhau Daji Lad Museum, Mumbai, for CAMP's exhibition *The Country of the Sea*

Inverting ideas of unity and abstraction, this work treats the ports along the coasts as cities of their own country. It brings the coast of Africa uncannily close to that of the Indian subcontinent. The work unfixes the land, and fixes the volatile sea instead, providing a visual metaphor for speaking of institutions, taking into account their own sense of stability from the perspective of movement and migration.

Digging into the Past to Unearth the Future

Hans Ulrich Obrist

In discussing the future of curatorial practice, the future of the institution is inevitably called into question. In searching for new possibilities, we should not only look to our present, or even toward the future, but also study the past, since there is an entire history of unrealized art institutions, which in their dormant state have the potential to inform what an institution of the twenty-first century could be.

The unrealized museum proposed by Édouard Glissant is one such example. Glissant (born in 1928 in Martinique, died in 2011 in France) was one of the most important writers and philosophers of the last century. His poems, novels, plays, and theoretical essays provide a 'toolbox' that I use every day in my praxis as a curator.

His idea for a museum in Martinique teaches us a great deal about the state of current institutional structures, and the risk of homogenizing forces of globalization. Glissant called attention to means of global exchange that do not homogenize culture, but instead produce a difference from which new things can emerge. At the beginning of his trajectory he was preoccupied with issues of national identity in view of colonial histories. This formed the subject of his first novel, *La Lézarde* (1958, published in English as *The Ripening* in 1959), in which he considered the blend of languages and cultures as a decisive characteristic of Antillean identity. His native Creole was formed from a combination of the languages of French colonial rule and African slaves; it contains elements of both, but it is itself something independent and unexpectedly new. On the basis of these insights, he later observed that there are similar cultural fusions all over the world, and he began to expand on the idea of creolization, applying it to a worldwide process of continuous intermixing. Glissant notes that "creolisation is a process which never stops," and it is this idea of continuous motion that links to his idea for an institution for the twenty-first century; its structure is informed by that of the fragmentation of the archipelago, not by the single mass of the continent.[1]

As a structural metaphor, the archipelago is highly significant for what we show; it is within this constellation of islands, and by extension, the blend of cultures, that the idea of creolization manifests itself. Archipelagic thought and practice make it impossible to identify any individual or collective body as fixed and finite. As Glissant says: "I can change through exchange with the other without losing or deluding my sense of self."[2] The geography of the archipelago is also important for Glissant. An archipelago has no center, but comprises a string of islands and cultures. Archipelagic thought, which endeavors to do justice to the world's diversity, is the antithesis of continental thought, which often lays claim to absoluteness and imposes its singular

1
Glissant, Édouard. *Mémoires des esclavages* (Paris: Gallimard / La Documentation française, 2007) p. 91.

2
Ibid.

worldview on others. Glissant coined his museum as an institution of *mondialité.* This word—*mondialité*—is difficult to translate into English. Suggestive of 'globality,' it reaffirms the forms of worldwide exchange regarding the thinking of what a public space can be, and how to facilitate diverse reflections through diverse experiences, but yet it recognizes and preserves diversity. Rather than disengaging from globalization completely, Glissant encourages the affects of feedback within local and global contexts. He asks how we can react to individual circumstances in such a way as to produce difference, as opposed to assimilation. The archipelago idea urges us to support smaller context-specific institutions for the twenty-first century.

The ideas of Glissant continue to be relevant to Paul B. Preciado's conception of the museum. Preciado's unrealized projects have more recently become an important touchstone for my investigation. As a format in itself, the exhibition has always been problematic for Preciado: the issue takes root in the lack of use-value in much of contemporary exhibition-making. Preciado questions how one can conceive of a de-colonial or anti-colonial exhibition format, in which we can develop actual usage. This idea extends to the institutions that house these exhibitions. In a conversation I had with Preciado and the artist Philippe Parreno, we discussed the question of what an institution of the twenty-first century could be, where an art museum would not only contain objects, but also quasi-objects (as defined by Michel Serres),[3] non-objects (live elements such as performance), and hyper-objects (in reference to the writings of Timothy Morton).[4]

A second and crucial outcome of this re-thinking of objecthood within the museum is the reconsideration of disciplines. We should rid ourselves of rigid classification, avoid the word 'interdisciplinary,' and instead talk about what Preciado refers to as different "intensities."[5] Within the context of the institution, the bringing together of different intensities generates a new set of relationships to bodies, and Preciado extends this connection to how an institution can consider our interaction with animals and the dead.

The threads that draw these examples together—art, politics, the idea of a counter-hegemonic practice, the archive, and education—all form a constellation of possibilities with which we can gain a new outlook on the future of the art institution. This idea of thinking through the spaces of an institution and resisting its homogenization marked the beginning of my practice as a curator. Rather than linking this particular relation to only space, however, I would like to also consider the homogenization of time.

The Russian art critic, patron, and ballet impresario Sergei Diaghilev is an important inspiration for this idea of curating in

3
Michel Serres, *The Parasite* (Minneapolis, MN: University of Minnesota Press, 2007).

4
Timothy Morton, *Hyperobjects: Philosophy and Ecology after the End of the World* (Minneapolis, MN: University of Minnesota Press, 2013).

5
Beatriz Preciado, *Testo Junkie: Sex, Drugs and Biopolitics in the Pharmacopornographic Era* (New York, NY: The Feminist Press at the City University of New York, 2013) p. 115.

time rather than in space. After years of organizing painting exhibitions, he moved away from an object-based practice, and connected the worlds of visual art and literature by bringing works by Picasso or Goncharova together with important literary figures. Diaghilev invited Anton Chekhov to edit a literary journal, while also working with Igor Stravinsky, whom he commissioned to write *The Rites of Spring* (1913). Most notably, Diaghilev invented his own institution, the Ballet Russes, which functioned between 1909 and 1929, and which, rather than operating out of a fixed location, moved all over the world in the form of a *Gesamtkunstwerk.*

The influence of Diaghilev was at the forefront of a project that I curated with Philippe Parreno in 2007, called *Il Tempo del Postino* (The Postman's Time) for the Manchester International Festival. Parreno and I discussed how art does not dictate the length of time a visitor stands in front of it, rather it is one of art's universal characteristics that it allows its audience their own control over time. With this in mind, *Il Tempo del Postino* was intended as a reversal of conventional modes of viewing, with the artists delivering their work to the viewer within a very specific timescale.

Following an introductory speech given by Parreno performing as a ventriloquist, a piece by Liam Gillick opened the show, and recurred at each of its intervals: a playerless piano on stage was accompanied by a recording of Gillick's attempt to play a Portuguese revolutionary song he had once heard from memory. The event continued with works by Matthew Barney & Jonathan Bepler, Trisha Donnelly, Dominique Gonzalez-Foerster and many more. In short, the project was an experiment for a time-based group exhibition within the live context of a festival.

Such examples question the pre-existing structures of exhibition-making in the twenty-first century. However, the issue of alternative forms of curatorial practice is not limited to single exhibitions, and I would like to discuss a new model for an institution that is in this respect in the process of being developed. Art collector, producer, and patron Maya Hoffmann invited Gillick, Parreno, and curators Tom Eccles, Beatrix Ruf, and myself, to form a group to plan an experimental art center with her, far from any capital city. The LUMA Foundation, a creation, production, and exhibition center specializing in contemporary art, is situated in Arles, in the marshland of France's Camargue, and represents Hoffman's goal to connect an art center to ecology. In 2012 we developed the exhibition *To the Moon via the Beach* within the ancient Roman amphitheater of Arles. This site had a charged, pre-existing function. For the duration of the exhibition the amphitheater was transformed: the arena was covered in mountains of sand from the beach, and then, little by little, formed into a moonscape which a team of sand sculptors. This work in progress acted as the backdrop for a series of interventions by twenty artists of different generations, who reacted to this shifting 'stage,' and produced works in and around the arena. At the end of the exhibition, all the sand was moved to Arles's Parc des Ateliers, a former railway construction site, which was accessible to the public as part of a temporary playground. It was then used once again in the foundations of the forthcoming LUMA center. As the philosopher Michel Serres once said, part of today's fundamental revolution within art could be to open oneself up to living species, to life, and to nature.[6] The LUMA Foundation was conceived with this very approach in mind: as an art center that was built from and maintains connections with the fabric and ecology of its surroundings.

The ideas underlying the LUMA project resonate with those of the English architect Cedric Price (1925-2003) and his unrealized architectural proposal of *The Fun Palace*. Conceived with the theater director Joan Littlewood as a 'laboratory of fun,' and a 'university of the streets,' *The Fun Palace* was imagined as a complex for cultural projects comprised of fixed and moving elements where ownership is less important. It would allow users to make their own decisions and to interact freely with the spaces of the institution. Price and Littlewood said: "A 21st century museum or art centre will utilise calculated uncertainty and conscious incompleteness to produce a catalyst for invigorating change."[7]

When I assumed the role of curator for the Swiss Pavilion at the 14th International Architecture Exhibition in 2014, and within the Biennale's context of re-examining the fundamentals of architecture over the past century, I focused the Swiss Pavilion on Price, and the Swiss sociologist Lucius Burckhardt (1934-2003), whose work resonates with and continues to inspire new generations. Both were serial inventors, and *The Fun Palace*, designed by Price and Littlewood as a transdisciplinary cultural center, is emblematic of our own era. It lends itself more to the choreography of twenty-first-century time-based exhibitions than to the object-based displays of the twentieth century; it fosters a more communal experience, largely free to operate outside its material limits, and ventures into other realms of human experience.

Among Burckhardt's many inventions, meanwhile, is that of Strollology, the science of going for a stroll, which he implemented at the University of Kassel. In his analysis of what marks an urban space, he went far beyond the facades or architecture of streets and squares, taking into account, for instance, the dirt in the neighborhood, or the darkness of the night. Design, he

6
Michel Serres, Interview with Hans Ulrich Obrist, in *032c*, No. 25, Winter 2013-2014.

7
Cedric Price, private interview with Hans Ulrich Obrist, 1997.

said, is invisible, and architecture must contemplate the environmental and social circumstances that outweigh the city resident's visible environment by far.

Few of Price and Burkhardt's buildings were realized, but their drawing practice constituted a tool for redefining architecture and remains as evidence of their ability to anticipate our contemporary times. Therefore I placed their archives at the center of the show in the Swiss pavilion. Through a variety of materials—photocopies, watercolors, sketches, and videos—the archives reflect not only their common ground, but also the profound difference between them: Price, as an architect, questioned the surrounding physical reality throughout his projects, while Burckhardt, as a sociologist, faced the need to change the 'now' by looking at categories of problems.

A dramaturgy—conceived by Tino Seghal, with Herzog & de Meuron, Lorenza Baroncelli, Atelier Bow Wow, Dominique Gonzalez-Foerster, Dorothea von Hantelmann, Philippe Parreno, and Asad Raza—enveloped Price and Burckhardt's production, selecting drawings from the archive and re-presenting them to the public. Jacques Herzog and Pierre de Meuron said of the exhibition, "The longer we worked on it and thought about it, the less 'physical' the exhibition concept became, so that, in the end, only Lucius and Cedric's mental universes were floating in space."

In response to the question of archiving and how architecture can be given a new life within a twenty-first-century art institution, we proposed the idea of an archive on wheels. At the start of the day the pavilion would be empty, but as more and more visitors entered the space, trolleys would be wheeled in with the aim of initiating an ongoing series of conversations. Over the six months of the Biennale, dozens of emerging researchers (knowledge assistants replacing museum guards) would activate this portable archive in ways that would not only engage the viewers in conversation, but would also engage their own practices and enable reflections through experience. This time-based choreographing of the space was fundamental to engendering a space in motion, whereby more unexpected layers were added across the duration of the project. A replica of *The Fun Palace* was put on wheels, as Price had always wanted it to be, and Burckhardt's mental universes were suspended in a dynamic presentation. A summer academy was organized by Lorenza Baroncelli and Stefano Boeri, and throughout the Biennale each day another group appropriated the pavilion and converted it into their own reality.

In an essay titled "Art and reality from the standpoint of cultural anthropology," from 1943, Margaret Mead writes:

[I]n primitive societies, the artist is not a separate person, having no immediate close relationship to the economic processes and everyday experiences of his society. The concept of the artist whose gift sets him apart, or who only becomes an artist because his life history has set him apart, is almost wholly lacking. The artist, instead, is the person who does best something that other people, many other people, do less well. His products, whether he be a choreographer or dancer, flutist or pot-maker, or carver of the temple gate, are seen as differing in degree but not in kind from the achievements of the less gifted among his fellow citizens. The concept of the artist as different in kind is fatal to the development of any adequate artistic form, which will satisfy all of the sensibilities [...] Our own Middle Ages as well as many great cultures of the past developed complete harmonious rituals that involved every type of sense experience and the concept of the artist and the related concept of fine arts are both special bad accidents of our own local.[8]

Through revisiting the anthropologist Mead's criticism of the exhibition, and by including an art historians reflecting *in vivo* on the experience of the exhibition, Von Hantelmann's text, produced during the exhibition, puts in question the relevance of this medium today. Denoted by its title—*Lucius Burckhardt and Cedric Price: A stroll through a fun palace*—the project was an attempt to create junctions, to explore the ritualized meeting points that can occur within the structure of a twenty-first-century art institution in motion.

One of Price's stipulations regarding his proposal for *The Fun Palace* was that its existence should be temporary. He felt that everything should have a limited life span, and that his model of an institution, if ever realized, should only exist for ten or twenty years. This notion of temporality as it relates to architecture is a crucial component of the Serpentine Galleries' annual pavilion commission. An art institution can be pictured structurally as a house: there is the moment when the foundations of the institution are set, and then throughout its lifetime additions take shape.

The pavilion commission is one of these additional wings to the Serpentine Galleries. Conceived in 2000 by Julia Peyton-Jones as a way in which the institution could continually reinvent itself, the pavilion commission began life with a temporary structure designed by Zaha Hadid. Since this point of inception, the project has continued a curatorial approach to commissioning architecture, a model of working with leading and emerging practitioners within this field in order to produce a temporary structure on the lawn outside the Serpentine Gallery in

8
Margaret Mead, "Art and Reality from the Standpoint of Cultural Anthropology," in "Art and Reality: A Symposium," George Boas, C. L. Watkins, and Margaret Mead, *Collage Art Journal*, Vol. 2, No. 4, May 1943, pp. 119-121.

Kensington Gardens. As Peyton-Jones comments: "The pavilion's temporality and extremely fast programme can provoke architects into experimentation and a deployment of public space. As well as being encapsulations of their creators' oeuvres, the pavilions can also act as a significant spur to the expansion of their ideas, while conventional buildings can often stifle ambition."[9] The commission was also intended to widen the scope of architectural innovation within England, which at the time was fairly insular.

When I joined the Serpentine Galleries in 2006 as Co-Director, Julia and I invited Rem Koolhaas with Cecil Balmond to design the pavilion of that year. The centerpiece of their design was an ovoid-shaped inflatable canopy that floated above the Gallery's lawn. Made from translucent material, the structure was illuminated from within at night. The canopy was raised into the air, or lowered to cover the amphitheater below, depending on the weather.

I believe that we need a Black Mountain College for the twenty-first century: a place where multiple disciplines are allowed to intersect. This would maintain the framework of a school, but within the context of an exhibition space or museum. This bringing together of disciplines, or intensities, as Preciado would say, informed the structure of the Serpentine Marathon, which began in 2006 in line with Koolhaas and Balmond's 'Speech Bubble' pavilion.

The first Marathon was based on the interview format, whereby Koolhaas and I interviewed practitioners from all over London in order to construct a partial portrait of the city. Starting at 6 pm one evening, and finishing 24 hours later, we interviewed individuals from a spectrum of fields and disciplines, from artists and writers to scientists and historians.

The following year we worked with Olafur Eliasson on the pavilion commission. He was key to rethinking the format of the 2007 Marathon; he believed that ultimately the event was still a conference and that we needed to hybridize its format further. His solution was to propose a time-based experiment whereby participants were given time to perform an experiment in public. Since Eliasson's Experiment Marathon, the two-day event has continued to evolve. In 2008 we staged the Manifesto Marathon. Both a gesture toward the nearby Speaker's Corner in Hyde Park, and an opportunity to question the value of the manifesto in the twenty-first century, this Marathon also marked the first collaboration with Eric Hobsbawm, who would become an advisor on subsequent Marathons. The Manifesto Marathon was followed by the Poetry Marathon in 2009, in Kazuyo Sejima and Ryue Nishizawa's pavilion. In 2010, the Map Marathon raised the issue of how we can conceive of

9
Julia Peyton-Jones, "Fast Forward Architecture," *Serpentine Gallery Pavilion 2005*; Designed by Alvaro Siza, Eduardo Souto De Moura with Cecil Balmond – Arup, ed. Melissa Larner (London: Serpentine Gallery and Trolley, 2005) pp. 34-35.

map-making within the digital age. This theme of the digital was continued with the 2011 Garden Marathon, where we looked at the differences between the Internet and the analog garden.

Memory Marathon in 2012 was the last project involving Hobsbawm, before he passed away. His important claim was that in our digital age we may think that there is more information, but this does not necessarily mean that there is more memory. Perhaps amnesia is the key danger in the age of the digital. This idea led to a collective protest against forgetting, with a diverse set of practitioners questioning the role of memory in the twenty-first century.

In 2013 we held the 89plus Marathon. Together with Simon Castets, I have begun an investigation charting the work of those born in or after 1989—the first generation to have grown up with the Internet, and which makes up half of the world's population. *89plus*, as we call the project, is a form of international research that follows the development of this generational shift through various platforms, including conferences, books, periodicals, and exhibitions. In twenty to thirty years' time—the intended duration of the project—we are very interested to see how their practices will have developed in the course of time. One of the big questions of the twenty-first century is how to foster collective action. In the age of the Internet the potential to join, to come to shared engagement, is there, so we consider what that would mean in relation to display.

Castets and I decided on residencies as a way of supporting emerging artists from all over the world in a more sustained way. The *89plus* project is not about predicting future creation, but rather about bringing together individuals whose voices are only starting to be heard. So far 5,000 artists from all over the world have responded to our open call, and uploaded information about their respective practices onto our platform. Since we started in 2013, we have also conducted on-site research in Hong Kong, Singapore, and Cape Town. Wherever we go, we interview local practitioners, and then develop public panels out of our conversations. This February, in Cape Town, we developed one for the annual design conference INDABA (meaning 'business' or 'meeting' in Zulu). One of the panelists, artist Bogosi Sekhukhuni, had previously never left South Africa for very long, so we invited him to do a residency in Paris, where he could develop his video diary and make other work. Right now, he is working on a film about his ancestors who fought against the Boers, and his time at the Google Cultural Institute allows him access to the technology he needs for research and production.

The Internet has caused a crisis of representation, dislocating the experience and curatorship of art from the sacred space of the gallery or the museum, but moreover, altering the relationships of time and space. Another consequence is the algorithmic control of the 'filter bubble'—the recommendation systems utilized by online companies whereby users become stuck in a static, ever-narrowing version of themselves. It prevents users from being exposed to any information that might be in disagreement with their viewpoints, de facto isolating them within a coherent ideological environment, what Eli Pariser, who coined this concept, calls a personal ecosystem. For Pariser, the power of these mechanisms goes against the original nature of the web, which was supposed to stimulate openness, now instead generating closed systems of knowledge, harmful to both society and individuals. We have observed through the *89plus* research that many artists are critically addressing this concept of the filter bubble. The condition was underlined, for instance, in the work of young filmmakers and artists using moving images such as Sarah Abu Abdallah, Darja Bajagić, Bogosi Sekhukhuni, Simon Lässig, or Valia Fetisov.

For the *89plus* generation, questions of display and community become fundamental, while we are aware that the role of the digital is just beginning to be explored in the world of exhibitions. What we intend to achieve through our project is to understand how traditional notions of authorship and cultural heritage are changing. Many of these artists have an instant technological understanding and technological know-how at their fingertips, and rely on different social platforms to showcase new ideas and culturally iconoclastic approaches. We are already starting to witness visionary acts of digital curating, and the field of curating will surely change as a generation native to digital tools begins to develop new formats.

By listening to this generation that has grown up in an entirely new world, we can learn something about our future twenty-first-century art institutions. As John Kenneth Galbraith wrote, "Change comes not from men and women and their minds, but it comes from the change from one generation to the next."[10] If we believe in this assumption, how can we track, document and present such change? But also, what are the implications outside of the art world? Can we, in addition, help a new generation take advantage of their special and historic circumstances? These are the questions that our *89plus* project explores, while bringing together individuals whose places of origin are as different as their practices.

One of the things we can learn from this generation is their multidimensional ability, and it's not a coincidence many of the

10
John Kenneth Galbraith, *Money: Whence It Came, Where It Went* (Boston, MA: Houghton Mifflin, 1975) p. 231.

89plus artists mention Etel Adnan as an influence. Adnan originally wanted to be an architect, or rather an urbanist, but when the Lebanese civil war interrupted her studies, she became one of the greatest poets of our time. Her poetry led to her plays, and incredible novels, like *Sitt Marie-Rose* (1977), which is one of the most profound books about the civil war in Lebanon. She also wrote *The Arab Apocalypse* (1989), a book of poems showing that war is the worst form of extinction, and it announces many more wars to come. Her small landscape paintings, often of Mount Tamalpais, near Sausalito, in Northern California, however, are much less dark. She has always had this dream of getting her art into the world in a Bauhaus kind of way, so she also makes murals and textile works, works with craft, and as a filmmaker.

Today there is an urgent need to bring together the many dimensions in which art can manifest itself, and Adnan provides an example in bringing us her cartographies, drawings, films, leporellos, notebooks, novels, paintings, plays, poems, political journalism, tapestries, and teaching. Adnan sees public art as a way to humanize the environment, and these works form therefore an important part of her oeuvre. In her own words: "Decent or beautiful public work is democratic because even a poor person can walk in a beautiful environment and have his spirit uplifted. We painters do an elitist type of work; nevertheless it has its place because it's intellectual and spiritual. But we badly need public works."

In a discussion of the future of curatorial practice, specifically as it relates to the art institution, the question of extinction is particularly resonant. Gustav Metzger told us that "as artists we need to take a stand against the ongoing erasure of species, even when there is little chance of ultimate success. It is our privilege and our duty to be at the forefront of the struggle. While humanity has moved through extreme crises in the past, time and speed are of the essence."[11] Metzger felt that if we talk about climate change rather than extinction, nothing will ever change, and it was due to this urgency that the Serpentine Extinction Marathon was developed as a platform from which to call for political and social change. This was not only an opportunity to address the extinction of species, but it was also concerned with the extinction of language and cultures. To return to Édouard Glissant's words, it is the forces of globalization that lead to a flattening out of diversity; the production of difference is stunted and homogeneity dominates.

The process-based approach to programming that is embedded within all of the Serpentine Marathons, as diverse as their subjects may be, is indicative of the extended and ongoing nature of these projects. In relation to my purposes in this text, it

11
Gustav Metzger, 2014.

raises the important question of how, in the twenty-first century, we can develop possibilities within institutions that have what Fernand Braudel calls a *longue durée*.[12] Within the current structure of museums there is an implicit temporality to exhibition-making. I believe this structure should be replaced by a longevity and continued engagement with artists and ideas that counteracts the instantaneity, which characterizes a lot of the current models of programming.

We began with a consideration of models from the past, notably Glissant's conception of a museum in Martinique, and how such alternatives could inform a contemporary reworking of an institution for the future. The documentary filmmaker Adam Curtis argues that today we live in a static culture. We are obsessed with going back to the past and recycling it in a way that is both unimaginative and damaging. In the context of the digital age, our ability to record, archive, and access an unknowable plethora of information is leading to a fossilization rather than a renewal. We have become cannibals, obsessed with the past and terrified of transgressions from established conventions.[13]

This process of becoming stuck implies that we are not able to access the future. Within the frame of Curtis's vision of contemporary world stasis, the institution becomes a graveyard, the curator nothing but a macabre gravedigger slowly disintegrating the past. But it is through examples such as Glissant's museum of *mondialité*, or through the productive feedback loops that Price and Littlewood envisaged with *The Fun Palace*, that we could begin to not only envisage an alternative future, but also escape from our static state and find a way to access it.

12
Fernand Braudel, "Histoire et sciences sociales: La longue durée," in *Annales. Histoire, Sciences Sociales*, Vol. 13, No. 4, October 1958, pp. 725-753.

13
Rob Pollard, "Adam Curtis: We don't read newspapers because the journalism is so boring," *The New Statesman*, February 14, 2014, available online at http://www.newstatesman.com/culture/2014/02/adam-curtis-interview (accessed November, 2015).

In Search of a Flashlight: The Intimate Politics of the Curatorial

Vivian Ziherl

Preface

Capital curates the aesthetic at an intensifying global scale, but not without regional particularities and counter circulations.[1] Across tiered, cross-contaminating art worlds, differing forms of capital pursue differing ideals of art.[2] Curators are among those who moderate these form-giving processes through the pragmatic means of production.

Contemporary art discourse tends to self-substantiate through theoretical rhetorics, often resulting in a disciplinary space that has a weak critical purchase for procedural knowledge. Concurrent with shifts among the Euro-American left, post-1989 contemporary art often prefers to be justified 'in theory.' The priority of business imperatives and the neoliberal consensus is routinely challenged critically, less often in practice.

In a similar vein, Fred Moten and Stefano Harney call upon Fredric Jameson to stress the paradox of academic dependence upon "Enlightenment-type critiques and demystification of belief and committed ideology, in order to clear the ground for unobstructed planning and 'development.'"[3]

Amid these trajectories, Curatorial Studies has emerged as a quasi-academic discipline concurrent with the expansion of the American university model in its debt-restructured mode. Scholarly and professional platforms seek to build curatorial/exhibitions historiographies, regional area studies, and disciplinary critique simultaneously. This in itself need not be a problem. What remains backgrounded in rehearsed academic forms such as the conference is the nature of the discipline as a labor bloc in the first instance. Crudely put, something like a curatorial class-consciousness is needed—as 'curatoriat,' as a self-critiquing 'curatocracy,' or complex version thereof. What follows is in effect a pamphlet drafted toward a public lecture among curators in late 2014. These preface notes are included in re-considering the original text, which has been re-worked in order to transcribe its intentionally performative invective.

The text comprises roughly three parts. The opening segment stakes a claim toward curating understood in the era of what Angela Mitropoulos has called "intimate self-management."[4] Its style is intentionally performative, referencing testimonies of the 1904 Congress of the Second Internationale to stress a break from the cultivated curatorial persona.

The second part derives from conversations that arose around research of artist Susanne M. Winterling into the early 1940s correspondence between novelist Carson McCullers and the journalist Anne-Marie Schwarzenbach.[5] In spirit it also draws upon Leela Ghandhi's narration of dissident collaborations through British-Indian friendships during the fin de siècle.[6]

1
The formulation of the post-1989 curation of the aesthetic is borrowed directly from an interview with poet, researcher, and critic Rachel O'Reilly, who casts this frame in pointing to the particularization of imperial processes needed to make meaningful museological and contemporary art interest in 'decolonization' as a concept-metaphor. The reference is from Part 1 of the interview, available online at http:// www.internationaleonline.org/opinions/74_what_do_we_talk_about_when_we_talk_about_decolonisation_part_1 (accessed October 3, 2015)

2
In mind here is Elizabeth A. Povinelli's discussions of the world-making and form-producing effects of circulatory systems. See "Routes/Worlds," *e-flux Journal*, No. 27, 2011. Available online at http://www.e-flux.com/journal/routesworlds/ (accessed October 3, 2015) In addition see Goankar and Povinelli, "Technologies of Public Forms: Circulation, Transfiguration, Recognition," *Public Culture*, Vol. 15, No. 3, 2003, pp. 385-397.

3
Fredric Jameson, *Late Marxism: Adorno, or, the Persistence of the Dialectic* (London: Verso, 1990), p. 43, quoted in Fred Moten and Stefano Harney, "The University and the Undercommons: Seven Theses," *Social Text* 79, Vol. 22, No. 2, Summer 2004.

4
Mitropoulos develops this concept as a means to locate transformations in the social contract amid the eroding boundaries between domestic and public spheres and the coercive organization of capitalist futurity, examined through the shifting politics of the household. See Angela Mitropoulos, *Contract and Contagion: From Biopolitics to Oikonomia* (New York, NY: Minor Compositions, 2012).

5
A small facsimile publication of the remaining letters was published in 2014 with Kunstverein Amsterdam, with a preface by Susanne and myself. The publication was accompanied by the exhibition *Complicity*, featuring works by painter Romaine Brooks, and architect and designer Eileen Grey.

The closing salvo of the third part should not be mistaken as an argument for male, female, hetero/homosexual/queer as generalizable curatorial categories. The point is rather to address—in the most literal way—the intimate politics of curation.

The text was written against a backdrop of instances where artists collectivized to demand financial-ethical accountability, such as those at the Biennale of Sydney and the São Paulo Biennale.[7] The alignment and intervention of curators (or lack thereof) influenced the unfolding and aftermath of such campaigns profoundly. A scrupulous Curatorial Studies may locate within these controversies knowledge of the multiple actors that express curatorial oversight, as well as a more compelling account of the artist/curator relationship than that of an embattled dialectic of control versus autonomy.

The arrangements of state and private interests that finance contemporary art vary across contexts. These are to be assessed within the light of ongoing imperial and anti-colonial projects. Research reflecting upon non-metropolitan art and curatorial histories has done much to critically historicize 'the contemporary' as a non-neutral periodizing term.[8] Efforts of agreement-making and protocol-drafting may also offer much in learning of how regional and circulatory legacies produce current asymmetric conditions of curatorial decision-making that are in turn conditioning—of and conditioned—by the work of artists, among others.

Abstract

"There is no need to fear or hope, but only to look for new weapons," posits Gilles Deleuze in his "Postscript on Societies of Control."[9] But what if the best new weapons are old ones in disguise? Drawing upon recent work with the Dutch horizontal feminist institution If I Can't Dance, I Don't Want To Be Part Of Your Revolution, conjecture around the notion of 'aesthetic solidarity' with artist Susanne M. Winterling, and research into the global imaginaries of the Australian frontier for IMA Brisbane—this presentation will attempt to posit a set of practices that may yet support the rebellious desires of the working curator.

Scene 1: A Congress of Curators

As a certain preamble, I am going to read from a book that was recently given to me by the artist, poet, and activist Gregg Bordowitz. It is called *Flashlights of the Amsterdam Congress* by Daniel de Leon, and it was published by the New York Labor News Company in 1929.

De Leon was a Curaçao-born Dutch-American lawyer, and later co-founder of the International Workers of the World who had attended the Sixth Congress of the Second International. His 'Flashlights' are subjectively written recollections of

6
Leela Gandhi, *Affective Communities: Anticolonial Thought, Fin-de-Siècle Radicalism, and the Politics of Friendship* (Durham, NC: Duke University Press, 2006).

7
Both boycott efforts concerned the question of political accountability through arts funding—regarding offshore detention of asylum seekers in Australia, and BDS compliance during the period of the Gaza bombardment respectively. However, they differ in terms of the constituency of their action and the vexed matter of intersecting local and internationalist priorities. A discussion of the São Paulo campaign by curator Galit Eilat appears in this volume. A discussion of the Biennale of Sydney campaign from local and international standpoints is available via the Melbourne-based journal *Discipline* here: http://www.discipline.net.au/biennale-of-sydney-2014-and-transfield/ (accessed October 13, 2014) as well as a commentary by *Discipline* editor Helen Hughes here: http://blog.frieze.com/on-the-boycott-of-the-2014-biennale-of-sydney/ (accessed October 13, 2014).

8
An excellent and prescient example of this is Indian critic and curator Geeta Kapur's address to the Third Havana Biennale in 1989. See Geeta Kapur, "Contemporary Cultural Practice: Some Polemical Categories," in *Making Art Global (Part 1): The Third Havana Biennial 1989*, eds. Rachel Weiss *et al.* (London: Afterall, 2011).

9
Gilles Deleuze, "Postscript on Societies of Control," *October*, Vol. 59, Winter 1992, pp. 3-7

speeches made in the Congressional committee. As transcribed notations the short texts capture the instant of public address and highlights above all else the 'character' of the delegates.

In his preamble de Leon stresses that to understand a speech requires an understanding of the speaker's language and literature, and he considers at length the question of "Sentiment as Force" within the dynamics of the Internationale.

The glimpses of these flashlights afford the insight that within such structures of public representation the work of politics is performed as much as it is reasoned. Likewise the fate of becoming a caricature of one's own intentions is an unavoidable and often humorous fact. For example, de Leon notes:

> *Van Koll's speech sounded as he looks, dull and bovine. His face had no more expression when he speaks than a pitcher of water when the water is flowing out. Indeed the only time during the whole congress when I noticed an expression on his face was when he got through reeling of his speech and Mrs Clara Zeitken of the German delegation was rendering a German translation thereof.*
>
> *Ms Zeitken is the exact opposite of Van Koll. Dull and Bovine as he is, she bubbles over with animal spirit. Into whatever she translated, even if it was a motion to adjourn, she threw the fire of thrilling impassioned declamation.*

[Pause]

> Let us not be mistaken comrades; we live in a time of high crypto-fascism. Not since the robber barons of the 1820s has the world witnessed such uncompromising, illegitimate power concentrated through the vector of raw wealth. Yet the aggressive capitalists of our time do not merely accumulate bullion and push the wheels of its machinery into overdrive, they sit astride a disaggregated systemic construct that alienates labor not only from its products, but also from itself at the most profound and subjective level.
>
> As capital becomes massively mobile, through the abstractions of finance, the territorial and vertical band of the ethico-juridical nation-state narrows and becomes evermore rigid, militarized, and prone to purges and violent acts of exclusion. We see the evidence: the asylum seekers abandoned in their attempts to reach Europe and my own Australia; the expulsion of the poor from access to the means of health and welfare through austerity reform; the agitation of separatist struggles in Hong Kong, Kurdistan, Palestine,

and Catalunya, to name a few; the dispiriting post-'Spring' regimes of the Levant and the Maghreb; the conservative governments of celebrated democracies such as India, Australia, Canada, and Turkey.

Comrades, I fear truly that within our near future the hatred currently fueled by extractive injustice will show its true face. Perhaps this will have a silver lining. Perhaps at this point our foe will become locatable, tangible, defeatable. In the meantime we drift in the serpentine flows of power described by Deleuze in his 1992 article in *October* magazine, "Postscript on Societies of Control." A 'generalized crisis' exists in the transition from the disciplinary to the control society, argued Deleuze therein, as—despite collectivized social bids for emancipation from the eighteenth- and nineteenth-century enclosures of the hospital, the school, the barracks, and the prison—these structures have instead disarticulated into modular flows of pernicious instrumentalizing power, at once decentralized and yet ever more hegemonic. As scholar Gayatri Chakravotry Spivak has so incisively remarked: "Globalisation takes place only in capital and data. Everything else is damage control."[10]

It is at this juncture that I make my intervention—a plea to take good care of one another. To dust off this maimed, near-abandoned notion of the left: 'solidarity.' To radicalize, reformulate, re-inhabit it. For us to practice solidarity *every time* as a first resort, and *always* as a committed response to conditions of uncertainty. But what might it mean—for us, the humble curatoriat—to practice 'solidarity'?

[Pause]

Scene 2: On Aesthetic Solidarity

In 1940, in New York, at an evening of drinks hosted by the literary family of the Manns, the Swiss journalist Anne-Marie Schwarzenbach (1908-1942) and the American novelist Carson McCullers (1917-1967) had a chance encounter. Although they would never meet again, a strong bond was forged, and thereafter followed a chain of correspondence that continued until Schwarzenbach's untimely death in 1942.

It is clear throughout their exchange of letters that to categorize these only as 'love letters' is to radically foreclose their potential value to us now. They are not so much offering each other their 'hearts' so much as their strength and endurance in carrying on the work of committing truths to paper through their literature, and this despite the quite unbearable nature of their surrounds.

10 Gayatri Chakravorty Spivak, *An Aesthetic Education in the Era of Globalization* (Cambridge, MA: Harvard University Press, 2013).

Both struggled to sustain queer lives and relationships, and both were in regions of extreme structural racism. Shortly after their meeting McCullers returned from New York to her home of Georgia in the segregated South, and Schwarzenbach traveled to colonial Belgian Congo where she contributed to writing the global histories of the Euro-Centered 'World War' in her dispatches to the *Zürcher Zeitung.*

[Pause]

I am proposing here that—as we have heard, the school, the expo pavilion, the opera could be a model for curating—the relational correspondence of Anne-Marie Schwarzenbach and Carson McCullers could be taken just as well as our example for curatorial practice.

I make these remarks at a time when the traditional modern bonds of the factory floor are systematically obstructed—and to a population of workers whose self-insularization, self-instrumentalization, and self-precaritization are exemplary among professions.

And so we may ask—what is it to be in 'aesthetic solidarity'? What is to be allied through the effortful project of enduring the subjective experiences of injustice, and of transcribing these through the medium of the self into material form? How might an 'aesthetic solidarity' be summoned in a time of dematerialization and fragmentation of labor relations such as we are seeing currently?

Here Gayatri Spivak's return to Schiller's *Letters on the Aesthetic Education* (1756-1763) may offer a useful elaboration. Schiller—observing the radical redefinition of Empire undertaken in his time—has cause to note that "A revolution does not last in the absence of subjects trained in the practice of freedom."[11] In response, Spivak argues that this amounts to a "training of the imagination for epistemic performance," incisively summarized as "the habit of the ethical."[12]

Spivak most expressly situates this need in the time of Globalization—which she claims has "rendered obsolete the historical ways of knowing things."[13] In terms of curatorial histories there are a number things that can be footnoted here regarding an aforementioned de-neutralization of 'the contemporary,' and of what it might mean to become perceptive toward third-worldist and non-aligned histories.

11 *Ibid.*

12 *Ibid.*

13 *Ibid.*

And so I posit this concept of Aesthetic Solidarity, as a mode of poetic relation—to borrow from Édouard Glissant—gained through practice and profound self-investment. As an orientation that activates the ethical impulse, and that is—I feel—essential to curatorial practice.

I would argue that the ethical sense must be one of those activated and excited, in the Kantian meaning of the aesthetic as excitation, or quickening.

[Pause]

Scene 3: Feminism After Feminism

I'd like to introduce myself a bit further.

I live in Amsterdam, but grew up in Brisbane, Australia. I am a butch-femme, 31-year-old, DTF, versatile, HIV-negative, witch-pagan, Caucasian, cis-gendered woman.

My status is tired, overworked, angry, willful, determined, happy, grateful.

I am grateful for the traditions that I stand within, for a lineage of radical queers, and a venerable history of lesbian parrhesia that I am attempting to speak within today.

I stand within a tradition of women of the antipodes, and with the legacy of reckoning with this history and its ongoing imperial processes.

I *attempt* to speak in these traditions. I borrow from Fred Moten in noting such an effort is aspirational—it means that, when all is said and done I hope, I desire that the results might be counted toward these collectivities.

A queer-feminist politics resides exactly with the problems of desire. Of the processes of reckoning and self-truth that are demanded in coming to terms with desiring other than what is given. Do we—as the curatoriat—desire the status quo? How can we act as desiring curators?

This is our task. This we must attempt together. It is very good that we can come together and discuss BDS, but until we can discuss BDSM we have not yet begun...

[Pause]

I am blessed to work within a structurally feminist institution. It is called If I Can't Dance, I Don't Want To Be Part Of Your Revolution. It is named after the Lithuanian-born anarchist Emma Goldman. It was initiated by a joint effort among three women, and remains at base an institution premised in linkages.

I will briefly parse the institutional structure.[14] If I Can't Dance, I Don't Want To Be Part Of Your Revolution currently functions through two-year commissioning cycles called editions. In effect this gives the organisation a temporal rather than a physical architecture. Each edition is led by a thematic focus such as 'Theatricality,' 'Feminism, its Legacies and Potentials,' 'Masquerades,' 'Affect,' or the current 'Appropriation and Dedication.' This thematic guides the process of commissioning four new works by artists, and four new 'Performance in Residence' projects, which support an open and eccentrically conceived notion of research. There is a reading group that ties things together and forms a spine for this ongoing work.

Without the physical architecture of a gallery or presentation space each commission confronts a suite of fundamental questions anew: What should it be? Where should it be? Should it be a book, a film, a theater performance, something in public space? If a performance, should it be in partnership with Tate Modern, or with the Stedelijk Museum? Should it be in a theater, or should it be in the basement of a half-constructed building in the South of Amsterdam? In this way the institution constitutes a process of constant linkage, relationship building, and recalibration among institutional rates of exchange.

It is an institution based upon relational binds, on trust, upon relationships, and we are constantly subject to guest/host dynamics. However, like any organism unorthodox to its holding environment, If I Can't Dance... experiences allergic reactions. It suffers from the burden of self-explanation that classically marks difference.

Conventionally curatorial authorship is read toward architecture in the bricks-and-mortar sense—and as such If I Can't Dance... is vulnerable in terms of recognition and credit. It happens not altogether infrequently that commissions we have so tenderly nurtured over two years are attributed to our host institutions. Sometimes host institutions overlook accurate credits within communications documents. Sometimes event institutions decline to amend these when asked, and argue word-length, publication deadlines or other reasons.

[Pause]

I want to argue that the practice of aesthetic solidarity—in our profession and in general—is very much a matter of small things.

14
An expanded discussion and particular consideration of the temporal arrangement of the organization was published in Paul O'Neill and Mick Wilson, *Curating Research*, (London: Open Editions, 2015).

It is the perpetual effort of self-work: upholding the ethical habit. As desiring curators we may consider what a curatorial problem is. For example, the mystery of the ongoing demographic lack of 'great women artists.' To this I think we all know the truth. Beyond all the barriers of gender representation lies the unspoken libidinal economy of curating. You know it, you've experienced it, you've probably been complicit in it—but I will spell it out nonetheless.

As a female artist: one is structurally positioned as a potential object of desire for a male curator, and in competition with women artists and curators, for the attentions of male artists and curators.

As a male artist: one is positioned as a fraternal colleague to male curators, and as a possible subject of desire to female curators.

There is an entire well-networked Euro-American demimonde of gay male artists, curators, critics, and collectors based upon such libidinal flows and exchanges.

As a lesbian, things remain much as Queen Victoria is claimed to have put it: one hardly exists.

It is in this kind of practice that our solidarity will find its form—in quasi-events, to borrow loosely from Elizabeth A. Povinelli. In hastily made decisions, dashed-off emails, and their consequences. What I am calling for is a constant and purposive effort.

Women: if you feel yourself moving into competition with a female colleague, artist or curator, in the presence of a powerful man—struggle against it; perhaps name it to each other, de-link from it.

Men: if you find yourself mentally framing a woman artist in condescending or dismissing terms if she perhaps appears demure or coquettish, refuse this within *your*self; support and mirror a confident, intellectually driven attitude in the women you are dealing with.

Gay men—women who aren't divas aren't invisible.

This is an epistemic performance. These are effortful acts of shifting within our curatorial day-to-day struggle, led first by that imagination of the otherwise that—as arts workers—is supposed as our stock in trade.

The author would like to thank the artists Anjalika Sagar, Suzanne Winterling, Greg Bordowitz, and Jonas Staal, as well as scholar Rosalind Morris for their generosity in the preparation of this text.

Qalqalah: Falling out of Memory

Sarah Rifky

The First Part, a Story

In keeping with time, before I tell you a story and talk about the future, let us travel back to the past. Let us go back to Cairo in January 1977. The capital is on fire and the Egyptian Bread Riots are rippling through the city. They are tearing the liberal policies of Sadat's *infitah* to pieces. In a small apartment in Giza, a woman, a poet, not particularly religious, wakes up from her sleep. Placing one hand on her five-months-old bump, she whispers a few words to dispel nagging spirits. She was visited by the prophet in her sleep. In the dream he said, "Give your child a good name." A good name does not necessarily mean a name with a good meaning, but, more importantly, a name that would ensure a good and prosperous future. The first act of language is always that of giving a name. This child is born. She gives her child a name: Qalqalah.

It is worth noting that Qalqalah grows up to become an artist, but this account is not about that. We are interested in what happens a long time after she was born. In 2048 Qalqalah turns 71. She is an unusual woman in all respects. It all started with the name she was given. Qalqalah, a very Arabic sounding word, is not a name; it is a motion in language, a phonetic vibration, a bounce or an echo, over certain letters of the Arabic scripture that make up the words 'Kt Bgd'—in colloquial slang, in Egyptian dialect that is, the words would mean 'a cat for real.'

Although it is easy to understand how Qalqalah came to be an artist (in the context she found herself in, the type of family she was brought up in) no one can historically determine exactly when art as a vocation, as we understood it in 2014, became obsolete. Some argued that everyone had become an artist, or no one was, but neither of these things really matters. The pressing question is: When did art as art cease to exist? It is vaguely said to have been around the 2030s, shortly after the economy had finally and completely collapsed. The collapse was more of a systematic meltdown, felt and accepted, and didn't come with a bang or a boom or a clearly identifiable event. The fact of the future was that the economy, predicted for so long to collapse, had collapsed. Finally. The unimaginable had finally arrived, and with it the order of the world changed radically, much faster than anyone could have imagined possible.

Qalqalah now lives in the United Arab World, a conglomerate of corporations, where as a citizen she takes up her place as a linguist, serving the greater good of UAW (often pronounced by Arabic speakers as: WOW, which also signified the letter *waw*). The *waw* is the twenty-seventh letter of the Arabic alphabet, of the *abjadiya*. It represents the number six and belongs to the element of air. It symbolizes the mystical promise of total assent, and it denotes the universal aspect of the whole according to some mystics. Already in the eleventh century, Ibn al-Arabi gives quite some attention to *waw* in a booklet dealing with the letters *waw*, *meem*, and *nuun*. We find out that *waw*, a letter, is the first perfect number. By other sheikhs we are told that *waw* corresponds to the quality of dying when you are still alive, which, of course, is part of the message.

Ten centuries later, in the twenty-first century, linguists and translators have found a good place in the new social scheme of UAW. This is an unexpected turn of things; who would have thought that linguists and translators would be well-compensated positions in this future, which I speak to you in present tense? Not only that, but to work with words, and words as numbers, are skills that are held in high regard in the era of new corporations. Qalqalah had been lucky; as a young person she hadn't opted to study languages, but she was naturally attuned to many, having grown up with six. Qalqalah's parents were both poets, and she had married into a family of librarians, from the former Kingdom. In her old age Qalqalah regrets never having had children, like many of her generation, but she thinks of every word she speaks as giving birth to new meaning.

In the winter of 2048, Qalqalah is invited to attend a closed meeting at the prestigious University of the Future Post-Sense (UF-PS). The university is situated in a former parliamentary building in a town that was once known as Bern in Switzerland. The overhaul of the school into a sort of think tank was part of the larger education reform movement on a continental scale, and was meant to ensure that those schools and universities didn't shut down following the economic collapse of the early 2030s. Universities realigned themselves with new corporate bodies with the promise that they would bring in returns on investment pretty quickly.

This is a time when philosophy is prized for bringing in fast results and where ideology is incubated, as it has failed to simply emerge in the previous decades, despite ongoing political tumult and hyper-action. The closed convention Qalqalah is invited to is one in a series organized worldwide. She often declines invitations for events where she finds herself bored with the lack of imagination of the scholars and researchers present... In her eighth decade of life, she finds that pretty much anything that was worth saying has already been said. The effect of recycling language is tiresome to her ears. Qalqalah has lived through a lot. Organizers of such conventions are often younger avid types who have no memory of a past, but sense something akin to nostalgia for it.

It is true of people born in the 2000s that they have a different experience of memory; they are an entirely different type of human altogether. Save for those who were born into families of time separatists and idealists, who had tried to extract themselves from the system, which were very few. The younger generations had very short attention spans, and, contrary to what one would imagine, they continuously made up human life; they had no real connection to narrative. Whereas in previous decades the premise of being human was based on a continual history, narrative mimesis, and the ability to retell one's life in stories, now narrative is produced in the instant, and it disappears as soon it speaks.

Organizers of the convention are interested in Qalqalah, as she is a first-hand witness to the early waves of uprising and recounted revolutions and occupy movements in the early 2010s and 2020s. She has lived through regional wars, and was part of the dissident movements that caused the collapse of the nation-state system in the Eastern hemisphere in her youth. Not that much good had come out of that. But, like many people at this time, Qalqalah has trouble recollecting memories of her past. Suffering from attention disorders, narrative fatigue, and spiritually struggling with psychotic breaks means that Qalqalah isn't as lucid as we are today, in 2014. Or maybe one could say she is more lucid, just in a way that disagrees with post-1950s psychiatry. For the Bern convention, she is tasked with piecing together something that resembles a political narrative, a type of history, of the political time cracks since 2010.

She is useful to the world because she is a survivor, and a thinking witness to revolutions and uprisings that preceded the imagined yet unpredictable collapse of the nation-states in the early 2030s. This sounded familiar. Qalqalah herself, like many of her generation, has trouble recollecting memories of her past. She suffers from attention disorders, mental fatigues, and, like many of her generation, spiritually struggles with repeated psychotic breaks. Didn't we already say this before? At the meeting she is tasked with piecing together a coherent narrative of political changes in former Egypt. She struggles to remember a distant past beyond the hyper-capital conglomerate of the new United Arab World.

The conference in 'Bern' draws on conscious and unconscious thought and behavior, paving the economy toward a post-linguistic future. Qalqalah is suspicious of institutions, yet thrives on language. She has an innate understanding that there is no future post-language, which she developed as the daughter of polyglot poets and in her brief marriage into a family of librarians. On the fringes of the conference, she finds herself among a self-proclaimed group of 'monolingual activists' from the Indo-European worlds. She attends their meetings and embarks on a set of impossible questions about the future of a region. Is a political paradigm shift possible through a rediscovery of other languages? Is speaking more than one language a form of treason masked as knowledge?

Speaking so many languages, it is impossible to think, she thinks. To think in her native Arabic father-tongue, Qalqalah has to unlearn her other glossal skills. She has an inkling that if she sets out to investigate linguistic facts and little known secrets of the Arabic language, in its chronographic dimension, it would be possible to approach the future differently. Arabic allegedly does not have a future tense. What does it mean for a language not to encompass a future in speech? And what are the political implications of introducing new tenses to old languages?

If we had more time, we would find out about Qalqalah's travels, memories, and thought between the future-present and the present-past. About how she studies the fundamental forms, the shapes of the letters of the Arabic alphabet, and their corresponding quantitative values, where the quality of meaning is in fact encrypted in numbers, but for now we have to move to the second part.

The Second Part, a Picture of a Story

This picture is meta-pragmatic: here talk talks about talk, about an echo of sound in talk, which tells us about language, and, ultimately, about what language is, namely, an age-old institution, if not the first. Qalqalah, like all women in language, is followed. Readers and scholars will follow her into the annals of history; they will dust off memories and file away reason, in an effort to recover political hope. I am often gripped by the realization that the effort of preserving and reviving the past might soon be replaced with something else. How does this affect our earthly desire? Every effort of writing is marked by something otherworldly, a yearning that draws the ghosts of old stories into the ones we are writing now. Every effort of exhibition-making is the same, always determined by past artworks forming indices and traps for everything that is yet to be made.

Digressions often form the thesis of a work. I wanted you to read about Qalqalah. I wanted to create a word-image of this phonetic action and motion. I wanted you to regard her name as an occupation of a set of letters in language, lingering vibration, voiced. She is a character of our present, more than the future. She looks back from the future onto our present, and we follow her glances. She stops, and we imagine a revolution in time. Revolution. When adrenaline soars we often find ourselves with something to defend. The last time this happened, I was following the sound waves of a man, a speaker at a conference. What he said threw me off. To what extent do we respond to everything we feel addressed by?

There are a few ways to strike a response: Interrogate common syntax. Think about what you speak. Learn from drawings, don't be a photograph. Invent stories and lose them. Losing them allows for them to be found. Organize, form institutions. In the long run, instituting is about creating reasons for working and acting, that don't hinge on desire. Someone asked: "What is our object of knowledge? How do we write and how do we speak?" Answering from my memory, remembering something someone else said: "We can only think about one thing, when we think about something else." Think about it, or think about something else.

The exhibition is always implied within curatorial practice, like institutions are when language is spoken. Yet the curatorial embraces far more things than the unique talent set of exhibition-making. Regularly, someone will ask me: "What do you do?" Sometimes I will respond: "I read exhibitions, like books, and occasionally I write." I will say: "I am not a professional writer of books; in fact I have been more of a bookkeeper, in both senses of the word." I collect and keep books I like, and for a number of years I have kept the financial books of Beirut in Cairo. Books, like artworks, are material; they are objects, autonomous, and important. Arriving at the East Coast this summer, I overheard a student boasting about the book collection in miles at the bottom of the steps of Harvard's Widener Library. The strange thing is that in my mind I recall him giving a figure in kilometers. While editing, I realize my memory errs, and I am comforted by the thought that some cities have shorter histories than others, and, like language, systems of measures are never quite the same everywhere.

Beirut is a three-year-old institution, like a book with a beginning and an end. Bakhtin would describe it as an utterance, which is better than being a word or a sentence. Within the rubric of what we were doing at Beirut, then, and engaging with the persistent question "What is an institution?," we invited the historian Hussam Ahmad to speak. Ahmad was piecing together fragments of the francophone cultural scene in Cairo between 1919 and 1939. The narratives of the artistic and literary circles that had sprung up in Egypt during the interwar period have not been assimilated or made visible as part of Egypt's cultural history yet. In his research, Ahmad revisited the role of groups such as Les Essayistes, and L'Association des Amis de la Culture Française en Égypte, which attracted cosmopolitan crowds, high-profile local as well as foreign intellectuals, and received regular coverage in Egypt's francophone press. Exhibitions were held in private homes and in galleries, which no longer exist, not even in memory. This paints a picture of a worldlier Cairo, more refined, understatedly cosmopolitan.

The recollection of it is in black of white, of its time. Feeling for the image is nostalgia. I overheard an academic and an artist vehemently agree the other day that we must be suspicious of nostalgia and its effects. I am mindful of the task of the historian. I often think about whether going back really helps shift our imagination toward the future, and whereas I am more suspicious of history than nostalgia, I think the currency of time is well spent in archives with things, documents, and objects that have fallen out of memory. It is like storytelling, for the future looking back.

Implicit to these multiple digressions is Beirut. What is Beirut? Beirut does not exist... In practice, the case study is always implied. Delineating method congeals practice into crystalline forms, predictable and recognizable before they even become. It fixes things at the frontal lobe of our imagination's brain. Hard-line realist curators tend to fight back against this type of curatorial constructivism. It is not at a time, we can only think of one thing, when we think of something else. In 2012, the cultural and political climate in Cairo was imploring us for an art institution, a site was required from which to grapple with the question: "What is the role of art at this complicated time of insurgency (now bygone...)?" The questions multiplied, and became articulated in doing, in work, in practice—not only in storytelling, or in theory. One question became a cornerstone to our mission: How do we think of institution building as a curatorial act? The institution is a body, a fictitious body in a legal sense, as much as it is a language. In other discourses it is a host, as well as a guest. In inventing institutions, the mind becomes future-oriented; in imagining the institution, the myth of the stable rational thing that makes an institution slowly becomes undone. There is thinking's unclad descent to a generative place, where the animation of soul and mind can become. The mind starts to work, hovering. Unsure, we start to draw lines between ideas. We picture associations to these references. Slowly, they outgrow us, they possess us, exercising their autonomy, they inspire and morph, transfusing, and for glimmers of moments these creations become feverish delusions. In this unstable state, institutions between thought and being, will learn from artworks.

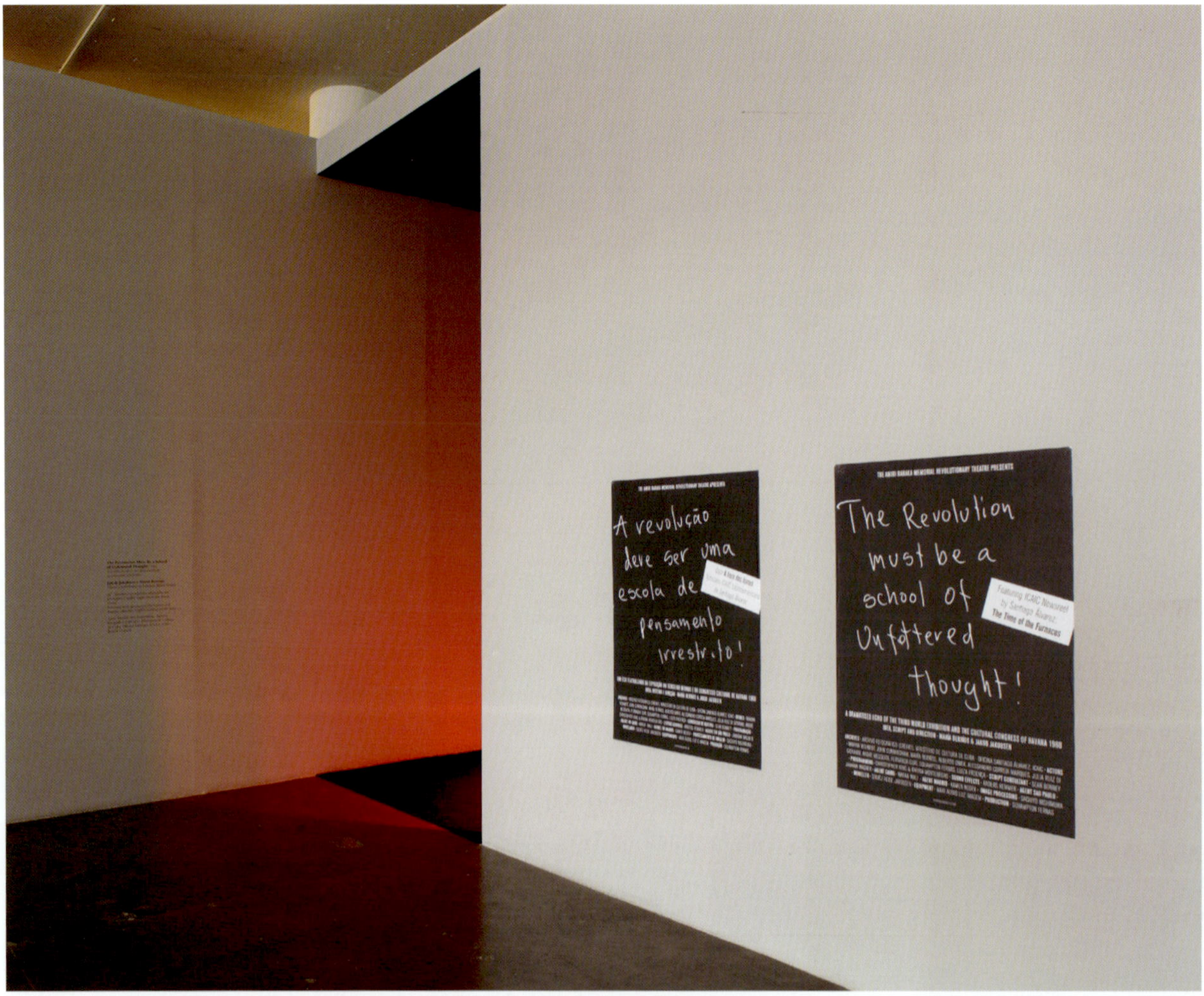

Maria Berrios & Jakob Jakobsen, *The Revolution Must Be a School of Unfettered Thought*, 2014
Installation (mechanical theater of sound, light, video, and images; poster; tabloids), variable dimensions, 30 min. 45 sec.

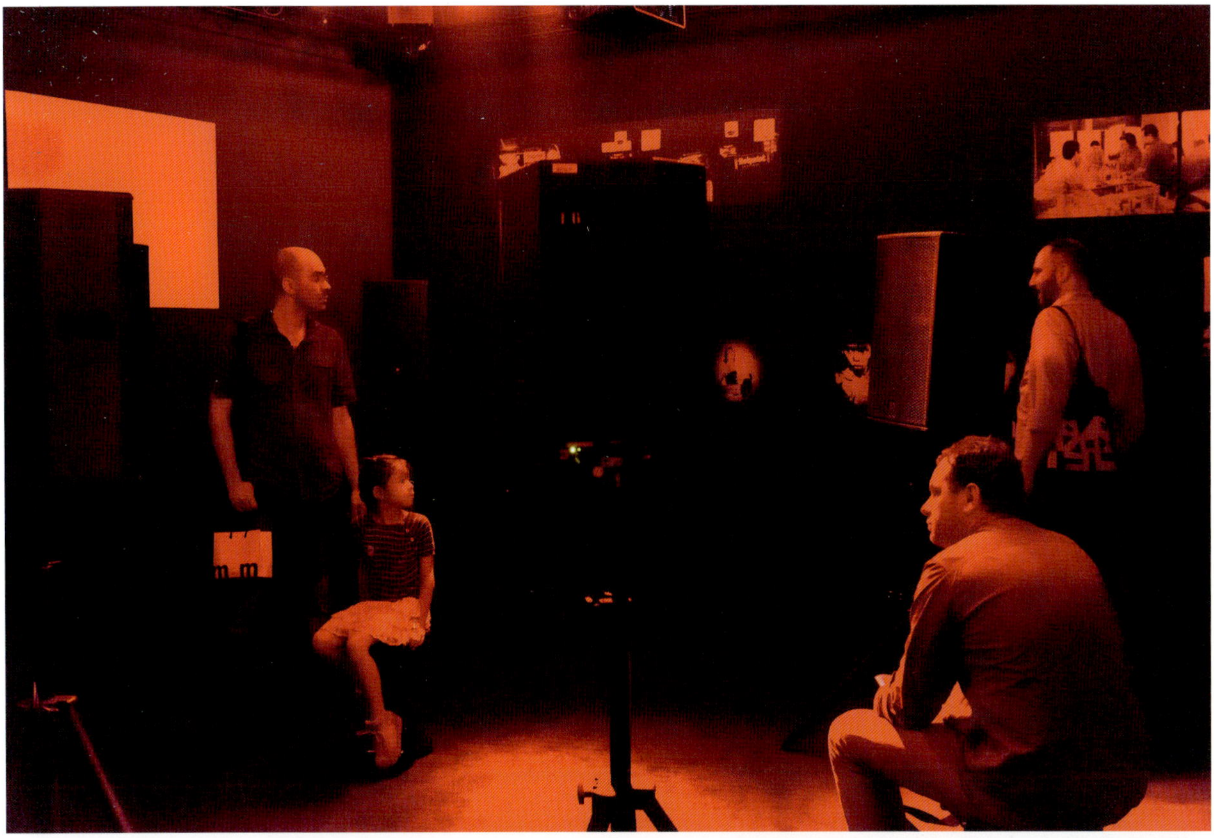

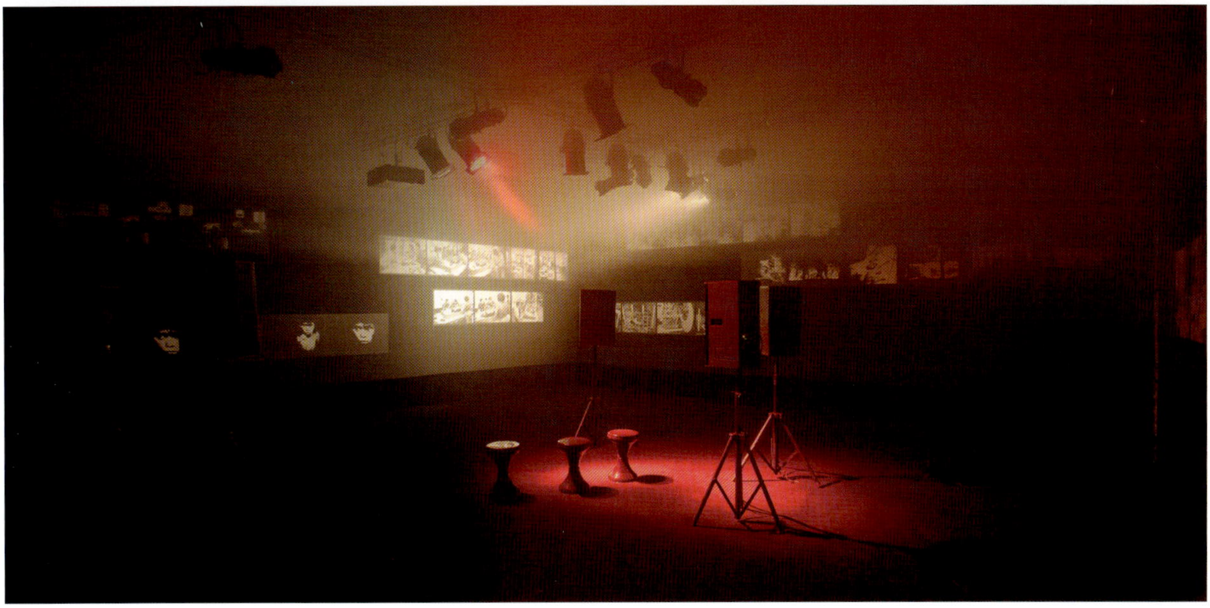

Sigmar Polke, *Untitled (Venice, empty pavilion et al.)*, undated (1983-1986)
Film stills / 16mm transferred to video, color, silent, 28 min. 29 sec.

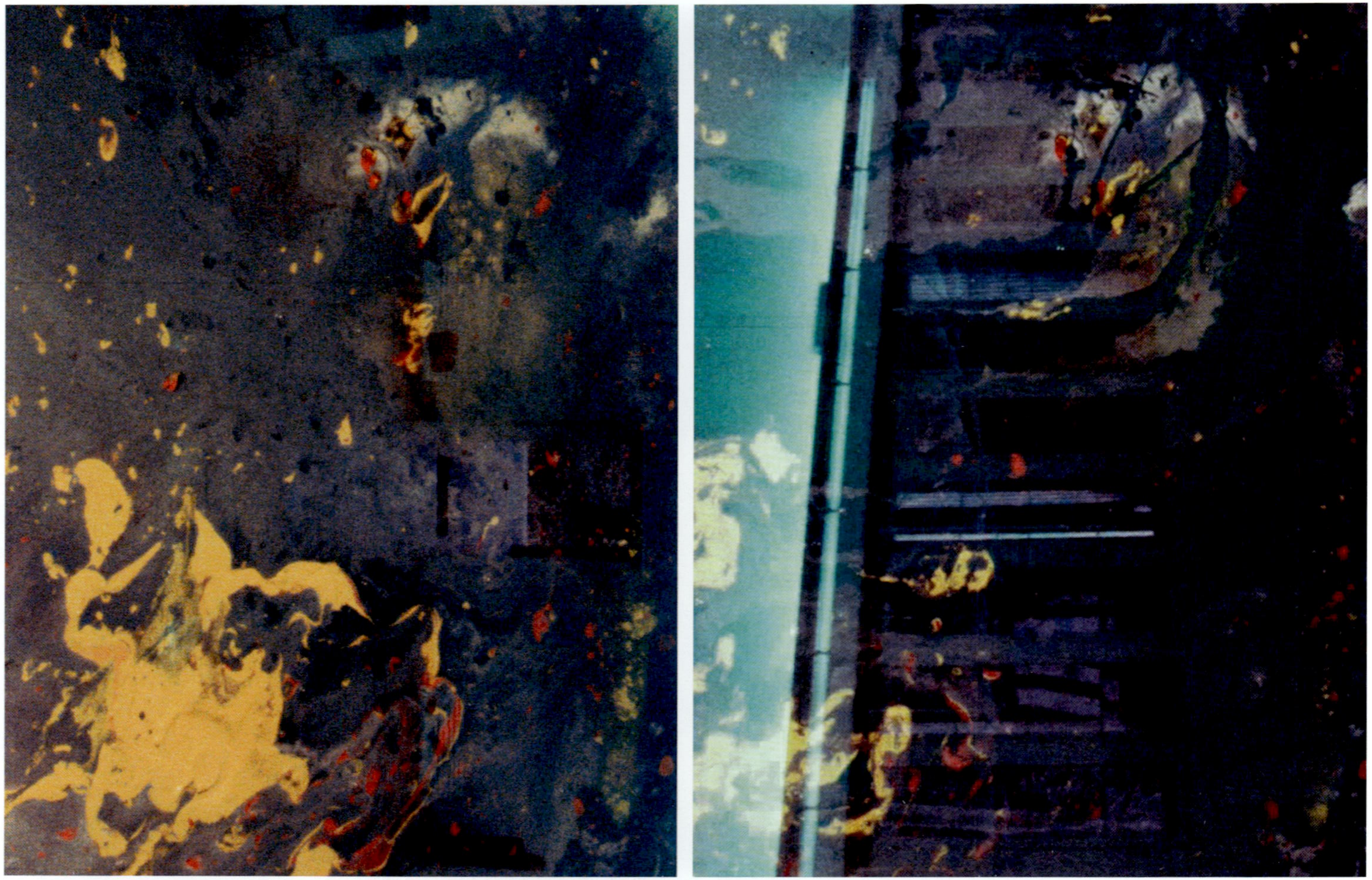

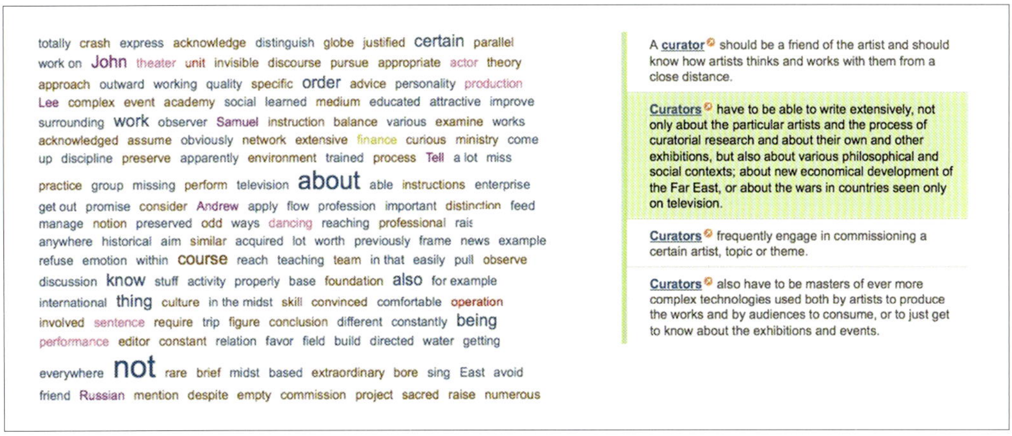

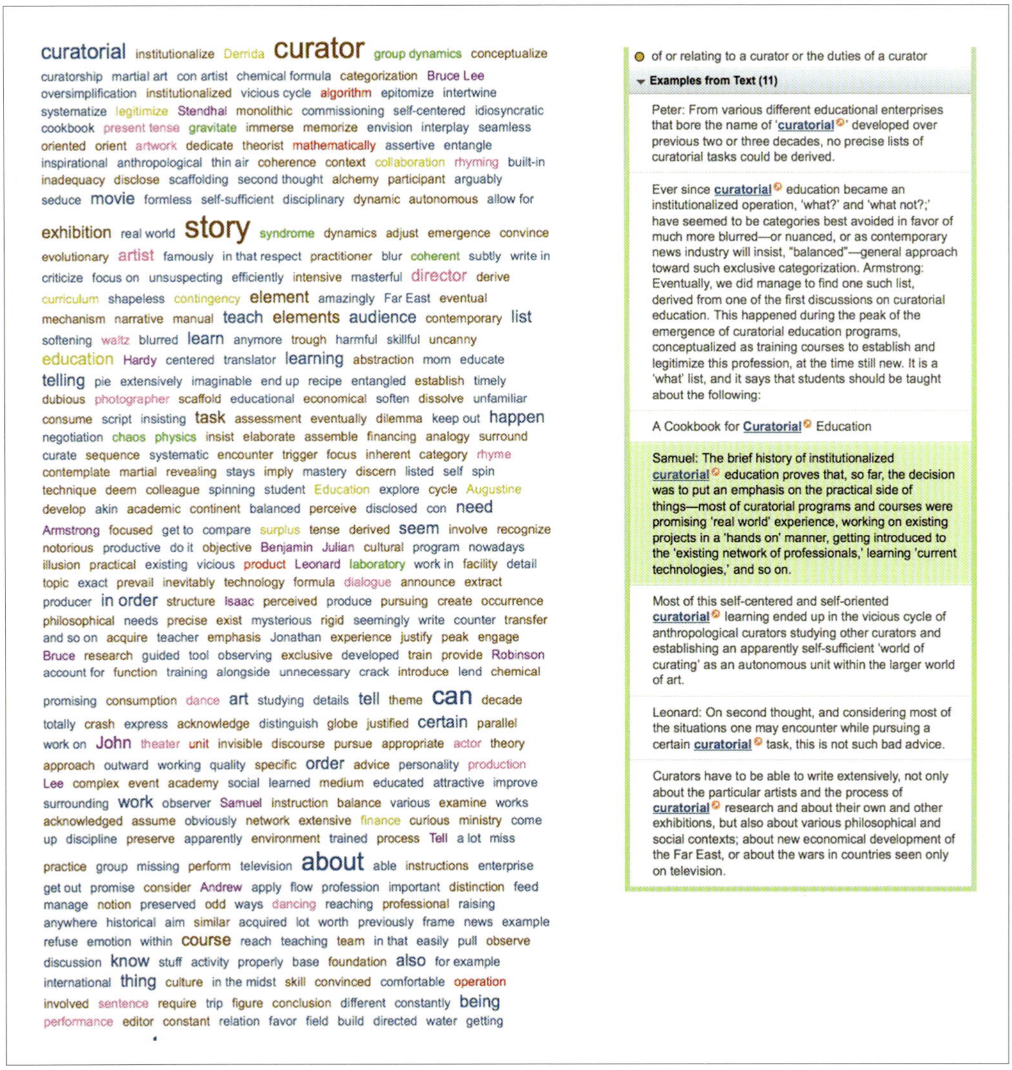

AlchemyAPI, Screen Shot, January 9, 2016 (www.alchemyapi.com/products/demo/alchemylanguage)

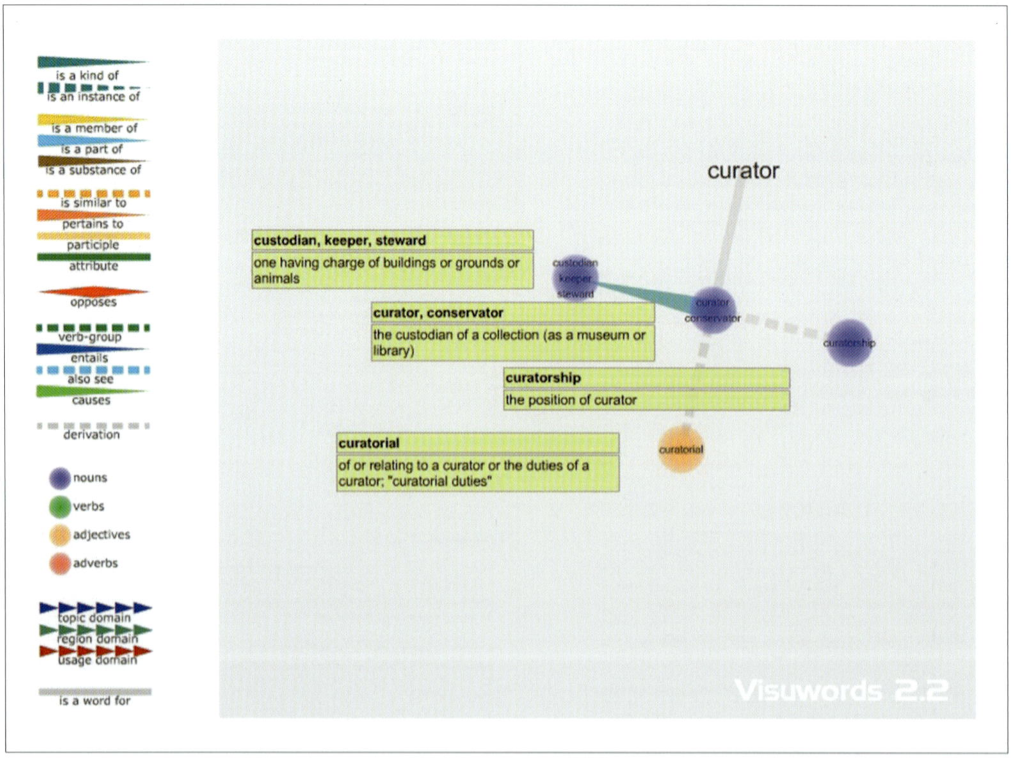

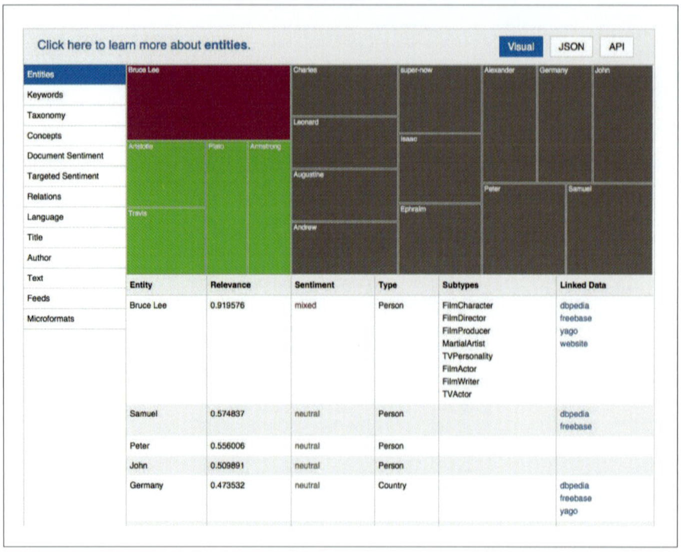

Entity	Relevance	Sentiment	Type	Subtypes	Linked Data
Bruce Lee	0.919576	mixed	Person	FilmCharacter FilmDirector FilmProducer MartialArtist TVPersonality FilmActor FilmWriter TVActor	dbpedia freebase yago website
Samuel	0.574837	neutral	Person		dbpedia freebase
Peter	0.556006	neutral	Person		
John	0.509891	neutral	Person		
Germany	0.473532	neutral	Country		dbpedia freebase yago

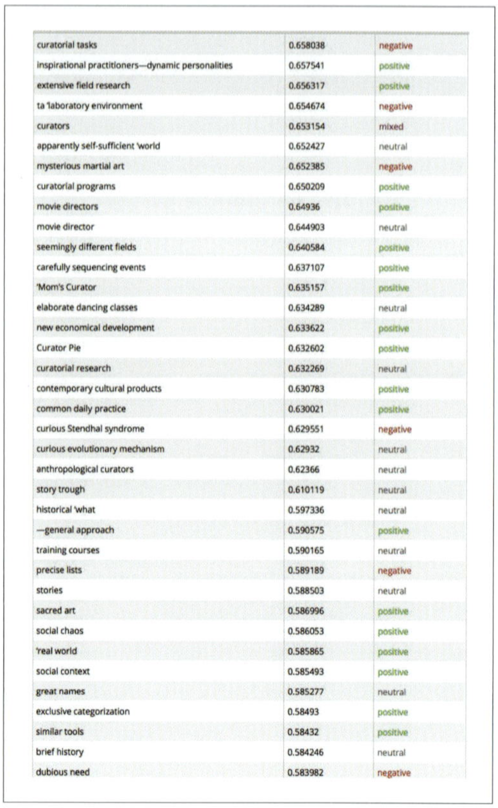

curatorial tasks	0.658038	negative
inspirational practitioners—dynamic personalities	0.657541	positive
extensive field research	0.656317	positive
ta 'laboratory environment	0.654674	negative
curators	0.653154	mixed
apparently self-sufficient 'world	0.652427	neutral
mysterious martial art	0.652385	negative
curatorial programs	0.650209	positive
movie directors	0.64936	positive
movie director	0.644903	neutral
seemingly different fields	0.640584	positive
carefully sequencing events	0.637107	positive
'Mom's Curator	0.635157	positive
elaborate dancing classes	0.634289	neutral
new economical development	0.633622	positive
Curator Pie	0.632602	positive
curatorial research	0.632269	neutral
contemporary cultural products	0.630783	positive
common daily practice	0.630021	positive
curious Stendhal syndrome	0.629551	negative
curious evolutionary mechanism	0.62932	neutral
anthropological curators	0.62366	neutral
story trough	0.610119	neutral
historical 'what	0.597336	neutral
—general approach	0.590575	positive
training courses	0.590165	neutral
precise lists	0.589189	negative
stories	0.588503	neutral
sacred art	0.586996	positive
social chaos	0.586053	positive
'real world	0.585865	positive
social context	0.585493	positive
great names	0.585277	neutral
exclusive categorization	0.58493	positive
similar tools	0.58432	positive
brief history	0.584246	neutral
dubious need	0.583982	negative

This page, top: Visuwords, Screen Shot, January 9, 2016 (www.visuwords.com)

Bottom left and right: VocabGrabber, Screen Shot, January 9, 2016 (www.visualthesaurus.com/vocabgrabber)

Opposite page: VocabGrabber, Screen Shot, January 9, 2016 (www.visualthesaurus.com/vocabgrabber)

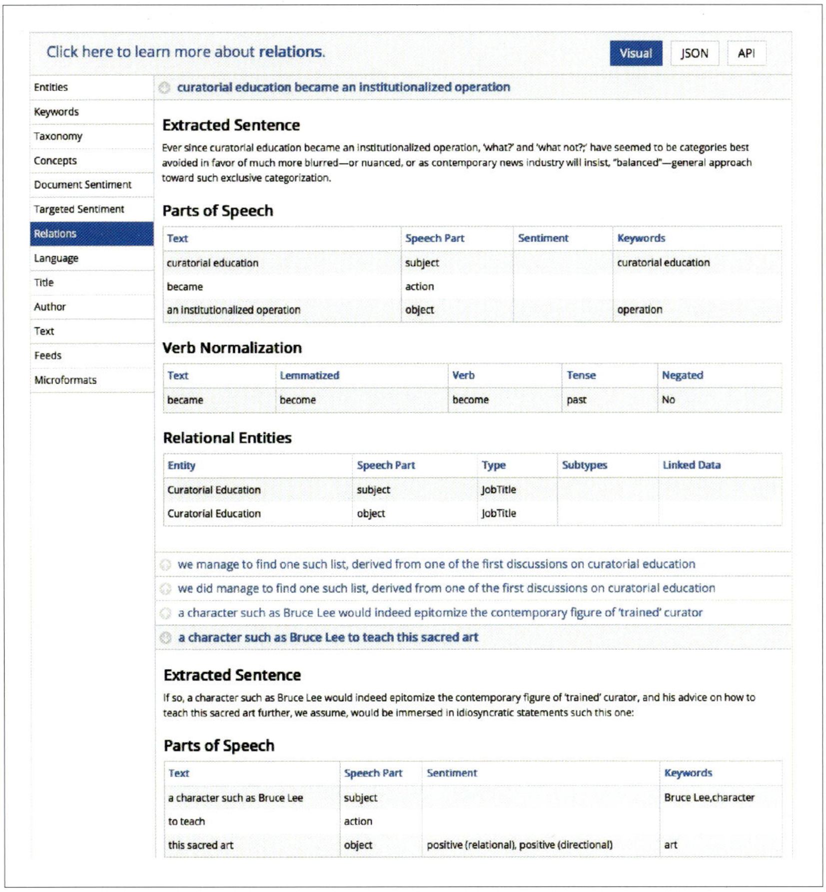

Click here to learn more about relations.
Visual
JSON
API
Entities
Keywords
Taxonomy
Concepts
Document Sentiment
Targeted Sentiment
Relations
Language
Title
Author
Text
Feeds
Microformats
curatorial education became an institutionalized operation
Extracted Sentence
Ever since curatorial education became an institutionalized operation, 'what?' and 'what not?,' have seemed to be categories best avoided in favor of much more blurred—or nuanced, or as contemporary news industry will insist, "balanced"—general approach toward such exclusive categorization.
Parts of Speech
Text
Speech Part
Sentiment
Keywords
curatorial education
subject
curatorial education
became
action
an institutionalized operation
object
operation
Verb Normalization
Text
Lemmatized
Verb
Tense
Negated
became
become
become
past
No
Relational Entities
Entity
Speech Part
Type
Subtypes
Linked Data
Curatorial Education
subject
JobTitle
Curatorial Education
object
JobTitle
we manage to find one such list, derived from one of the first discussions on curatorial education
we did manage to find one such list, derived from one of the first discussions on curatorial education
a character such as Bruce Lee would indeed epitomize the contemporary figure of 'trained' curator
a character such as Bruce Lee to teach this sacred art
Extracted Sentence
If so, a character such as Bruce Lee would indeed epitomize the contemporary figure of 'trained' curator, and his advice on how to teach this sacred art further, we assume, would be immersed in idiosyncratic statements such this one:
Parts of Speech
Text
Speech Part
Sentiment
Keywords
a character such as Bruce Lee
subject
Bruce Lee,character
to teach
action
this sacred art
object
positive (relational), positive (directional)
art

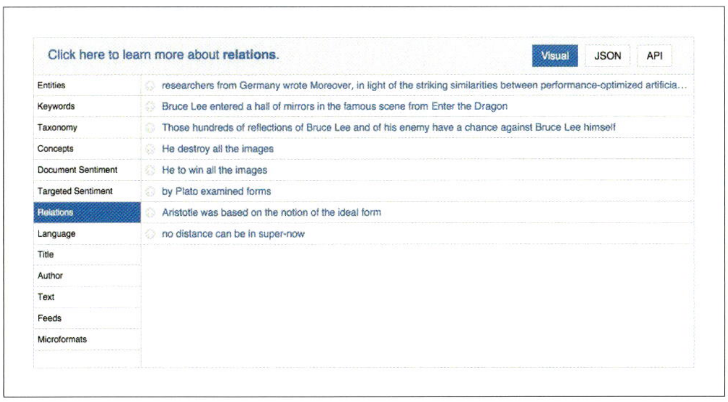

Click here to learn more about relations.
Visual
JSON
API
Entities
Keywords
Taxonomy
Concepts
Document Sentiment
Targeted Sentiment
Relations
Language
Title
Author
Text
Feeds
Microformats
researchers from Germany wrote Moreover, in light of the striking similarities between performance-optimized artificia…
Bruce Lee entered a hall of mirrors in the famous scene from Enter the Dragon
Those hundreds of reflections of Bruce Lee and of his enemy have a chance against Bruce Lee himself
He destroy all the images
He to win all the images
by Plato examined forms
Aristotle was based on the notion of the ideal form
no distance can be in super-now

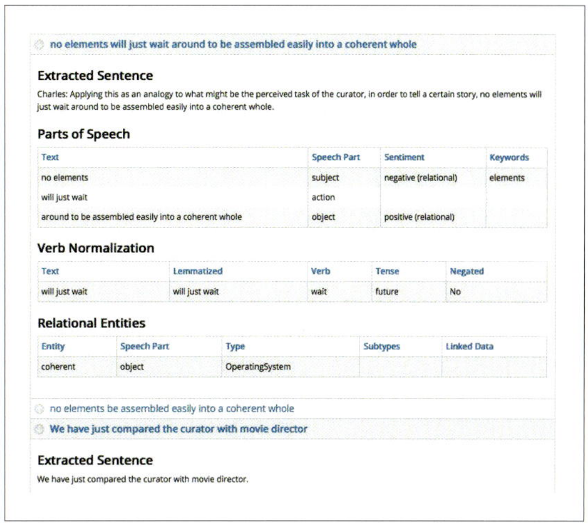

no elements will just wait around to be assembled easily into a coherent whole
Extracted Sentence
Charles: Applying this as an analogy to what might be the perceived task of the curator, in order to tell a certain story, no elements will just wait around to be assembled easily into a coherent whole.
Parts of Speech
Text
Speech Part
Sentiment
Keywords
no elements
subject
negative (relational)
elements
will just wait
action
around to be assembled easily into a coherent whole
object
positive (relational)
Verb Normalization
Text
Lemmatized
Verb
Tense
Negated
will just wait
will just wait
wait
future
No
Relational Entities
Entity
Speech Part
Type
Subtypes
Linked Data
coherent
object
OperatingSystem
no elements be assembled easily into a coherent whole
We have just compared the curator with movie director
Extracted Sentence
We have just compared the curator with movie director.

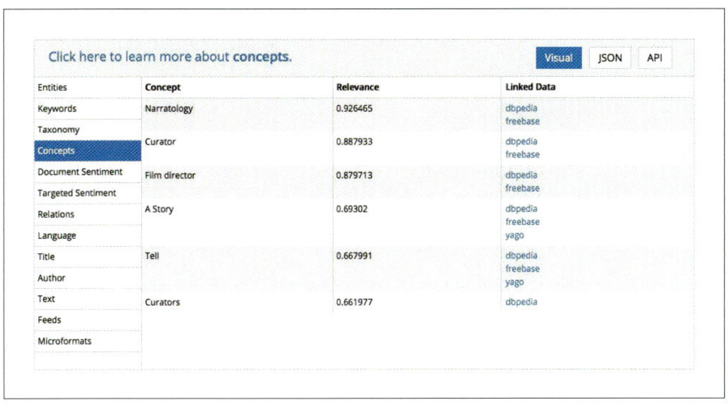

Click here to learn more about concepts.
Visual
JSON
API
Entities
Keywords
Taxonomy
Concepts
Document Sentiment
Targeted Sentiment
Relations
Language
Title
Author
Text
Feeds
Microformats
Concept
Relevance
Linked Data
Narratology
0.926465
dbpedia
freebase
Curator
0.887933
dbpedia
freebase
Film director
0.879713
dbpedia
freebase
A Story
0.69302
dbpedia
freebase
yago
Tell
0.667991
dbpedia
freebase
yago
Curators
0.661977
dbpedia

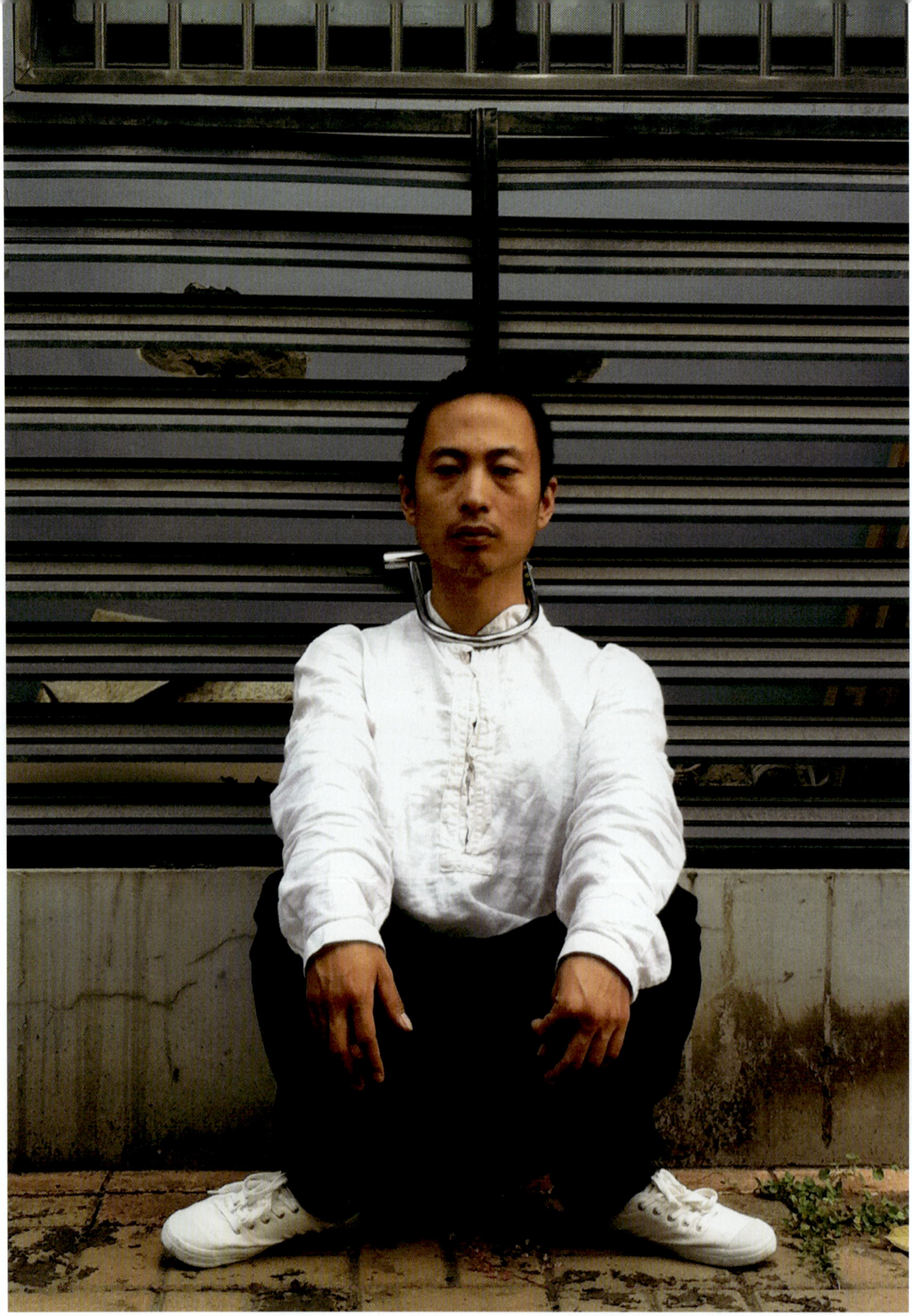

Li Liao, Spring Breeze, 2011
Performance, single channel
digital video (color, sound),
126 min. 39 sec.

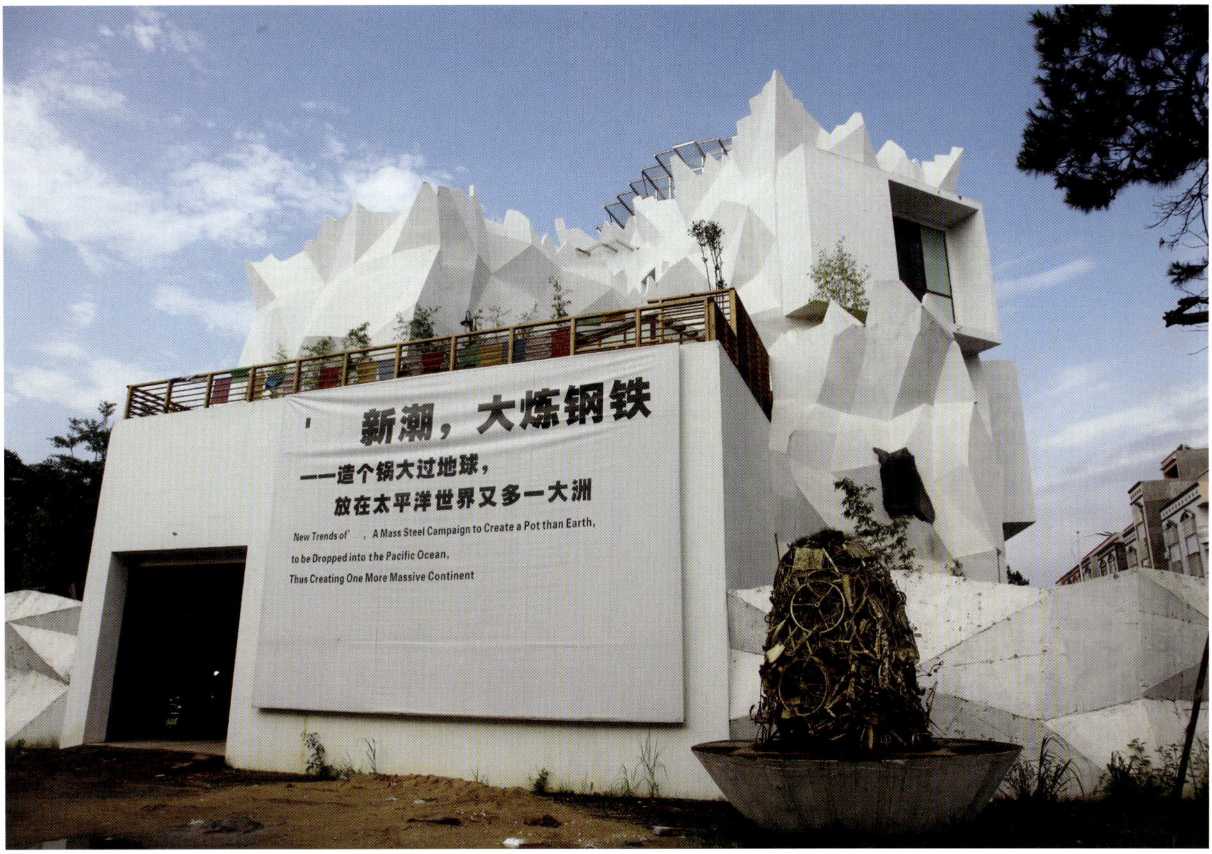

Above:
Zheng Guogu, in collaboration with Yangjiang Group, *58 New Wave, Big Steel Making*, 2008
Installation, scrap iron, displayed outside the studio of the Yangjiang Group

Following spread, left:
Maryam Jafri, *The Day After*, detail of Maryam Jafri, *Independence Day 1934–75*, 2009–ongoing, at Bétonsalon—Centre for art and research, Paris, 2015

Right:
Maryam Jafri, *The Day After*, detail of Heilihanta Rajaonarison, photographs from ANTA fund, at Bétonsalon—Centre for art and research, Paris, 2015

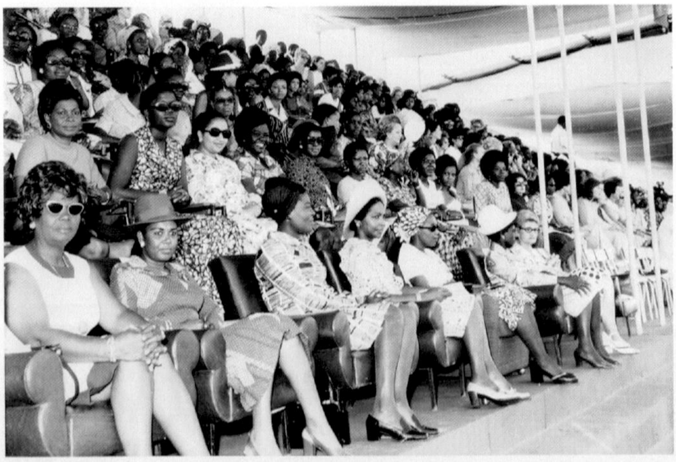

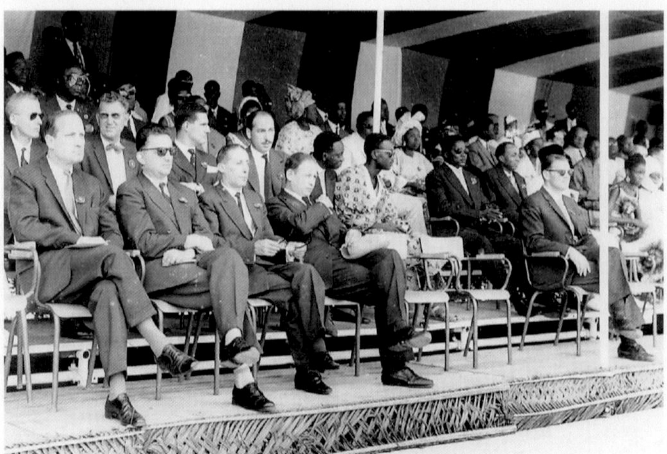

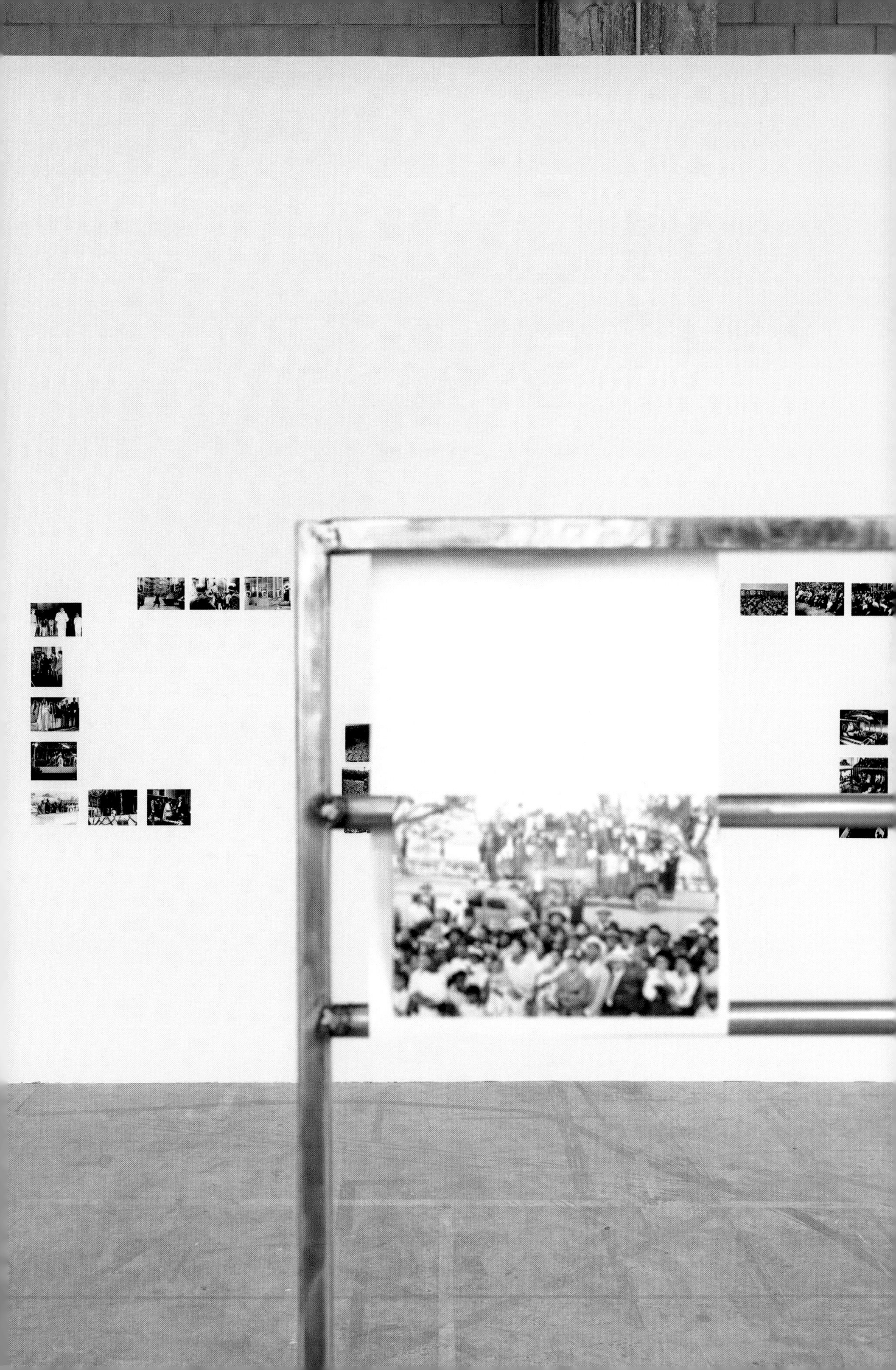

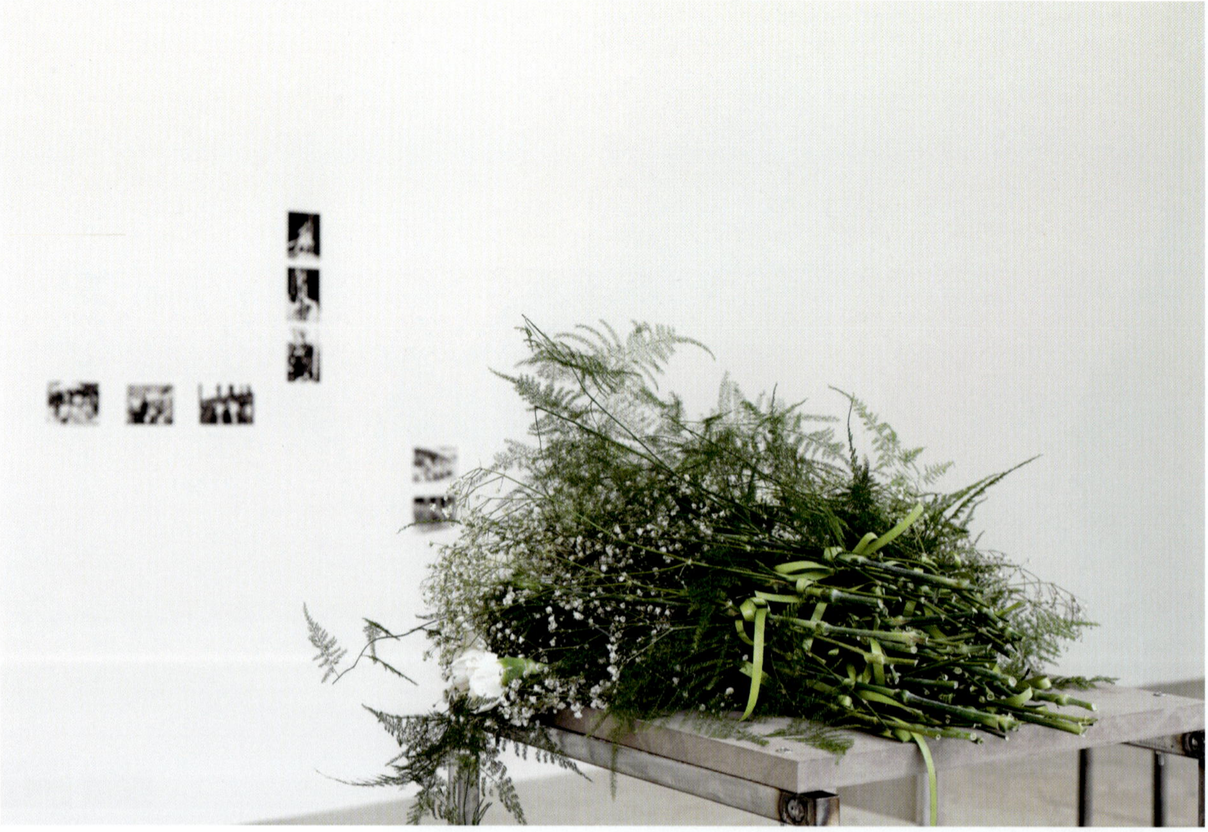

Above:
Maryam Jafri, *The Day After*, view of Kapwani Kiwanga, *Flowers for Africa, Federation of Mali*, 2012, at Bétonsalon–Centre for art and research, Paris, 2015

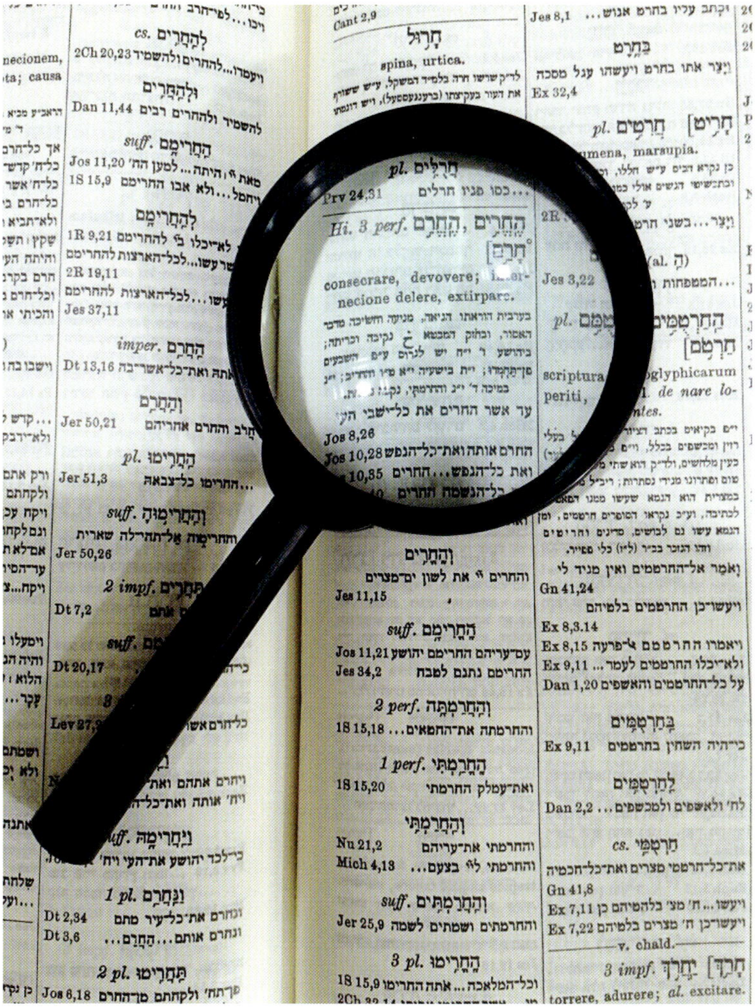

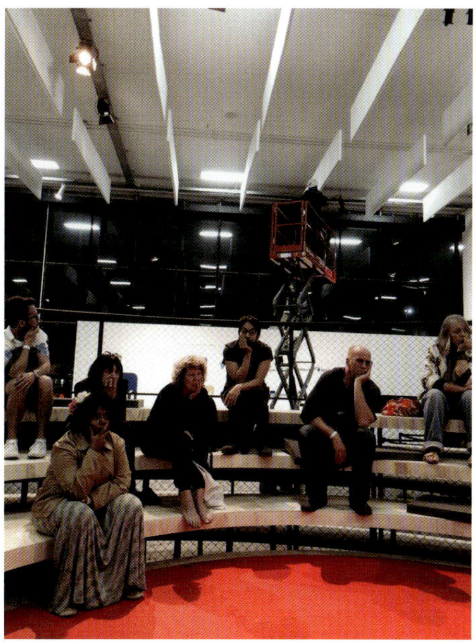

This page, top:
Cross-references

Bottom:
A 7 pm meeting

Following spread:
Bik Van der Pol, *Turning a Blind Eye*, 2014
Installation shot from press preview 31st Bienal de São Paulo, September 1, 2014

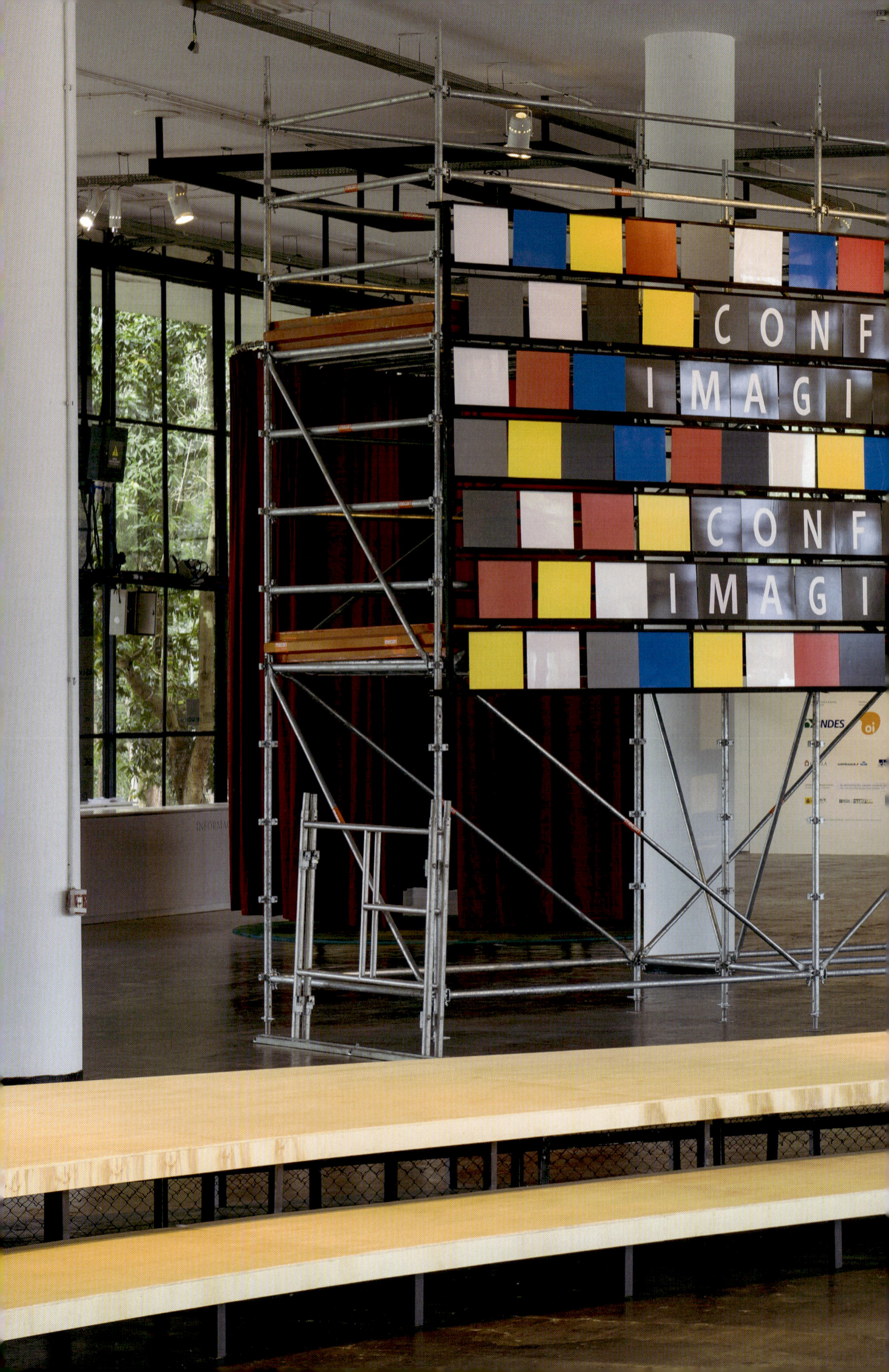
CONF
IMAGI
CONF
IMAGI

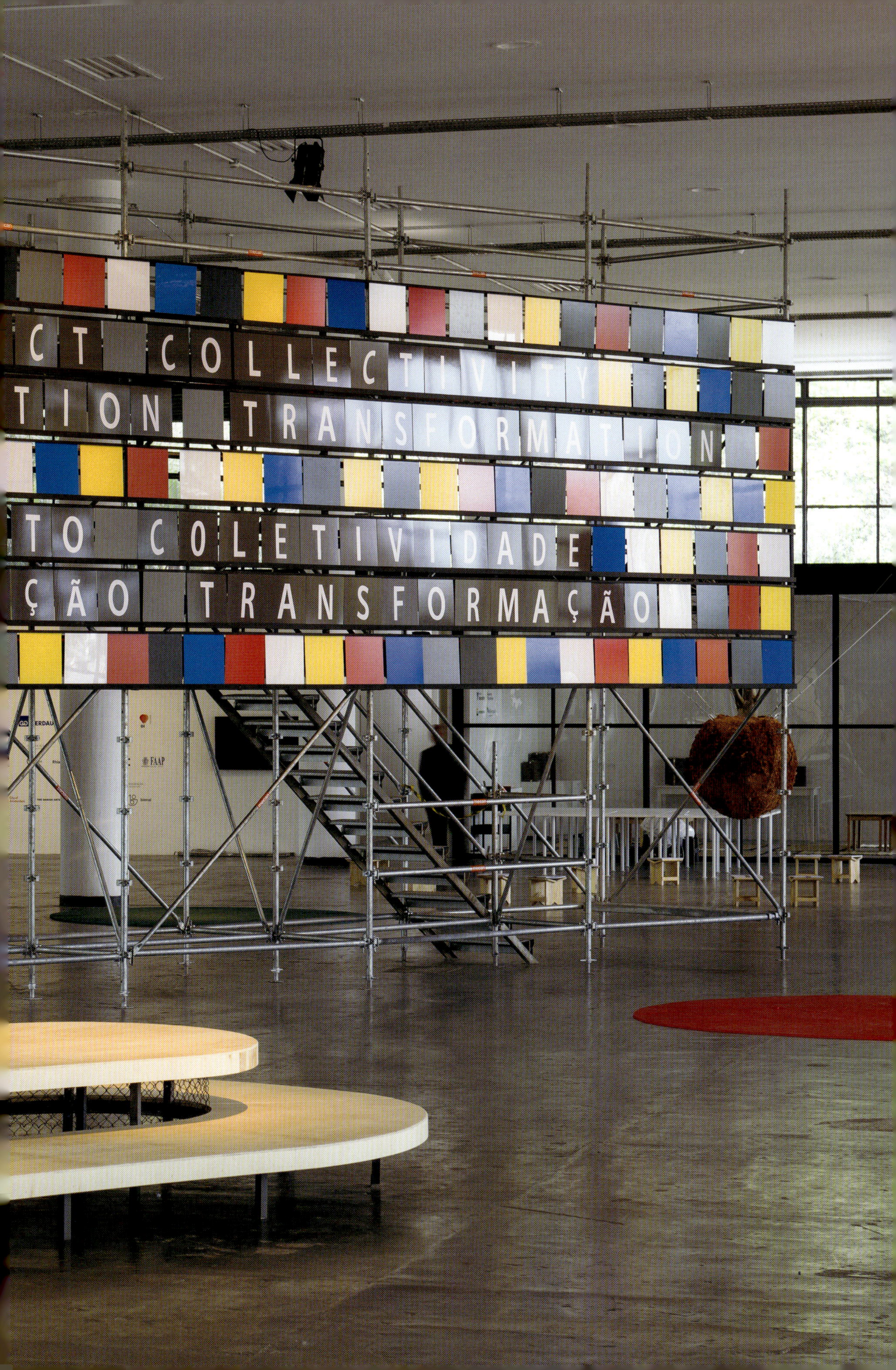
CT COLLECTIVITY
TION TRANSFORMATION
TO COLETIVIDADE
ÇÃO TRANSFORMAÇÃO

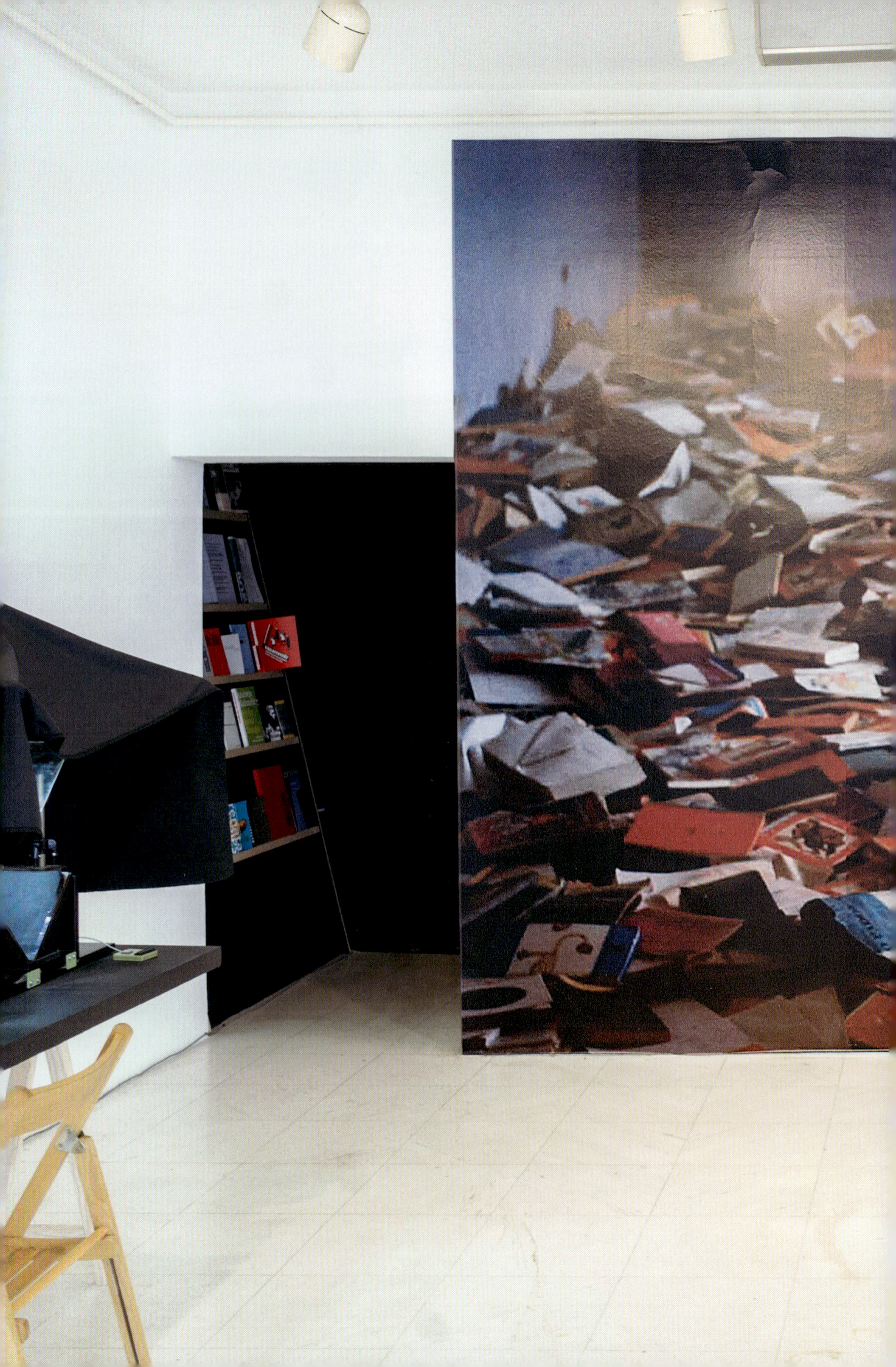

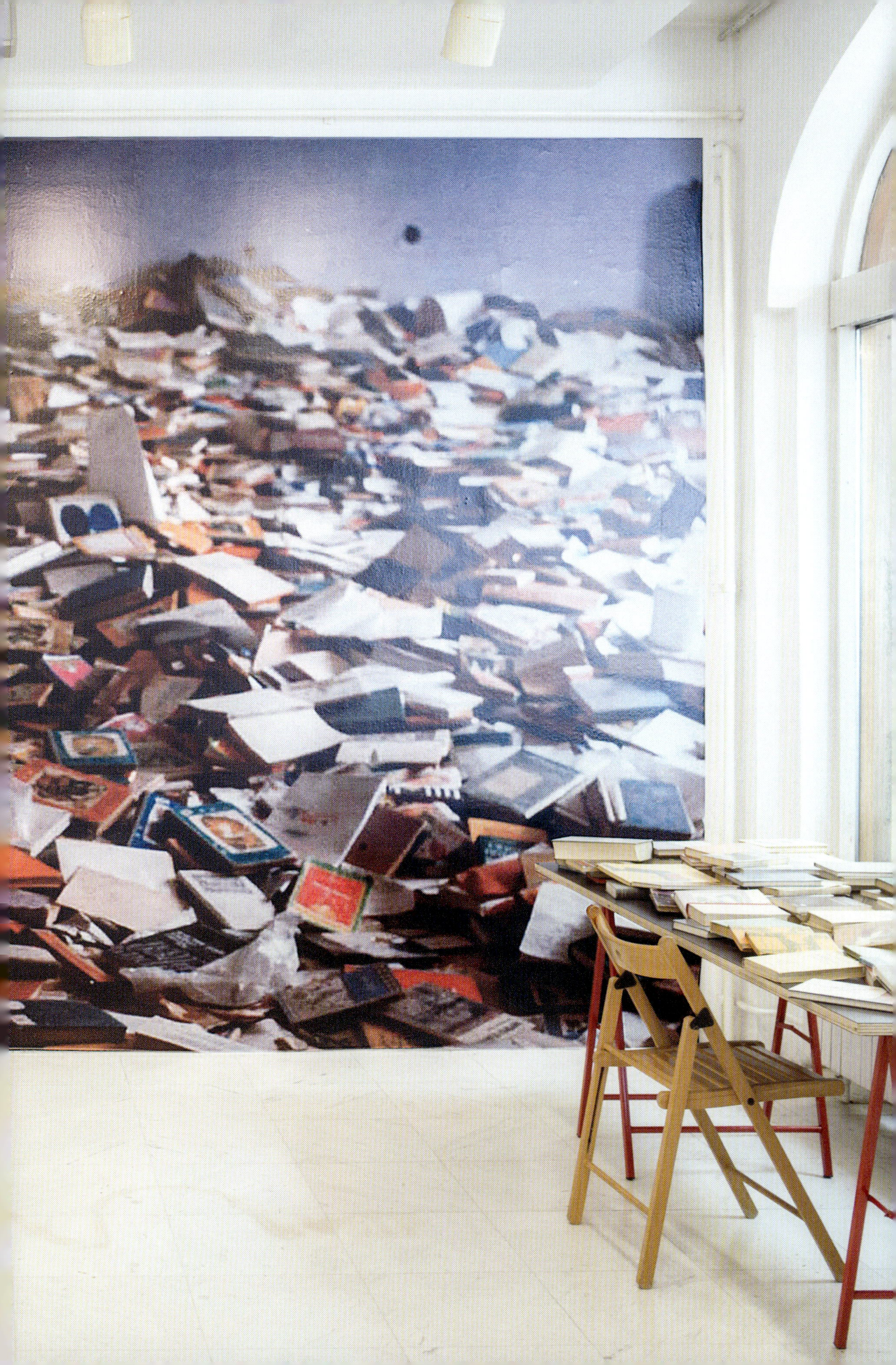

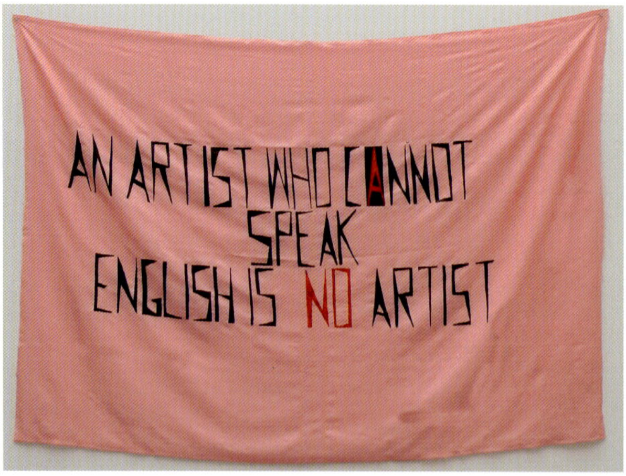

005.94

A public library is:

- free access to books for every member of society
- library catalog
- librarian

With books ready to be shared, meticulously cataloged, everyone is a librarian.

When everyone is librarian,
library is everywhere.

http://www.memoryoftheworld.org

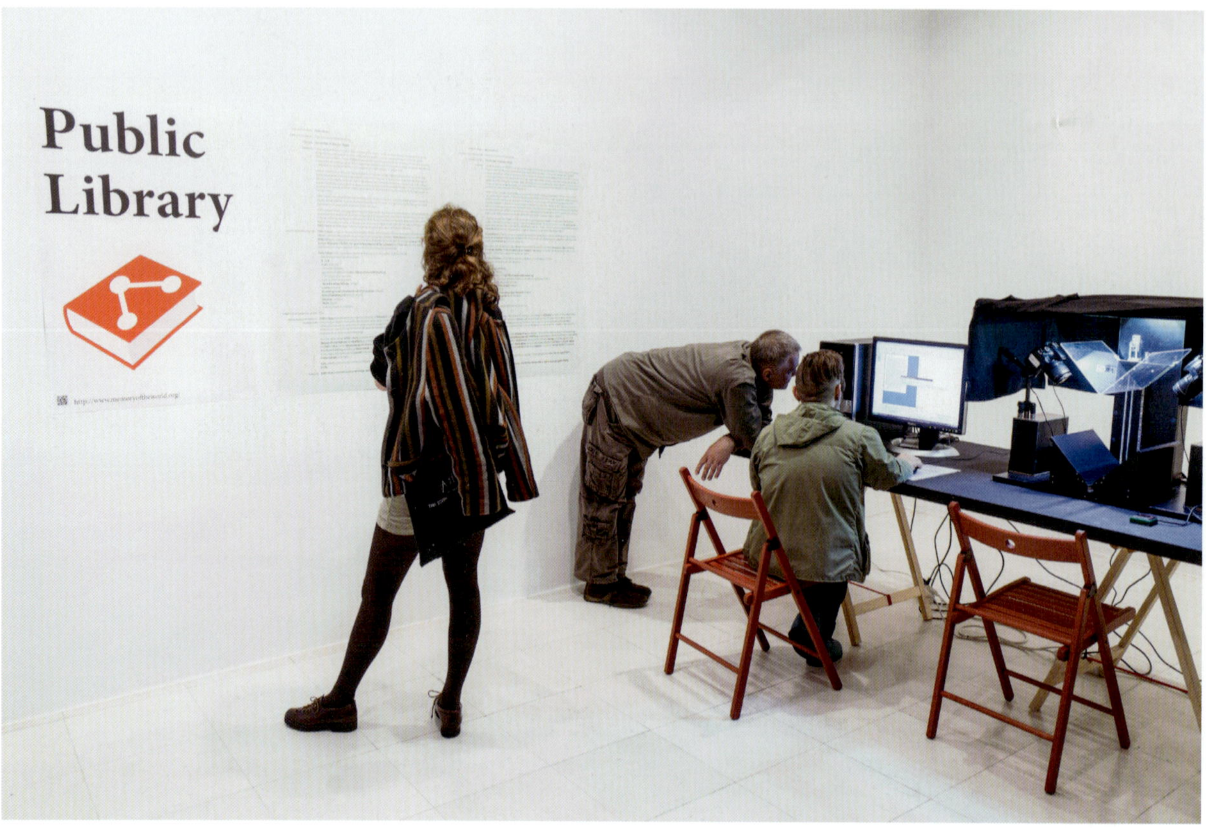

Previous spread:
Installation view exhibition/action *Written-off, on the occasion of the 20th anniversary of the Storm* at Gallery Nova, 2015

This page, top left:
Mladen Stilinović, *An Artist Who Cannot Speak English Is No Artist*, 1992

Top right:
Public Library info card

Bottom:
Installation view *Public Library* exhibition, Gallery Nova, Zagreb, 2015

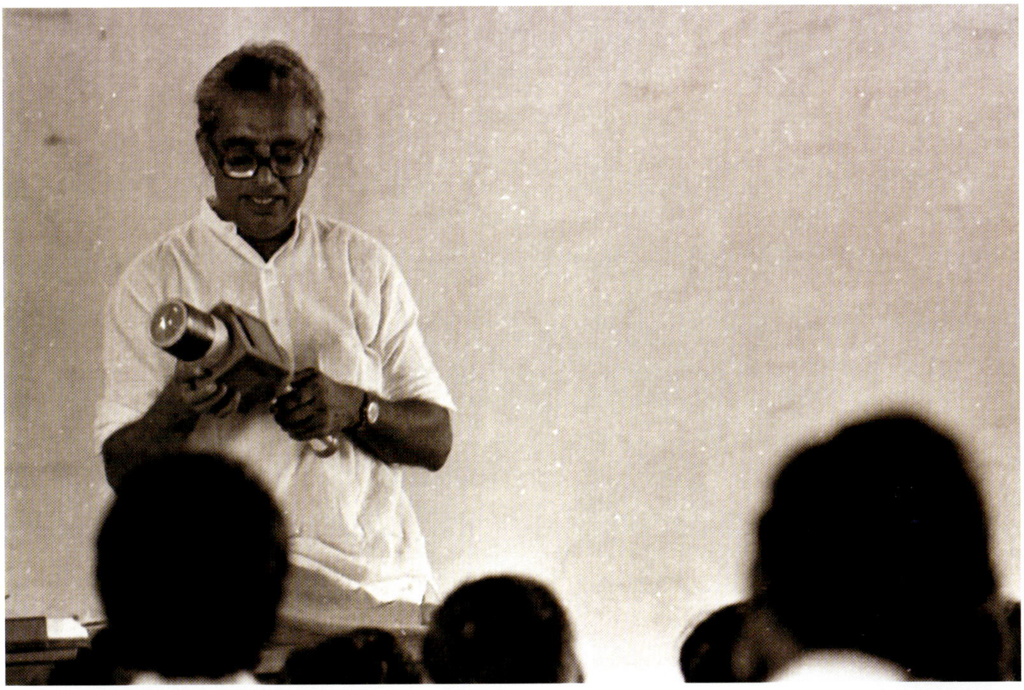

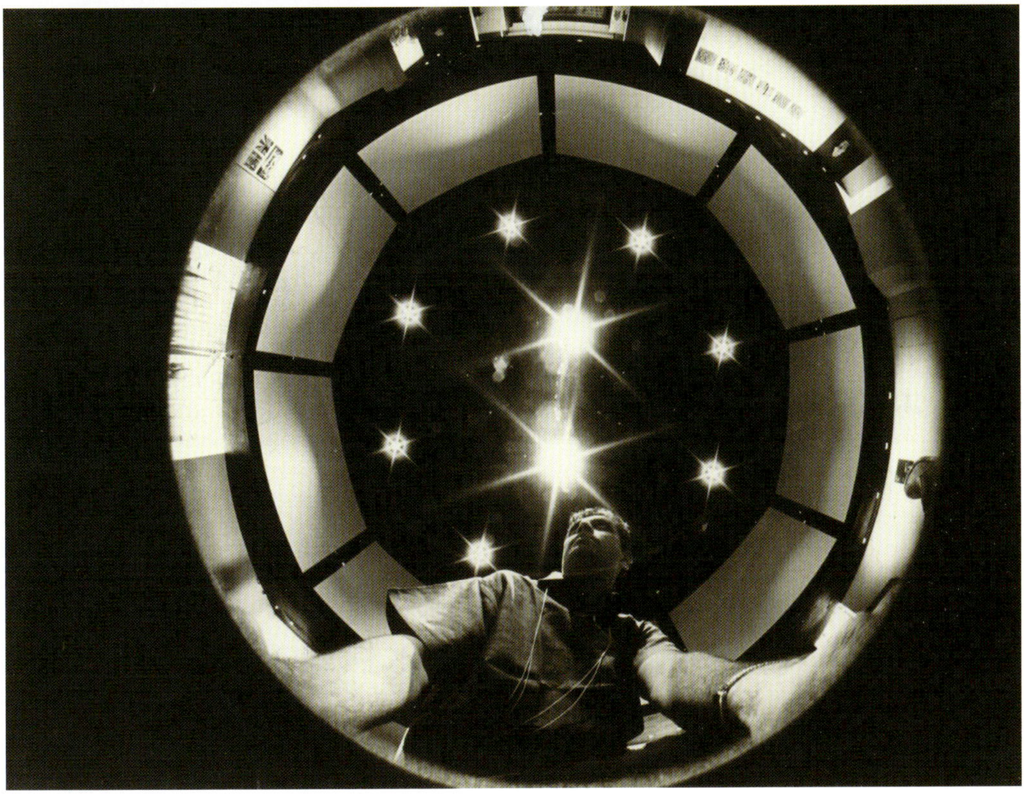

Top:
Dashrath Patel demonstrating a torch-operated projector made from a cardboard box and magnifying glasses for activists working in villages without electricity

Bottom:
Dashrath Patel's self-portrait at the India pavilion, Montreal Art Fair 1967. He is surrounded by a nine-screen, 360° projection of *A Journey in India*

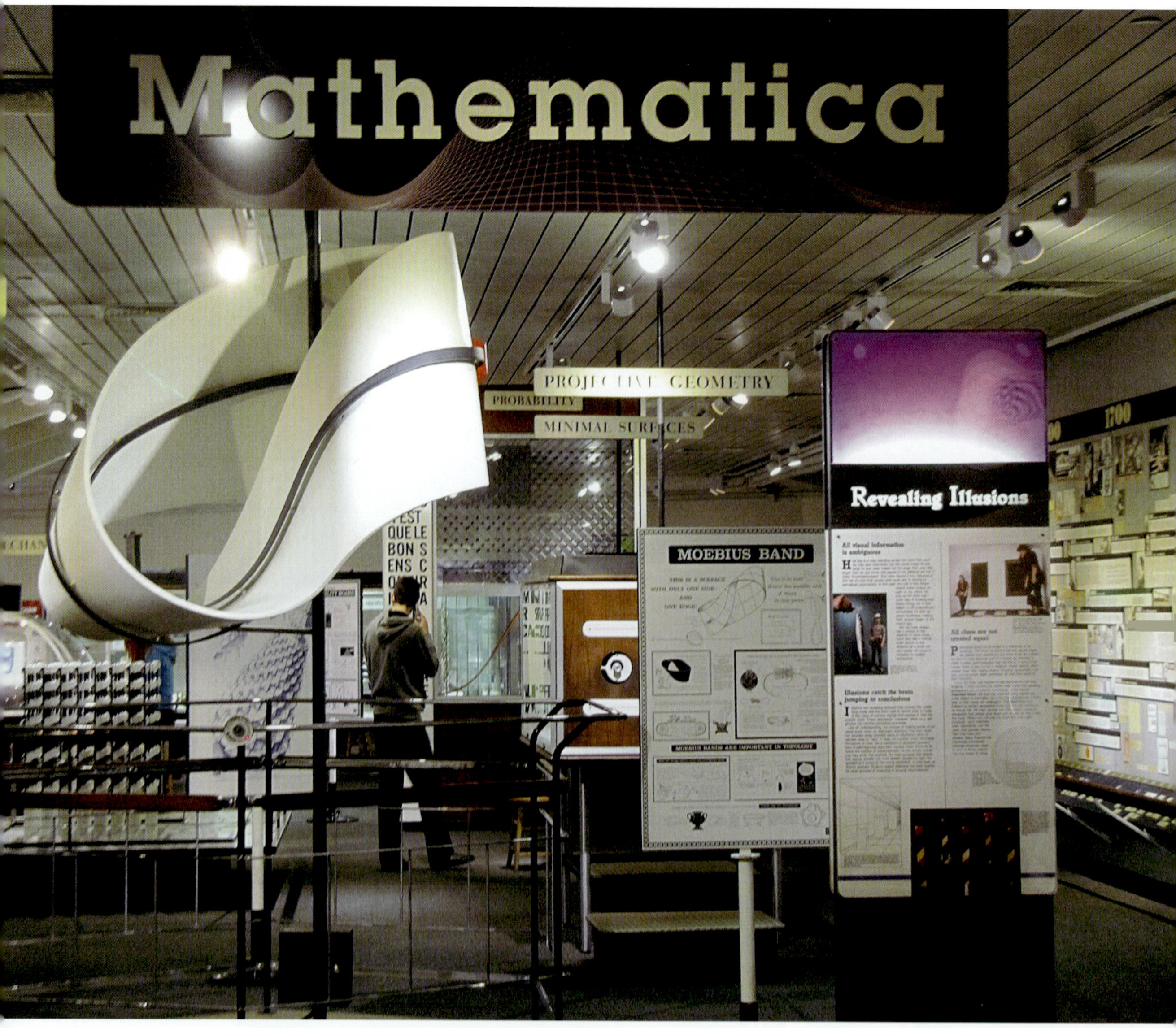

The Eameses' *Mathematica* exhibition, housed in the New York Hall of Science

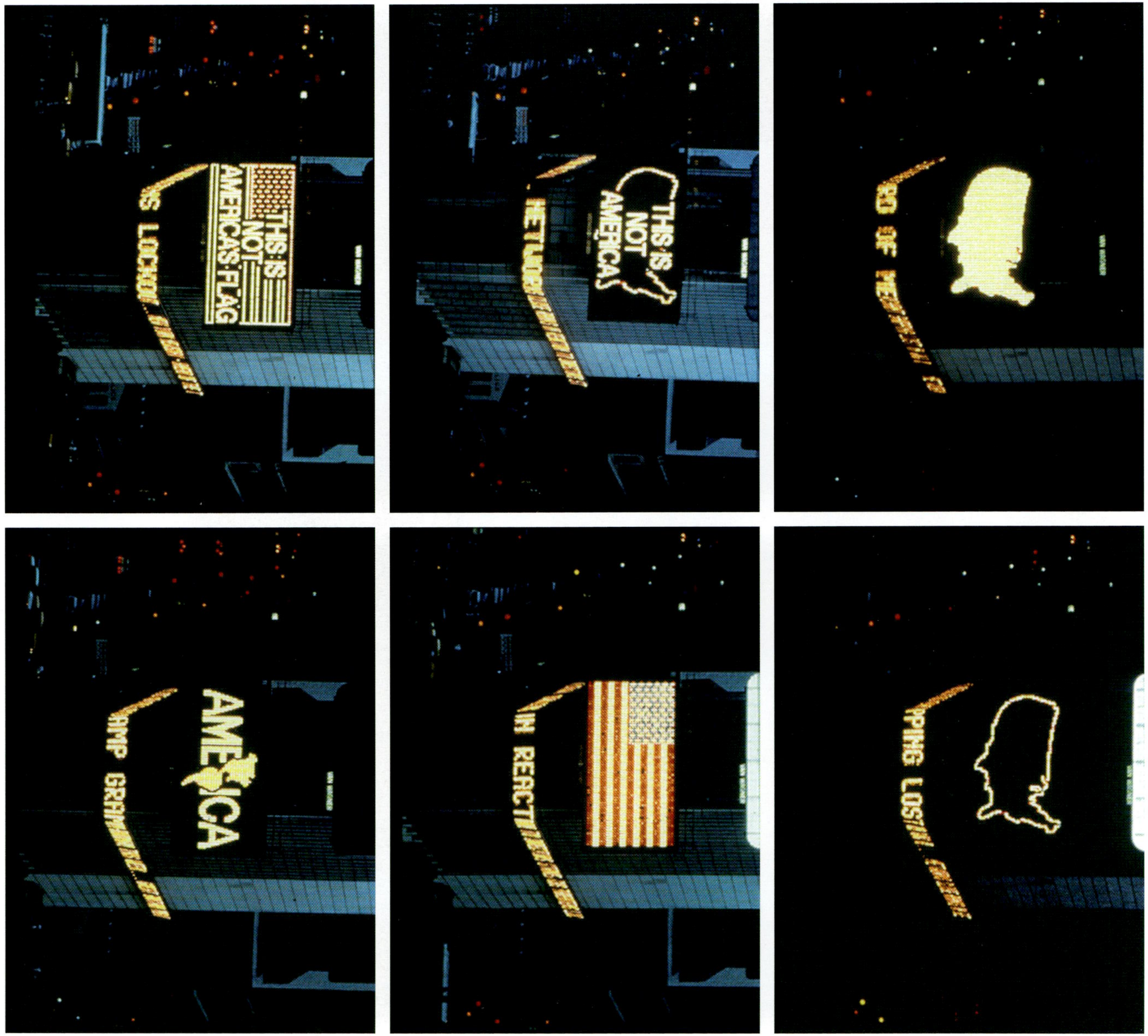

Alfredo Jaar, *A Logo for America*, 1986
Public intervention at Times Square, New York

Following spread:
Collaboration between CAMP and Clark House Initiative, *Country of the Sea*, 2015, (detail) solar-exposed cyanotype on cotton fabric, 5 × 16 feet, commissioned by Dr. Bhau Daji Lad Museum, Mumbai, for CAMP's exhibition *The Country of the Sea*

Inverting ideas of unity and abstraction, this work treats the ports along the coasts as cities of their own country. It brings the coast of Africa uncannily close to that of the Indian subcontinent. The work unfixes the land, and fixes the volatile sea instead, providing a visual metaphor for speaking of institutions, taking into account their own sense of stability from the perspective of movement and migration.

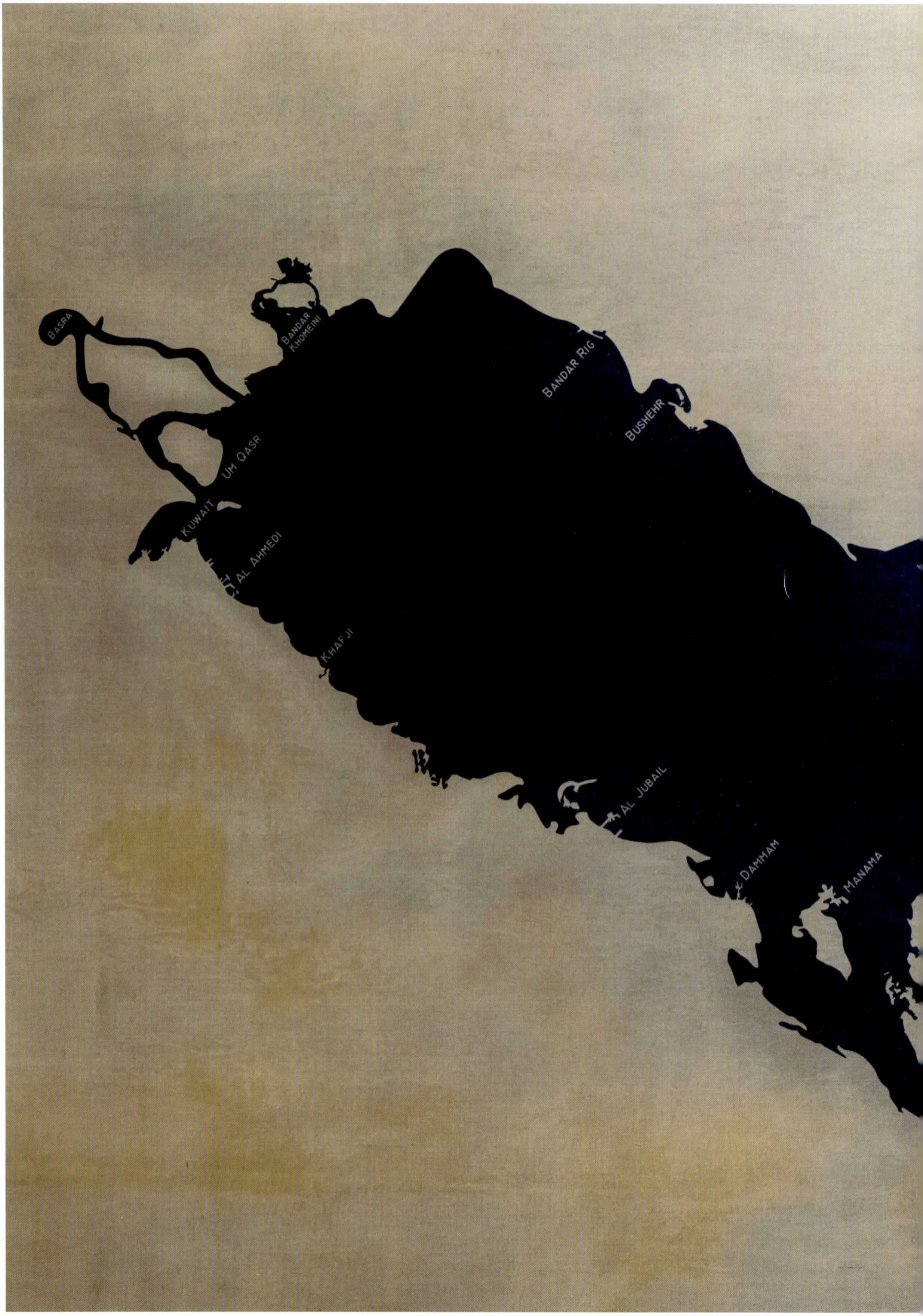
BASRA
BANDAR KHOMEINI
BANDAR RIG
BUSHEHR
UM QASR
KUWAIT
AL AHMEDI
KHAFJI
AL JUBAIL
DAMMAM
MANAMA

Bandar Abbas
Hormuz
Queshm
Sirik
Khasab
Bab-Al-Musandam
Bandar Lengeh
Asaloyeh
Bandar-e-Charak
Kish Island
Ras-Al-Khaimah
Khor Fakkan
Fujairah
Abu Musa Island
Umm-Al-Quwain
Siri Island
Sharjah
Dubai
Ras Laffan
Al Khor
Abu Dhabi
Doha
Mesaieed
Al Marfa
Ruwais

Contributors' Biographies

Nancy Adajania is a cultural theorist and curator based in Bombay. Her recent book, *The Thirteenth Place: Positionality as Critique in the Art of Navjot Altaf* (Bombay: The Guild Art Gallery, 2016) is an artist monograph that folds within it the history of leftist politics and the women's movement in India. She was Joint Artistic Director of the 9th Gwangju Biennale (2012), and has curated a number of exhibitions including a cycle of video art for *Sights and Sounds: Global Film and Video*, Jewish Museum, New York (2015). In 2013 and 2014, Adajania taught the curatorial practice course at the Salzburg International Summer Academy of Fine Arts. In 2014, she curated the hybrid exhibition-publication project *Sacred/ Scared* (Latitude 28/*TAKE on Art magazine*, Delhi), interweaving the expressive with the discursive by linking the exhibition to a transdisciplinary anthology. Adajania has proposed several new theoretical models through her extensive writings on media art, public art, biennial culture, transcultural art practices, and the relationship of art to the public sphere. She has lectured on these subjects at numerous venues, including Documenta 11, Kassel; ZKM, Karlsruhe; Transmediale, Berlin; the Center for Curatorial Studies Bard College, New York; Haus der Kulturen der Welt (HKW), Berlin; and the 3rd FORMER WEST Research Congress: Beyond What Was Contemporary Art, Vienna. Since the late-1990s, Adajania has written consistently on the practices of four generations of Indian women artists. She is the editor of the monograph *Shilpa Gupta* (Prestel, 2010), and co-author of *The Dialogues Series* (Popular Prakashan/ foundation b&g, Bombay 2011). She was research scholar-in-residence at BAK/ basis voor actuele kunst, Utrecht, 2010 and 2013. Her monographic essay on Sheba Chhachhi's art, "Obey the little laws and break the great ones: A life in feminism," is forthcoming.

Mélanie Bouteloup is a co-founder and the current director of Bétonsalon—Centre for art and research. Over the last ten years, she has curated numerous projects in various forms that anchor research in society on process-based, collaborative, and discursive levels, following different time spans, in cooperation with various local, national, and international organizations. In 2012, Mélanie Bouteloup was associate curator with artistic director Okwui Enwezor of the Paris Triennale—an event organized on the initiative of the Ministry of Culture and Communication/ DGCA, the Centre National des Arts Plastiques, and the Palais de Tokyo.

Nikita Yingqian Cai lives and works in Guangzhou, where she is currently Associate Director and Chief Curator at Guangdong Times Museum. She has curated such exhibitions as *A Museum That is Not* (2011), *Jiang Zhi: If This is a Man* (2012), *You Can Only Think about Something if You Think of Something Else* (2014), and *Roman Ondák: Storyboard* (2015). She is also organizing the paracuratorial series at Guangdong Times Museum, which features an annual seminar, and related publication. These seminars have included *No Ground Underneath: Curating on the Nexus of Changes* (co-organized with Carol Yinghua Lu, 2012), *Active Withdrawal: Weak Institutionalism and the Institutionalization of Art Practice,* (co-organized with Biljana Ciric, 2013), *Cultivate or Revolutionize? Life between Apartment and Farmland* (co-organized with Binna Choi, 2014), *Between Knowing and Unknowing: Research in-and-through Art* (2015). During the de Appel Curatorial Programme in 2009-2010, she co-curated *I'm Not Here. An Exhibition without Francis Alÿs,* with the other participants. Her writings have appeared in a number of publications and magazines, and she is a contributing writer to *LEAP*, *Artforum.com.cn, Arttime*, and *Yishu Journal of Contemporary Chinese Art*.

Luis Camnitzer is a German-born Uruguayan artist and writer who moved to New York in 1964. He was at the vanguard of 1960s Conceptualism, working primarily in printmaking, sculpture, and installations. Camnitzer's artwork explores subjects such as social injustice, repression, and institutional critique. Though Camnitzer resides in New York, his practice is invested in Uruguay and the whole of Latin America via debates around ideas of post-colonialism, conceptualism, and pedagogy. He represented Uruguay at the Venice Biennial in 1988. He taught at the State University of New York, College at Old Westbury 1969-2000, and is now professor emeritus.

Eddie Chambers is a curator and writer of art criticism. He has since the early 1980s been involved in the visual arts, particularly the practice of Black-British artists. He holds a PhD from Goldsmiths College, University of London, and is a Professor in the Art History Department of the University of Texas at Austin. His publications include *Things Done Change: The Cultural Politics of Recent Black Artists in Britain*, published by Rodopi in 2012, and *Black Artists in British Art: A History Since the 1950s*, published in 2014 by I.B. Tauris. His current book project is *Roots and Culture: Cultural Politics in the Making of Black Britain*, which will be published by I.B. Tauris in 2016. His web site is www.eddiechambers.com.

Zasha Cerizza Colah is an art historian and curator, and is a member of the curatorial collaborative and union of artists Clark House in Bombay. Zasha is interested in cultural sovereignty and the way art addresses injustice and legal frameworks. Her curatorial work researches instances of collective imagination under situations of political exigency, political and philosophical motivations for choreography, and under-represented art historical narratives. Her writing is to appear this year in *20th Century Indian Art* (Skira), and *Curating Now* (Laurence King). She is currently also editing a publication on the art of Myanmar since the late 1980s, and on the history of curated exhibitions in India (Marg).

Galit Eilat is an independent curator, a writer, and the founding director of The Israeli Center for Digital Art in Holon (2001-2010). She was the co-founder and chief editor of *Maarav*—an online arts and culture magazine (2004-2010), and was a research curator at the Van Abbemuseum in Eindhoven (2010-2013). In 2012-2013 she was the President of the Akademie der Künste der Welt. Recently she co-curated the 31st São Paulo biennial. She has published in periodicals and is the editor of numerous books.

Liam Gillick (b.1964) deploys multiple forms to expose the new ideological control systems that emerged at the beginning of the 1990s. He has developed a number of key narratives that often form the engine for a body of work: *McNamara* (1992 onward), *Erasmus is Late* and *Ibuka!* (1995 onward), *Discussion Island/Big Conference Center* (1997 onward), and *Construction of One* (2005 onward). Gillick's work exposes the dysfunctional aspects of a modernist legacy in terms of abstraction and architecture when framed within a globalized, neoliberal consensus. His work extends into structural rethinking of the exhibition as a form. In addition he has produced a number of short films since the late 2000s, which address the construction of the creative persona in light of the enduring mutability of the contemporary artist as a cultural figure: *Margin Time* (2012), *The Heavenly Lagoon* (2013), and *Hamilton: A Film by Liam Gillick* (2014). Gillick is currently completing a book on the genealogy of the contemporary artist titled *Industry and Intelligence: Contemporary Art Since 1820* for Columbia University Press. Gillick's work has been included in numerous important exhibitions including documenta and the Venice, Berlin, and Istanbul Biennales—representing Germany in 2009 in Venice. Solo museum exhibitions have taken place at the Museum of Contemporary Art in Chicago, the Museum of Modern Art in New York, and Tate in London. Gillick's work is held in many important public collections, including the Centre Pompidou in Paris, the Guggenheim Museum in New York and Bilbao, and the Museum of Modern Art in New York. Over the last twenty-five years Gillick has also been a prolific writer and critic of contemporary art—contributing to *Artforum*, *October*, *Frieze*, and *e-flux Journal*. He is the author of a number of books including a volume of his selected critical writing. High profile public works include the British Government Home Office (Interior Ministry) building in London, and the Lufthansa Headquarters in Frankfurt. Throughout this time Gillick has extended his practice into experimental venues and collaborative projects with artists including Philippe Parreno, Lawrence Weiner, and Louise Lawler.

Vladimir Jerić is media researcher, author, and media editor based in Belgrade. The founding member of music collective Darkwood Dub (1988-2008, band still active), Creative Commons Serbia (Public Lead, 2007-2013) and TEDx Belgrade (Board member & Event Moderator, 2010–present), Vlidi is also a former member of Prelom Kolektiv (2005-2010), teaching assistant at the faculty of Media and Communication Belgrade (2009-2012), field-producer from the region for SVT (Swedish National Television, 1999-present), editor for MTV Adria digital network (2009-2015), and technical director of a number of critical international exhibitions (2004-present). He is the author of critical texts and translations from the fields of media theory, social theory, and artistic practice. As the member of the board of critical journal *Red Thread* based in Istanbul, Vlidi is currently one of the editors working on the forthcoming issue dedicated to exploring the notion of 'dispossession.'

Koyo Kouoh is an exhibition maker and the founding artistic director of RAW Material Company, a center for art, knowledge, and society in Dakar. She is the curator of the artistic and education programmes of 1:54, Contemporary African Art Fair in London and New York. In 2015 she was appointed curator of the 2016 EVA International, Ireland's Biennial in Limerick. She has served in the curatorial teams for documenta 12 and 13, co-curated the biennial Rencontres de la Photographie Africaine in Bamako in 2001 and 2003, as well as collaborated in different capacities with the Dakar Biennial from 2000 to 2004. Her most recent projects include *Streamlines: Oceans, World Trade and Migration* at Deichtorhallen Halle für Aktuelle Kunst, Hamburg; *Body Talk: Feminism, Sexuality and the Body in the work of six African women artists* (2015-2016, WIELS, Konsthal Lund, FRAC Lorraine); Personal Liberties, a program comprised of three exhibitions, seminars, talks, performances, screenings, and a publication looking at freedom of speech, homosexuality, and homophobia in Africa (2014-2015) at RAW Material Company, Dakar; *Condition Report on Building Art Institutions in Africa*, a collection of essays resulting from the eponymous symposium held in Dakar in January 2012; *Word! Word? Word! Issa Samb and the undecipherable form*, the first monograph dedicated to the work of seminal Senegalese artist Issa Samb. Besides a sustained theoretical and exhibition program at RAW Material Company, she maintains a dynamic international curatorial and judging activity. In collaboration with Rasha Salti, Kouoh is working on *Saving Bruce Lee: African and Arab Cinema in the Era of Soviet Cultural Diplomacy*, a three-year research, exhibition and publication project that will unfold across various international institutions in 2017-2018. She lives and works in Dakar and sometimes in Basel.

Miguel A. López (Lima, 1983) is a writer, researcher, and Chief Curator of TEOR/éTica and Lado V in San Jose, Costa Rica. His work investigates collaborative dynamics and transformations in the understanding of and engagement with politics in Latin America in recent decades. His work also focuses on queer re-articulations of history from a Southern perspective. He has published in periodicals such as *Afterall*, *ramona*, *Manifesta Journal*, *e-flux Journal*, *Art in America*, *ArtNexus*, *Art Journal*, and *The Exhibitionist*, among others. He has recently curated *Teresa Burga. Estructuras de aire* (with Agustín Pérez Rubio) at the MALBA, Buenos Aires (2015); the section "God is Queer" for the 31st Bienal de São Paulo (2014); *Losing Human Form. A seismic image of the 1980s in Latin America* (with Red Conceptualismos del Sur) at the Museo Nacional Centro de Arte Reina Sofía, Madrid (2012-2013); and *Pulso Alterado* at the MUAC-UNAM, Mexico City (2013). Recent publications include *Caderno Sesc_Videobrasil 11: Alianças de Corpos Vulneráveis* (Videobrasil, 2016); two monographic books on the queer aesthetics of Sergio Zevallos, *The obscene death. Sergio Zevallos. Drawings 1982-1987* (AMIL, 2015), and *A wandering body. Sergio Zevallos in the Grupo Chaclacayo, 1982–1994* (MALI, 2014); *Giuseppe Campuzano. Saturday Night Thriller y otros escritos 1998-2013* (2013), a collection of writings by philosopher and drag queen Giuseppe Campuzano; *¿Y qué si la democracia ocurre?* (2012, co-edited with Eliana Otta) a book on visuality, politics, and democracy; a comprehensive catalogue on Peruvian conceptual artist Teresa Burga (2011, with Emilio Tarazona); and a queer issue of Argentine *ramona* magazine (2010, co-edited with Fernando Davis). López is co-founder of the independent art space Bisagra, active in Lima, Peru, since 2014.

Hans Ulrich Obrist (b. 1968, Zürich, Switzerland) is co-director of the Serpentine Galleries, London. Prior to this, he was the Curator of the Musée d'Art Moderne de la Ville de Paris. Since his first show *World Soup (The Kitchen Show)* in 1991 he has curated more than 300 shows. In addition to the exhibitions and marathon series curated at the Serpentine Galleries, Obrist notably curated *Etel Adnan In All Her Dimensions* at Mathaf in Doha; *Gerhard Richter: Pictures/ Series* at The Fondation Beyeler in Basel; and, with Liam Gillick and Philippe Parreno, the *The Solaris Chronicles* at LUMA in Arles (all 2014). In 2015 Obrist co-curated with Klaus Biesenbach the latest version of *15 Rooms* at the Long Museum in Shanghai; previous versions include *13 Rooms* at The Manchester International Festival in 2013, and *14 Rooms* at Art Basel in 2014. Obrist's *Art of Handwriting* project, which casts a light on the disappearance of handwriting in the digital age, currently takes place on Instagram and Twitter (@hansulrichobrist). Along with Simon Castets, he co-founded the *89+* research project in 2012, which was conceived as a mapping of the digitally native generation of innovators born in or after 1989. The research has been presented through conferences and exhibitions, including the 2015 show *Filter Bubble* at LUMA Westbau in Zurich, and *Poetry will be made by all!* at *After Babel* at Moderna Museet in Stockholm. In 2009 Obrist was made Honorary Fellow of the Royal Institute of British Architects (RIBA), in 2011 he received the CCS Bard Award for Curatorial Excellence, and in 2015 he was awarded the International Folkwang Prize. Obrist has lectured internationally at academic and art institutions, and is contributing editor to several magazines and journals. His recent publications include *A Brief History of Curating*, *Do It: The Compendium*, *Lives of the Artists, Lives of Architects*, *Ai Weiwei Speaks*, *Ways of Curating*, *The Age of Earthquakes* with Douglas Coupland and Shumon Basar, and new volumes of his Conversation Series.

Dr. Paul O'Neill is a curator, artist, writer and educator based in New York. He is Director of the Graduate Program at the Centre for Curatorial Studies, Bard College in New York. Paul has co-curated more than sixty exhibitions and curatorial projects across the world, and his writing has been published in many books, catalogs, journals, and magazines, and he is a regular contributor to *Art Monthly*. He is reviews editor for *Art and the Public Sphere Journal*, and an editor of Afterall's *Exhibition Histories* Series. He is on the editorial board of *FIELD* and *The Journal of Curatorial Studies*. He is editor of the curatorial anthology *Curating Subjects* (2007), and co-editor of *Curating and the Educational Turn*, with Mick Wilson (2010), both published by de Appel and Open Editions (Amsterdam and London), and author of *Locating the Producers: Durational Approaches to Public Art* (Amsterdam, Valiz, 2011), edited with Claire Doherty. He is author of the critically acclaimed book *The Culture of Curating and the Curating of Culture(s)* (The MIT Press, 2012). His most recent book, *Curating Research* (de Appel and Open Editions), co-edited with Mick Wilson, was published in 2015.

Tobias Ostrander is Chief Curator and Deputy Director for Curatorial Affairs at the Pérez Art Museum Miami. He was previously the Director of El Museo Experiemental del ECO, an alternative contemporary art space run by the Universidad Nacional Autónoma de México, Mexico City. From 2001 to July 2009, Tobias Ostrander served as the Curator of Contemporary Art Museo Tamayo, Mexico City. He has an MA from the Center for Curatorial Studies, Bard College.

João Ribas is Deputy Director of the Serralves Museum of Contemporary Art in Porto, Portugal. He was previously Curator at the MIT List Visual

Arts Center (2009-2013), and at The Drawing Center, New York (2007-2009). He is the winner of four consecutive AICA Exhibition Awards (2008-2011), and of an Emily Hall Tremaine Exhibition Award (2010). His writing has appeared in numerous publications and journals, including *Artforum*, *Mousse*, *Frieze*, *Afterall*, *Artnews*, and *Art in America.* His most recent publication, *In the Holocene,* was published by Sternberg Press (2015).

Sarah Rifky is a writer and curator based in Cairo, where she co-founded Beirut, an art space that thinks about institution building as a curatorial act, since 2012. She is founder of CIRCA (Cairo International Resource Center for Art), and was Curator at Townhouse Gallery of Contemporary Art in Cairo 2009-2011. She was a Curatorial Agent of dOCUMENTA 13 in Kassel, Germany. In 2010 she was Adjunct Professor of Art History and Theory at the American University in Cairo and co-managed MASS Alexandria, an independent study program for young artists in Egypt, with artist Wael Shawky. Rifky is author of *The Going Insurrection* (2011) and *Delusions of Reference: In Defense of Art* (forthcoming). She is co-editor of the artist book *Damascus: Tourists, Artists and Secret Agents* (2009).

Sumesh Sharma (1983) is a curator informed by alternate art histories that often include cultural perspectives informed by socio-economics and politics. Immigrant culture in the Francophone sphere, vernacular equalities, and movements of Black consciousness in culture are his areas of interest. He co-founded the Clark House Initiative in 2010. His Mres at the Université Paul Cézanne (2008) was an inquiry into artists' careers, and he was part of the Gwangju Biennale Curators Course 2010, as well as the first Independent Curators International's Curatorial Intensive in Bombay. He has been a resident at ISCP New York (2012), Kadist Art Foundation Paris (2013), and the Manifesta Online Residency (2013), Casa Masaccio Tuscany (2013), San Art in Ho Chin Minh City Vietnam (2014), and Para Site Hong Kong (2014). He is presently one of the curators of Dak'Art 2016, Senegal, and was ICI's 2014 Curatorial Fellow in Senegal, where he researched how the funding mechanisms in culture and institutional support of art institutions utilize the power structures put in place by colonial laws.

Dr. Simon Sheikh is a curator and theorist. He is Reader in Art and Programme Director of the MFA Curating at Goldsmiths, University of London. He is a correspondent for *Springerin*, Vienna, and a columnist for *e-flux Journal*, New York. He is a researcher for the ongoing *Former West* project, initiated by BAK in Utrecht, and working on a book about art and apocalypse entitled *It's After the End of the World*. He was Coordinator of the Critical Studies Program, Malmö Art Academy in 2002–2009. He was curator at NIFCA, Helsinki (2003-2004); director of Overgaden—Institute for Contemporary Art in Copenhagen (1999-2002); editor of the magazine Øjeblikket (1996-2000); and a member of the project group GLOBE (1993-2000). Curatorial work includes exhibitions such *Buck to the Future*, Museum of Contemporary Art, Roskilde; *Unauthorized*, Inter Arts Center, Malmö (2012); *Do You Remember the Future?,* Etagi, St. Petersburg (2011); *All That Fits: The Aesthetics of Journalism*, QUAD, Derby (2011); *Vectors of the Possible*, BAK, Utrecht (2010); *Kunstihoone*, Tallinn (2006); *Capital (It Fails Us Now),* UKS, Oslo (2005); *Circa Berlin*, Nikolaj—Copenhagen Contemporary Art Center (2005); *Naust,* Øygarden, Bergen, Norway (2000); *Models of Resistance*, Overgaden, Copenhagen (2000, with GLOBE); *In My Room, Nordic Video*, Musée d'Art Moderne de la Ville de Paris (1998); *Do-It-Yourself—Mappings and Instructions*, Bricks+Kicks, Vienna (1997); *Escape Attempts in Christiania*, Copenhagen (1996, with GLOBE); *I Confess,* Nikolaj, Copenhagen Contemporary Art Center (1995); and *Exclusion, Consul*, Århus (1993). Publications include the anthologies *On Horizons* (with Maria Hlavajova and Jill Winder, BAK, 2011); *Capital (It Fails Us Now)* (b_books, 2006); *In the Place of the Public Sphere?* (b_books, 2005); *Knut Åsdam* (monograph), *Fine Arts Unternehmen* (Zug, 2004); *We are all Normal*, with Katya Sander (Black Dog Publishing, 2001). A collection of his essays is forthcoming from b_books. Sheikh lives in Berlin and London.

Lucy Steeds is Editor of the *Exhibition Histories* research and publishing project of *Afterall* at Central Saint Martins, University of the Arts London, and she is Pathway Leader for the Exhibition Studies MRes course at Central Saint Martins. This two-year postgraduate research course takes as its starting point the work underpinning the *Exhibition Histories* book series, and, through this, supports students as they pursue their particular areas of interest. Her most recent publication is *Exhibition*, for the *Documents of Contemporary Art* series (Whitechapel Gallery and The MIT Press, 2014). She has a doctoral degree in cultural history from Goldsmiths College, University of London.

Jeannine Tang is Senior Academic Advisor and LUMA Foundation Fellow at the Center for Curatorial Studies, Bard College. She is an art historian and critic who received her MA and PhD from the Courtauld Institute of Art, London, and was previously a Terra Foundation fellow at the Smithsonian American Art Museum, and a Critical Studies participant at the Whitney Museum Independent Study Program, New York. Her writing has appeared in publications such as *Artforum*, *Art Journal*, *Theory, Culture & Society*, *Afterimage*, *journal of visual culture*, *Art India*, and *Broadsheet*, among others. She is working on a book project about convergences between contemporary art and the 1970s information age, and an exhibition on the galleries American Fine Arts Co. and Pat Hearn Gallery (in collaboration with Ann Butler and Lia Gangitano).

David Teh is a writer, curator, art advisor and researcher based at the National University of Singapore, specializing in Southeast Asian contemporary art. Before moving to Singapore, he worked as an independent curator and critic in Bangkok, realizing diverse projects including *Platform* (2006), *The More Things Change* (5th Bangkok Experimental Film Festival, 2008), *Unreal Asia* (55. Internationale Kurzfilmtage, Oberhausen, 2009), and *Video Vortex #7* (Yogyakarta, 2011). His most recent exhibition was *TRANSMISSION*, at the Jim Thompson Art Center in Bangkok (2014). David's writings have appeared in *Third Text*, *Afterall*, *Theory, Culture & Society*, *LEAP Magazine*, *Art Asia Pacific*, and *The Bangkok Post,* and his monograph on Thai contemporary art will be published in 2017 (The MIT Press). He is also a director of Future Perfect, a gallery and project platform in Singapore.

Jelena Vesić is an independent curator, writer, editor, and lecturer. She was co-editor of *Prelom—Journal of Images and Politics* and co-founder of the independent organization Prelom Kolektiv. Active in the field of publishing, research, and exhibition practice that intertwines political theory and contemporary art, she is also co-editor of *Red Thread*, a journal for social theory, contemporary art and activism and a member of editorial board of *Art Margins*. Vesić explores the relations between art and ideology in the field of geopolitical art history writing, focusing on experimental art and exhibition practices of the 1960s and 1970s in former Yugoslavia and Eastern Europe. She also writes on artistic labor and practices of self-organization in the environment of cognitive capitalism. Her recent curatorial projects are based on experiments with the form of lecture-performance and immaterial quality of the exhibits. These include: *Oktobar XXX: Exposition–Symposium–Performance* (2012-2013); *Exhibition on Work and Laziness* (2012-2015); and *On Undercurrents of Negotiating Artistic Jobs—Between Love and Money, Between Money and Love* (2013-2014).

What, How & for Whom/WHW is a curatorial collective formed in 1999 and based in Zagreb, Croatia. Its members are Ivet Ćurlin, Ana Dević, Nataša Ilić, and Sabina Sabolović, and designer and publicist Dejan Kršić. WHW organizes a range of production, exhibition, and publishing projects, and since 2003 has been directing city-owned Gallery Nova in Zagreb. "What?," "How?," and "For Whom?" are the three basic questions of every economic organization, and are fundamental to the planning, conception, and realization of exhibitions, and the production and distribution of artworks and the artist's position in the labor market. These questions formed the title of WHW's first project, in 2000 in Zagreb, and became the motto of WHW's work and the name of their collective. In 2009, WHW curated the 11th Istanbul Biennial, entitled *What Keeps Mankind Alive?* Recent projects include the festival Meeting Points 7 (2013 and 2014) in Zagreb, Antwerp, Cairo, Hong-Kong, Beirut, Vienna, and Moscow under the title *Ten thousand wiles and a hundred thousand tricks*; the exhibition *Really Useful Knowledge*, at the Museo Nacional Centro de Arte Reina Sofia in Madrid (2014); the exhibition *So, You Want to See*, at e-flux, New York (2015); and *A Retrospective by Appointment* by David Maljković, at Gallery Nova and several locations in Zagreb (2015).

Mick Wilson is the Head of Valand Academy of Arts, University of Gothenburg, Sweden (2012-), and formerly founder Dean of the Graduate School of Creative Arts and Media, Ireland (2008-2012). Prior to this he was the first Head of Research at the National College of Art and Design (2005-2007). He completed his doctoral thesis on the subject of *Conflicted Faculties: Rhetoric, Knowledge Conflict and the University* (NUI, 2006), and has been active in developing doctoral education across the arts as Chair of the SHARE Network (2010-2013); as a member of the European Artistic Research Network, EARN (2005-); and as a member of the working group for the Platform for Artistic Research PARSE (2013-). Ongoing projects include *the food thing* (2011-), *dead publics* (2009-), multi-stranded art, education and research projects, and *rhetor* (2007-). Edited volumes include *Curating Research* (2014), and *Curating and the Educational Turn* (2010), both with Paul O'Neill; and *Handbook of Artistic Research Education* (2013) with S. van Ruiten.

Vivian Ziherl is a critic and curator from Brisbane, living and working in Amsterdam. In 2015 Vivian established the multi-platform project Frontier Imaginaries through the IMA Curatorial Fellowship. She is curator of the 8th Jerusalem Show (2016)—a project of the Al Ma'mal Foundation for Contemporary Art and the Qalandiya International. From 2013 until 2015 she led the multi-part curatorial project Landings, presented at Witte de With Center for Contemporary Art, Rotterdam, and David Roberts Art Foundation, London, and NGBK, Berlin (as part of the Tagore, Pedagogy and Contemporary Visual Cultures Network), Stedelijk Museum Amsterdam, and other partner organizations (with Natasha Ginwala). In 2012-2014 she was a curator with If I Can't Dance, I Don't Want To Be Part of Your Revolution, including presentations with OCAT Shenzhen and STUK Leuven, among others. Vivian is editor of publications including *Gerry Bibby: The Drumhead* (Sternberg), *The Lip Anthology* (Kunstverein and MacMillan), and co-editor of the anthologies *Reading Feeling* and *ReReading Appropriation* (If I Can't Dance and Idea Books).

The Curatorial Conundrum What to Study? What to Research? What to Practice?

In November 2014, the Symposium *The Future Curatorial What Not and Study What?* Conundrum took place, organized by LUMA Foundation and CCS Bard, in partnership with Valand Academy of Arts, University of Gothenburg; Afterall Books: Exhibition Histories, and Central Saint Martins, University of Arts London; and de Appel arts centre, Amsterdam.

Center for Curatorial Studies, Bard College
November 6-8, 2014

Entitled *The Future Curatorial What Not and Study What? Conundrum*, the symposium included presentations by Nancy Adajania, Mélanie Bouteloup, Thomas Boutoux, Nikita Yingqian Cai, Luis Camnitzer, Eddie Chambers, Zasha Colah and Sumesh Sharma (Clark House Initiative Bombay), Common Practice New York (CPNY), Ivet Curlin (What, How & for Whom), Elvira Dyangani Ose, Galit Eilat, Annie Fletcher, Liam Gillick, Koyo Kouoh, Miguel A. López, Hans Ulrich Obrist, Tobias Ostrander, João Ribas, Sarah Rifky, Simon Sheikh, David Teh, Jelena Vesić and Vladimir Jerić, and Vivian Ziherl. The moderators and respondents were Suhail Malik, Paul O'Neill, Lucy Steeds, Jeannine Tang, and Mick Wilson.

The symposium was organized by Paul O'Neill and Tom Eccles (CCS Bard/LUMA Foundation), in partnership with Mick Wilson (Valand Academy of Arts, University of Gothenburg); Lucy Steeds, Yaiza Hernández, Charles Esche, and Alison Green (MRes Art: Exhibition Studies/ Afterall Books: Exhibition Histories and BA/ MA Culture, Criticism and Curation at Central Saint Martins, London); and Lorenzo Benedetti and Guus van Engelshoven (de Appel arts centre, Amsterdam).

The symposium was part of an ongoing collaboration between CCS Bard and the LUMA Foundation, which hosted previous symposiums organized by the two institutions. Both *The Human Snapshot* (2011), and *The Flood of Rights* (2013), organized collaboratively with Bard College's Human Rights Project, were held in Arles, and addressed the photographic image and human rights.

The symposium took place in a specially commissioned room in the Hessel Museum at Bard College designed by architects Pedro&Juana and Montserrat Albores Gleason (2014 Fundación Jumex Fellow at CCS Bard), as part of the exhibition *Hotel Palenque is not in Yucatán*, curated by Gleason.

Following the symposium the participants were invited to expand on their presentations and submit new texts, which has resulted in the book *The Curatorial Conundrum*.

LUMA Foundation

The LUMA Foundation was established by Maja Hoffmann in 2004 in Switzerland to support the activities of independent artists and pioneers, as well as institutions working in the fields of art and photography, publishing, documentary, and multimedia. The foundation produces and commissions ambitious artistic projects, combining a particular interest in environmental issues, human rights, education, and culture in the broadest sense.

The LUMA Foundation and LUMA Arles, founded in 2014 in support of the project in Arles, are currently developing an experimental cultural center in the Parc des Ateliers in the city of Arles, France, working with a core group of artistic consultants (Tom Eccles, Liam Gillick, Hans Ulrich Obrist, Philippe Parreno, Beatrix Ruf), the architects Frank Gehry and Annabelle Selldorf, and landscape architect Bas Smets. This ambitious project envisions an interdisciplinary center dedicated to the production of exhibitions and ideas, research, education, and archives, and is supported by a growing number of public and private partnerships. Construction started after the groundbreaking ceremony in April 2014, and the opening of the campus is scheduled for early 2018.

President, LUMA Foundation
Maja Hoffmann

Center for Curatorial Studies, Bard College

The Center for Curatorial Studies, Bard College (CCS Bard) is an exhibition, education, and research center dedicated to the study of art and curatorial practices from the 1960s to the present day. In addition to the CCS Bard Galleries and Hessel Museum of Art, the Center houses the Marieluise Hessel Collection, as well as an extensive library and curatorial archives that are accessible to the public. The Center's two-year MA program in curatorial studies is specifically designed to deepen students' understanding of the intellectual and practical tasks of curating contemporary art. Exhibitions are presented year-round in the CCS Bard Galleries and Hessel Museum of Art, providing students with the opportunity to work with world-renowned artists and curators. The exhibition program and the Hessel Collection also serve as the basis for a wide range of public programs and activities exploring art and its role in contemporary society.

CCS Board of Governors
Martin Eisenberg, *Chairman*
Leon Botstein, *ex officio*
Amy Cappellazzo
Lori Chemla
Marieluise Hessel, *Founding Chairman*
Maja Hoffmann
Audrey Irmas
Ruth Keating Lockwood
Patrizia Sandretto Re Rebaudengo
Melissa Schiff Soros
Michael Ward Stout

CCS Bard Staff
Tom Eccles, *Executive Director*
Paul O'Neill, *Director of the Graduate Program*
Tracy Pollock, *Director of Administration and Development*
Marcia Acita, *Director of Exhibitions and Operations*
Ann E. Butler, *Director of Library and Archives*
Ramona Rosenberg, *Director of External Affairs*
Amanda Bard, *Graduate Program Coordinator*
Karlene King, *Administrative and Development Coordinator*
Mark DeLura, *Preparator*
Amy Linker, *Registrar*
Bronwen Bitetti, *Librarian*
Ryan Evans, *Archivist*
Trian Mort, *Administrative Assistant*
George Acker, *Security Manager*

The Curatorial Conundrum
What to Study? What to Research? What to Practice?

Publishers
LUMA Foundation
Center for Curatorial Studies, Bard College
The MIT Press

Editors
Paul O'Neill, Mick Wilson, Lucy Steeds

Design
Project Projects, New York

Managing Editor
Gerrie van Noord, London

Printer
Die Keure, Belgium

LUMA Foundation
Breuerlakehouse
Im Hausacher 35
CH-8706 Feldmeilen
Switzerland

Center for Curatorial Studies, Bard College
Annandale-on-Hudson, NY 12504
USA
www.bard.edu/ccs/

The MIT Press
One Rogers Street
Cambridge, MA 02142-1209
USA
http//:mitpress.mit.edu/

ISBN: 978-0-262-52910-5

LUMA FOUNDATION

CCS BARD

UNIVERSITY OF GOTHENBURG

ual: university of the arts london central saint martins

DE APPEL ARTS CENTRE

Image Credits
The editors and publishers have endeavored to identify and contact all copyright holders of images used in this publication, but have not always been successful. If an image has not been identified, and you are aware of its origins and/or its copyright holders, please contact the Center for Curatorial Studies, Bard College, so we can ensure rectification in future editions.

p. 24/pp. 234-235: Reproduced with permission from the artists and Arquivo Histórico Wanda Svevo/ Fundação Bienal de São Paulo
p. 25/p. 236: © The Estate of Sigmar Polke / DACS, London
pp. 40, 43, 47/pp. 237-239: Screenshots courtesy the authors
p. 70/p. 240: Image courtesy of the artist
p. 71/p. 241: Image courtesy of the artist
p. 123/p. 242: Photograph © Aurélien Mole
p. 124/p. 243: Photograph © Aurélien Mole
p. 125/p. 244: Photograph © Aurélien Mole
p. 127/pp. 246-247: © Leo Eloy / Fundação Bienal de São Paulo
p. 131/p. 245 (top): Image Galit Eilat
p. 135/p. 245 (bottom): Image Galit Eilat
p. 140 (top)/p. 250 (top left): Courtesy the artist, photograph by Boris Cvjetanović
p. 143 (top): Photograph by Ivan Kuharić
p. 143 (bottom)/p. 250 (bottom): Photograph by Ivan Kuharić
p. 144: Photograph by Joaquín Cortés, Román Lores / Museo Nacional Centro de Arte Reina Sofía, Madrid
p. 145 (top)/pp. 248-249: Photograph by Ivan Kuharić
p. 145 (bottom): Courtesy the artist, photograph by Ivan Kuharić
p. 168 (top)/p. 251 (top): Image courtesy the Dashrath Patel Museum
p. 168 (bottom)/p. 251 (bottom): Image courtesy the Dashrath Patel Museum
p. 171/p. 252: Image courtesy Nancy Adajania
p. 178/p. 253: © Alfredo Jaar, courtesy Galerie Lelong, New York
p. 196, 204/pp. 254-255: Photo: Anil Rane